German Cultural Studies

German
Cultural Studies

An Introduction

Edited by Rob Burns

OXFORD UNIVERSITY PRESS
1995

Oxford University Press, Walton Street, Oxford OX2 6DP

Oxford New York
Athens Auckland Bangkok Bombay
Calcutta Cape Town Dar es Salaam Delhi
Florence Hong Kong Istanbul Karachi
Kuala Lumpur Madras Madrid Melbourne
Mexico City Nairobi Paris Singapore
Taipei Tokyo Toronto
and associated companies in
Berlin Ibadan

Oxford is a trade mark of Oxford University Press

Published in the United States
by Oxford University Press Inc., New York

British Library Cataloguing in Publication Data
Data available

Library of Congress Cataloging in Pulication Data
German cultural studies : an introduction / edited by Rob Burns.
Includes bibliographical reference (p.   ) and index.
1. Germany—Cultural policy—History—19th century.   2. Germany—
Cultural policy—History—20th century   3. Germany—Intellectual
life—19th century.   4. Germany—Intellectual life—20th century.
5. Arts, Modern—19th century—Germany.   6. Arts, Modern—20th
century—Germany.   I. Burns, Rob, 1949–   .
DD67.G47   1995
306'.0943—dc20   95–5109
ISBN 0–19–871502–1
ISBN 0–19–871503–X (pbk)

1 3 5 7 9 10 8 6 4 2

Typeset by Graphicraft Typesetters Ltd., Hong Kong
Printed in Great Britain
on acid-free paper by
Bookcraft Ltd.,
Midsomer Norton, Bath

Contents

List of Illustrations

List of Contributors

Keith Bullivant: Professor of German, University of Florida. Has published numerous studies of post-war German literature, including *Literature in Upheaval* (1974, with R. H. Thomas), *Realism Today* (1987), *The Future of German Literature* (1994), and (as editor) *The Modern German Novel* (1987) and *After the 'Death' of Literature* (1989).

Rob Burns: Senior Lecturer in German Studies, University of Warwick. Has published studies on working-class culture, *Arbeiterbewegung in der Weimarer Republik* (1982, with W. van der Will), and on the political culture of the Federal Republic, *Protest and Democracy in West Germany* (1988, with W. van der Will).

Godfrey Carr, Senior Lecturer in German and Business Studies, University of Warwick. Publications on German literature and thought in the twentieth century, including *Karl Jaspers as an Intellectual Critic* (1983).

Axel Goodbody: Lecturer in Modern Languages, Universty of Bath. Publications on twentieth-century German poetry and East German literature, including *Natursprache. Ein Dichtungstheoretisches Konzept der Romantik und seine Wiederaufnahme in der modernen Naturlyrik* (1984) and (as editor) *Geist und Tat: Writers and the State in the GDR* (1992, with D. Tate).

Stephen Lamb: Lecturer in German Studies, University of Warwick. Numerous publications on the Weimar Republic, including (as editor) *German Writers and Politics 1918–1939* (1992, with R. Dove) and various articles on the life and work of Ernst Toller.

Robin Lenman: Lecturer in History, University of Warwick. Various publications on nineteenth- and twentieth-century German history, including a study on the visual arts in Imperial Germany, *Die Kunst, die Macht und das Geld: Zur Kulturgeschichte des kaiserlichen Deutschland 1871–1918* (1994).

John Osborne: Professor of German Studies, University of Warwick. Numerous publications on the culture of Wilhelmine Germany, including *The Naturalist Drama in Germany* (1971), *Meyer oder Fontane? German Literature after the Franco-Prussian War* (1983), and *The Meiningen Court Theatre, 1866–1890* (1988).

Georgina Paul: Lecturer in German Studies, University of Warwick. Various publications on women's writing and on GDR literature, including *Subjective Authenticity: Contemporaneity and Commitment in the Works of Christa Wolf* (1990).

Anthony Phelan: Senior Lecturer in German Studies, University of Warwick. Has published widely on nineteenth- and twentieth-century German culture, including *Rilke: Neue Gedichte. A Critical Guide* (1993) and (as editor) *The Weimar Dilemma: German Intellectuals in the Weimar Republic* (1984).

C. Jane Rice: Associate Professor of German, University of Arizona. Various publications on GDR literature and women's writing.

Eda Sagarra: Professor of Germanic Studies, University of Dublin. Has published widely on the social history of Germany and on German literature, including *Tradition and Revolution* (1971), *A Social History of Germany 1648–1914* (1977), *Germany in the Nineteenth Century* (1980), and (as editor) *Deutsche Literatur in sozialgeschichtlicher Perspektive* (1989).

Dennis Tate: Senior Lecturer in Modern Languages, University of Bath. Has published extensively on GDR literature, including *The East German Novel: Identity, Community, Continuity* (1984), *Franz Fühmann: Innovation and Authenticity* (1995), and (as editor) *European Socialist Realism* (1988, with M. Scriven) and *Geist und Tat: Writers and the State in the GDR* (1992, with A. Goodbody).

Ian Wallace: Professor of German, University of Bath. Is founder/editor of *German Monitor* (formerly *GDR Monitor*) and has published widely on GDR cultural affairs, including *Volker Braun* (1986), *East Germany* (1987), and (as editor) *The GDR under Honecker: 1971–1981* (1981), *The Writer and Society in the GDR* (1984), and *The German Revolution of 1989* (1992, with G.-J. Glaeßner).

Wilfried van der Will: Professor of German, University of Birmingham. Has published extensively on the culture of the Third Reich and of postwar Germany, including *Pikaro heute* (1967), *The German Novel and the Affluent Society* (1968, with R. H. Thomas), *Protest and Democracy in West Germany* (1988, with R. Burns), and (as editor) *The Nazification of Art* (1991, with B. Taylor).

Introduction

ROB BURNS

WHEN some people hear the word 'culture'—as with Friedrich
Thiemann in Hanns Johst's play *Schlageter* (1933) or in the more
notorious but apocryphal case of Hermann Göring—they reach for
their revolver. In the light of the recent proliferation of publications, media debates, and academic courses concerned with cultural studies, others may be more inclined to reach for their
dictionary. Of the many meanings of culture listed there, two are
of relevance: the aesthetic and the anthropological. In Britain cultural studies originated with the attempts by Richard Hoggart and,
above all, Raymond Williams to shift the critical focus from the
one meaning of the term to the other: from the traditional, narrow
view of culture as coterminous with the arts to the broad, anthropological and extended sociological use of the word to indicate a
'whole way of life', the entire mental and material habitat of a
distinct people or other social group. As Williams pointed out, the
latter sense of culture has the considerable merit of highlighting a
general system. In contrast with analytical perspectives that
compartmentalize life in its various aspects (the economic, the political, the spiritual, and so on) the notion of culture as a 'whole
way of life' evokes 'a specific and organized system of acted and
activated practices, meanings, and values'.[1] Williams applied this
approach in the two texts commonly seen as marking the inception
of cultural studies in Britain, namely *Culture and Society* (1958) and
The Long Revolution (1961). Here he challenged the then dominant
paradigm of literary studies as epitomized by the work of F. R.
Leavis, for whom culture was to be equated exclusively with 'high
culture'. While the latter continued to be of interest to Williams,
his overriding concern was to explore the relations between works
of art and popular culture. Since culture was to be understood as
the 'whole way of life' of a particular society, the cultural consumption and self-expression of the working class was deemed to be as

1 Raymond Williams, *Culture* (London, 1981), 209.

legitimate an object of enquiry as the discourse of an educated élite. Culture was thus conceived in the broadest sense as encompassing the fabric of everyday life, 'the points at which real lives intersect with cultural forms and commodities, the point at which new patterns and "structures of feeling" find expression and surface right along and across the landscape of the social'.[2] And yet, notwithstanding the democratic impulse behind Williams's project, the recuperation of excluded experiences, the model of cultural studies he pioneered in the late 1950s attracted criticism for its assumption that 'a group or class acts freely and constitutively through its cultural expressions, that the working class lives in an enclave separated from the rest of the social formation and is therefore able to make up for itself its "own" culture'.[3]

In Germany the main impetus for the development of cultural studies came from the 'Critical Theory' of the Frankfurt School, in particular as elaborated in the essay 'Kulturindustrie. Aufklärung als Massenbetrug', the fourth chapter in Max Horkheimer and Theodor Adorno's *Dialektik der Aufklärung*. First published in the USA in 1944 (in a mimeographed edition) but hugely influential in the 1960s when their ideas helped shape the thinking of the West German student movement, Horkheimer and Adorno's analysis pointed in the opposite direction to the culturalism of Raymond Williams. Indeed, Adorno subsequently explained that they had opted for the term 'culture industry', in preference to their original choice of 'mass culture', precisely in order to exclude the notion of

2 Angela McRobbie, 'Revenge of the 60s', *Marxism Today*, 12 (1991), 25.
3 Antony Easthope, *Literary into Cultural Studies* (London and New York, 1991), 72.
4 Theodor W. Adorno, 'Résumé über Kulturindustrie', in *Ohne Leitbild. Parva Aesthetica* (Frankfurt am Main, 1967), 60 and 62–3.
5 Max Horkheimer and Theodor W. Adorno, 'The Culture Industry: Enlightenment as Mass Deception', in *Dialectic of Enlightenment*, trans. John Cumming (London, 1973), 120. Subsequent references to this edition.

a culture that arises spontaneously from the masses themselves. On the other hand, Adorno insisted, the word 'industry' was not to be taken literally; it referred to the standardization and rationalization of the methods of dissemination and not, that is to say, to the actual process of cultural production.[4]

The chief feature of the culture industry, according to Horkheimer and Adorno, is its standardizing effect, for 'culture now impresses the same stamp on everything' and its various branches 'make up a system which is uniform as a whole and in every part'.[5] The mere 'semblance of competition and range of choice' should not be mistaken for a truly pluralist culture; rather, 'something is provided for everyone so that no one may escape' and 'the ruthless unity in the culture industry is evidence of what will happen in politics' (p. 123). Moreover, the process of standardization extends to human experience itself, for under advanced capitalism 'amusement is the prolongation of work' in so far as, if it is to remain pleasure, it must not demand mental effort or independent thinking. Thus, paradoxically, 'what happens at work, in the factory, or in the office can

Rob Burns

only be escaped from by approximation to it in one's leisure time' (p. 137). The culture industry amounts to 'mass deception' because it constantly 'cheats its consumers of what it perpetually promises' (p. 139):

What is decisive today is . . . the necessity inherent in the system not to leave the customer alone, not for a moment to allow him any suspicion that resistance is possible. The principle dictates that he should be shown all his needs as capable of fulfilment, but that those needs should be so predetermined that he feels himself to be the eternal consumer, the object of the culture industry. Not only does it make him believe that the deception it practises is satisfaction, but it goes further and implies that, whatever the state of affairs, he must put up with what is offered. The escape from everyday drudgery which the whole culture industry promises . . . the paradise offered by the culture industry, is the same old drudgery . . . . Pleasure promotes the resignation which it ought to help to forget. (pp. 141–2)

In this process of cultural depravation Horkheimer and Adorno attribute particular significance to what they term the 'technical media'. Writing in the mid-1940s they could, of course, only speculate about the development of television, noting that 'its consequences will be quite enormous and promise to intensify the impoverishment of aesthetic matter'. The 'stunting of the mass-media consumer's powers of imagination and spontaneity' is, then, typified by the cinema, with its 'alliance of word, image, and music . . . derisively fulfilling the Wagnerian dream of the *Gesamtkunstwerk*—the fusion of all the arts in one work' (p. 124). In particular, film is condemned for the passive role it imposes on the spectator, 'far surpassing the theatre of illusion' and leaving 'no room for imagination or reflection on the part of the audience' (p. 126). In its pernicious effects the cinema is outdone only by the radio, 'the progressive latecomer of mass culture', for the technical structure of the commercial radio system makes it 'immune from liberal deviations such as those the movie industrialists can still permit themselves in their own sphere' (p. 159). In reaching this judgement Horkheimer and Adorno were clearly influenced by three factors: the way in which in America radio programmes were permeated by advertising, the fact that the audience received its entertainment free of charge, and the use to which broadcasting was put under National Socialism:

In bringing cultural products wholly into the sphere of commodities, radio does not try to dispose of its culture goods themselves as commodities straight to the consumer. In America it collects no fees from the public, and so has acquired the illusory form of disinterested, unbiased authority which suits Fascism admirably. The radio becomes the universal mouthpiece of the Führer. (p. 159)

While the Nazis demonstrated an undeniable sophistication in their exploitation of the radio for propaganda purposes, for Horkheimer and Adorno this was greatly facilitated by the authoritarian properties of the medium itself. For 'the inherent tendency of radio is to make the speaker's word, the false commandment, absolute. A recommendation becomes an order' and does so, it would appear, whether the voice in question is that of an announcer extolling a particular brand of soap or Goebbels exhorting the German nation to mobilize for 'total war'.

The fact that certain types of modern popular culture were singled out for special criticism did not mean that Horkheimer and Adorno saw the traditional forms of 'high art'—literature, drama, painting, etc.—as remaining uncontaminated by the culture industry; nor, as their discussion of the difference between 'light' and 'serious' art indicated, did they attack the development of mass culture *qua* mass culture, that is, on the élitist grounds that it attracted a popular audience. 'Light' art as such, distraction, is not, they insist, a decadent form, nor a betrayal of the 'purity' of bourgeois art. The latter, the realm of disinterested contemplation evoking a world of freedom in contrast to the reality of the material world, was always the preserve of a minority, withheld from those 'for whom the hardship and oppression of life make a mockery of seriousness. Light art has been the shadow of autonomous art . . . the social bad conscience of serious art' (p. 135). The truth which bourgeois art necessarily lacked because of its social exclusiveness thus endowed light art with the semblance of legitimacy. Yet this division between the classes, to which the existence of the two types of art attests, is precisely what the culture industry attempts to reconcile by absorbing light art into serious art and vice versa. The ensuing fusion leads not only to the 'intellectualization of amusement' but also to the 'depravation of culture' (p. 143). Hence the abolition of educational privilege as effected by the culture industry does not in fact 'open for the masses the spheres from which they were formerly excluded, but, given existing social conditions, contributes directly to the decay of education and the progress of barbaric meaninglessness' (p. 160). Moreover, a change is brought about in the nature of the work of art, for 'what is new is not that it is a commodity but that it deliberately admits it is one; that art renounces its own autonomy and proudly takes its place among consumption goods', thus depriving human beings of 'precisely that liberation from the principle of utility which it should inaugurate' (pp. 157–8). In other words, firmly embedded in capitalist production, culture is now an integral part of what it was once presumed to challenge and transcend.

The one-dimensional, purely affirmative character Horkheimer and Adorno ascribe to culture under capitalism is most apparent at the end of the essay where they assert that technically as well as economically advertising and the culture industry effectively merge, in both cases transforming 'technology into a procedure for manipulating human beings' (p. 163). The political function ultimately fulfilled by the culture industry is thus made palpably clear: 'it becomes a vigorous and prearranged promulgation of the status quo, the irrefutable prophet of the prevailing order'; in short, it 'acts as an instrument of domination' (p. 147). Furthermore, the more firmly established the position of the culture industry becomes, 'the more summarily it can deal with consumers' needs, producing them, controlling them, disciplining them, and even withdrawing amusement' (p. 144). Allied to their prognosis that 'no limits are set to cultural progress of this kind', such an argument makes it difficult to resist the conclusion—one which is further underscored by the following passage—that Horkheimer and Adorno are here positing nothing less than total human manipulability:

As naturally as the ruled always took the morality imposed upon them more seriously than did the rulers themselves, the deceived masses are today captivated by the myth of success even more than the successful are. Immovably, they insist on the very ideology which enslaves them. The misplaced love of the common people for the wrong which is done them is a greater force than the cunning of the authorities. (pp. 133–4)

Notwithstanding the cabalistic overtones of the last phrase, Horkheimer and Adorno were clearly not seeking to explain ideological manipulation of this kind in terms of some crude conspiracy theory. While, under certain circumstances, it might readily be combined with overt political manipulation, the production and consumption of mass culture is, in their view, essentially governed by 'the same kind of unconscious force as the "blind" economic determinism of capitalist society as a whole'.[6] Despite or perhaps because of this the charge has frequently been levelled at the Frankfurt School that its critique of culture under capitalism lacked historical specificity and failed to distinguish sufficiently between the differing political contexts of cultural production. Hence some critics have argued that the trauma of National Socialism led Horkheimer

6 Phil Slater, *Origin and Significance of the Frankfurt School* (London, Henley, and Boston, 1977), 124.

and Adorno to conflate the culture industry and Nazi totalitarianism so that they tended to judge the liberal, bourgeois society that existed in America, for example, solely in terms of its fascist potential;[7] while others have discerned a basic antipathy towards technology in *Dialektik der Aufklärung*, as a consequence of which technological rationality 'becomes the rationality of domination *per se*, monopoly capitalist culture becomes industrial culture'.[8]

In the light of such criticisms, Germany during the period covered by this study—which, indeed, begins shortly after the establishment of industrial capitalism—provides a highly instructive model on which to test the thesis of the culture industry; and not least because, in the notably dynamic but often traumatic advance from unification in 1871 to reunification in 1990, Germany underwent so many dramatic changes in relation to its economic structure and political culture:

1. **Imperial Germany (1871–1918)**: where the transition from liberal to monopoly capitalism, superintended by the political structures of the *Obrigkeitsstaat* (the authoritarian state), ushers in the industrialization of culture;

2. **the Weimar Republic (1918–33)**: where Fordism, the standardization of commodity production, is established against the political and cultural backcloth of modernism;

3. **the Third Reich (1933–45)**: where economic modernization is steered towards production for war, and a centrally organized ideology of social unity, reinforced by terror, denies all cultural pluralism;

4. **the German Democratic Republic (1949–90)**: where a centralized, state-run economy is constructed under the auspices of socialism, with culture primarily under the control of the Socialist Unity Party (SED);

5. **the Federal Republic (1949–68)**: where the 'restoration' of capitalism is attended by the extensive Americanization of culture but only a partial democratization of the political culture;

6. **the Federal Republic (1968–90)**: where the development towards a post-industrial society is paralleled by the growth of an active, participative democracy and of a postmodern, postmaterialist culture.

In exploring the changes sketched out here, all the chapters in the present volume engage implicitly or explicitly with Horkheimer and Adorno's thesis in so far as they chart the growth of (or reaction against) modernism, outline the diversification (or centralization) of the institutions of cultural production, and trace the extent

7 Martin Jay, *The Dialectical Imagination: A History of the Frankfurt School and the Institute of Social Research 1923–50* (London, 1973), 297.
8 Diane Waldman, 'Critical Theory and Film: Adorno and "The Culture Industry" Revisited', *New German Critique*, 12 (1977), 56.

Rob Burns

to which culture in any given period functions as an instrument of ideological manipulation or critical enlightenment. Moreover, the volume as a whole is weighted towards the development of Germany since 1945, that is, the period subsequent to the appearance of *Dialektik der Aufklärung*.

If, at this point, we anticipate one of the conclusions reached by our discussion of post-war Germany, then this is because it qualifies a key aspect of Horkheimer and Adorno's argument, namely the thesis of total manipulation. In an essay published in 1941 Horkheimer could still write, with just a glimmer of optimism: 'One day we may learn that in the depths of their hearts, the masses, even in fascist countries, secretly knew the truth and disbelieved the lie, like catatonic patients who, only at the end of their trance, make known that nothing has eluded them.'[9] Yet, as we have seen, by the time of his collaboration with Adorno on *Dialektik der Aufklärung* Horkheimer's hope that the masses might prove not totally manipulable had evidently been extinguished. Similarly, when almost twenty years later, in an essay of 1963, Adorno returned to the question of the culture industry, he saw no reason to revise any of his original conclusions. However, in a radio lecture about leisure time delivered shortly before his death in 1969 Adorno did, somewhat grudgingly, concede that 'the integration of consciousness and leisure time, it seems, is not yet complete after all. The real interests of individuals are still strong enough to resist total manipulation up to a point'.[10] While our analysis endorses this judgement, it also goes further than simply noting the enduring capacity of individuals to withstand total manipulation. For, as will become especially clear from our discussion of the Federal Republic since 1968, the capitalist industrialization of culture and communication, highly advanced though it most assuredly is, has itself not been fully realized. Rather, in a way not foreseen by Horkheimer and Adorno, the expansion and diversification of the culture industry opened up spaces in the public sphere where a non-manipulative, even critical employment of the means of cultural communication was possible. In short, culture is the site of critical resistance as well as ideological manipulation.

In this respect at least the present volume can be aligned with that form of cultural studies which, in Meaghan Morris's memorable phrase, balks at the choice in cultural theory between 'cheerleaders and prophets of doom'[11] and seeks to reconcile the two paradigms of 'culturalism' (with its emphasis on cultural practice as constitutive and empowering) and 'the culture industry' (with its focus on a consensus mass culture saturated with imposed meaning).

9 Max Horkheimer, 'Art and Mass Culture', *Studies in Philosophy and Social Science*, 9 (1941), 304.
10 Theodor W. Adorno, 'Freizeit', in *Stichworte: Kritische Modelle 2* (Frankfurt am Main, 1969), 66.
11 Meaghan Morris, 'Banality in Cultural Studies', *Block*, 14 (1988), 24.

To quote the editorial statement of *Cultural Studies*, an international journal founded in 1987: 'Cultural studies, committed to the radically contextual, historically specific character of cultural practices . . . aims to identify and examine those moments when people are manipulated and deceived as well as those moments when they are active, struggling, and even resisting.' Similarly—to return to the starting-point of our discussion—Raymond Williams sought in his later work to harness together the idealist and materialist approaches to the sociology of culture with his notion of culture as a 'realized signifying system'; that is to say, as 'the signifying system through which necessarily (though among other means) a social order is communicated, reproduced, experienced, and explored'. What distinguishes this conception, Williams contends, is the convergence between, on the one hand, 'the anthropological and sociological senses of culture as a distinct "whole way of life", within which, now, a distinctive "signifying system" is seen as essentially involved in *all* forms of social activity' and, on the other hand, the more specialized (albeit more common) sense of culture as 'artistic and intellectual activities', though these are now much more broadly defined to include 'not only the traditional arts and forms of intellectual production but also all the signifying practices', from language through the arts and philosophy to film, journalism, and television.[12] It is part of the project of cultural studies that this broad conception of culture should be complemented by a similarly expansive definition of politics, which accordingly is taken to mean the workings of social relations of power. For, as Angela McRobbie has argued, 'it is in culture that we see long-term and deep social change take root, and it is also in culture that opposition to certain kinds of change is manifest, whether this opposition is planned or else seemingly organic, the result of buried but tenacious discontent'.[13] Like the present volume, such an analysis might appear to err on the side of the 'cheer-leaders', but—to leave Adorno with the last word—'it would be in tune with the prognosis that consciousness cannot be totally integrated in a society in which the basic contradictions remain undiminished'.[14]

12 Williams, *Culture*, 13.
13 McRobbie, 'Revenge of the 60s', 25.
14 Adorno, 'Freizeit', 67.

Imperial Germany: Towards the Commercialization of Culture

ROBIN LENMAN,

JOHN OSBORNE,

EDA SAGARRA

IF, as the Basle historian and cultural critic Jacob Burckhardt observed on resuming his lectures on the French Revolution in the summer of 1871, European history since 1789 had been the history of revolution, 'Germany's revolution' (Disraeli) of 1871 was of a different order from the rest. Standing Clausewitz's dictum concerning the relationship of war and politics on its head, Bismarck had throughout the so-called wars of unification (1864–71) retained both the diplomatic initiative and political control over the campaigns. In the winter of 1870–1, even though military victory in the Franco-Prussian War was still uncertain, the Prussian Prime Minister and his officials embarked on a massive twin-track operation: the opposition of the German princes to unification under Prussia was individually and systematically overcome, while simultaneously a Reich constitution, drawing heavily on that of the North German Confederation (1867–71), was drafted as both formal and symbolic instrument of that unification.

From the outset, however, certain internal contradictions in Bismarck's construct were evident. On the one hand, the Second Empire defined itself as a constitutional state (*Rechtsstaat*) and the first Reichstag (1871–4), elected on the basis of universal manhood suffrage and dominated by the National Liberals, the Chancellor's partners in government, put through a substantial programme of legislation. It included a commercial code for Germany, with the Reichsmark as the currency, and civil and political rights for Germany's Jews. On the other hand, this state, characterized by extraordinary economic dynamism and social dislocation, was denied by its neo-feudal political strait-jacket the opportunity to evolve structures appropriate to modern industrial capitalism. From the outset, Bismarck resolutely refused to concede those constitutional measures which were axiomatic for a *Rechtsstaat*, namely ministerial responsibility to parliament and budgetary control of the army. Combining in his person the posts of Prussian Prime Minister and Foreign Minister with that of Imperial Chancellor, he underpinned both the power of the executive and Prussia's domination of the Empire by resisting the creation of Reich ministries and working through permanent civil servants whose careers he controlled. Moreover, the position of the Emperor as the only genuine institutional link between Prussia and the Empire proved a major obstacle to evolutionary political growth; at the same time, as Wilhelm II's period of personal rule (1896/7–1915) would demonstrate, the system failed to provide safeguards against arbitrary rule and its resultant inefficiencies. The Emperor appointed and dismissed governments; the Chancellor was responsible to him alone. Only once, and then in unusual circumstances, did the Reichstag succeed in having a Chancellor dismissed (Bülow in 1909).

The most flagrant anomaly was the position of the army. It was indeed 'the absolutist kernel of Prussian-German constitutionalism'.[1] Anchored in the Prussian royal prerogative, the army became, apart from the limited budgetary influence of the Reichstag, effectively independent of civilian control. The situation was aggravated under Wilhelm II, who repeatedly—though not always with the support of the military—attempted to use the army as an instrument of civilian control. Yet paradoxically it did perform an integrating function. For many, military service was remembered in a positive light; and the uniform, which even Bismarck and after him Chancellor Bethmann Hollweg (1909–16) wore in the Reichstag, had positive associations for very large sections of the population. Its representational character, signifying experience of nationhood, was widely associated with pleasurable social occasions.

The speed of national unification in 1871 led to a restoration of confidence among most Germans in the traditional role of the state as provider of ideological as well as material needs. Certainly it seemed in the aftermath of 1871 as if the gap that had developed in Germany since the late eighteenth century between the state and society was now being closed. Burckhardt might in private anticipate Nietzsche's anxiety with his vision of 'a teleological view of

1 Wilhelm Deist, 'Die Armee in Staat und Gesellschaft 1890– 1914', in Michael Stürmer (ed.), *Das kaiserliche Deutschland: Politik und Gesellschaft 1871–1918* (Darmstadt, 1976), 312–39 (316).

Robin Lenman, John Osborne, Eda Sagarra

world history from Adam onwards in terms of German victories, culminating in 1870–1';[2] but it was clear that the authorities' understanding of the role of culture in the reinforcement of this process owed much to their ability to harness the educated middle classes as opinion-makers. The pace of Germany's victory also led—not least because of developments in communications and the perceptible rise in living standards over the previous two decades—to increased expectations among the subjects of the new German Emperor. Thus the protracted economic downturn following the stock exchange crash in 1873 administered a shock, whose severity was out of proportion to its actual impact and which goes far to explain the characterization of the post-unification decades as 'the age of neurosis'.[3] Even more relevant was the impact of demographic and social factors. Germany's population rose from 10,059,000 to 64,926,000 between 1871 and 1910. In 1871 some 64 per cent of Germans lived and worked in communities of less than 2,000 and only 12.5 per cent in towns of 20,000 or more; in 1910 the corresponding figures were 40 per cent and 34.7 per cent. From the 1890s onwards, as Germany entered a massive boom period in its economy (1896–1913), the resultant dislocations were reflected with particular force in the transformation of its political culture.

The manipulation of political culture by the ruling élites, notably the military, the agrarians, and the major industrialists, took *inter alia* the form of systematic promotion of mass organizations such as the War Veterans, Navy and Defence Leagues, and the School Leavers Association (Jungdeutschlandbund). Yet of equal significance, at a time when German political parties were being transformed from 'groups of notables' to modern mass organizations, was the extent of self-mobilization of specific strata and economic groups in the lower ranks of society. Principal among these were the petty-bourgeois sectional interest groups and the peasant leagues, accompanied, like satellites, by a myriad of radical fringe groups, all seeking access to mass cultural networks. Almost all could be seen as a response to the high profile and sophisticated organization of the German labour movement which, even after the lapse of Bismarck's anti-socialist legislation (1878–90), the state authorities still sought systematically to marginalize. German Catholics, responding to their marginalization in the *Kulturkampf* of the 1870s and 1880s, shared an almost equal capacity with the Social Democratic Party (SPD) for creating an effective, nation-wide organization in pursuit of their special interests. Indeed, the degree to which Germans generally in the later decades of the Empire were democratized by their identification with sectional or ideological interest

2 Jacob Burckhardt, *Briefe*, ed. Max Burckhardt (10 vols.; Basel and Stuttgart, 1949–86), v (1963), 184.
3 Hans Rosenberg, *Große Depression und Bismarckzeit: Wirtschaftsablauf, Gesellschaft und Politik in Mitteleuropa* (Berlin, 1967), 56.

groups is a key feature of the age; it is well exemplified in the women's movement. Within a mere seven years of the lifting of the ban on their right to organize (1908), the German women's movement became the third largest in the world; under its umbrella organization, the Association of Women's Organizations, it numbered some 1.5 million members in 1914.

Thus the half-century following the proclamation of the German Empire in the Hall of Mirrors at Versailles saw the development of conditions which prepared the way for the commercialization of culture. It should, however, be said that the principal exponents of this analysis of the culture industry, Horkheimer and Adorno, did not construct their arguments with reference to the Imperial Germany in which they were born. From the perspective of American exile they argued that the delay in the process of industrialization and the surviving legacy of an absolutism independent of market forces afforded in Germany a certain protection to cultural institutions: universities, theatres, opera houses, museums, and orchestras; and it might indeed be argued that significant cultural patronage from the provincial courts, stripped in Bismarckian Germany of political power, was directly involved in some of the most enduring cultural achievements of the period: the theatre reforms which emanated from the Duchy of Meiningen, Wagnerian opera, which benefited from the patronage of King Ludwig II of Bavaria, and the Artists' Colony established in Darmstadt by Grand Duke Ernst Ludwig, which led to the foundation of influential organizations dedicated to the improvement of industrial design, the Werkbund (1907) and, during the Weimar period, the Bauhaus.

On the other hand, there may be reasons for calling into question the periodization proposed by Horkheimer and Adorno. The development of the commercial theatre and the popular press during the Wilhelmine period already points to the emergence of a passive and socially undifferentiated mass audience. Furthermore—and this is reflected in the decision to devote a substantial part of this chapter to the creation and dissemination of visual culture in both its traditional and innovative forms (the 'technical media')—a distinct pre-eminence was already being acquired by the visual sense, identified by Adorno as the sense most representative of the culture of advanced industrial society.[4] Recent research has also begun to emphasize the bureaucratization of culture and the professionalization of its administration, made possible by the continued buoyancy of municipal tax receipts under the Empire.[5] In the development and organization of cultural institutions which secured increased participation by the masses a significant role was

4 Theodor W. Adorno, *Versuch über Wagner* (Frankfurt am Main, 1974; first pub. 1952), 92–3.
5 Peter Merkl, 'Urban Challenge under the Empire', in Jack R. Dukes and Joachim Remak (eds.), *Another Germany: A Reconsideration of the Imperial Era* (Boulder, Colo., and London, 1988), 61–72 (70).

Robin Lenman, John Osborne, Eda Sagarra

assumed by a third force, consisting of the modern state itself, local government, and sectional interest groups.

The Concept of Culture in Imperial Germany

An examination of the concept of culture itself, as it figured in public discourse at the time, leads to similarly ambivalent conclusions. Despite many conscious attempts to bring culture before a wider public, despite the aspirations of marginalized and minority groups expressed in the avant-garde, despite the resistance in the regions to the dominant culture emanating from the Imperial capital, there remains a certain static quality in the use of the concept, so that at the end of the period Clara Zetkin, a representative socialist woman, could still declare: 'The art of socialism . . . will be an extension of the grand, classical, bourgeois [*bürgerlich*] art.'[6] Less surprisingly Thomas Mann, an equally representative bourgeois male, could reassert: 'The German is synonymous with the *Bürgerlich*; if spirit [*Geist*] in general is of *bürgerlich* origin, then this is particularly true of the German spirit; German culture [*Bildung*] is *bürgerlich*.'[7]

This continuity is spectacularly manifest in the appeal made to culture in the context of the two wars which respectively mark the beginning and end of the Second German Empire. The National Liberal *Bildungsbürgertum*, the educated professional middle classes who had been in conflict with Bismarck since the constitutional crisis of 1859, were not just progressively won over to *Realpolitik* by the victories in the three wars of unification; they sought to claim these victories as their own. The Battle of Königgrätz (1866) had, according to the Leipzig geography teacher Oskar Peschel, been won in the classroom. The army and the aristocracy were, of course, inclined to dispute this. The military theorist Hohenlohe-Ingelfingen declared: 'The brilliant saying of one of our most talented men: "Our victories were won by the German schoolmaster", is only partially true. They might more justly be said to have been won by our N. C. Officers';[8] and in the 1890s the claim was contemptuously dismissed by *Ministerialassessor* von Rex in Fontane's *Der Stechlin* (1899): 'for my part I would rather award the palm to the needle gun or to old General Steinmetz, who was many things, but certainly no schoolmaster'.[9] In 1870, however, when Prussian troops had again set out to fight, German culture had not stood idly by. The regiments were sent on their way with the sound of those *male* voice choirs, which represented German musical culture at grass-

6 Franz Mehring, *Kunst und Proletariat* (Stuttgart, 1911), 6–7. Quoted from Vernon L. Lidtke, *The Alternative Culture: Socialist Labor in Imperial Germany* (New York and Oxford, 1985), 197.

7 Thomas Mann, *Betrachtungen eines Unpolitischen*, in *Gesammelte Werke in zwölf Bänden* (Frankfurt am Main, 1960), xii. 107.

8 Prince Kraft zu Hohenlohe-Ingelfingen, *Letters on Infantry*, trans. N. L. Walford (London, 1889), 22–3.

9 Theodor Fontane, *Werke, Schriften und Briefe*, ed. Walter Keitel and Helmuth Nürnberger (Munich, 1962–), 1. *Romane, Erzählungen, Gedichte*, ed. Walter Keitel, v (1966), 54.

roots level, ringing in their ears: 'How instantly then, on the banks of the Rhine as well as those of the Memel, did . . . every singing club . . . break out into a song which had up to then been totally unknown, "Die Wacht am Rhein".'[10] On their lips, or in their rucksacks, were further martial words by contemporary poets as divergent as the conservative veteran of the Wars of Liberation (1813–15), Hans Ferdinand Maßmann, and Georg Herwegh, an advocate of socialist revolution and a subsequent critic of the nationalism of the new state. Georg Hesekiel summed up the joy of participation after decades of exclusion as follows:

> As they march forth to battle, proud soldiers of the line,
> O Lord in heaven above me, they're singing a song of mine!
> Now I need grieve no longer, but calmly claim what's mine:
> 'As they marched forth to battle, they sang a song of thine!'[11]

During the campaign the armies were accompanied and their exploits recorded by writers and artists such as Gustav Freytag, Anton von Werner, Louis Braun, and Theodor Fontane. When they returned in triumph in 1871 writers such as Julius Rodenberg made their contribution with poems and festival dramas which would be brought out annually on 2 September, the anniversary of the Battle of Sedan.

Again the victories were celebrated as a triumph for culture, specifically German, national-liberal, Protestant culture, over the 'decadence' of the Latin rival. The prevailing tendency is recorded by Zola in words he attributes to Otto Günther, a Prussian Guards officer, in his novel *The Débâcle*:

'You can see, Paris is burning. . . . it was bound to come. . . . A grand piece of work!' Otto . . . raised his arm as though delivering a reproof. He was about to speak with the vehemence of that cold, hard, militaristic Protestantism that can always quote verses of the Bible. But . . . his gesture had been enough, it had expressed his racial hatred and his conviction that he was in France as a judge sent by the Lord of Hosts to chastise a perverse people. Paris was burning as a punishment for centuries of wickedness, for the long tale of its crimes and debauches. Once again the Germanic tribes would save the world and sweep away the last remains of Latin corruption.[12]

After the military victories it was the turn of German culture to consolidate and colonize. The *Deutsche Rundschau* claimed a place alongside the *Quarterly Review* and *La Revue des deux mondes* as a flagship of national culture. Through the German and then the European tours undertaken by the Duke of Meiningen's company, modern director's theatre was introduced to Brahm in Berlin, Irving

10 Hohenlohe-Ingelfingen, *Letters on Infantry*, 261.
11 Franz Lipperheide (ed.), *Lieder zu Schutz und Trutz: Gaben deutscher Dichter aus der Zeit des Kriegs im Jahre 1870 und 1871* (4 vols.; Berlin, 1871), i. 110.
12 Émile Zola, *The Débâcle* (1892), trans. Leonard Tancock (London, 1972), 485.

Robin Lenman, John Osborne, Eda Sagarra

in London, Antoine in Brussels, and Stanislavsky in Moscow. The itinerant orchestra of the same court, under the direction of Hans von Bülow, introduced equally far-reaching changes in orchestral practice, contributing by its example to the founding of the Berlin Philharmonic Orchestra in 1882. The pre-eminence which these changes gave to the orchestral conductor served, furthermore, to establish an institutional base for some of the greatest composers of the period: most notably Mahler in Vienna, and two of Bülow's successors in Meiningen, Richard Strauß and Max Reger. The element of cultural imperialism behind such activities was proudly recognized in Germany: 'After the great task of national unification had been completed, he [Duke Georg II] set out at the head of a great army of artists in order, in a series of bloodless triumphs, to proclaim the glory of the nation before all peoples.'[13]

On the outbreak of the First World War the situation was no different from that of 1870, except that the rucksacks contained even more of the same or similar anthologies:

even the noise of world war does not silence the voice of song. The love of music is too deeply rooted in the heart of our people. These great times teach us once again that our joys and our sorrows are bound up with German song. Wherever our troops take their leave from home, songs of folk and fatherland ring out, songs accompany them as they march into enemy cities and villages, our young company goes singing into the attack, and in hours of rest songs are also a source of refreshment: as it did for the old Germanic armies, song also arms our warriors and strengthens their hearts.[14]

Even the sensitive Rilke paid his tribute in the 'Fünf Gesänge' of 1914.

There followed countless poems, sermons, essays, and lectures expressing support for a war seen as the fulfilment of the mission to defend and propagate German spirit and culture, with titles such as *Die welthistorische Bedeutung des deutschen Geistes* (Rudolf Eucken) or *Mobilmachung der Seelen* (Fritz Lienhard). Among the weightiest was the manifesto of 4 October 1914, addressed to the 'world of culture' by ninety-three of the most prominent German intellectuals, including the General Director of the Berlin Royal Library, founding president of the Kaiser Wilhelm Society for the Advancement of Science (now the Max Planck Gesellschaft) and the country's leading Protestant theologian, Professor Adolf von Harnack.

The fragility of these apparently solid proprietorial claims on culture by a particular section of German society can be shown by the simple juxtaposition of the names of David Friedrich Strauß

13 Alfred Klaar, 'Herzog Georg von Meiningen: Ein Nekrolog', *Shakespeare Jahrbuch*, 51 (1915), 93.
14 Kommission für das deutsche Volksliederbuch (ed.), *Volkslieder für gemischten Chor, Partitur* (Leipzig, 1915), i. pp. v–vi.

and Friedrich Nietzsche, or Adolf von Harnack and Karl Barth. Nietzsche's and Barth's vigorous denunciations in youthful works of great power (*Unzeitgemäße Betrachtungen*, 1873–6; *Der Römerbrief*, 1918) of the confusion which permitted their liberal forebears to misuse culture for national and military ends were destined to contribute to a revision of the concept itself with far-reaching effects outside the period under discussion.

The Cultural Formation of the Public

A real need for integration in the newly unified state was clearly felt in the 1870s by the *Bildungsbürgertum*, the acknowledged exponents of the classical conception of German culture. This received expression in the titles and the editorial programmes of such literary journals as *Im neuen Reich* (1871–, ed. Alfred Dove) and the *Deutsche Rundschau* (1874–, ed. Julius Rodenberg), which brought together eminent contributors like Gottfried Keller, Theodor Storm, Conrad Ferdinand Meyer, Paul Heyse, Theodor Fontane, Louise von François, Marie von Ebner-Eschenbach, Gustav Freytag, Georg Brandes, Wilhelm Dilthey, Wilhelm Scherer, Erich Schmidt, Carl Justi, Hermann Grimm, Konrad Fiedler, Heinrich von Sybel, Theodor Mommsen, Eduard Hanslick, and Max Lenz. It was the hope of the *Bildungsbürgertum* that the new state would finally provide an appropriate political form for a national culture. There was, especially outside Prussia, some unease that unity had been imposed by political actions from above, rather than emerging in the slow, organic growth (*Bildung*) of the nation, and so Gustav Freytag, as if reserving judgement, broke off his cycle of novels, *Die Ahnen* (1872–80), in which he retrospectively constructs a pedigree for the Second Empire, at the emotive date of 1848. Similarly the South German liberal Friedrich Theodor Vischer, though willing to take the spoils, deplored their provenance; he assented, according to Fontane, 'without reservation to the events of the year 1870, in particular the reconstruction of the German Empire. It was only the architect who displeased him. "It is regrettable that it had to be Bismarck of all people who brought this about."'[15] The fear of again being left to observe from the sidelines while others participated in the national success was, however, very great. It meant that the educational reforms initiated in the 1870s produced a mixed response.

These reforms, promulgated from 1872 onwards by the Prussian Minister of Education, Adalbert Falk, were designed to produce an

15 Theodor Fontane, *Aus den Tagen der Okkupation, Werke, Schriften und Briefe*, 3. *Aufsätze, Kritiken, Erinnerungen*, iv. *Autobiographisches*, ed. Walter Keitel (1973), 703.

Robin Lenman, John Osborne, Eda Sagarra

educational system more fitted to the needs of a modern industrial state than the repressive one that had been in place since the measures introduced by von Raumer after the disturbances of 1848. The new legislation brought about a widening and modernizing of the curriculum, with an emphasis on scientific subjects at the expense of religious instruction, and it increased state control, for instance through the ministerial prescription of school textbooks (purchased, as in Germany today, by parents). It led to a gradual upgrading of the *Realschule* and the establishment of technical universities, including the Königliche Technische Hochschule, founded in Berlin in 1879 and moved, in 1883, to new premises in Berlin-Charlottenburg where, with the active support of Werner von Siemens, one of a number of entrepreneurs who recognized the need for a skilled labour force, it established itself as a centre of excellence in electrical engineering. This strengthening of vocational education was energetically supported at the turn of the century by Kaiser Wilhelm II himself, interested as he was in securing Germany's position in world markets. It was on the direct intervention of the Kaiser that the technical universities were given the right to award doctorates in 1899. By imperial decree of 26 November 1900 the *Gymnasien, Realgymnasien*, and *Oberrealschulen* were formally given equal status.

Vociferous protests were made against Falk's reforms. Some came, of course, from the Roman Catholic Church, against whose influence the measures were directly aimed as part of the anti-Catholicism which constituted one plank in Bismarck's policy of national consolidation, and which the liberals characteristically saw, in the formulation of the distinguished pathologist, Rudolf Virchow, as a struggle for culture (*Kulturkampf*). Reservations were also voiced by the Junker class, whose patronage of schools on their estates was threatened. The *Bürgertum*, whose interests the reforms were designed to further, responded with mixed feelings. On the one hand, there is evidence of a desire to appropriate the achievements of technology. As Dubslav observes of 'his' schoolmaster in Fontane's *Der Stechlin*: 'When Koch discovers tuberculin or Edison plays you an opera at a distance of fifty miles . . . then my Krippenstapel will show you that he already had the idea thirty years ago.'[16] Others were inclined to dematerialize technological achievements by wishfully interpreting them as secondary manifestations of German *Geist*: 'Everything technical and organizational is also born of the spirit and is a representation of spirit.'[17] On the other hand, there arose a significant body of conservative cultural criticism which saw in the transformation of schools into vocational institutions a threat

16 Fontane, *Werke, Schriften und Briefe*, 1. v. 54.
17 Karl König, *Neue Kriegspredigten* (Jena, 1914), 25.

to traditional humanistic culture. As early as 1872 this found voice in Nietzsche's lectures, 'Die Zukunft unserer Bildungsanstalten', identifying the educational system as a thinly disguised means of recruiting servants for the state, and arguing for the restriction of education to a minority of élite leaders.

The differing reactions of *Gymnasial-* and *Volksschullehrer* suggest that the recurrent attacks on contemporary 'materialist' tendencies were in part an expression of the fears of a social group who felt their status as the representatives of German culture to be under threat. That threat was, in fact, fairly slow to take concrete form; not only did the *Abitur*, the passport to the universities, remain the prerogative of the *Gymnasien* until 1900, but the cost of higher education and the social ethos created by the student corporations continued to militate against participation from outside the male *Bildungsbürgertum*.[18] Yet by 1911 the participation rates at university by males from the lower middle class as well as the *Bürgertum* generally had, by modern standards, reached a satisfactory level, and even the significant under-representation of Catholics in the educational system had begun to redress itself.[19]

Following the demands made by Luise Otto-Peters in the 1850s, and the Frauenbildungsverein, founded in 1865, the Wilhelmine period saw growing pressure from among the early women's movement for changes in the education and training of women. Prominent voices included those of Fanny Lewald, Hedwig Dohm, and Helene Lange, but their efforts were slow to take effect. The young Anna Mahr in Hauptmann's *Einsame Menschen* (1891) is a student at the University of Zurich, where women had been admitted since 1864, and where Ricarda Huch (in voluntary exile for personal and economic reasons) and Rosa Luxemburg (a political refugee) took their doctorates in the 1890s. In 1894, when Käthe Windscheid became the first woman to be awarded a doctorate by a German university (Heidelberg), the Prussian Ministry of Education still maintained the principle that 'Girls' High Schools are a quite different kind of educational institution from those institutions which in Prussia are described as High Schools in the narrower sense and to which only members of the male sex have access.'[20] In Prussia it was not until 1908 that girls' schools were given equal status with boys' schools, and university entrance opened to both sexes.

A certain unease at the educational reforms is evident in the ambiguities informing some of the imaginative writing of the 1880s, which was already beginning to grapple with one of the dominant themes of early modern literature: the alienation of the intellectual. The hero of Theodor Storm's *Der Schimmelreiter* (1888) is a self-

18 Fritz K. Ringer, 'Higher Education in Germany in the Nineteenth Century', *Journal of Contemporary History*, 2 (1967), 123–38 (136–7).
19 Fritz K. Ringer, *Education and Society in Modern Europe* (Bloomington, Ind., 1979), 108; and Ronald J. Ross, 'Catholic Plight in the *Kaiserreich*: A Reappraisal', in Dukes and Remak (eds.), *Another Germany*, 73–94 (78–80).
20 Quoted from Max Bucher *et al.* (eds.), *Realismus und Gründerzeit: Manifeste und Dokumente zur deutschen Literatur, 1848–1880*, (2 vols.; Stuttgart, 1975–6), i. 252.

taught technocrat, whose work (dike-building in eighteenth-century Frisia) represents a solitary achievement, carried through despite the resistance of a superstitious, seemingly ineducable society. His tale, admiringly narrated by none other than the village schoolmaster, remains nevertheless ambivalent because, lacking any deep bond to the community, Storm's hero pursues his aims as much for personal aggrandizement as for the general good.

Criticism of education becomes more explicit in a number of literary works published around the turn of the century devoted to the sufferings of the adolescent schoolboy: Holz and Schlaf, *Der erste Schultag* (1889), Thomas Mann, *Buddenbrooks* (1901), Hermann Hesse, *Unterm Rad* (1903), Heinrich Mann, *Professor Unrat* (1905), the Austrian Robert Musil's *Die Verwirrungen des Zöglings Törleß* (1905), the Swiss Robert Walser's *Jakob von Gunten* (1909). In several of these works education becomes associated with problems of sexuality (including homo-eroticism) which, in the wake of the writings of Freud and others, begins slowly to claim a place in public debate. Only Wedekind in *Frühlings Erwachen* (1891) considers the plight of the uneducated adolescent female—unless one includes the anonymously published *Josefine Mutzenbacher: Die Lebensgeschichte einer wienerischen Dirne, von ihr selbst erzählt* (1906). This frankly pornographic narrative, believed to be by Felix Salten (better known as the author of *Bambi: Eine Lebensgeschichte aus dem Walde* (1923; filmed 1942)), is a first-person account of the experiences of a Viennese prostitute. It is recounted in a way which acknowledges the existence of female sexuality with far greater force than the pioneers in this field, Wedekind and Schnitzler, although in a manner far removed from that of the contemporary champion of female sexuality, Helene Stöcker. For Josefine Mutzenbacher it is the absence of education that is significant; many of the first group of works proceed by the examination of personal and intimate experiences, but they do so in order to criticize the overbearing pressure of a school system perceived as increasingly functional in character, and in which even the surviving elements of the classical humanist tradition were being undermined.

A characteristic expression of this unease takes the form of an anti-modernist yearning for a rescue from what were felt to be the fragmenting tendencies of intellectualism, technology, and materialism. This was to develop both popular and élite strands, with offshoots in counter-cultures and subcultures of remarkable tenacity. For the most extreme exponents, such as the right-wing Alldeutscher Verband, the Wilhelmine Reich represented no more than an interim arrangement, and its adherents greeted the outbreak of war in 1914 as an opportunity for the purification of the nation into the *Volk*.

In early Imperial Germany such thinking had its most important focus in the romantic nationalism of the Bayreuth circle, and drew both its inspiration and its abidingly anti-Semitic tendency from the writings of Richard Wagner. It was further developed in the work of Paul de Lagarde, whose cultural-critical essays, *Deutsche Schriften* (1878–81), after first circulating only among small groups of enthusiasts, entered the mainstream of public debate in the more conservative climate after 1878. A decade later Nietzsche began to secure attention with his critique of contemporary 'decadence' in *Also sprach Zarathustra* (1884, 1892), and, on a more popular level, Julius Langbehn's anonymously published *Rembrandt als Erzieher, von einem Deutschen* (1890) met with enormous success. Support for this defence of the values of Germanic 'culture' against those of Western 'civilization' was found in the work of Houston Stewart Chamberlain, and further developed in the writings of Moeller van den Bruck. The debate was to continue throughout the war and into the Weimar Republic in the writings of Thomas and Heinrich Mann, and in the programme of 'Conservative Revolution' espoused by Thomas Mann and Hugo von Hofmannsthal. During the Wilhelmine period the most notable, but most exclusive, manifestation of cultural-conservative opposition was the George-Kreis, a group of writers assembled around a charismatic leader and dedicated to an anti-materialist, anti-liberal, and anti-egalitarian programme for the ultimate benefit of the *Volk*.

The sympathy of the Naturalist writers with the early Social Democratic movement gave to their cultural criticism a different political complexion. Many were nevertheless attracted to the views of Langbehn and in the 1890s largely withdrew from the industrial metropolis for the peace of rural Friedrichshagen. Even some of those who, like Bruno Wille, had been directly involved in the theoretical debates of the Social Democratic Party and in institutions such as the Freie Volksbühne gave up their political engagement and espoused a utopian cult of 'social aristocracy' designed to eliminate the conflicts of modern life. Gerhart Hauptmann documents this change in *Einsame Menschen*, taking as his hero a young intellectual from the *Bildungsbürgertum*, equally alienated from his devout parents with their simple, pre-Darwinist Christian faith, the values of the modern natural sciences, as exemplified by Du Bois-Reymond (at the time Director of the Physiological Institute and Rector of the University of Berlin), and the radical politics of his shaven-headed friend Braun. Partaking of a variety of contemporary

Robin Lenman, John Osborne, Eda Sagarra

reformist attitudes, Hauptmann's Vockerat resides in Friedrichshagen, is inclined to interrupt the action of the play with gymnastic exercises and lakeside walks, and is attracted to the notion of a new kind of non-matrimonial relationship between the sexes.

Many of the groups which emerged during this period, often forming their own communities, rejecting the *Gesellschaft* of modern urban life in favour of the *Gemeinschaft* of agrarian society, saw themselves as seeking a 'third way' between socialism and capitalism. They are too numerous to list exhaustively, but it ought to be noted that certain of those who were inspired by this desire to return to nature—for instance, the Worpswede community, the artists who gathered in the garden-suburb of Hellerau (Dresden), where Jacques-Dalcroze was invited in 1910 to found his School of Dance, and Rudolf Steiner's Anthroposophische Gesellschaft— exercised an important influence both on individual artists (Rilke, Paula Modersohn-Becker, Hesse, Else Lasker-Schüler, Kandinsky, Franz Marc, Jawlensky, Adolphe Appia, Diaghilev, and, at a later date, Josef Beuys and Michael Ende) and on the development of the arts in Germany and elsewhere. Dismissed contemptuously by Naphta in Thomas Mann's *Der Zauberberg* (1924), they drew their support largely from the educated middle classes and their interests covered an enormous range of activity including education, dress, alternative medicine, vegetarianism and diet, and animal rights. Certain of the manifestations of this subculture entered the mainstream of German cultural life, and even gave new words to the language: *Freie Waldorfschule, Eurhythmie, Kneippkur, Reformhaus, Demeter* products; although there can be few who would now recognize their Jaeger outfits as originating in the reforms of Gustav Jäger, who argued in his book *Die Normalkleidung als Gesundheitsschutz* (1880) for the exclusive use of animal fibres in clothing.

Literary Culture

In the following examination of the development of literary culture attention will be focused on what were still the three most important institutions for its dissemination, and the three most important sources of employment for the writer: the book trade, the press, and the theatre. All of these institutions, which had languished during the economically and intellectually morose situation after 1848, received new impetus from a number of changes which either coincided with, or followed directly from, the foundation of the new Reich in 1871. Among the most notable were the removal of restrictions on the right to practise trade (*allgemeine Gewerbefreiheit*), which facilitated the founding of new publishing houses and theatres; the introduction of a unified postal system, which permitted the expansion and intensification of the publishers' distribution network; and the standardization of copyright legislation throughout the Empire, which put the marketing of intellectual property on a sound footing. Changes to the legislation on censorship in the unified Press Laws (*Reichspressegesetze*, 1874) were initially greeted optimistically, but were two-edged in their effect, leaving the initial decision as to confiscation or prohibition of public performance in the hands of the local police authorities rather than the judiciary. Their liberalizing tendency was, in any case, seriously constrained by the anti-socialist legislation.

Although the period of rapid economic growth came to an abrupt end in 1873, and the recovery of 1879 proved short-lived, the upturn in the book trade which had begun in the late 1860s continued, the number of new publications rising from 10,563 in 1868 to 15,191 in 1881. At the same time the number of publishing houses grew rapidly, and the location of so many of them in the Imperial capital meant that Berlin came to replace Leipzig as the major publishing centre, without, however, inhibiting the development of regional centres of book and journal publishing, such as Hamburg, Stuttgart, Dresden, or Munich. Increased price competition and more modern forms of distribution confronted booksellers with the problems associated with the challenge to the Net Book Agreement in Britain in the 1990s, until discounting was outlawed in 1887 by the reforms which bear the name of Alfred Kröner. The decisive turning-point in the development towards mass literacy occurred between 1850 and 1870, and by 1880 illiteracy was virtually eliminated in Prussia, save for certain pockets east of the Elbe. The growth of academic education and the increase in the number of schools was rapidly reflected in the shape of the market: in the 1870s education displaced theology as the largest category of books published.

The year 1867 saw the end of timeless copyright, freeing classic works by writers who had died before 9 November 1837, the distribution of which had been restricted by the pricing policy of the publisher Cotta. Henceforward the symbolic function of the classics as a sign of socio-cultural prestige was served by the production of luxury editions (*Prachtwerke*)—a practice which still survives. Although the public of the traditional outlets remained a middle-class public, from now on the techniques of mass marketing began to be employed to bring the classics to a wider readership. The publishers Brockhaus and Hempel developed series of works sold by subscription, the latter's *Nationalbibliothek*, backed by a massive marketing campaign, immediately acquiring as many as 40,000 subscribers; while an even more radical change was brought about by the publisher Reclam, whose *Universalbibliothek* opened challengingly with Goethe's *Faust* in 1867. At a price of 2 groschen, less than a twentieth of the price asked by Cotta, the cheap paperback sold 20,000 copies in a matter of months, to establish a new and enduring concept in the German book trade.

In general, however, books, particularly recent belles lettres, continued to be relatively highly priced and book purchase remained at a low level even among the educated middle classes; 'a German who *buys* a book is a special kind of person,' observed a contributor to the *Preußische Jahrbücher* in 1884.[21] The commercial lending libraries, whose subscription and borrowing charges were modest, reached a significantly larger public. Borstell's *Leihbibliothek* in Berlin, the biggest in Germany, had a stock of 600,000 books in 1898. This included 2,316 copies of Freytag's *Soll und Haben*, 1,688 of Dahn's *Ein Kampf um Rom*, and 1,285 of Marlitt's *Goldelse*; and works of canonical status such as Keller's *Der grüne Heinrich* (630 copies) and Meyer's *Jürg Jenatsch* (618). But by the 1880s they too had passed their peak, being replaced as purveyors of fiction by the public libraries and the newspaper press.

It was not easy for a writer to survive financially unless he or she belonged to the select few with private resources, such as Conrad Ferdinand Meyer, or a professional post, such as Gottfried Keller or Theodor Storm. Journals and newspapers, which published short works or longer works in serial form, often prior to publication, provided a better source of income than book publishers. The *Novelle*, the classic German short narrative genre, thus experienced a golden age in the years 1870–90, benefiting also from the political correctness of its foreshortened view of history as a collection of momentous events decided by Great Men, providence, or fate. Its leading exponents, Keller, Storm, Meyer, and the pre-eminent theorist, Paul Heyse, were assiduously courted by Rodenberg and guaranteed publication in the *Deutsche Rundschau*. The principal contemporary work of narrative theory, *Beiträge zur Theorie und Technik des Romans* (1883), by the commercially successful Friedrich Spielhagen, was clearly influenced by the exigencies imposed by the desirability of pre-publication in serial form: proscribed were expansive reflections, psychological details, and anything at all dubious in a moral sense. Particular success was enjoyed in the serialized novel by a group of women writers of whom the best known is Eugenie Marlitt.

21 'Der deutsche Sortimentsbuchhandel', *Preußische Jahrbücher*, 53 (1884), 90; quoted from Bucher *et al.* (eds.), *Realismus und Gründerzeit*, i. 239.

Her stereotyped romances on the Cinderella theme contributed largely to the increased circulation of the family journal *Die Gartenlaube*, which reached a record level of 378,000 in 1881.

The marginalization of politically progressive or stylistically experimental authors, who lacked a readership among the middle classes, led in the 1880s to the formation of small literary circles and societies, which correspond to the Secessionist movements in the visual arts, and out of which German Naturalism emerged. Naturalism in particular brought with it a new generation of periodicals which spearheaded the literary avant-garde in the early twentieth century. The most successful of these journals, *Freie Bühne für modernes Leben*, was responsible for the first publication in Germany of works by Gerhart Hauptmann, Dostoevsky, Zola, Maupassant, Strindberg, Schnitzler, d'Annunzio, Thomas Mann, Hofmannsthal, Wilde, and Hesse, establishing a close connection between the publisher Samuel Fischer and many of the writers of early modernism. As a statement of its intention to challenge the dominant culture represented by the *Deutsche Rundschau* it changed its title to *Neue deutsche Rundschau* in 1894 (since 1904 *Die neue Rundschau*).

At the popular end of the spectrum colportage represented a significant extension in the form of book distribution, by which a variety of works, including classics and works of reference, such as Brehm's *Tierleben* and *Meyers Konversationslexikon*, were sold on a door-to-door basis. Certain publishers specialized in this field, commissioning work which appeared in instalments in weekly journals such as Münchmeyer's *Deutsches Familienblatt* or Spemann's *Guter Kamerad*, at low cost (10 Pf), following specific formulas or conventions, and designed to appeal to a clearly targeted (proletarian) audience. Although it contributed to the development of a mass market, this form of distribution failed during the 1890s to survive competition from the *Illustrierten*, which were aimed at a wider, non-class-based readership.

By far the most successful exponent of the colporteur-novel was Karl May, whose prolific output is best known for adventure stories, usually set in exotic lands and propagating the image of the benevolent colonist who understands the natives, but remains patronizingly aware of the superiority of Western European values and technology. Criticized as a purveyor of *Schund* (trash), his books, along with those of Eugenie Marlitt, were excluded by dedicated Social Democrat librarians from the workers' libraries which began to flourish in the 1890s after the lapse of the anti-socialist laws. However, in 'Old Shatterhand' and his 'blood-brother' Winnetou,

Robin Lenman, John Osborne, Eda Sagarra

May created figures of great significance for the cultural formation of subsequent generations of Germans of all social classes.

The changes referred to above reflect both institutional changes and changes in reading habits. As far as the latter are concerned particular importance attaches to the continuation of a trend characteristic of the reading revolution of the nineteenth century, namely the shift from intensive reading, the repeated, reflective reading of a limited body of material, to extensive reading of more and increasingly varied material. The consequences of these changes were recognized by the newspaper and periodical press at an earlier stage than the book trade. On its first publication in 1866 *Die deutschen Zeitschriften und die Entstehung der öffentlichen Meinung*, a polemical study by Heinrich Wuttke which deplored the contemporary subversion of the classic role of the press as a medium of information, preparing people to participate in public debate, made little impact; but it reappeared in a much quoted and imitated third edition in 1875. The principal motif in this critique was once again the threat to the traditional concept of *Bildung* posed by commercialization and the emergence of a mass public.

The need for an increase in information during the political upheavals and wars which preceded unification had had commercially beneficial consequences for the newspaper press, leading to an increase in the number of pages and the publication of extra editions. With the founding of the *Berliner Tageblatt* (1872) a new kind of newspaper began to emerge, the *Generalanzeigerpresse*, although initially its development was inhibited by the economic depression of the 1870s. No longer exclusively dependent on the traditional method of distribution by subscription, the new papers secured the basic part of their income from advertisers. In 1883 the *Berliner Lokal-Anzeiger* was founded by August Scherl (whose publishing house was to provide the basis for the Hugenberg concern during the Weimar Republic) as a Sunday paper with an edition of 200,000; from the outset its costs were largely covered by advertising revenue, without any charge other than a delivery charge of 10 Pf. It settled down in 1885 as a daily paper with a circulation of 150,000, and the proprietor reverted to distribution by subscription at a monthly cost of 1 mark. Editorial policy thus came increasingly to be determined by the market, that is to say, by the advertisers, so that the paper could no longer lay claim to the role of representative of public opinion. There was undoubtedly a significant broadening of the readership, but this was accompanied by a shift in the function of the news content towards raising and maintaining circulation in a competitive situation. In these circumstances readers tended to become consumers, both in the sense of passive absorbers of the material supplied, and purchasers of the goods and services advertised.

A parallel development took place in the popular periodical press. The middlebrow family journals of the mid-century, despite their proclamation of a non-political programme, can be seen to articulate a distinct ideological position, namely that of lower middle class, liberal nationalism. Before the turn of the century, however, such journals had been supplanted by the *Illustrierten*, a new kind of journal which did not cultivate the loyalty of a particular circle of subscribers, but created its own public in the competition of street sales. The first example, the *Berliner Illustrirte*, founded by the Ullstein publishing house in 1891, and selling at 10 Pf. per issue, soon reached a circulation of 40,000. The content of the *Illustrierten* included the serial novel, local news, popular science, and topical items of cultural and social interest with immediate and direct appeal.

Since the mid-century efforts had been continually made to exploit illustration in the press. The final breakthrough came only in the Wilhelmine period, which saw significant technical improvements (for instance, in the process of stereotyping and half-tone engraving, and the introduction of the rotation machine which permitted the simultaneous printing of text and image). The consequence was to be a change in reading habits, most evident in the press but by no means confined to it, in which the image itself figured as an immediately comprehensible vehicle of complex information with a high claim to authenticity. Even though it was only the static illustration that was initially available, a variety of attempts to integrate the text with a series of pictures pointed to a desire to add motion, and thus heralded major developments in the image-dominated culture of the twentieth century.

Although the first Berlin cinema was opened in 1899, it was only towards the end of the Wilhelmine period that this new medium began to assume real importance. The cinema was destined to become more prominent a part of mass culture than the theatre, but developments in the practice of theatre pointed in the same direction. There is even a certain paradigmatic quality about the history of the theatre in Berlin from the middle of the century, when the virtual monopoly position of the court theatre, housed in Schinkel's famous Königliches Schauspielhaus and administered by a retired Prussian officer, Botho von Hülsen, was unchallenged, to the end of the Imperial period, when the spectacular productions of a professional theatre director, Max Reinhardt, clearly anticipate the style of Hollywood.

Prior to 1848 Berlin had only three theatres and until the 1870s there was very little growth. The first concession to be granted since 1842 had permitted the opening in 1848 of the Friedrich-Wilhelmstädtisches Theater, to be the site of some of the major developments in mainstream theatre up to the First World War; but at the time the concessionaire, Deichmann, had to undertake not to compete with the royal theatres, which thus maintained their monopoly of the classic repertoire. Things changed significantly with the introduction of *allgemeine Gewerbefreiheit* in 1869 and 1871; paragraph 32 of the new legislation referred expressly to the theatres, so that establishments could now be opened with almost total freedom. This brought Germany to the position established in England by the Theatre Regulation Act of 1843, when the patents of Charles II, limiting the legitimate spoken drama to the theatres of Covent Garden and Drury Lane, were revoked. Urban growth, the emergence of a new theatre audience, and the speculative atmosphere of the post-war period gave rise to frenzied activity. The first year of *allgemeine Gewerbefreiheit* saw the building of ninety new theatres, and over the next fifteen years the total number of theatres in the Reich increased threefold, to approximately 600.

Among the many changes which took place as the modern commercial theatre began to develop, symptomatic importance attaches to theatre buildings, theatrical production, the relation of the actor and the public, and the rise of the director. Instructive examples can be drawn from the practices of the Meiningen Court Theatre, firstly because of its perceived role in theatre reform and secondly because it so obviously occupies a transitional position between court and commercial theatre, competing, as it did from 1874 onwards, with the Königliches Schauspielhaus from its Berlin base at the Friedrich-Wilhelmstädtisches Theater.

The great model for theatre architects of the time was provided by Charles Garnier's Paris Opéra (1875), a monument to the culture of the *haute bourgeoisie* of the nineteenth century, reflecting in its location in Haussmann's rebuilt Paris and its own external and internal architecture the hierarchy of a society dominated by this social class and providing it with a forum for self-display.[22] It also represented a culminating point, for as the composition of the theatre audience in modern urban society became more diverse, so theatre architecture was modified. Gradual change is evident in the series of theatres designed by Fellner and Helmer in the last

22 Michael Hays, *The Public and Performance: Essays in the History of French and German Theater, 1871–1900* (Theatre and Dramatic Studies, 6; Ann Arbor, 1981), 3–6.

two decades of the century, with a significant reduction of the ancillary social space, and an increase and redistribution of the functional (audience) space. Radical stimulus to change came from the innovations of Richard Wagner at the Festspielhaus in Bayreuth, where the whole theatre space was brought under the control of the artistic director.

Meiningen provides an interesting illustration of the trend, because the theatre was burnt down in 1909 and rebuilt in a way which preserves certain of the features of the older type: the central royal box and the hierarchical division of the audience by the provision of separate staircases, buffets, and cloakrooms for the various categories of seats. The new design, however, continued the movement in the direction taken by the theatres built after 1885, which had already been evident in the modifications the Duke of Meiningen had made to the theatre after taking over the artistic direction in the late 1860s: the size of the auditorium was increased for commercial reasons, and it was restructured in a 'democratizing' spirit to minimize differences between privileged and less privileged perspectives. A design for a single-level, raked, semi-circular, amphitheatre-type auditorium had been submitted, but was declined in favour of the more conventional plan of a local architect. The boxes, traditionally the place of the aristocracy, were replaced by an upper circle, of which it has been said: 'these seats are undefined; they bring neither prestige nor odium. They confer an inestimable privilege . . . that of seeing without being seen. . . . Whoever sits in the upper circle strives to forget that the boxes used to exist.'[23] As the audience came to be drawn increasingly from the lower middle class, the element of self-presentation by the audience as a social class was diminished in favour of an emphasis on the shared experience of the theatrical event in a uniform setting.

The darkening of the auditorium during performance, as practised by the Meiningen company and by Wagner in Bayreuth; the increasing sophistication in the use of stage lighting, pioneered at this time by Hugo Bähr of Dresden; the subordination of the text to non-verbal elements in theatrical art; the separation of stage space and audience by the proscenium arch, further emphasized by illusionist means in the architecture of Wagner's Festspielhaus; the concealment of entrances and dressing rooms for actors and actresses—all these developments combined to force a change in the role of the audience to that of passive recipient, only watching, no longer participating. At the same time they favoured a change to an acting style in which actors seem to deny the presence of an audience and perform only for each other. Applause in mid-scene

23 Theodor W. Adorno, 'Natural History of the Theatre', in *Quasi una Fantasia: Essays on Modern Music*, trans. Rodney Livingstone (London and New York, 1992), 73–4.

Robin Lenman, John Osborne, Eda Sagarra

was therefore discouraged, and performers were expressly forbidden to acknowledge audience response by taking a bow, as Ludwig Barnay (an actor of an older school) none the less did—across the body of the dead Caesar—when playing Antony in *Julius Caesar* with the Meiningen company in London in 1881. In this respect the apparent eccentricity of King Ludwig II of Bavaria reveals itself as curiously progressive. His *Separatvorstellungen*, performances mounted exclusively for a solitary spectator in a darkened theatre, subverted the normal relationship of actor and audience.

Power was thereby taken away from both the audience and the performer, who hitherto had enjoyed a certain autonomy in matters of casting and a certain degree of freedom in such matters as costume, improvisation, and attendance at rehearsal. Power, codified in written rules with sanctions including summary dismissal, now accrued to the director, who emerged in these years as an interpreter imposing his conception of the text by all available means on an audience which was beginning to acquire some of the characteristics of an undifferentiated mass public, open to manipulation.

In 1882 the Friedrich-Wilhelmstädtisches Theater was reopened as the Deutsches Theater by the entrepreneur Adolf L'Arronge, only to disappoint the high expectations expressed on behalf of the early Naturalist movement by Heinrich Hart in the pioneering journal *Kritische Waffengänge* (1882–4). It was not until after the new literary movement had made its breakthrough in a private venture modelled on Antoine's Parisian Théâtre Libre, the Berlin Freie Bühne, that the Deutsches Theater became the home of men eager to assume the role of professional director: the autocrat, Otto Brahm, and his renegade pupil, the 'magician', Max Reinhardt. In a development parallel to that taking place in the press, theatre thus began to lose its function as a forum for public debate, becoming instead a vehicle of education, indoctrination, or diverting entertainment for commercial ends.

Although the audience was widened to include the lower middle classes, the theatre remained by and large financially out of reach of working men and women; in the 1870s ticket prices at the Königliches Schauspielhaus ranged from 1 to 7 marks. The Berlin tours of the Meiningen company had provoked competition in the form of special performances of the classics at much lower prices, 0.30–2 marks, which, in 1875, played to packed houses in the normally bad month of May. It was not, however, until the 1890s that systematic attempts were made to provide theatre for the people. At the same time the *Volksbühnenbewegung* (People's Theatre Movement) is, in its early history, paradigmatic of the problems of organized socialism in developing an alternative to dominant bourgeois culture.

The Freie Volksbühne was established in 1890 in Berlin on the initiative of Bruno Wille, following the model of the Freie Bühne and with a significant element of common membership among its founders. But whereas the latter was conceived as a self-consciously élite group, dedicated to furthering the literary avant-garde, the primary concern of the Freie Volksbühne was to bring a new public into the theatre. Ticket prices were uniform, seats being allocated by lottery, and performances consisted in part of special productions and, increasingly, productions 'bought in' from those currently in repertory in the commercial theatres. Once it became clear that the aim of Wille and his supporters, who were associated with the radical wing of the Social Democratic Party, was also to create a link between organized socialism and literary modernism, they were swiftly pushed aside. Wille was replaced by the Marxist critic Franz Mehring, who was alienated by the pessimistic determinism of modern Naturalist doctrine, and much less interested in encouraging the development of a specifically working-class literature than in claiming for the proletariat the great works of the classic writers, notably Lessing and Schiller. Mehring's view prevailed both here and in the wider debate about Naturalism at the Party Congress in Gotha in 1896, confirming the orientation of the SPD towards traditional high culture. The Freie Volksbühne flourished all the same, along with workers' theatrical clubs, singing clubs, cycling clubs, and gymnastics clubs, providing an alternative culture in the form of separate organizations parallel to their bourgeois counterparts, but not yet dedicated to any specifically working-class content. It remains today an important feature in German theatre life, with an honourable and distinguished history.

Visual Culture: The Institutional Framework

Late nineteenth-century Germany experienced an upsurge of image production closely comparable with its boom in book and journal publication and similarly sustained by the country's dynamic industrial economy and by the growth of an increasingly urbanized, culture- and entertainment-hungry public. There were other links too: many painters doubled as book-illustrators; exhibitions and museums were dominated by historical and literary subjects; and the early cinema was closely related to mass-produced popular fiction. Between 1871 and 1918 tens of thousands of artists (both

Robin Lenman, John Osborne, Eda Sagarra

'fine' and commercial), reprographic workers, professional and amateur photographers, and eventually photo-journalists and film-makers created hundreds of millions of images at all levels of value, durability, and aesthetic pretension.

Fine art developed within an institutional framework already well established by 1871. High-quality, low-cost training was provided by academies in the Empire's various art centres, most notably Dresden, Düsseldorf, and Munich. Equally important and similarly attractive to foreigners (such as the Norwegian painter Edvard Munch) was the emergence of a modern art market. Central to this process was the proliferation since the post-Napoleonic period of art unions (*Kunstvereine*): societies of mainly lay art-lovers which organized exhibitions, in many cases founded galleries, and generally promoted middle-class interest in art and collecting. (The widespread use of a lottery system offset initial reluctance to spend money on pictures.) Major groups, such as those of Saxony and Rhineland-Westphalia, had many affiliated branches, numerous members in Germany and abroad, and large incomes from which they financed works of 'patriotic' monumental art. Academy salons, mainly established in the eighteenth century, continued through the nineteenth, although they were increasingly dominated—in Munich eventually controlled—by artists' own groups. National and international exhibitions, whether academy- or artist-sponsored, grew steadily in size, popularity, and financial turnover: the Berlin Academy's centenary salon in 1886, for example, showed work by nearly 1,500 artists, attracted over a million visitors, and achieved a million marks' worth of sales.[24] After 1871 the art trade continued to expand, with dealers functioning as elements of order in the ocean of art production, either by themselves or in collaboration with art unions and artists' societies: Paul Cassirer's relationship with the Berlin Secession and Herwarth Walden's with the Blue Rider painters were among the most fruitful in the history of modern art. After unification, too, the market became increasingly integrated, with national and regional exhibition circuits, a network of links between dealers at home and abroad, and considerable foreign participation. By the 1880s Berlin's increasing dominance as a training centre and market was attracting growing numbers of artists. But for historical and political reasons the centralization process was less complete than in other cultural fields; Dresden, Munich (Germany's principal art-export centre), and even Darmstadt remained important, and by 1914 the Rhine-Ruhr industrial region was becoming one of Europe's richest art markets. Finally, although later than in Britain or France, demand was diversifying, with prints, water-colours, and

24 *Die Kunst für Alle* (15 Sept. 1887), 377.

other 'minor' media gradually attracting more interest and higher prices alongside the highly finished oil painting. Both internationalization and diversification benefited the pre-war avant-gardes, which attracted foreign buyers and produced large quantities of work in minor media. In the background modern commercial art and industrial design were developing, encouraged by progressive groups like the Werkbund.

Essential to the formation of a 'public sphere' within which works of art could be discussed and evaluated was the development of an art press. Specialist journals ranged from Wilhelm Lübke's scholarly *Zeitschrift für bildende Kunst* (1866), with its topical supplement *Die Kunstchronik*, to Friedrich Pecht's more popular *Kunst für Alle* (1885) and Bruno Cassirer's pro-Secessionist *Kunst und Künstler* (1902). Much more widely circulated, and aggressively anti-academic and anti-Victorian, was Georg Hirth's *Jugend* (1896), which reproduced work by mainly younger artists and, as its advertising pages revealed, catered for a young, style-conscious, and affluent middle-class public. But there was also extensive coverage of art in the ordinary press, from illustrated magazines like *Die Gartenlaube* to newspaper *Feuilletons*. The *Deutsche Rundschau*'s critic Hermann Grimm—academic art historian, author of bestselling artist-biographies, essayist, lecturer, and *habitué* of the Berlin salons—was one of many talented communicators interpreting art for the public at large. At the same time innovations in reprographic technology, linked with names such as Albert, Obernetter, and Meisenbach, were revolutionizing art publishing and making painting a semi-mass medium. Self-consciously modern journals like *Jugend* and the satirical *Simplicissimus* owed much of their appeal to three-colour printing, and the low-cost reproductions of firms such as Seemann, Bruckmann, and Hanfstaengl were the visual equivalent of Reclam's slot-machine editions of literary classics.

Art in Imperial Germany was not simply an ornamental luxury, but had major symbolic and didactic functions: both as part of the cultural 'identity kit' indispensable to a new nation and as a medium for communicating historical facts, myths, and political values. This was conspicuously true of the outsize monumental paintings which, though more realistic, continued the tradition set by Peter Cornelius and Alfred Rethel in the first half of the century. Paid for by a mixture of dynastic, state, municipal, and art-union funds (hence, partly, their complex and sometimes contradictory symbolism), they ranged from the murals in the restored Imperial Palace at Goslar, uniting 'Red Beard' Frederick Barbarossa and 'White Beard' Wilhelm I, to the acres of decorated wall-space in schools, lawcourts, and city halls all over Germany. Still more spectacular, costly, and symbol-laden were the ubiquitous three-dimensional monuments constructed since the end of the Napoleonic Wars, culminating in Wilhelm II's reign with scores of Bismarck towers and the gigantic Leipzig *Völkerschlachtdenkmal* inaugurated in 1913. On another level, art was a kind of mirror and symbolic integration-mechanism for the liberal, Protestant, and, in its own estimation, culture-creating middle class. Clearly, for the large proportion of the 'respectable' population which belonged to art unions, attended salons, and read about art in the press, works of art in the broadest sense (not only paintings and sculpture, but also buildings and *objets d'art*) made visible the historical role of the German *Bürgertum* since the end of the Middle Ages, and helped it to position itself politically and culturally in relation to other key groups in society. 'What was [architecture] in the last century', asked Lübke in the first issue of the *Zeitschrift für bildende Kunst*, 'but the handmaiden of a degenerate aristocracy, for whose debauched life, opulent festivals, and strength-wasting pastimes it furnished the coquettishly decorated stage?' Now, however, buildings expressed a way of life which 'in manly labour and the earnest grasp of material and spiritual aims has thrown the main force of development back into the natural centre, into the *Bürgerstand*'.[25] Not only the aristocracy was excluded from this materially and spiritually creative nucleus of the nation, but also reactionary and unpatriotic Catholics, and culture-less and equally unpatriotic workers. Such assumptions and stereotypes underlay Imperial Germany's major debates about museums and public patronage, the nature of acceptable mainstream art, and the images suitable for working-class consumption.

By 1871 the formation of great public art collections was well under way. As part of an ambitious programme to increase his capital's prestige King Ludwig I of Bavaria had created the Glyptothek for classical sculpture, the Alte Pinakothek for the cream of the huge Wittelsbach collection of old-master paintings, and the Neue Pinakothek for modern German and foreign art. Friedrich Wilhelm III of Prussia and Grand Duke Ludwig I of Hesse also made some of their art treasures accessible in public museums. But important new collections were created by private citizens, such as Johann Friedrich Städel in Frankfurt, and Ferdinand Wallraf and the Boisserée brothers in Cologne. The 262 modern pictures assembled by Heinrich Wagener in Berlin formed the nucleus of the Berlin National Gallery. Finally, as already mentioned, many art-union galleries eventually became autonomous or semi-autonomous civic museums: for example, the Leipzig Museum of Fine Art,

25 'Die heutige Kunst und die Kunstwissenschaft', *Zeitschrift für bildende Kunst*, 1 (1866), 4.

established in 1848; the Hamburg and Bremen Kunsthallen; and many lesser institutions.

For historical and political reasons it was unlikely that unification would produce national art institutions and patronage-mechanisms above the level of the individual state. Bismarck's constitution gave the Reich a minimal role in cultural matters (except for press and copyright legislation), and the smaller states, especially Saxony and Bavaria, regarded their capitals' long-established cultural prestige as a counterweight to Prussia's dominance in the new Empire. Bavaria in particular consistently opposed Berlin-based initiatives in the visual arts and further hardened its line as the Imperial capital began to threaten Munich's position as Germany's premier art centre. Long-standing demands for a national museum of modern art were never realized, and the Berlin National Gallery founded in 1861 was, and continued to be, a Prussian institution. The Germanic National Museum, established in Nuremberg in 1852 and supported by city, Bavarian, and eventually Reich funds, remained the only properly national institution of its kind in the Empire.

There was more scope for development on issues such as the funding of public galleries, the content of Germany's major modern collections, and the wider role of museums in society. The century between 1815 and 1914 witnessed a transformation of the balance between dynastic, state, and other funding of the visual arts, as of music and the theatre. In 1815 practically every German art collection of more than local importance was owned by royal or princely houses, supervised by court appointees, and accessible only to an élite. By the eve of the First World War these galleries not only coexisted with many non-royal ones but were supported largely by public grants and private donations, managed by professionals, and visited annually by tens of thousands of people; the most important ones had even been designated as inalienable national property. Behind this change was the idea that art collections were part of a national heritage and a resource for *Bildung* and, as tourism increased, an economic asset which must be tended regardless of individual rulers' attitudes. In fact, even if all the arts are considered, pre-1918 Germany only mustered a handful of really important and innovative royal patrons: Ludwig I and Ludwig II of Bavaria, Friedrich Wilhelm IV of Prussia, Georg II of Saxe-Meiningen, and the last Grand Duke of Hesse, Ernst Ludwig. Moreover, especially after 1871, cultural hyperactivity by a monarch was not necessarily welcome. This was true to a degree of Emperor Wilhelm II; but above all of the 'dream king' Ludwig II, one of history's most extravagant royal art-lovers. Though intensified by personal eccentricity

Robin Lenman, John Osborne, Eda Sagarra

and political frustration, Ludwig's taste for exoticism, and for visual illusion created by elaborate gadgetry, was far from unique, and his passion for Wagnerian music-drama anticipated a vast cultural phenomenon. But his building schemes had no wider economic or educational purpose, and even their stimulus to the applied arts was largely fortuitous. He also neglected the royal art collections and saw painting mainly as an adjunct to his theatrical and architectural projects; and the Munich School's prosperity during his reign (1864–86) owed virtually nothing to the Crown. This indifference was deeply resented and the sense that dynastic and national interests had parted company was an important reason for the large increase in the state's art budget after the King's death in 1886.

In principle, public spending on the arts was nothing new. Academies in particular, but in some cases also museums, had long been supported by taxpayers' money, for both economic reasons—the improvement of manufactures—and political ones, especially in newly acquired territories. (Efforts after 1871 to improve the Strasburg art collections under the guidance of Wilhelm von Bode, later Director of the Prussian Museums, were similarly motivated.) In the aftermath of unification Saxony and Prussia both increased their spending far beyond what their dynasties could have afforded, and between 1876 and 1913, in its efforts to give Berlin the trappings of an Imperial capital, the Prussian state spent more than 70 million marks on the city's museums alone. By 1900, too, more and more municipalities were making regular grants to museums and commissioning murals for their public buildings.

But the shift from royal to public funding was only one aspect of a more complex process. Political and financial constraints prevented art budgets from keeping pace with rapidly rising art prices as collecting increased and American millionaires entered the market. Although records were broken mainly by old masters (in 1904 Rembrandt's *Blinding of Samson* cost the Städel Institute the astronomical sum of 336,000 marks), major Realist and Impressionist works—such as Courbet's *Stone-Breakers*, bought by the Dresden Gallery—were also fetching six-figure sums after the turn of the century. This complicated the debate about whether Germany's representative modern galleries should continue to buy mainly German work from the local salons or become international in scope. The commitment of directors such as Karl Woermann in Dresden and Hugo von Tschudi in Berlin, then Munich, to the latter course antagonized conservative, often Francophobic purchasing-committees (and Kaiser Wilhelm II), and artists jealous of their hold on public funds. A solution lay in Bode's practice of trading expert advice to collectors for promises of future donations, and of forming friends' associations (*Museumsvereine*) to support particular galleries. Comparable strategies in the more controversial modern area enabled the Mannheim Kunsthalle to acquire Manet's *Execution of Maximilian* and the Neue Pinakothek to obtain the magnificent Tschudi Donation (funded by the director's circle of rich acquaintances) of Realist and Impressionist paintings. In Hamburg, Kunsthalle-director Alfred Lichtwark drew on private wealth to enrich an undistinguished collection with large numbers of Romantic and Realist paintings, works by Berlin Secessionists such as Liebermann, Corinth, and Slevogt, and commissioned Hamburg views by Vuillard and Bonnard. The Elberfeld Museum, a classic civic foundation which opened in 1902, became in 1911 the first public gallery to house a Picasso and, largely thanks to its friends' association headed by Baron August von der Heydt, acquired a collection of Post-Impressionists, Fauves, and works by Wassily Kandinsky and other avant-garde painters. Though the 'Americanness' of these new practices was tempered in royal capitals by the use of honours to reward donors, its overall effect was to increase directors' independence from monarchs, artists, and bureaucrats; and to bring rich private individuals into the taste-formation process of which museums were increasingly a part.

While Romantic notions of the museum as a temple-like space for the contemplation of genius persisted in some quarters, the growth of academic art history made collections systematically organized by periods and schools more and more the norm. By the 1870s the Leipzig Museum was also sponsoring lectures and other activities, and Imperial Germany's professional curators increasingly regarded themselves as active promoters of *Bildung*, with Max Lehrs and H. W. Singer at the Dresden Gallery's Print Room playing a major educative role. But the most comprehensive programme was Lichtwark's in Hamburg. In his inaugural address on 9 December 1886 he announced his intention to make the Kunsthalle not a museum 'which stands and waits, but an institution which actively intervenes in the artistic education of our population';[26] and during his long period in office (1886–1914) his activities included lecturing, publishing, and supporting Hamburg's amateur painters, photographers, and print-makers. He was also prominent in the German art education movement, which aimed to brighten up schools, bring children into museums, and promote good-quality reproductions and illustrated books. Like many of his contemporaries, from Wagnerites to Werkbund members, Lichtwark was driven by a belief in art—in the broadest sense of an aesthetically harmonious

26 Alfred Lichtwark, 'Die Aufgaben der Kunsthalle', in *Drei Programme* (Berlin, 1902), 29.

Robin Lenman, John Osborne, Eda Sagarra

environment—as an antidote to materialism, alienation, and social conflict. In detail he was convinced that art education should emphasize looking and visual enjoyment rather than book-learning, and that people could best approach art via works close to them in time and subject-matter: hence his acquisition of (accessible) contemporary paintings and his creation of a gallery of local landscapes and portraits. He was in many respects conservative. In practice most of his efforts were directed at the middle class; and women's place in his aesthetic grand design was as home-makers and amateurs, not as professional artists. But his energy, personal magnetism, and vision of the museum as a bridge between art and life made him one of the giants of the Imperial German art scene.

High-Cultural Images

As late as 1914 much of the vast output of Germany's numerous painting schools fell into the classic salon categories of genre and landscape; variously influenced by Dutch, French, and British models, identified since the early nineteenth century with the art unions, and sustained economically by tourism. Still important, too, after 1871 was large-format historical colourism. Its most eminent practitioner, Berlin Academy-director Anton von Werner, completed the first version of his celebrated *Die Kaiserproklamation zu Versailles* in 1877 and the last in 1913. Although the photographic detail and waxworks illusionism of this kind of painting had long been criticized (in 1867 Munich's leading critic, Friedrich Pecht, had remarked that microscopes were for examining lice, not heroes), the public money spent on it and its privileged position in academic curricula continued to be justified in terms of its assumed value as patriotic and monarchical propaganda. New young recruits to the specialism included Arthur Kampf, who began in the 1880s as a radical Naturalist before turning to the large-scale historical canvases which kept him in business well into the Third Reich.

If history-paintings influenced public consciousness it was also because they were endlessly reproduced as prints and textbook illustrations, and matched by parallel developments in the theatre, most notably the pedantically authentic realism identified with the Meiningen Court troupe. Historical colourism also overflowed into *Künstlerfeste*, elaborate costume pageants organized to mark artistic events like Dürer anniversaries and great national occasions like the homecoming of the victorious armies in 1871 and the completion of Cologne Cathedral in 1880. History specialists such as Hans Makart

1. Anton von Werner, *Im Etappenquartier vor Paris, 1870* (1894).
(Oil on canvas, 120 x 158 cm.)
Anton von Werner (1843–1915) was one of the Second Reich's most prolific conventional
painters, and a determined opponent of the modernism associated with groups like the Berlin
Secession. He owed his meteoric early success to the Franco-Prussian War, during which he used
his friendship with the Grand Duke of Baden to gain access to military headquarters. In France he
witnessed the proclamation of the Empire, made invaluable contacts with Germany's military and
political élite, and gathered picture-material on which he drew for more than forty years. This
painting, showing Prussian officers relaxing in the requisitioned Château de Brunoy, exemplifies
the theatrical composition and ultra-illusionistic detail for which Werner was famous.
Symbolically, it deftly balances the soldier fire-lighting to combat the intense cold with the
officer who sings a Schubert song to exorcise the French rococo frivolity all around.

were famous both as painters and festival-designers; the historical banner-paintings created in 1871 ended up as wall-decorations in schools; and the Cologne city fathers commissioned murals to immortalize their pageant. There was also an overlap between art and visual entertainment, especially the commercial panorama in which the combination of painted scenery, three-dimensional objects—boats, cannon, dummy soldiers—and clever lighting effects achieved a degree of realism unsurpassed until the coming of the cinema. (A portent for the future was the 360° *cinéorama* at the 1900 Paris Exhibition which featured coloured moving images of an aerial journey across Europe and Africa filmed from a balloon by several synchronized cameras.) Executed by teams headed by eminent artists such as Werner and Louis Braun, these productions were hailed by critics as serious works of art.

Historical colourism and its small-scale genre offshoots flourished in a particular architectural and decorative setting. Although many styles found favour in the historicist 1870s and later, those of the *Dürerzeit* or German Renaissance—roughly from the late fifteenth century to the Thirty Years War—acquired particularly intense patriotic, urban-bourgeois, and Protestant associations in the aftermath of unification. Their revival was perceived as a symbol of German emancipation from French aesthetic hegemony and, again in contrast with France, as a reaffirmation of mercantile and artisan rather than aristocratic traditions. Albrecht Dürer, who had long been venerated by artists as a kind of secular patron saint, now increasingly became a national hero. 'Those who do not know him', proclaimed Grimm, 'lack the knowledge of part of our history; but for those who do know him the sound of Dürer's name being spoken is like Germany, fatherland.'[27]

The German Renaissance or *altdeutsch* vogue owed much to the 1876 Munich Applied Art Exhibition (its motto was 'the works of our fathers'—more popularly, 'every man his own Fugger'), appropriately heralded by a vast 'Charles V' pageant. One of the show's principal backers was the Munich publicist Georg Hirth, who spelled out the symbolism of the revival in his book *Das deutsche Zimmer der Renaissance* (1880) and published albums of sixteenth-century designs as a resource for craftsmen and manufacturers. Among other things Hirth enunciated a 'national' colour code, with browns, old golds, and dark reds, reminiscent of forests, the wine-harvest, and autumn, identified as both fundamentally German and 'natural'. (It was no accident that browns dominated the palette of the Brückner atelier of Coburg, which provided the decorations for both Meiningen and Bayreuth.) With its dark panelling, opaque windows, and

27 *Albrecht Dürer*[2] (Berlin, 1873), 44.

urgemütlich bays and alcoves, the *Dürerzeit* interior was a kind of domestic stage set which transported its 'cast' to a period both rich in patriotic associations and remote from the modern 'struggle for existence'. At the same time, although the term *altdeutsch* also implied solidity and traditional craftsmanship, nineteenth-century synthetic materials and devices such as collapsible panelling adapted it to the budget and living conditions of the modern urban apartment-dweller. Whether fake or genuine, this was the setting for which much mainstream art was created, not only in the 1880s but for decades thereafter; indeed, for many people it probably remained the dominant domestic style until well into the 1920s. Although the rich might match their antique furniture and fittings with genuine (especially Dutch) old masters, ordinary buyers turned to comparably detailed and dark-toned contemporary works in the manner of artists like Wilhelm Diez and Franz Defregger, who, both personally and through the hundreds of painters they trained, dominated an important section of the art market from the 1870s until after the First World War.

The strength of historicism with all its ramifications hindered the acceptance in Germany of so-called *plein-airisme*: essentially a development of mid-century Realism characterized both by rejection of narrative subject-matter and by the effort to capture fleeting effects of light and atmosphere. There were several reasons why, during the 1880s and 1890s, the movement was constantly attacked by conservatives. In the first place, prominent *plein-airistes* like Max Liebermann had strong links with Paris, and in Imperial Germany's Francophobic atmosphere the style fitted all too easily into a discourse of Germanness versus Frenchness which identified the latter with superficiality, empty virtuosity, and materialism. Such prejudices were doubtless coloured by a nagging sense of cultural inferiority and an awareness that influences across the Rhine flowed strongly from west to east. Secondly, the *plein-airistes'* loose brushwork and sketch-like selective detail offended against the notions of effort and 'finish' fundamental to orthodox criteria of artistic value. Finally, their high-key palette flouted 'national' colour conventions—hence the rejection as garish and unnatural of works such as Fritz von Uhde's *Trommelübung* of 1883, a picture of bandsmen practising on a bright spring day.

However, in what amounted to a minor revolution in taste international *plein-airisme*, identified in Germany by the 1890s with the anti-academic Secession movement, gradually won over the country's more adventurous art-buyers. The growing popularity among rich collectors of German Secessionism and French Impressionism

Robin Lenman, John Osborne, Eda Sagarra

and Post-Impressionism doubtless owed much to their inherently pleasing and unproblematical quality at a time of rapid urbanization and worrying social problems. But attacks on them by Wilhelm II and Anton von Werner also gave these movements an attractively oppositional flavour for wealthy and successful people eager for aesthetic independence in an authoritarian society. Important too, especially in Berlin, was the highly effective marketing operation conducted by Paul and Bruno Cassirer, who promoted *pleinairisme* as a fashionable and bankable commodity via the collections of their relatives, friends, and business associates. Their allies included the leading art-critics Julius Meier-Graefe and Richard Muther, and Hugo von Tschudi, who began to acquire Impressionist works for the Berlin National Gallery.

By 1914, despite the protests of cultural nationalists, Germany had some of the world's finest collections, public and private, of modern French art. The Secessions were part of the art establishment and had a secure position on the market. Still outside this circle of accepted non-academic artists, though on the threshold of recognition, was Germany's disparate pre-war avant-garde. Its precursors had been the Realists around Wilhelm Leibl in the 1870s; Berlin Naturalists of the 1890s such as Hans Baluschek and Käthe Kollwitz; and the three great outsiders of Central European painting, Hans Thoma, Max Klinger, and the Swiss Arnold Böcklin, who, by the turn of the century, after years of isolation, had achieved virtual cult status. The term avant-garde covers artists who varied greatly in age, national origin, and artistic orientation, who responded in highly individual ways to influences ranging from German Romanticism to contemporary movements in Paris and Russia, and the 'primitive' art of Russian and Bavarian peasants, and of Africa and Polynesia. Particularly important were the Dresden *Brücke* group, formed in 1905, which espoused an idyllic, erotically charged ruralism before succumbing to the fascination of Berlin; and the artists around Kandinsky and the *Blaue Reiter Almanach* published in Munich in 1912, who aspired to a completely non-representational 'spiritual' art. There were also more isolated figures such as Emil Nolde, the pioneer abstract painter Adolf Hoelzel, and the naïve Expressionist Paula Modersohn-Becker. What linked them, however, was rejection of the surface or 'optical' naturalism of *pleinairisme* and the belief that art should seek to express inner psychic states, or spiritual realities beyond the visible material world.

Although they attracted predictable abuse from many quarters and clashed fiercely with leading Secessionists, avant-garde artists were, nevertheless, not wholly isolated. Their affinities with Romanticism,

the interest of some of them in Rudolph Steiner's fashionable occult theories, and their debts to Van Gogh and Munch, both widely
known in Germany by the 1900s, created important points of contact with the cultural élite. Sales, too, were increasing by 1914. The
First World War, although it disrupted the international market,
killed a number of artists, and temporarily removed the Russians
from the German art scene, probably accelerated the process of
recognition. New groups proliferated, new patrons entered the field,
the activities of Herwarth Walden and other avant-garde dealers
continued, and inflation created a growing demand for objects of
value from which radical artists also benefited. In June 1917 Paul
Klee, whose wartime breakthrough was one of the avant-garde's
major success stories, told Walden that *Der Sturm* was no longer an
appropriate title for his journal: 'Culturally we already have world
peace now, and it is only to the elderly gentlemen that our creed
[still] seems like a tempest.'[28]

Images for the Masses

On her wedding day in 1901 the Bavarian writer Lena Christ was
presented by the regulars of her stepfather's Munich pub with a
large steel engraving of (an ominous portent for the marriage) Franz
Defregger's *Andreas Hofers letzter Gang*.[29] Just as the pub with its
rentier and artisan customers was part of a world very different
from that of the modern, tourist-thronged Löwenbräukeller on the
nearby Stiglmaierplatz, so the choice of picture—a salon sensation
of 1878—suggests a huge taste-lag between the cosmopolitan clien-
tele of Munich's smart city-centre galleries and the lower echelons
of 'respectable' society. Below that lower-middle-class level it seems
unlikely that artist-created images had more than minimal impact.
Exhibitions and museums were effectively closed to the working
class, for practical, financial, and psychological reasons, and the
panorama also seems to have been a largely middle-class spectacle.
'Only rarely', commented a socialist pamphlet of 1909, 'does a light-
ray of art reach the bare, harsh dullness of the worker's life.'[30] The
art education movement did, it is true, campaign to embellish what
one teacher described as 'the desolate prison walls of our class-
rooms', and to bring illustrated books and lithographs within reach
of the working class. One series of pleasing but bland and traditional prints—some of them by artists close to Ferdinand Avenarius's
conservative *Kunstwart*—was endorsed by the education committee
of the SPD; which was hardly a surprise, given the aim of prominent

28 Otto Karl
Werckmeister, *The
Making of Paul Klee's
Career, 1914–20*
(Chicago and London,
1989), 96.
29 Lena Christ,
*Erinnerungen einer
Überflüssigen* (Munich,
1970), 224.
30 Bildungsausschuß
der SPD (ed.),
*Künstlerischer
Wandschmuck: Eine
Anregung und ein
Verzeichnis* (Berlin,
1909), 5.

Robin Lenman, John Osborne, Eda Sagarra

socialists to increase their followers' access to mainstream culture and given the use of conventional fine-art imagery (even Germanic motifs by Hugo Höppener (Fidus)) in the Party's propaganda. However, the aesthetically conservative official culture of the SPD and its affiliated trade unions was not necessarily that of its members; quite apart from the fact that even in 1914 only a quarter of Germany's geographically, ethnically, and confessionally highly diverse industrial proletariat belonged to the labour movement at all.

Until the spread of the cinema at the turn of the century, and in rural areas for much longer, the masses' visual diet remained overwhelmingly dominated by newspaper illustrations and the popular prints (*Bilderbogen*) mass-produced since the eighteenth century in places like the Brandenburg town of Neu-Ruppin. In the heyday of this industry its output was enormous, with Neu-Ruppin firms turning out some 3 million images in 1870–1 alone. Subject-matter, which was stringently vetted by the authorities, ranged from devotional images—a very high proportion—to portraits of statesmen and heroes, views, battle-scenes, and sensational events such as shipwrecks (later airship crashes) and natural disasters. As with pulp literature, distribution took place efficiently via networks of regional depots and thousands of pedlars who brought their wares both to peasants and urban tenement-dwellers. But the print trade was truly international, with firms like E. G. May in Frankfurt am Main shipping wagonloads of prints eastwards to Russian Poland, westwards to France and Spain, and overseas; while from beyond the Rhine the products of French firms like Wentzel in Wissembourg (Alsace) reached, on the eve of the Franco-Prussian War, Warsaw, Prague, and Vienna. These images crossed social as well as national boundaries. Praising the topical prints of the Neu-Ruppin firm of Gustav Kühn, Theodor Fontane confessed:

I have seen lingering with visible interest in front of these pictures people who would have been simply appalled at their artistic quality. But the power of the subject-matter overcame them, and they (and I myself) counted with quiet satisfaction the corpses of Danish casualties without feeling any twinge of their artistic consciences.[31]

As a child Fontane had been fascinated by the ubiquitous travelling peepshows which displayed similar prints in portable, box-like viewers. There were also fairground panoramas in which much larger painted images, created by specialist firms, were displayed in booths; while *Bänkelsänger* elucidated sequences of sensational painted pictures by reciting ballads or *Moritaten*. All these types of visual entertainment remained popular through the 1920s and 1930s (a

31 *Schilder, Bilder, Moritaten*, exhibition catalogue, Museum für Volkskunde im Pergamon-Museum (Berlin, 1987), 52.

Bänkelsänger appears in the film *Hitlerjunge Quex*, 1933), and in parts of eastern Germany until the establishment of television in the 1950s. Finally, too, there were 'original' oil paintings for the home, serially produced in picture factories and sold by travelling dealers, so-called *fliegende Händler*, some of whom eventually rose into the regular art trade.

Important at a more elevated level were projected images. Familiar since well before 1800, these improved rapidly during the nineteenth century thanks to better lenses and light-sources which also made possible special effects such as dissolves, back-projection, and 'phantasmagoric' apparitions on smoke. Thousands of finely painted glass slides were offered for hire by firms such as Liesegang in Düsseldorf and Krüss in Hamburg. Late nineteenth-century magic-lantern shows were elaborate affairs, incorporating recited texts and often music, and ranging from travelogues and educational programmes to scenes from Dante, the *Odyssey*, and the Nibelung legend: subjects which, like the venues and admission prices, indicate that this was a middle-class form of 'improving' spectacle.

By 1871, more than three decades after the creation of the first photographic images, photography in Germany was advancing technically and commercially by leaps and bounds. Many of the refinements available by the turn of the century had been invented or improved by German firms, and in 1913 Oskar Barnack created the prototype of the revolutionary Leica 35 mm. miniature camera. The photographic portrait business had expanded rapidly, ranging eventually from lavishly appointed, electrically lit salons for the rich and famous to travelling operators who made cheap ferrotypes of servant-girls and army conscripts. The photograph album became an obligatory drawing-room accessory and a repository for studio-created fantasies. (If the results were sometimes bizarre, they were hardly more so than the images of Ludwig II being rowed through the Linderhof grotto in his cockleshell boat.) In the 1890s, partly as a reaction against the aesthetic mediocrity of commercial photography, an amateur artistic movement developed which soon became associated with the painting Secessions in cities like Dresden and Munich. But one of its earliest and liveliest centres was Hamburg, partly because of links with British pictorialism, partly because of energetic encouragement by Lichtwark, who regarded art photography, especially portraiture, as yet another means of improving public taste and in 1893 inaugurated an annual series of international photo-salons in the Kunsthalle. Other significant developments before 1914 included the early documentary photography of Waldemar Titzenthaler and August Sander. Finally, although it developed only slowly after the invention of the half-tone process at the beginning of the 1880s, photo-journalism was establishing itself by the turn of the century, with Berlin as its main centre and gateway to the international news-photograph market. But Germany's first publicly subsidized photography school opened in 1900 in Munich, the *Münchener Illustrierte Zeitung* was founded in 1909, and the city acquired its own corps of photo-journalists. One of them was Hitler's later photographer Heinrich Hoffmann, who took the world-famous photograph of Munich citizens, including Hitler, euphorically celebrating the outbreak of the First World War.

By the late nineteenth century projected photographic slides were being used for both education—Hermann Grimm was one of the first to illustrate lectures on art history with them—and entertainment. The Berlin *Kaiserpanorama* (1883–1939), described nostalgically by Walter Benjamin as 'an aquarium of distance and time',[32] allowed customers to view a succession of coloured stereoscopic images rotating within a cylindrical apparatus; and by the early 1890s mutoscope-type slot-machines enabled single viewers to experience the illusion of movement. The convergence of technologies to produce projected motion pictures was only a matter of time, and this occurred on 1 November 1895 when the brothers Max and Emil Skladanowsky demonstrated their *Bioskop* at the Berlin Wintergarten. Technically more viable, however, was the Lumière brothers' apparatus unveiled in Paris at the end of December and soon leased exclusively in Germany to a slot-machine firm affiliated to the Cologne chocolate-manufacturer Stollwerck. Its first demonstration at the company's canteen on 16 April 1896, followed by public shows at trade fairs and other venues across the country, has been described as 'the film medium's true hour of birth in Germany'.[33]

In fact, notwithstanding the capitalist and consumerist implications of the Stollwerck connection, the cinema had important links with older forms of popular spectacle: Max Skladanowsky was a trained slide-painter, another brother joined the circus, and their father was a former showman of projected 'phantasmagorias'; early films, like *Moritatenbilder*, were often explained by a man with a pointer; and initially the cinematograph functioned as a peripatetic vaudeville and fairground 'attraction'. After 1900, as in America, film shows increasingly became a fixed form of mainly urban entertainment, and by 1914 Germany had some 2,500 cinemas, over 200 of them in Berlin. In the same period important technical improvements took place, many of them (including an early sound system) associated with the formidably inventive and versatile Oskar Meßter,

32 Winfried Ranke, 'Magia naturalis, physique amusante und aufgeklärte Wissenschaft', in Detlev Hoffmann and Almut Junker (eds.), *Laterna Magica: Lichtbilder aus Menschenwelt und Götterwelt* (Berlin, 1982), 11.
33 Martin Loiperdinger, 'Wie der Film nach Deutschland kam', *Kinntopp: Jahrbuch zur Erforschung des frühen Films*, 1 (1992), 117.

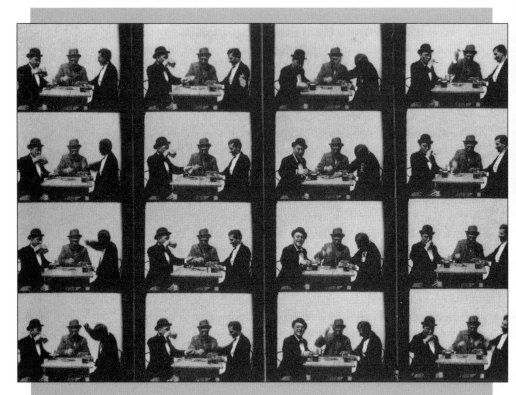

2. Max Skladanowsky, 'Lebende Bilder' (1898).
Max Skladanowsky (1863–1939) and his brother Emil had experimented with the creation of
'living photographs' from the mid-1880s, and in 1892 created a motion-picture camera using
Kodak celluloid film. In preparation for their historic début on 1 November 1895 they filmed a
series of variety turns in different Berlin locations, including a boxing kangaroo in front of the
Busch Circus. The Bioskop apparatus used for the 15-minute Wintergarten show had two lenses
and transport mechanisms, and projected alternate images from two circular strips of film; its
limitations led the brothers subsequently to adopt single-lens projectors of the type soon
developed by Oskar Messter. Max Skladanowsky remained moderately successful as a maker of
comedies and actuality films and created a lucrative parallel business with photographic 'flicker-
books' of scenes like the 1898 one above.

who has been described as 'Germany's first all-round cinema-owner-inventor-director-producer-distributor'.[34] Other notable figures included Carl Geyer (film-processing) and Guido Seeber (special effects, and the camera-work on films such as *Der Student von Prag*, 1913, and *Der Golem*, 1914), but the most significant developments were commercial and organizational, especially the emergence by 1910 of a modern distribution network and a star system centred on actresses such as Asta Nielsen and Henny Porten. The resulting growth of profitability and investment stimulated the production side—increasingly concentrated in Berlin—of an industry hitherto overwhelmingly dominated by imports, and began to attract talent from mainstream culture: stage directors such as Max Reinhardt, actors like Paul Wegener and Albert Bassermann, and writers like Gerhart Hauptmann and Arthur Schnitzler.

In the beginning, however, cinema as a form of cheap mass entertainment had evoked a fiercely negative establishment response, which for several reasons was probably stronger in Germany than in other countries. In the first place, early films were closely related in subject-matter and tone to the lurid pulp novels and *Groschenhefte* which had long been denounced as a threat to lower-class and juvenile morality; but moving pictures were assumed to be far more harmful. Secondly, early films' strong appeal to women, to which the industry readily responded, provoked a predictable outcry about perils to the family: part of a larger anti-modern and anti-urban discourse in which increasing leisure opportunities for women outside the home (in dancehalls and department stores as well as cinemas) featured prominently. Worrying too was the cinema's wordlessness, in a society in which a literary high culture was widely regarded as the foundation of both individual *Bildung* and national identity. A fascinating article in 1910 claimed that film's prime means of expression was 'romanic' gesticulation, whereas *Geist* could be mediated only by words, and ominously described how a Monsieur Decroix of Pathé was giving the necessary training to German actors.[35] In short, the hoped-for absorption of civilized culture by the masses, essential for social stability, was apparently being thwarted by a *Geist*-less, foreign-dominated medium appealing solely to instinct. These concerns were largely shared, moreover, by Germany's *Bildung*-conscious socialist intelligentsia, who viewed commercial entertainment as a threat to their own projects, both political and cultural.

From the outset, films were subjected to rigorous police censorship, by 1914 centred in the individual state capitals and increasingly influenced by Berlin norms. (It is interesting to contrast the

34 Thomas Elsaesser, 'Wilhelminisches Kino; Stil und Industrie', *Kintopp: Jahrbuch zur Erforschung des frühen Films*, 1 (1992), 18.
35 Walter Turszinsky, 'Kinodramen und Kinomimen', in Jörg Schweinitz (ed.), *Prolog vor dem Film: Nachdenken über ein neues Medium 1909–1914*, (Leipzig, 1992), 21–6.

minimal response to cinema's exclusion, on dubious legal grounds, from the protection of the 1874 Press Law, with the spectacular and successful protest campaign of 1900 led by bourgeois and socialist intellectuals against proposed obscenity legislation which might have threatened 'serious' art). More positively, the so-called *Reformkino* movement agitated for more edifying cinema programmes, although their demands for documentaries and educational films had little impact on the public's taste for sensation and drama. By the eve of the war, however, observers like the sociologist Emilie Altenloh and some socialist critics were beginning to relate film entertainment to the nature of industrial life and work, and to acknowledge the legitimacy of pure recreation and escapism as against paternalist notions of 'improvement'.

In her classic study of the cinema completed in 1913, Altenloh pointed to the striking diversification of the market which had taken place in the previous five years.[36] Cinemas by this time ranged from primitive *Kintopps*, in which the auditorium was periodically sprayed with disinfectant, to elaborate picture palaces with house orchestras, uniformed ushers, and prices to match: for example, the 1,000-seat Leipzig Königspavillon which opened in April 1913 with a gala showing of Enrico Guazzoni's *Quo Vadis?*. (Continuing public ambivalence, however, was revealed by the outcry at Kurt Pinthus's use of his theatre column in the *Leipziger Tageblatt* for a review of the film.) Such multireel costume spectaculars, some of them featuring international stage stars like Sarah Bernhardt, were the Trojan Horse by which cinema entered the citadel of mainstream culture, while popular audiences watched American thrillers and westerns and other sensational fare. Although in 1914 all sections of the market were still dominated by foreign productions, German output and even exports were increasing. Quality, too, was respectable. Indeed, it seems likely that German films of this period have been unfairly neglected in favour of the classics of the 1920s; and that, for instance, the comedies of the Skladanowsky brothers and the thrillers of Heinrich Bolten-Baecker compared well with their foreign counterparts. Finally film-makers, together with German writers like Pinthus, were formulating a film aesthetic which went beyond mimed stage plays and recreations of Böcklin paintings. 'The real poet of the film', declared the actor-screenwriter Paul Wegener in a lecture in 1916, 'must be the *camera*.'[37]

Conditions between the outbreak of war in 1914, which eliminated most film imports, and the stabilization of the currency in 1924, which reopened the floodgates to foreign competition, vastly stimulated German output. Wartime demand for escapist entertainment,

36 *Zur Soziologie des Kinos: Die Kinounternehmung und die sozialen Schichten ihrer Besucher* (Hamburg, 1977; first pub. Jena, 1913).
37 'Von den künstlerischen Möglichkeiten des Wandelbildes', in Schweinitz (ed.), *Prolog vor dem Film, 336.*

Robin Lenman, John Osborne, Eda Sagarra

newsreels, and propaganda for both German and neutral audiences increased the number of production companies from twenty-eight in 1913 to 245 in 1919. Already before 1914 both political and other organizations had begun to recognize film's propaganda potential; and 1913 saw the release of a three-part epic about Queen Luise of Prussia: a prototype of the patriotic spectaculars which were to be so popular in subsequent decades. By the middle of the war, systematic and large-scale use of film propaganda was playing an increasing role in the total-mobilization plans of the High Command, especially Quartermaster-General Erich von Ludendorff, who strongly favoured state intervention in the film industry. Eventually, after various preliminaries and continuing military pressure, the Universum-Film AG (Ufa) was formed in December 1917, with financial backing from the Reich, the Deutsche Bank, and industrialists such as Alfred Hugenberg, and facilities bought from Meßter and other entrepreneurs. This was no short-term measure, but was intended to meet Germany's anticipated propaganda needs even after the end of hostilities; and in its post-war form Ufa remained a pillar of what was during the 1920s the world's most important film industry after Hollywood. The political thinking behind the initiative, lucidly elaborated in a memorandum of October 1917, would eventually be implemented much more thoroughly by the Nazis.[38]

This chapter began by noting in Imperial Germany a certain tension between dynamic economic development and political backwardness. The same tension extends to within the cultural sphere for, as a casual observer can see even after the destruction of two world wars, it is an epoch whose public monuments, providing as they did a historical pedigree for the new state, seem to contrast starkly with what has subsequently come to be valued most among its intellectual achievements: the critical challenge to tradition and history which emanated from the spiritual fathers of the Modern—Marx, Nietzsche, and Freud. The preceding examination has shown this ambivalence to be very deeply rooted in the cultural institutions of the period as they adapted to industrial capitalism, hence the question raised about the periodization proposed by Horkheimer and Adorno. A reasonable answer would be not to push back, but to lower the threshold which marks the inception of the commercialization of culture, the manipulation of a passive mass audience by a large production apparatus. There is indeed evidence to support the view of Jürgen Habermas that the later nineteenth century saw an important weakening of the institutions which underpinned

38 'Bild- und Filmamt: Der Propagandafilm und seine Bedingungen, Ziele und Wege (Oct. 1917)', in Wilfried von Bredow and Rolf Zurek (eds.), Film und Gesellschaft in Deutschland: Dokumente und Materialien (Hamburg, 1975), 73–87.

a 'reasoning' as opposed to a 'consuming' public sphere. The continuation of this process on the one hand, and, on the other, the project of re-establishing an active relationship between the social and the aesthetic contribute decisively to the cultural tensions of the immediately following decades.

Suggested Further Reading

There is a significant body of literature devoted to the culture of Imperial Germany in all its aspects; many of the most interesting contributions take the form of illustrated exhibition catalogues. A few selective pointers to further reading on topics covered in this chapter are offered below.

The following works give a wide-ranging picture of the culture of the period or significant aspects of it:

Aspekte der Gründerzeit, exhibition catalogue, Akademie der Künste (Berlin, 1974).

Evans, Richard J. (ed.), *Society and Politics in Wilhelmine Germany* (London, 1978).

Hamann, Richard, and **Hermand, Jost,** *Epochen deutscher Kultur von 1870 bis zur Gegenwart* (Munich, 1971–), i. *Gründerzeit* (1971); ii. *Naturalismus* (1972); iii. *Impressionismus* (1972); iv. *Stilkunst um 1990* (1973).

Hermand, Jost, *Old Dreams of a New Reich* (Chicago, 1992).

Hohendahl, Peter Uwe (ed.), *The Origin of Mass Culture: The Case of Imperial Germany (1871–1918)* (New German Critique, 29 (spring/summer 1983)).

Stern, Fritz, *The Politics of Cultural Despair* (Berkeley and Los Angeles, 1961).

There are a number of books on specific cultural centres or regions, including:

Abrams, Lynn, *Workers' Culture in Imperial Germany: Leisure and Recreation in the Rheinland and Westphalia* (London, 1992).

Georg II. und der Historismus: Ein Kulturideal im Zweiten Deutschen Kaiserreich exhibition catalogue, Staatliche Museen Meiningen, Schloß Elisabethenburg ([Meiningen], 1994).

Haxthausen, Charles W., and **Suhr, Heidrun** (eds.), *Berlin: Culture and Metropolis* (Minneapolis and Oxford, 1990).

Jelavich, Peter, *Munich and Theatrical Modernism: Politics, Playwriting and Performance* (Cambridge, Mass., and London, 1985).

Viel Vergnügen: Öffentliche Lustbarkeiten im Ruhrgebiet der Jahrhundertwende, exhibition catalogue, Ruhrlandmuseum (Essen, 1992).

Der westdeutsche Impuls, 1900–1914: Kunst- und Umweltgestaltung im Industriegebiet, exhibition catalogues (Cologne, Essen, Düsseldorf, Hagen, Krefeld, Wuppertal, 1984).

The development of the education system is treated in:

Ringer, Fritz K., 'Higher Education in Germany in the Nineteenth Century', *Journal of Contemporary History*, 2 (1967), 123–38.

Ringer, Fritz K., *Education and Society in Modern Europe* (Bloomington, Ind., 1979).

Robin Lenman, John Osborne, Eda Sagarra

There are a number of important contributions to the history of the book trade, the press, and the growth of the reading public, including:

Fullerton, Ronald A., 'Creating a Mass Book Market in Germany: The Story of the "Colporteur Novel" 1870–1890', *Journal of Social History*, 10 (1976–7), 265–83.

Lerg, Winfried Bernhard, and Schmolke, Michael, *Massenpresse und Volkszeitung* (Assen, 1968).

Martino, Alberto, *Die deutsche Leihbibliothek: Geschichte einer Institution (1756–1914)* (Wiesbaden, 1990).

Schenda, Rudolf, *Volk ohne Buch: Studien zur Sozialgeschichte der populären Lesestoffe 1770–1910* (Frankfurt am Main, 1970).

Wittmann, Reinhard, *Geschichte des Buchhandels: Ein Überblick* (Munich, 1991).

Parallel developments in the institutional framework of the visual arts are treated in:

Hochreiter, Walter, *Vom Musentempel zum Lernort: Zur Sozialgeschichte deutscher Museen 1800–1914* (Darmstadt, 1994).

Lenman, Robin, *Die Kunst, die Macht und das Geld: Zur Kulturgeschichte des kaiserlichen Deutschland 1871–1918* (Frankfurt am Main, 1994).

Mai, Ekkehard, Pohl, Hans, and Waetzoldt, Stephan (eds.), *Kunstpolitik und Kunstförderung im Kaiserreich: Kunst im Wandel der Sozial- und Wirtschaftsgeschichte* (Kunst, Kultur und Politik im Kaiserreich, 2; Berlin, 1982).

Teeuwisse, Nicolaas, *Vom Salon zur Secession: Berliner Kunstleben zwischen Tradition und Aufbruch zur Moderne 1871–1900* (Berlin, 1986).

Thiekötter, Angelika, and Siepmann, Eckhard (eds.), *Packeis und Preßglas: Von der Kunstgewerbebewegung zum Deutschen Werkbund* (Werkbund-Archiv, 16; Berlin, 1987).

With, Christopher, *The Prussian Landeskunstkommission 1862–1911: A Study in State Subvention of the Arts* (Kunst, Kultur und Politik im deutschen Kaiserreich, 6; Berlin, 1986).

The Secessionist movements and the growth of artists' colonies are documented in:

Makela, Maria, *The Munich Secession: Art and Arts in Turn-of-the Century Munich* (Princeton, 1990).

Paret, Peter, *The Berlin Secession: Modernism and its Enemies in Imperial Germany* (Cambridge, Mass., and London, 1980).

Wietek, Gerhard (ed.), *Deutsche Künstlerkolonien und Künstlerorte* (Munich, 1976).

The cultural impact of the early women's movement in Germany has been the subject of much recent work, such as:

Berger, Renate, *Malerinnen auf dem Weg ins 20. Jahrhundert: Kunstgeschichte als Sozialgeschichte* (Cologne, 1982).

Evans, Richard J., *The Feminist Movement in Germany 1894–1933* (London, 1976).

Frederiksen, Elke (ed.), *Die Frauenfrage in Deutschland, 1865–1915: Texte und Dokumente* (Stuttgart, 1988; first pub. 1981).

Sagarra, Eda, 'The German Woman Writer 1900–1933: Socio-Political Context and Literary Market', in Brian Keith-Smith (ed.), *German Women Writers, 1900–1933: Twelve Essays* (Lampeter, 1993), 1–22.

A comprehensive study of working-class culture is given in:

Lidtke, Vernon L., *The Alternative Culture: Socialist Labor in Imperial Germany* (New York and Oxford, 1985).

Among studies of the development of new media are:

Jacobsen, Wolfgang, Kaes, Anton, and **Prinzler, Hans Helmut**, *Geschichte des deutschen Films* (Stuttgart and Weimar, 1993).

Kaes, Anton, *Kino-Debatte: Texte zum Verhältnis von Literatur und Film 1909–1929* (Munich, 1978).

Kaufhold, Enno, *Bilder des Übergangs: Zur Mediengeschichte von Fotografie und Malerei in Deutschland um 1900* (Marburg, 1986).

Robin Lenman, John Osborne, Eda Sagarra

2

Weimar Culture: The Birth of Modernism

STEPHEN LAMB

ANTHONY PHELAN

In his well-known discussion of modernity as an incomplete project ('Die Moderne—ein unvollendetes Projekt'), Jürgen Habermas, arguably the most significant post-war critic in the Frankfurt School tradition, suggests that in the course of the nineteenth century a consciousness emerged which reduced the Modern to a mere resistance to the past and its legacy. At this point the optimism of an eighteenth-century understanding of modernity was already in decline. Enlightenment thinkers expected the arts and sciences to harness the forces of nature, to give meaning to the world, to promote moral progress and social justice, and ultimately to guarantee human happiness. Horkheimer and Adorno traced out the way in which this positive project for human and social development had been hijacked by the instrumental rationality of capitalism. What had been progressive and emancipatory had become, in the growth of the culture industry, coercive and exploitative.

The transformation of cultural production occurred as a result of crucial social, technical, political, and artistic developments in the inter-war period. In the 1920s and early 1930s there are still remnants of the old project of a liberated humanity. Indeed, when Habermas is casting about for an instance of the reintegration of the specialized spheres of science and scholarship, politics, and art, he cites narratives of workers discovering a personal—that is, moral and political—relation to works of art.[1] It is precisely that active relation between the social and the aesthetic which characterized

1 Habermas's allusion is to Peter Weiss's novel *Die Ästhetik des Widerstandes*, set—at that moment—in 1937. See Jürgen Habermas, 'Die Moderne—ein unvollendetes Projekt', in *Kleine Politische Schriften* (Frankfurt am Main, 1981), iv. 444–64.

so many cultural projects in the Weimar years, from the Bauhaus to popular illustrated papers, and from the documentary theatre to Dadaist montages. What was progressive in Weimar culture was informed by aspirations derived from a basic tenet of modernism: the belief that technological change could effect a positive transformation of the environment and an improvement of the human condition.

Introducing a new edition of his essays from the 1920s and 1930s, Ernst Bloch recalled in 1962 that the famous Golden Twenties were a time of transition. Extremists on both left and right saw the first German democracy not as an end in itself, but the incidental means by which a new Germany was to be created, whether as a socialist utopia or as the national community of a *Volk*. A look back to the Weimar years from the post-war period, across the gulf of the Third Reich, confirms their reputation for cultural vitality and innovation. The great Weimar icons—Dietrich in *Der blaue Engel*, Brecht's cigar and leather jacket, Klemperer at the Kroll Opera—still hold out a promise which National Socialism interrupted and our own postmodernity has yet to fulfil.

Defending Tradition: The Reaction against Modernity

The sense of transition celebrated by Bloch was an altogether less attractive prospect for Thomas Mann, who announced, in his essay 'Gedanken im Kriege', published in November 1914, that the Great War was a crusade in defence of German *Kultur*. Mann believed that his key terms *Kultur* and *Zivilisation* had been subject to imprecise and arbitrary usage in the press, so his own definitions and use can bear closer examination. He explains the meaning of culture in partly military terms as unity, style, form, self-control, and discipline. This creative force has the task of transfiguring and subduing the 'darker, hotter world' of irrational (chthonic) powers which underlie all societies.[2] This *Kultur* is opposed by Mann to all the French liberal traditions of *Zivilisation*: liberty, equality, and fraternity, all of which he dismisses as the 'cosiness of the social contract'.[3] None of this meant, however, that Thomas Mann was not actively interested in progressive social institutions, though the Dionysian tone and Nietzschean reminiscences of what he had to say might easily give that impression. In reality he is keen to cite the achievements of Wilhelmine society—hospitals, elementary schools, scientific institutes, luxury steamers, railways—and quotes comparative statistics on the British, French, and German educational systems in

2 Thomas Mann, 'Gedanken im Kriege', in *Von Deutscher Republik. Politische Schriften und Reden in Deutschland* (Gesammelte Werke in Einzelbänden), ed. Peter de Mendelssohn (Frankfurt am Main, 1984), 8.
3 Ibid. 9.

Stephen Lamb and Anthony Phelan

support of his claim that 'our social empire' has more of the future in it than the Western democracies. So, for Mann, Bismarck's national insurance scheme is a measure of German modernity when compared with the relative backwardness of England and France.

Less than five years after Mann's attack on liberalism the political form which was the target of his polemic, *Advokaten-Parlamentarismus* (lawyers' parliamentarism) in a republican state, was constitutionally established in Germany. A humiliating military defeat had resulted in the dismantling of older social and political structures. The Hohenzollern and Wittelsbach monarchies had been deposed; universal suffrage was in place; what had been condemned, in the French state, as the 'unclean, plutocratic Bourgeois Republic' had now overtaken the 'warrior-like conservatism' of the German soul.[4] The conditions of the Versailles Treaty forced one of the world's most powerful industrial and military nations to renounce its military might and its status as a leading imperial power. Germany's first parliamentary, democratic, and republican state came into being, in circumstances which encouraged many Germans with a background like Thomas Mann's to share his fears that 'the nation of metaphysics' and of *Bildung* was being engulfed by social and cultural anarchy.

Clearly enough there was a substantial change after 1918, but what was threatened—and what was it threatened by? It was no accident that Mann chose to quote figures, from a Spanish newspaper, on the educational establishments in the warring nations of 1914. Yet these very institutions, through which the traditions of literary and scientific culture are transmitted, were challenged by popular forms and, perhaps above all, by technological developments in the aftermath of the war. Of course, what had been assertive and self-confident in Wilhelmine Germany, drawing on national pride and the military triumphs of 1870, was destroyed by military defeat at the hands of powers which all embodied alien liberal traditions; but the pluralism which emerged in the Weimar years was inexorably driven by the forces of modernity to which Mann had also in part laid claim—a social security system, progressive research and development—in 'Gedanken im Kriege'. The mechanization and 'machine culture' which had developed on the battlefields of Europe, and the changed ways of seeing brought about by such things as the use of aerial photography for reconnaissance purposes, were merely symptoms of the expanding capitalist exploitation of technology. Horkheimer and Adorno rightly stress the degree of protection from the market mechanism enjoyed by the education system and by institutions of high culture;[5] but Mann and his class

4 Ibid. 16.
5 Max Horkheimer and Theodor W. Adorno, 'The Culture Industry: Enlightenment as Mass Deception', in *Dialectic of Enlightenment*, trans. John Cumming (London, 1973), 132–3.

felt the threat none the less. In the long run the rigid conceptual framework of his definition of culture in 1914 could not encompass the rapid growth of popular access to new media. Yet the pluralism of the post-war period was not confined to new or popular forms, such as photography, film, or cabaret. The culture which the *Bildungsbürgertum* had seen as somehow above the grubby world of politics had been irredeemably politicized by events.

This process can be gauged by Mann's own negotiation of the new Republican set-up. In the course of the 1920s Mann embarked on the ambitious project of persuading his readers in the educated middle class that the new political arrangements were not alien to German tradition but that Social Democrats such as Friedrich Ebert, the first President of the Republic, actually extended that tradition. The case Mann made out for democracy, for the Republic, and eventually for socialism is a heady mixture of Novalis and Hölderlin, Marx, Wagner, and Walt Whitman. And yet, his rhetoric did no more than measure the difficulty of the ideological task Mann had set himself. In the end, in an essay of 1928, the 'socialist class' is declared to be conducive to culture.[6] This cuts both ways: Mann recognizes that the Weimar state is now guaranteed uniquely by the Social Democrats, who are therefore the last resort of the 'parliamentary centre' and the values of the middle class; on the other hand, in a very general sense he accepts the left as the only possible demonstration in *real terms* of the pluralism and openness of Weimar.

To its opponents, however, including many of Thomas Mann's own former conservative allies, the Weimar Republic could never be anything but a socialist *closure*, the replacement of one hegemony by another.

Weimar Germany's Modernist Political Project: Theory and Practice

6 Thomas Mann, 'Kultur und Sozialismus', in *Von Deutscher Republik*, 267.
7 The complete text of the Weimar constitution, together with analysis, can be found in Hans-Joachim Winckler, *Die Weimarer Demokratie* (Berlin, 1963). For an English translation see Elmar M. Hucko (ed.), *The Democratic Tradition: Four German Constitutions* (Oxford, 1987), 147–90.

The project of establishing a pluralist consensus in the Weimar Republic could confront its supporters and detractors alike with parliamentary deadlock and coalition politics, on the one hand, and with violent extra-parliamentary struggles, on the other. The new democratic structures which made contestation possible were established in the constitution, which was approved on 31 July 1919 by the National Assembly sitting in Weimar.[7] The values and principles it enshrined show that the decision to convene in Weimar was not simply dictated by a need to get away from the upheavals in Berlin. The choice of the former residence of German culture's

Stephen Lamb and Anthony Phelan

two greatest sons, Goethe and Schiller, reflected a desire amongst the designers of the constitution that the new Republic should turn its back on Germany's nationalist and authoritarian past and promote instead the cosmopolitan universalist values of *Humanität* and *Bildung*.

With its emphasis on personal freedom, universal suffrage for all above the age of 20, equality before the law, the right to assembly, freedom of thought, and the right to form political parties and independent trade unions, the Weimar constitution embodied a central concern of modernism, the desire for greater equality and emancipation. Above all it was intended to produce a society based on tolerance, mutual respect, openness, and democracy, where the social, political, and economic conditions that had given rise to the carnage of the First World War would be banished once and for all. In practice, however, various negative factors were to prevent a genuine democratization of German society after 1918. Foremost amongst these was the crippling task of reorganizing an economy not only devastated by four years of war, but also forced to meet the massive reparations payments that had been imposed by the Allies. Although the German economy briefly recovered from the instability of the early years and the 'galloping inflation' of the autumn of 1923 with the introduction of the *Rentenmark*, and indeed achieved a degree of stability in the mid-1920s, largely as a result of a massive infusion of private capital predominantly from the USA, the Wall Street Crash of October 1929, and the subsequent withdrawal of that capital, inflicted a fatal blow, resulting in unprecedented unemployment levels, widespread impoverishment, and political polarization.

Nothing illustrated the tragic discrepancy between the theory and practice of democracy in Weimar Germany better than its system of proportional representation, providing as it did for parliamentary representation on the basis of the total number of votes cast nation-wide. No party ever received an overall majority, and consequently the history of the Weimar Republic was one of constantly changing, unworkable minority coalition governments. Between June 1920 and March 1933 there were no fewer than eight general elections and twenty-one different cabinets. As Erich Fromm, an associate of the Frankfurt School, observed ironically in his *Fear of Freedom* (1941), democracy in the Weimar Republic worked only too well.[8] The Reichstag was an all too accurate reflection of conflicting interests and classes in the Republic, many of which were fundamentally opposed to any form of compromise and therefore unwilling to pay even lip-service to the constitution's basic principles.

8 Erich Fromm, *Fear of Freedom* (London, 1941).

One such principle was contained in Article 109, which asserted that men and women had equal civil rights and duties. This simple formulation reflected the high expectations of women that the new state would mark a radical departure from Germany's long-established patriarchal traditions. These expectations had already become apparent when 80 per cent of newly enfranchised women cast their vote in the January 1919 elections for the National Assembly. In some respects the 1920s saw undoubted changes in women's social status. A notable feature of the urban scene was the so-called *neue Frau*, a woman with independent income, assiduously following the latest fashions, reading women's magazines, and dancing the newest American dance styles, such as the Charleston. Her androgynous look (defeminized clothes, emphasizing straight lines, and *Bubikopf* short-cut hair-style) reflected a widespread desire on the part of aspiring independent women to match men in terms of opportunities and achievement. In reality women were largely absent from managerial and professional positions, and job opportunities were limited to the burgeoning white-collar sector, in 'women's jobs', such as typing and secretarial work, or the retail sector (sales). The agonizing of the eponymous heroine of Irmgard Keun's novel *Gilgi. Eine von uns* (1931), torn between her love for a handsome malingerer and her desire for economic and social independence, shows that the notion of the *neue Frau* was in part a media-created consumerist myth, and that the freedoms available to women in Weimar Germany were in reality considerably restricted. It would take more than a sentence in the constitution to change the long-established behaviour patterns and attitudes of both sexes. In the traditional male professions expectations of gender equality were largely unfulfilled. Even by 1931 only 0.5 per cent of lawyers and 5.6 per cent of doctors were female, and the 30 per cent of teachers who were women were almost exclusively restricted to the primary sector. Similarly in that year only 17 per cent of students in higher education (19,000) were women. In the minds of many influential conservative men, gender equality was inextricably linked with the general relaxation of sexual taboos, the increase in pregnancy rates outside wedlock, and above all the vociferous but unsuccessful campaign against Paragraph 218 of the Criminal Code, which stipulated up to five years for abortion. This hotly debated issue produced some of the most contentious drama of the period, notably Carl Credé's § 218 and Friedrich Wolf's Zyankali, which played to packed houses throughout Germany. Here, from a socialist perspective, the playwright drew on his own experience as a practising doctor to contrast the ease with which a bourgeois *neue*

Stephen Lamb and Anthony Phelan

Frau procures an illegal termination with the fatal result of the unemployed working-class girl's back-street operation. For many women in Weimar Germany the failure to secure the right to an abortion was symptomatic of wider barriers on the road to real equality, and represented another example of expectations raised by the constitution, but frustrated by entrenched conservative interests.

The latter were epitomized by the armed forces, whose membership was almost exclusively anti-republican. The overwhelming majority of the officer class were trained in, and still derived their values from, the Wilhelmine Empire. They deeply resented the humiliating conditions attached to the Versailles Treaty, in particular the loss of one-seventh of German territory, the 'sole guilt clause', the reduction of the army to 100,000 men, and the abolition of conscription. The notion that Germany had been 'stabbed in the back' became common currency in military circles, where every opportunity was exploited to undermine the new democratic social order. Paramilitary groups such as the Freikorps and the Stahlhelm, whose violent methods had already been in evidence in the assassination of communist leaders Rosa Luxemburg and Karl Liebknecht in January 1919 and in the brutal suppression of the Munich *Räterepublik* in the spring of the same year, were instrumental in staging the Kapp *putsch* of March 1920. This threat to the fledgling democracy was thwarted only by a general strike throughout the capital. The title of Theodor Plievier's novel *Der Kaiser ging, die Generäle blieben* (1930) represents an accurate summary of the powerful influence exercised by the armed forces, which throughout the Republic remained a state within a state. The same was true of the legal sector. Although the constitution prescribed an independent judiciary subject only to the law, the vast majority of legal practitioners were, like the officer class, incorrigibly prejudiced against the new democratic republic, which they viewed as little more than a socialist conspiracy. The huge discrepancy between sentences meted out to offenders from the right and left became a recurrent theme in the work of left-wing writers such as Kurt Tucholsky, Ernst Ottwalt, and Ernst Toller.

With education it was a similar story of unfulfilled democratic aspirations. Although the constitution stipulated free primary and secondary education for all, according to 'ability and inclination, not the social and economic status or religion of the parents', and exhorted education authorities to promote 'the spirit of German nationhood *and* international reconciliation',[9] in reality a decent secondary education and access to the tertiary sector remained almost

9 Hucko (ed.), *Democratic Tradition*, 181.

exclusively the preserve of the middle class. Even in those regions which came under the political control of reform-minded Social Democrats (Thuringia, Prussia, Saxony, and Hamburg) little progress was made in combating the enormous influence of factionalism in denominational schools. As in the judiciary and the armed forces, the great majority of education administrators, curriculum designers, and teachers, especially in the arts and social sciences, had little respect for the new ideals of republicanism. In the universities a similar situation obtained. Although the 1920s saw a 55 per cent increase in the number of people in higher education (from 72,000 in 1912 to 111,000 in 1928), the vast majority of undergraduates remained aggressively nationalistic and sworn enemies of the *Sozi-Republik*, like the disaffected anti-hero of Joseph Roth's violent novel *Das Spinnennetz* (1930), an impecunious law student who falls in with a gang of fervent anti-republicans dedicated to assassinating leftists and Jews. Roth offers fascinating insights into the psychopathology of student nationalism, which, despite the ostensible demise of the Wilhelmine order, had changed little since Heinrich Mann's eponymous 'man of straw', Diederich Heßling, had bullied his way into the upper echelons of that society's political and economic élite.[10]

A further factor conducive to the malfunctioning of democracy in Weimar was the widespread lack of consensus. The Weimar Republic was conceived as a state in which no single party, class, or interest group should be allowed to dominate. The constitution required the state to play a neutral role, mediating between conflicting interests, and its basic rationale was to guarantee the freedom of the individual. Yet the imperative expressed in the first article of the constitution that state power derived from the people presupposed the kind of politically sophisticated, democratically committed citizenry which was conspicuously absent from the Weimar stage.

Analysing the 'Psychology of Nazism', Fromm noted that Hitler was well aware of the Germans' difficulties in embracing a more open society that required active participation in the body politic: offered choice, many citizens in the 1920s experienced a profound 'fear of freedom'. Faced with the disorientating complexity of pluralism and its apparent inability to guarantee economic security (by early 1933 there were 6 million unemployed), many frustrated and resentful Germans ultimately opted for the certainty of totalitarianism. This 'fear of freedom' was not, however, typical of all sections of the population. Non-aligned leftists and liberals in the cultural sphere wholeheartedly embraced, and actively worked to extend,

10 Heinrich Mann, *Der Untertan* (Berlin, 1905).

Stephen Lamb and Anthony Phelan

the new freedoms offered by the constitution. It was their commitment to democracy which provided one of the main motivating forces behind Weimar culture. But one of the tragedies of that culture was that it never gained acceptance by certain significant social classes, whose allegiances were ultimately to help determine the fate of the Republic.

Prominent among these were the educated middle class and the petty bourgeoisie. For the former the Republic was an alien imposition, embodying socialist values hostile to their nationalist traditions and promising only political, economic, and cultural instability. They profoundly resented the infiltration of German culture by foreign influences, both American and Russian, and never lost their deep suspicion of technological change. Thomas Mann in particular was well aware of the Republic's unpopularity with this grouping, and in his speeches, especially after the assassination in 1922 of the Jewish industrialist and first Foreign Minister of the Republic, Walther Rathenau, he determined to canvass the support of the educated middle class for the beleaguered Republic. The title of his key speech of that year, 'Von deutscher Republik',[11] reveals a concern to emphasize the compatability of two apparent opposites: republicanism and German traditions. Mann recognized the danger of the middle class equating its own feeling of decline with that of the German nation *per se* and, albeit with initial reluctance, he came to acknowledge that the era of old middle-class hegemony in German history had passed with the end of the war.

Correlatively, the new middle class of white-collar workers employed in administrative jobs in banks, industry, trade, transport, and in other areas of the service sector, gradually increased in significance. This was essentially the product of the thorough rationalization of industry which took place in Germany in the mid-1920s as a result of the massive influx of American capital, together with its associated production techniques of Taylorism and Fordism. By 1930 the new middle class accounted for approximately 3.6 million employees, with 1.35 million in industry and 2.25 million in sales jobs. Sociologically it occupied an intermediate position between the industrial proletariat and the professional middle class. Although some 30 per cent of this new class were members of trade unions, on the whole they regarded organized labour activity as *infra dig.*, a sign of industrial working-class attitudes. In the pathetic figure of Pinneberg in the bestselling novel *Kleiner Mann, was nun?* (published at the height of the Depression in 1932) Hans Fallada gives a poignant and sympathetic portrayal of the quiescent unskilled white-collar worker, tragically exposed to the whims of his employers and

11 See Thomas Mann, 'Von deutscher Republik', in *Von Deutscher Republik*, 125–6; see also 29, 118–20.

without a trade union for support. Although Pinneberg and his kind initially eschewed identification with any political party, the rapid deterioration of the economy after October 1929 rendered this class increasingly susceptible to the anti-democratic, anti-modernist rhetoric of National Socialism.

In short, the Weimar Republic was a period in which both politically and socially Germany continued to undergo profound modernization. By the mid-1920s German culture, whether defined in the broad sense as the way in which people structure their lives as social beings, or in the more traditional sense as the totality of a nation's highest artistic endeavours, had been transformed to the point of unrecognizability. Political pluralism, the principle on which the Republic was founded, created an environment which facilitated a massive and rapid extension of cultural activities. The modernization of industry and the economy in the mid-1920s, together with the growth in technology and the increase in disposable income and leisure amongst the old middle class, the petty bourgeoisie, and even sections of the industrial working class, meant that Weimar culture became a crucible of diverse and often conflicting elements of bewildering complexity. Artists across the entire cultural spectrum, from literature to film, from music to photography, from architecture to painting, eagerly seized the opportunities offered by the new openness to experiment with new forms and ideas, redefining or reinventing culture and, crucially, making it for the first time in German history a mass phenomenon. Culture, both by and for the people, became a defining feature of German society in the 1920s. Ironically, it was precisely the intensity and bitterness of French-style party-political conflict which propelled culture into the centre of the political arena, not to its detriment, as Thomas Mann had feared in 1914, but to its benefit.

Definitions of Culture

The extent of this sea change in the nature of German culture is demonstrated by Thomas Mann's 1928 essay 'Kultur und Sozialismus'. Here the erstwhile champion of the automony of art acknowledges that *Kultur* and politics were no longer mutually exclusive spheres. Mass audiences for mass circulation media could scarcely be encompassed by traditional patrician or élitist ways of understanding what a culture was. What Mann calls the 'socialist class' (for so long held in deep suspicion by the educated middle class) is entrusted by him with no less a task than preserving the traditional

Stephen Lamb and Anthony Phelan

heart of German self-understanding in the new democratic future. Systematically blurring the lines between political discourse and cultural activity, Mann asserts the need for *Geist* ('the inwardly realized state of knowledge achieved already and in fact by the summit of humanity') to become manifest in the material world of legislation, constitutionality, and European coexistence.[12]

Mann's sense that the cultural future of the Republic now lay with a 'socialist class' relates to two quite different ways in which the socialist movement, in its various forms, had laid claim to the arts and the media. Although it is notoriously difficult to establish concrete historical points of reference in Mann's rather abstract considerations, his use of *Geist* in the context of socialism indicates an allusion to the radical Expressionist movement known as Activism. Mann refers explicitly to 'the activist spirit' which he had taken to task during the war in his *Betrachtungen eines Unpolitischen* (1918). When he mentions the 'consequences demanded by the activist spirit',[13] there can be no doubt that he is referring to the public proclamations of the Activist group around Kurt Hiller, with its yearbook *Das Ziel*.

Hiller had been the intellectual impresario and ideologist of the early pre-war Berlin Expressionist poets, orchestrating their critical response to Wilhelmine industrialization in Der neue Klub and the 'neopathetic cabaret' which it mounted. Hiller's life-long project was to make that critical impulse an active participant in the political life of Germany, and after the events of November 1918 he believed that intellectuals should extend and consolidate a cultural revolution in schools and universities, the theatre, the press, and the law ('Ein Ministerium der Köpfe', 1919). At the time of the workers' and soldiers' councils at the end of 1918, the Activists duly formed a 'political council of intellectual workers' under Hiller's chairmanship, though they received very short shrift from the executive council of Berlin workers. Hiller's belief that cultural institutions should be turned around by a self-appointed intellectual élite for the benefit of a revolutionary transformation of society nevertheless persisted throughout the period—and even survived, in exile with Hiller, into the 1950s. This Activist position in Weimar, still alluded to by Thomas Mann in 1928, is a measure of the extent to which the interests of a traditionally 'liberal' culture could only be promoted by direct engagement with democratic politics, which Mann takes to be the politics of the left.

The promotion of revolutionary politics as a cultural project was typified by the Munich *Räterepublik* between November 1918 and May 1919, and its association with writers and intellectuals such as

12 'Kultur und Sozialismus', 267.
13 Ibid. 261.

Kurt Eisner, Gustav Landauer, Erich Mühsam, and Ernst Toller. The jockeying for power which marked its varying phases was the consequence of a struggle between those who sought to establish a parliamentary form of democracy and those who believed in the more participatory practice of the workers' councils (*Räte*). Eisner, as President, although fundamentally committed to parliamentary democracy, was quick to establish a Council of Intellectual Workers in November 1918, alongside the workers' and soldiers' councils. Among its members were a number of well-known writers, including Heinrich Mann and Toller. Inaugurating the new Bavarian Republic with a performance of Beethoven's emancipatory *Leonore No. 3 Overture*, Eisner hoped that Schiller's old ideal of freedom attained through beauty (from the *Briefe über die ästhetische Erziehung des Menschen*) could finally be spread from an educated élite to the whole of society—as beauty through freedom. That is to say, the whole enterprise of a grass-roots democracy was viewed as a cultural as well as political venture, and thus truly a *Weimar* republic in accordance with the spirit of the constitution. In pursuit of these aims Eisner and, after Eisner's assassination in February 1919, Landauer, a sort of Commissar for Popular Enlightenment, concentrated on institutions which disseminated cultural values, such as the education system and the theatre. But in the end this confidence in the renewal of humanity through the idealistic principles of *Geist* foundered on political, military, and economic realities beyond its cultural control.

The more durable among the cultural producers close to the traditions of the Activists were perhaps those associated with the so-called non-aligned left based in Berlin. Kurt Tucholsky, in the influential Berlin journal *Die Weltbühne*, and later Erich Kästner developed a very flexible satire, critical of the imperfections of Weimar society and its state, but also exploiting the full range of a new popular journalism, ranging from the 'Couplet' and cabaret song to the revolutionary reportage practised by the 'rasender Reporter' Egon Erwin Kisch. Authors like these mounted a penetrating critique of Weimar, from a position of liberal humanism, without simply imposing the values of high culture *de haut en bas*. However, their relationship with the organized parties of the left was difficult. Walter Benjamin denounced their humanism as the last gasp of bourgeois individualism; and none of Tucholsky's attempts to negotiate the role of the intellectual in the Communist Party (KPD) came to anything. Toller's unsuccessful attempt in 1919 to find a middle way between the centralist authoritarianism of the Communist Party and the gradualist approach of Social Democracy earned him the contempt of both. After the demise of the Independent Social Democratic Party (USPD) in 1922, the non-aligned left found it increasingly difficult to find an effective forum for their radical, independent socialism.

However, some of the most striking developments in the political appropriation and use of culture were promoted by political parties in the context of the working-class movement. The Social Democratic Party (SPD) had traditionally viewed culture with suspicion, as essentially middle-class in origin and intent, and therefore inappropriate to the purposes of the working-class struggle. At most the Social Democratic promotion of a proletarian lay theatre had an educational aim which survived into Brecht's conception of the didactic play (*Lehrstück*). Nevertheless, before the war a number of organizations connected with the SPD promoted sport and gymnastics, choral singing, and even tourism—as well as amateur dramatics. After the successes of the working class in 1918/19 and the increasing confidence they brought, there was a growing sense among socialists that, alongside political struggle and the economic resistance from the trade unions, a counter-cultural space was needed. The middle years of the Republic saw a great blossoming of organizations, supported by the Communist Party and the Social Democratic Party, providing for workers' leisure, education, and practical training in various cultural skills: Proletarian Free-Thinkers, Nudists' Clubs, Worker Speech Choirs and Dance Groups, Worker Photographers (whose pictures were used by John Heartfield), Radio Clubs, and Film-Makers.

Enormous numbers were actively involved in these organizations. Almost half a million people sang in workers' choral societies in the Weimar Republic; and the performances of works for speech choir (involving a kind of collective dramatic speech) were often conceived on an epic scale as the climax of festivals and celebrations laid on by the parties of the left and the trade unions. Apart from a few texts by Ernst Toller and Bruno Schönlank, few of these organizations left behind accessible artefacts, but the movement associated with the Communist Party that promoted proletarian writing of various kinds exemplified the issues of aesthetic intention involved—and the controversy which emerged within the Party itself.

Once the 'revolutionary crisis' of 1918–19 had passed, and the hoped-for violent overthrow of the state was deemed no longer feasible in the light of the Republic's gradual stabilization in the early 1920s, the KPD, as part of its effort to establish a basis of mass membership, developed factory cells and with them factory newspapers. To these publications 'worker correspondents' were encouraged to contribute accounts of their day-to-day experience in the workplace. Their ranks eventually contributed important members to the BPRS (League of Proletarian Revolutionary Writers, founded in 1928): Willi Bredel, Erich Grünberg, Hans Marchwitza, and Ernst Ottwalt. Developing a highly simplified form of naïve realism, works such as Bredel's *Maschinenfabrik N & K* (1930) reflect the increasing material impoverishment of the working class and its organization as a movement. The representation of class divisions was not the exclusive territory of the proletarian authors; similar trends were clear in writers as different as Fallada (in *Kleiner Mann, was nun?*, for instance) and Arnold Zweig, as illustrated by the often schematic approach to social stratification in his epic war novel *Der Streit um den Sergeanten Grischa* (1927). What was striking about the specifically proletarian novel was its tight focus on its own class interests. Here working-class experience was isolated in a functional and instructive narrative. Other authors developed the accounts of first-hand experience provided by the worker correspondents to create critical reportage addressing the class-based nature of Weimar institutions, such as Ernst Ottwalt's ironically titled 'factual novel' on the legal system *Denn sie wissen, was sie tun* (1931) or Ludwig Turek's autobiographical *Ein Prolet erzählt* (1930). Yet both of these forms of proletarian writing eventually attracted the ferocious criticism of Georg Lukács, the most influential cultural theorist of the Communist Party.

In essays in the Party journal, *Die Linkskurve*, Lukács complained that in abandoning the broad sweep of the 'bourgeois novel' (of Balzac and Tolstoy) 'proletarian writing' and reportage succumbed to the very processes of reification which the working-class movement and all revolutionary politics were designed to resist. By pursuing a detailed sense of realism and objective authenticity Bredel and Ottwalt, he claimed, had merely reproduced the powerful objectivity of the commodity in consumer capitalism, so that the detail, reified as an authentic fact, retained an authority independent of the larger movements of history, of political change, or of human aspiration. Such a critique now seems far-fetched, but Lukács was acutely aware of the forms taken by the classic effect of alienation analysed by Marx from the *Economic and Philosophical Manuscripts* of 1844 onwards. The products of human labour (commodities for sale in the market) apparently become magically endowed with independent power, as objects of desire, as commodities with exchange values—as much as the things people actually need in their daily lives. Fallada gives a touching and amusing account of such an

Stephen Lamb and Anthony Phelan

emergent consumerism in the dressing-table episode of *Kleiner Mann, was nun?* and in the whole setting of the department store.

We do not have to accept the whole of Lukács's Marxist social psychology to appreciate the significance of the structural parallel he is trying to establish. The point would not necessarily be that the obsession with authenticity in proletarian writing somehow corresponds to the importance of the commodity as desirable item in consumer capitalism; rather, Lukács can be seen to suggest that changes in the production process itself, in factories modelled on those of the USA and guided by the principles of Taylorism and Fordism, largely responsible for German capitalism's temporary stabilization in the mid-1920s, had effects far beyond the immediate sphere of the economy. Such an intensification of productivity could not be successfully resisted, he suggests, by an impoverished realism which simply replicated its forms.

A question emerged in this argument which continued to recur on the left well after the collapse of the Republic: how could a cultural critique of Weimar society and the compromised Weimar state be mounted in forms which essentially still belonged to the culture of capitalism and the bourgeoisie? One answer (the one preferred by Lukács and ultimately the official line of Stalinist aesthetics) was that the 'socialist class' must inherit the older forms, in order to renew them fully once its struggle for power is over. But another influential answer was that existing forms could be revolutionized from the inside, as it were. It was Brecht's answer, as much in his operas and epic theatre—with their radical redefinition of traditional forms and expectations—as in his enthusiastic espousal of the popular milieux of boxing and cycle racing thrown up as part of a new leisure industry. In this respect Brecht's understanding of the issue seems more fundamentally in touch with modern developments than Lukács's or even Thomas Mann's. Theirs is still an essentially high view of culture, informed by the traditions of *Geist* and European realism; Brecht, on the other hand, repeatedly addresses the problem of form, of commodification, and consumption, as well as questions of working-class organization, in his plays from the late 1920s onwards, such as *Die Dreigroschenoper* (1928), *Die Heilige Johanna der Schlachthöfe* (1931), *Die Mutter* (1931), and *Die Maßnahme* (1931).

Brecht's fascination with the boxing ring and the sports stadium as public arenas indicates his commitment to work in the expanding cultural sphere of industrial capitalism. In the course of the stable middle years of the Republic, and above all with the development of the new cultural technologies of photography, radio, recording, and cinema, any simple belief that the liberal cultural values could be inherited or carried forward in a pluralism marked by the advent of a new political class (Mann's 'socialist class') was swamped by the sheer variety of cultural production which was now made possible. There was only one fully public debate on the limits of cultural expansion in these middle years. It too centred on an attempt to arrest diversification, this time by means of state censorship laws.

Modernism and its Malcontents

The simmering resentment in conservative circles against Weimar modernism and the cultural degeneracy it allegedly encouraged came to a head in a protracted and heated Reichstag debate in 1926 on a motion, proposed by the German National People's Party, which sought to ban 'trash' and 'filth' from publication, performance, or screening.[14] For members of the Catholic Centre Party and their allies further to the right economic prosperity had produced a dangerous development towards 'economic individualism and Mammon', which threatened to destroy the classical and religious foundations of German culture. Offering a fascinating mixture of conservative and progressive ideas the Catholic deputy Georg Schreiber called for a campaign against the profit motive in culture and a struggle for the 'soul' of the German worker, proclaiming that the restoration of German national dignity in the aftermath of the ravages of the First World War could not be achieved by politics and economics alone. The conservatives' mission was to reassert the best traditions of Germany's cultural heritage by stemming the influx of alien cosmopolitanism which, they lamented, was engulfing Germany in a tide of commercialism. Their fears were underlined in more extreme fashion by the Nationalists, who railed against the 'excesses of destructive sensual pleasure' and the worship of 'the body, nudity, and lasciviousness'. Germany, they proclaimed, was faced with nothing less than a moral decline of Roman proportions.

At the other end of the political spectrum, the Communists lambasted the proposal as a thinly disguised attempt to increase state control over art, designed to impose bourgeois standards of morality on newly emerging proletarian culture. Citing the effective banning of Eisenstein's *Battleship Potemkin* by local censorship boards in Württemberg, they pointed out that regional governments had already made use of legal powers ostensibly designed to preserve

14 The text of the 'Schund- und Schmutzdebatte' is reprinted in Hermann Haarmann *et al.* (eds.), *Das war ein Vorspiel nur. . . Bücherverbrennung Deutschland 1933. Voraussetzungen und Folgen* (Berlin, 1983), 156–86.

Stephen Lamb and Anthony Phelan

moral decency in order to ban politically unacceptable works of art. Opposition to the proposal also came from the Social Democrats, who feared that the absolute freedom of art was being jeopardized by concessions to petty-bourgeois philistinism. Eduard David, in a speech on the day in December 1926 when the proposal was passed by a majority of 92 votes, expressed particular concern that the decision to devolve decisions on censorship to regional testing commissions (*Landesprüfstellen*) meant a return to the pre-unification spirit of petty provincialism (*Kleinstaaterei*), and therefore a threat to the cultural integrity of the Republic. Thus he saw 3 December 1926 as a black day for German culture. Appealing in vain to the traditions of cultural liberalism in the Centre and Democratic Parties, he proclaimed that the freedom of art was a cornerstone of the constitution and that any form of censorship was an attack on the very foundations of the Republic.

A more balanced contribution to the debate came from Theodor Heuß, the Democratic Party deputy (and subsequently the first President of the Federal Republic). Deploying arguments which anticipate more recent debates in Britain, he reluctantly supported the measure on the grounds that the need to protect young people transcended absolute artistic freedom. Although he rejected the right of the state to intervene in matters of cultural expression, he nevertheless advocated the need for a 'social policy for the soul'. This apparently contradictory stance typified the complexity of a debate whose very intensity, both inside parliament and on the pages of newspapers and cultural magazines, mirrored the importance attached to cultural matters by all political parties in the Republic. When the censorship measures were passed, Heuß was forced to resign his position as president of the German Writers' League, which was opposed in principle to all forms of censorship.

The parliamentary debate was merely a prelude to an even more lively public dispute. Groups of prominent members of the non-aligned left, proclaiming the sanctity of spiritual freedom, lined up against a rag-bag of ultra-conservative and nationalist organizations, such as the German Women's League against Degeneracy in the Life of the German People, the Richard Wagner Society, and the German National Teachers' League, all of which zealously followed the call to organize against the alleged corruption of the German spirit that they saw as endemic in the new Weimar culture. The panoply of works banned by some of the new regional censorship committees was very broad indeed. That it included not only popular French magazines with fascinating titles such as *Paris Flirt*, *Frivolités*, *Paris Plaisirs*, and *Eros*, but also Soviet films and Brecht's début play *Baal* merely confirmed the worst fears of those opposed to the legislation.

The debate on trash and filth, coming as it did in the mid-1920s, when the distinctively new cosmopolitan, commercialist character of Weimar culture was becoming increasingly apparent, provided telling evidence of the extent to which culture remained a burning political issue. Many who supported the legislation did so out of a conviction that the Republic's claim to be the legitimate home of Germany's classical cultural heritage was a hollow one. In their estimation the reality, by the mid-1920s, was tasteless commercialization and a total loss of standards.

For the remainder of the Republic's precarious existence culture was to remain at the forefront of political debate. Less than two years after the legislation was passed, the hitherto disparate forces of the right combined to form the so-called Kampfbund für Deutsche Kultur (Combat League for German Culture), whose aim was to rescue German culture from destruction by alien forces. Using a potent cocktail of militarist and racist ideology and constantly harking back to Germany's betrayal in the First World War, the League's manifesto spoke in apocalyptic terms of the need to restore a truly Germanic culture. It was signed by some sixty academics, clerics, and writers, and many of the most prominent members, such as Alfred Rosenberg, Hanns Johst, Baldur von Schirach, Winfried Wagner, Adolf Bartels, and Robert Ley, were after 1933 to become prominent figures in Nazi culture. With its excessively bureaucratic organization (it had sections covering all aspects of cultural activity) the League was essentially a forerunner of Joseph Goebbels's Reichskulturkammer, which after 1933 presided over the *Gleichschaltung* of all aspects of cultural life in Germany. It was precisely cultural producers' engagement with the modernity of the Weimar Republic, their extension of boundaries, moral and artistic, political and geographic, that the Nazis sought to resist in their pursuit of censorship.

Neue Sachlichkeit: The Weimar Structure of Feeling

The passing of the censorship measures did not, however, substantially hamper cultural production in Weimar. The hallmarks of the middle period of the Republic, from 1924 to 1929, were a continuing diversity in the arts and an astonishing willingness to experiment. Weimar was highly aware of its own modernity and of the process of modernization taking place in design and production, including that of culture itself. This is true whether we consider

Stephen Lamb and Anthony Phelan

films such as Walter Ruttmann's collage of everyday urban life *Berlin, die Sinfonie einer Großstadt* (1927), Fritz Lang's ideologically naïve but technically pioneering *Metropolis* (1927), or the disruptive avant-garde modernism of Berlin Dada. By the mid-1920s the term or slogan that emerged to characterize the modern style was *Neue Sachlichkeit*. The phrase is not easily translated: it involves a new objectivity, not, as John Willett has pointed out,[15] in relation to physical objects, but more abstractly to matters in general (*Sachen*), a matter-of-factness he has translated as New Sobriety. *Neue Sachlichkeit* entails a cool assessment of modern society, sometimes merely registering the development of modern technologies, at others fiercely critical of social mores and their glittering adepts.

Neue Sachlichkeit covers a very broad range, from styles of painting and design, through the influence of technology and mechanization, to American popular forms such as jazz and the deliberate search for a direct and popular literary style by figures such as Kästner and Tucholsky. This variety of reference suggests that *Neue Sachlichkeit* can properly be understood as an instance of what Raymond Williams has called a structure of feeling. It yields, that is, to systematic analysis but retains an element of emotional response in lived experience which is distinct from its economic or ideological determinations. In any event the sheer range of this 'unified style complex'[16] is a measure of the cultural diversity and pluralism of the Weimar years.

The phrase was first used explicitly by Friedrich Hartlaub in the summer of 1925 as the title of an exhibition of paintings mounted at his Mannheim gallery. However, the term was in circulation well before this date, and by 1928 it had even been used as the title of a Berlin revue. By this time there was a degree of ironic distance towards the process of social and technical progress, implying a critique of merely economic development and a moral scepticism towards economic or technological development 'for its own sake'. Earlier in the period, this objectivity turned away from what seemed excessively emotional and rhetorical in the cultural forms which had preceded it from the turn of the century to the early 1920s, including both the pretensions of Wilhelmine society and the self-indulgence of its Expressionist critics, whether in the apocalyptic gestures of Der neue Klub or the mystical utopianism of painters such as Emil Nolde and Franz Marc. The tone of the middle years of Weimar demanded a cooler approach and a clinical sense of planning for an improved future. Hence the second connotation of *Neue Sachlichkeit* is a commitment to practical and realizable goals. Such a new sobriety offered a useful contrast to the intoxication of

15 See John Willett, 'Plan and Apologia' to *The New Sobriety: Art and Politics in the Weimar Period 1917–1933* (London, 1978).
16 See Jost Hermand, 'Unity within Diversity? The History of the Concept "Neue Sachlichkeit"', trans. Peter and Margaret Lincoln, in Keith Bullivant (ed.), *Culture and Society in the Weimar Republic* (Manchester, 1977), 167.

both Expressionist utopias and nationalist ambitions in the early years of the First World War—or for that matter the posturings of the militarist right wing in shocked defeat.

However, the objective appraisal of social processes which post-war progress seemed to demand was also available as an instrument of social critique. Such critique came simultaneously from diverse quarters. The Berlin revue *Es liegt in der Luft eine Sachlichkeit* (1928) satirizes the pure functionalism of avant-garde design in Weimar in much the same way that Brecht's *Tui-Roman* (1930–42) lampoons the typical Bauhaus chair as a fine thing until you try to sit on it. To the extent that *Neue Sachlichkeit* defines a characteristic mood in the art rather than merely in the design of Weimar, it entails a moral consideration of the values which impinge on the individual. But such a critique can just as easily slip into a quizzical or even cynical denunciation of any declaration of principle as in truth merely a tactical manoeuvre in a field without strategy. This is as true of Brecht's *Mann ist Mann* (1924) as it is of Döblin's chilling calculus of inner-city violence in his experimental novel *Berlin Alexanderplatz* (1931). In this important respect Weimar modernity was already postmodern in its transcendence of technical progress.

These various instances of objectivity as functionalism identify it as an important component of the structure of feeling registered in *Neue Sachlichkeit*. It is derived from the real changes in the underlying industrial technology of the 1920s, associated with the processes of mass production developed in the United States. Although the fundamental shift to methods of mechanized production, and away from handicraft and manufacture, had been accomplished in the 1890s, both motor-car production and the intensification of production techniques in the First World War made mass production a new feature of the middle years of the Republic. Production-line technology has a number of significant consequences. Production must be broken down into its simplest units, which are performed in a repetitive way by one worker (or group of workers) responsible for that phase of the accumulative process which, at the end of the production line, yields the final product. The individual worker's contribution is limited to the efficiency and consistency with which it is performed. Skill is required only to the extent that it serves the process itself; craftsmanship is no longer important, but the finished quality of the commodity itself increasingly is. Because these production processes are infinitely repeatable, there is little sense of uniqueness or creativity. Commodities are replaceable and interchangeable; and so are those who produce them. As we shall see, this is one of the themes addressed by Walter Benjamin

Stephen Lamb and Anthony Phelan

in his essay 'Das Kunstwerk im Zeitalter seiner technischen Reproduzierbarkeit'.

The simplification of individual actions in factory production and the need for the most profitable use of work-time and factory space subject industry to standards of rationalization which sociologists such as Friedrich Tönnies and Georg Simmel had already in the late nineteenth century recognized as typical of an urban industrial society. This means that design too becomes dominated by functional concerns and rejects the ornamental or decorative styles. Perhaps for the first time, the needs of industrial investment come to set the tone and style of everyday design, and that in turn provides a point of reference for artistic creativity.

The effects of this are seen most clearly in some of the paintings of the period. Apart from the direct thematic treatment of technological or industrial subjects (already parodied by Max Ernst's 1921 painting *Der Elephant Celebes* and certainly by Brecht's poem '700 Intellektuelle beten einen Öltank an'[17]), *Neue Sachlichkeit* can be detected, on the one hand, in the clarity of line and elimination of brush-strokes in an ex-Dada painter like Christian Schad and, on the other, in the clear ('veristic') representation of a corrupt reality in the work of Otto Dix and George Grosz. Schad's *Selbstbildnis mit Modell* (1927) shows the artist with immaculate precision, his torso covered by the green haze of a voile shirt so fine that it is utterly transparent. Behind him a model, naked but for the red stocking glimpsed on her thigh and the black ribbon at her wrist, is seen in profile with a strong nose and unpleasant scar. At her shoulder a single and emblematic narcissus stands in a vase; and beyond the transparent curtains behind her we see an urban industrial horizon against the darkening night sky. Like many of Schad's portraits from this period, the image has a photographic and even hyperreal clarity. Yet the details of the composition make it clear that this picture engages with the very nature of representation: there is nothing merely objective about it at all.

Otto Dix can produce a similar hyperreal effect in *Stilleben mit Witwenschleier* (1925), *Stilleben mit Kalbskopf* (1926), and even in his *Bildnis der Journalistin Sylvia von Harden* (1926), but the restless variety of his styles and the sheer violence in his drawings of war and of prostitution indicate that, in his work, objectivity or *Sachlichkeit* is in the service of a sharp social critique. Portraits reassert the significance of the individual, by exaggeration and distortion, against the mask-like homogenization of the human face in the calculus of mass production—or, for that matter, of mass politics! This reassertion of human value is even apparent in Dix's paintings of

17 Bertolt Brecht, *Werke* [Berlin and Frankfurt Edition], (Frankfurt am Main, 1988), xi. 174.

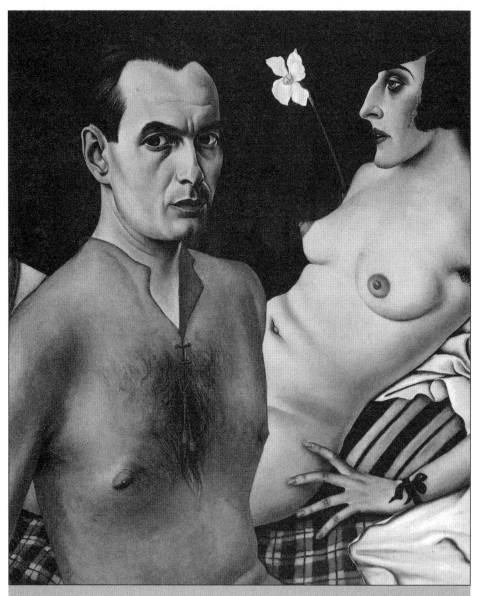

3. Christian Schad, *Selbstbildnis mit Modell* (1927).
Schad passed through the influence of modern movements such as Cubism and Expressionism and
was active in Dada, before he settled on a style derived from the old masters he had seen in Italy.
He moved back to Berlin in 1927 and was known as an extreme exponent of the objective manner.
Schad's self-portrait is both precise and erotically bohemian. The interplay of transparency in the
voile shirt and the curtain, the insistently two-dimensional presentation of the model's face
compared with the three-quarters view we have of Schad himself, and the relationship of the
flower to the narcissistic artist (whose shirt echoes the green of its stem) make it clear that this
picture asks what can be seen, what can be seen through, and what can only be alluded to
through symbolism. Schad quizzically moralizes the intense realism of the scene.

prostitutes and street scenes: where the cash nexus invades the intimacies of sexuality Dix's women are most vulnerable. The mere reproduction of reality is thus disrupted by an insistence on human values and on questions of meaning. Like Schad, Dix employs emblematic objects in the still lifes, in portraits, and in moralizing allegories such as *Melancholie* (1930), *Vanitas* (*Jugend und Alter*) (1932), and, supremely, *Großstadt* (*Triptychon*) (1928). Style and method, in Dix's work, are significant in their own right, not merely functions of objective reproduction and representation.

In other important fields functionality of design had a much more positive significance. Industrial rationality reduced the relative importance of style as an aesthetically motivated individual choice of line or colour, preferring instead the optimum coherence of production, mechanism, and purpose. In reality, however, there was a certain choice about styling in functionalism too, which simply liked the look of the machine and preferred an austerity of design to more ornamental or decorative possibilities.

This functional austerity became the characteristic design feature of Bauhaus architecture. Initially committed to adapting the principles of German classicism to modern industrial society, this élite academy of craft and design, founded with the active support of the Thuringian left coalition in Weimar in 1919 by the architect Walter Gropius, viewed itself as a 'republic of intellects', dedicated to the nurturing of a 'general, great, productive, intellectual, and religious idea'.[18] Its adoption, after moving to Dessau in 1923, of collectivist working principles and mass-production techniques for its wide range of products, including furniture, textiles, and buildings, heralded its gradual transformation into a socialist organization proclaiming the 'new unity of art and technology' and aiming for a mass market. Designers such as Gropius and Mies van der Rohe, as well as the architects Hannes Meyer and Bruno Taut, renounced the 'affectation' of traditional Imperial art, with its emphasis on ornateness and elaboration, in favour of new 'useful' forms of domestic design geared to the needs of an emerging mass consumer society. Responding to the drastic post-war accommodation shortage in large urban centres, Bauhaus designers, whose concern, according to Gropius's Marxist successor Meyer in 1928, was 'not the aesthetic process, but . . . social, technical, economic, psychic organization',[19] developed new construction techniques based on low-cost, ready-made materials assembled on site. In the later 1920s, whole estates were built on these lines in Berlin, Frankfurt, and Stuttgart. The extensive use of glass in Bauhaus factories and offices, intended to display the dignity of labour on the part of both their designers and

18 Magdalena Droste, *Bauhaus 1919–1933* (Cologne, 1990), 22.
19 Ibid. 190.

builders and those employed within, represented a new form of 'democratic' architecture, with principles of construction that were available for general inspection. Eventually everything from furniture to typography, from advertising to book-design would fall under the sway of this unsentimental approach. The Bauhaus commitment to social engineering, based on its utopian belief that a scientific approach to design and production would *ipso facto* alleviate environmental deprivation and improve living and working conditions for the urban masses, was yet another example of the modernist project underpinning some significant aspects of Weimar culture.

The advent of the Bauhaus tubular steel chair exemplifies the extent to which this sense of a modern technological society had distanced itself from the meaning of culture and style as understood by Thomas Mann and lovingly celebrated in the Second Empire furniture among which *Buddenbrooks* (1901) opens. The modernizing cultures of the 1920s were less likely to make traditional aesthetic demands of the artist and much more inclined to raise questions of utility, efficiency, and intention. From about 1926, this alternative standard in the arts crystallized around the term *Gebrauch* (use). The cult of artistic utility seems to have begun with the composer Paul Hindemith, who coined the term *Gebrauchsmusik* (utility music) by analogy with *Gebrauchsgraphik* (commercial art). Hindemith subsequently preferred the term 'communal music' (*Gemeinschaftsmusik*), and this throws important light on the sense of utility which was originally intended. Communal music would be works designed for performance with the skills and forces available in a given situation, that is, in a given community. Such performance might further train its executants in matters of technique or understanding; but its forms would not necessarily relate to the traditional genres. It would be tailored to its occasion.

There is a clear sense in which Brecht's *Lehrstücke* or teaching plays relate to Hindemith's model: these were works designed to enable young communists to explore political issues and to develop skills which are at once theatrical and political by playing out different roles in the same dramatic action. In the culture of the literary left, however, it was Kurt Tucholsky who offered a definition of functional poetry in his 1928 review 'Gebrauchslyrik'.[20] He sees such writing as directly contributing to political struggle by providing a means of educating the working class, with texts for street demonstrations or songs of solidarity. Perhaps Brecht's 'Einheitsfrontlied',[21] produced 'to order' rather later, is the best-known example of this functional view of poetic skills. But Tucholsky's journalism for the

20 Kurt Tucholsky, *Gesammelte Werke*, ed. Mary Gerold-Tucholsky and Fritz Raddatz (Hamburg, 1975), vi. 316.
21 Brecht, *Werke*, xii. 26.

Stephen Lamb and Anthony Phelan

influential Berlin cultural journal *Die Weltbühne*, as well as his verse, retains a sense of the local occasion, whether it is the appeal to international pacifism of works such as 'Der Graben' (1926)[22] or the very specific *aperçus* of his prose glosses and Wendriner stories. None of this writing is subject to traditional views of genre or style. Instead, it must take the autonomous forms and refashion (*umfunktionieren*) them. Erich Kästner's title for one of his own collections, *Ein Mann gibt Auskunft*, indicates the redefinition of a traditional form. The later *Lyrische Hausapotheke* (1936) echoes Brecht's first collection, the *Hauspostille* (1927). Calling verse collections 'Bert Brecht's Book of Household Devotions' or 'Dr Kästner's Poetical Household Remedies' ironically redefines the purpose of earlier sorts of 'practical' literature. In each case these books revert to models derived from the seventeenth century (baroque) or even earlier. Though Kästner appears to offer medical remedies, his *Hausapotheke* in fact prescribes cures for moral ills. As in the painting of Dix and Schad, Kästner's and even Brecht's poems take the psychological and spiritual temperature of the times: theirs is a cod functionalism which remains uncertain about the future, but celebrates the modernity of its own scepticism.

The Social Fabric on the Weimar Stage

The quest in popular print media—as well as in portraiture or poetry—for social and political relevance involved a shift away from the traditional idealism of their respective genres. In the theatre too 1918 represented a similar watershed. Even Hugo von Hofmannsthal, a modernist who recognized the difficulties of making connections with the classical tradition, regarded what was happening on the German stage after the end of the war as 'the dissolution of the higher German tradition'.[23] It was nothing less, he thought, than a crisis of everything that the theatre had stood for since the second half of the eighteenth century. A world of illusion, exhausted by its own over-long survival, was finally evaporating. In its belated inception in the eighteenth century German theatre had two decisive goals: it sought to be a moral and educational mirror for the improvement of the aspiring bourgeoisie; and it claimed to provide a national focus for German-speaking populations in widely disparate polities—to be in a special sense a *national* theatre.

The nationalization of the court theatres after 1918 represented a significant break with this tradition. Subsequently these *Hoftheater*

22 Tucholsky, *Gesammelte Werke*, iv. 571.
23 Quoted in Günther Rühle (ed.) *Theater für die Republik. Im Spiegel der Zeit 1917–1933* (Frankfurt am Main, 1977), 22.

of the old aristocratic residences became the national and provincial theatres (*Staats- und Landestheater*) which, along with those whose future finance was taken over at a municipal level, still provided the organizing institutional forms of the German stage, overseen by artistic directors (*Intendanten*) and financed by the public purse. While the *Volksbühne* movement continued to promote access to drama for a new audience, extended to include workers, attempts on the cultural left and by the theatrical trade union (Genossenschaft Deutscher Bühnenangehöriger) to extend workers' democratic control after the 'November Revolution' were largely frustrated in a reorganization of the theatre which relied both on public finance and private capital. Nevertheless, in 1919 these efforts were sufficient to provoke a 'memorandum' from Max Reinhardt and Richard Strauß, signed by many prominent actors, writers, and composers, in defence of individual artistic judgement against any principle of majority decision-making in the theatre. In the following year Reinhardt left Berlin for Vienna and Salzburg.

Max Reinhardt's departure is indicative of the changes in emphasis and approach which were working their way through the theatres of the Republic. He was probably the most prolific director in the history of the German stage, and he had drawn on a wide range of genres and styles to direct spectacular and even monumental productions of German and European classics, from Sophocles to Ibsen and from Schiller to Hauptmann. Although this eclecticism was seen by many as his greatest strength, in 1920 his production of Büchner's drama of revolution, *Danton*, which incorporated elements of Romain Rolland's more romantic version of the same material, met with weary scepticism in some reviewers: for Reinhardt's theatre of entertainment and theatricality, his cult of the drama as *Gesamtkunstwerk* requiring extravagant *tours de force* from designers and thousands of extras, was giving way to a new and more analytic kind of staging. The political functions which had been lost to an emphasis on education or on straightforwardly commercial entertainment before the war were restored to the most innovative theatre of the Republic. In this renewal Berlin retained its dominance.

The production of Ernst Toller's first drama, the anti-war play *Die Wandlung*, at the Tribüne theatre in Berlin in 1919 was groundbreaking for the new style. Expressionist productions abandoned the realistic representation of space found in naturalistic theatre and the illusionistic and decorative sets that went with it, in preference for the expressivity of the 'idea' sustained by a symbolic use of space and stage properties, and a discontinuous episodic action

Stephen Lamb and Anthony Phelan

(*Stationendrama*). But form and theme were also undergoing profound changes. The lifting of theatrical censorship and the freedom enshrined in the constitution permitted the performance of plays which before 1918 had either been banned or allowed only private performances. Georg Kaiser's *Gas* trilogy (1917–18), for instance, was put on at the Berlin Volksbühne in 1919. It channelled its Christian apocalyptic critique of technology through the motif of the poison gas deployed in the trenches of the western front—like the murderous effects of the gas, the consequences of technological development were unpredictable. Reinhold Goering's *Seeschlacht* (1917) developed a polyphonic form of symbolic disembodied voices to represent a spectrum of responses to the existential challenge of the Battle of Jutland. Such plays and their staging used a moment of historical crisis (the First World War) to reject the Reich and its values; but they also expressed the Oedipal rage of a whole generation which had been the major impulse in Expressionism for a decade. This *Vater–Sohn Konflikt* took to the stage in Arnolt Bronnen's *Vatermord* (1917) and Hasenclever's *Der Sohn* (1918), both of them violent assaults on Wilhelmine authoritarianism. It was the success of this generational revolt and the production style it inaugurated that drove Max Reinhardt from Berlin.

He returned in 1924: Expressionism's impact faded when its utopian spirit gave way to the matter-of-factness—the *Neue Sachlichkeit*—engendered by the relative economic stability of the mid-1920s. Its socio-critical energy was transferred to Erwin Piscator's brand of aggressively anti-romantic, multi-media production style, which sought to harness technological innovation for a new 'political theatre', expicitly Marxist in its orientation. Through his pioneering use of film and highly mechanized stage sets, Piscator attempted nothing less than a full-scale dramatization of Weimar politics—a *Totaltheater*, in which the complexity of political conflict was presented in its totality. Ironically, although Piscator intended to present the politics of the Republic to audiences previously excluded from the theatre, the sheer expense of his politicized *Gesamtkunstwerk* rendered the project ultimately unviable.

Toller's *Hoppla, wir leben!* was given this sort of treatment in Piscator's production at his own theatre (Theater am Nollendorfplatz) in 1927. Its panoramic action displayed the political accommodations of social democracy and the alienation of the old revolutionary socialist Karl Thomas from the new realities of the Republic. Toller's stage directions required film interludes—conveying the changing historical context from 1919 to 1927, for instance. Toller intended the play's dramatic action to be complemented by the new medium; however, film and stage action also functioned as contrasting or competing media. In realizing this technical innovation, Piscator recognized that the technical apparatus of his stage would seem alien and even hostile to actors working in the traditions of the 'bourgeois stage'. In the famous Grand Hotel scene of Act 3, Piscator's multi-level stage (*Etagenbau*) reveals the pathos of the disorientated and frustrated revolutionary seen against the elaborate stratifications of social power. What the scene in the radio station at the top of the hotel stresses, perhaps inadvertently, is that the political will of a party or even of a whole social class is always constrained by a world-wide economic, cultural, and even meteorological context which is ultimately beyond their control. And what can now be seen as anticipating the information revolution of the late twentieth century, including the advent of satellite television, casts doubt on the possibility of individual political action. Piscator's actors often felt they had a similar experience: the mechanization of the stage severely limited the scope of individual performances! Max Pallenberg's notoriously futile attempt to make himself heard above the noise of Piscator's conveyor-belt staging of Hašek's *Adventures of the Good Soldier Schweik* in 1928 is only the best-known case of an unintended alienation effect. As Piscator remarked, 'he was not the star of our production at all in the normal sense. It took a considerable effort of mind for this kind of man, who had had his formative training in Reinhardt's school, to do justice to this new mathematical kind of acting.'[24]

Max Reinhardt returned to Berlin to reclaim the stage for traditional theatre. His choice of a play by Goldoni (*A Servant of Two Masters*) from the *commedia dell'arte* tradition was designed to signal a return to the values of actorly theatre. However, other directors maintained their grip on a director's theatre (*Regietheater*) which remodelled even classical texts for political ends. Leopold Jessner's version of Schiller's *Wilhelm Tell* (1923) presented a solitary genius leading a movement of popular emancipation; his 1926 *Hamlet* became a republican critic of what was still rotten in the new Weimar state—a Claudius who resembled Kaiser Wilhelm II. While other directors also pursued this appropriation of a classical heritage for political ends (Karl-Heinz Martin in Büchner's *Dantons Tod*, Piscator in Schiller's *Die Räuber*), this significant change in Weimar theatre was given its definitive impetus by Brecht's attempt to redefine the classical tradition itself, reworking older ideas of form, content, and the function of performance on stage. Considering this shift of focus in 1929, the critic Herbert Ihering (one of a number of highly influential reviewers) was clear that Brecht's 1924 adaptation

24 Erwin Piscator, *The Political Theatre*, trans. Hugh Rorrison (London, 1980), 269.

Stephen Lamb and Anthony Phelan

of Marlowe's *Edward II* in the Munich Kammerspiele had given a new direction to classical production. Brecht sought to avoid current acting styles which played off emotion. In the most popular forms of the traditional repertoire, heavily reliant on subscription schemes, these were dominant. Instead he tried for a kind of historical objectivity by developing various techniques of distancing. *Die Dreigroschenoper* (1928) extended this effect of historical adaptation by a political use of parody. In his first play, *Baal* (1919), Brecht had already deployed this method to launch an ironic critique of Expressionism in general and, in particular, its inflated sense of the pathos of the isolated artist. Now parody served to unmask the political implications of the traditional bourgeois stage. Not only the action was to be exposed but 'also the mode of its literary and theatrical representation'.[25] Brecht's criticism encompasses both the musical conventions of opera and the Aristotelian notions of pity and fear. At the start of *Die Dreigroschenoper* the entrepreneurial Beggar King, Peachum, declares with disarming frankness that his business depends on arousing human pity. Brecht's point is that the function of pity in contemporary society must be re-examined because capitalist economies rely on the exploitation of human sympathy. But part of that re-examination also involved the traditional function of the actor to arouse pity on stage. Later, in his ambitious play about the Chicago meat markets, *Die Heilige Johanna der Schlachthöfe* (1931), Brecht deploys parody more fully, via allusions to Goethe's *Faust*, Schiller's *Die Jungfrau von Orleans*, and Hölderlin, to show how the position of theatre in high culture must also be analysed if its ideological commitments are to be changed.

Although Piscator and Brecht shared the same ideological position, their views of how the theatre should address politics differed radically. Whereas Piscator's *Totaltheater* insisted on direct engagement with contemporary issues, often making huge demands on audience and actors alike, Brecht preferred historical distance in the interests of reduced empathy and increased rational reflection. In spite of these differences they shared a commitment to an analytical practice of drama and even used the same phrase to describe their projects: Epic Theatre. In some respects the plays of Marieluise Fleißer transcend these differences in approach to social issues. *Fegefeuer* (1924) and *Die Pioniere von Ingolstadt* (1928) present very directly an airless and small-minded provincial existence beyond the great urban centres, but do so by reworking themes and scenarios from the classic tradition in Goethe or Büchner.

Several other developments aimed for contemporary relevance in less sophisticated ways, often involving lay actors. On the radical

25 Brecht, *Werke*, iii. 128.

left, the influence of *Proletkult* (proletarian culture) in the Soviet Union stimulated the growth of numerous proletarian troupes, variously called Das Rote Sprachrohr, Die Roten Raketen, and Die Roten Trommler, performing full-length pro-communist texts, and agitprop (agitation-and-propaganda) groups presenting street theatre or revue work in informal venues—outside factory gates, in community centres, or at workers' sports festivals. Piscator's *Roter Rummel* revue of 1924 was ground-breaking once again. However, the short sketch was more appropriate to schematic presentation and could not sustain a full argument, and in the later 1920s a documentary *Zeittheater* was developed by Piscator and drama groups associated with him as a forum for the investigation of topical social and political problems, such as the effects of the anti-abortion law in Friedrich Wolf's *Zyankali* (1929) and Carl Credé's *§ 218* (1930), and the treatment of young people in state care in Peter Martin Lampel's *Revolte im Erziehungsheim* (1928). It was no accident that the play proposed as part of its reform of children's homes the creation of drama groups for young people, or that Piscator's production of *§ 218* became a focal point for a nation-wide debate about abortion. Every serious development on the stages of the Republic had firmly recalled the theatre to its political responsibilities.

Weimar and the Meaning of Photography

26 Siegfried Kracauer, 'Die Photographie', in *Das Ornament der Masse* (Frankfurt am Main, 1977), 27–8.
27 The Deutscher Werkbund, established in 1907 by the architect Hermann Multhesius, was an association of artists, designers, and industrialists, whose aim was to improve the design of German goods. Among its early devotees were Bauhaus members Walter Gropius and Bruno Taut. It continued its activities throughout the Republic.

The challenge to traditional models of theatre came not only from the thematic shifts introduced by playwrights such as Toller or Brecht but also from the physical arrangement of the stage and the increasing mechanization of staging and sets by practitioners such as Piscator and Moholy-Nagy; the Bauhaus architect Gropius himself designed a performance space for Piscator of great flexibility and technical versatility. But the most radical challenge came from the increasing confidence of the new medium of photography. In the early 1920s the film industry had seen itself as producing filmed versions of literary material which lent legitimacy to the new and essentially popular form (and, of course, Hollywood in fact continued to live parasitically on printed media); similarly, as late as 1927, Kracauer's essay on photography mentions the fact that many early photographers had been painters and portraitists.[26] By the end of the decade, however, the autonomy and power of the photographic media had been recognized. The year 1929 saw the important international Werkbund exhibition 'Film und Foto' in Stuttgart;[27]

Stephen Lamb and Anthony Phelan

while, from a quite different ideological quarter, Ernst Jünger in *Der Arbeiter* (1932) denounced attempts to apply outmoded liberal concepts of culture to the new electrical media of film and radio.[28]

The first public wireless transmission was broadcast on 29 October 1923 by the recently founded Funkstunde AG Berlin from the offices of the Vox record company. It consisted of an hour-long programme of classical music on gramophone records, concluding with an infantry regiment band's rendition of 'Deutschland, Deutschland, über alles'. It was received by some 200 privileged Berliners on their individual headphones. The first live broadcast (of Franz Lehár's *Frasquita* from the Thalia-Theater in Berlin) took place on 18 January 1924. In the earliest phase of radio, a subscribing audience was slow to develop. Those interested in wireless were 'radio hams', committed to the active use of the new technology. However, they were unwilling to pay a licence fee merely to listen to programmes (mostly of news and music) produced by others. By reducing the licence fee and organizing clubs for wireless amateurs, the Reichspost encouraged the technical enthusiasts to become part of an audience of programme consumers. (The importance of home-made wireless sets and of the experience with the new technology which came from the First World War is well illustrated in the early part of Edgar Reitz's film *Heimat* (1984).) With the help of a widespread government campaign, encouraging people throughout the Reich to 'Become radio listeners', there were by 1926 a million radios in Germany, and by 1932 over 4 million.[29] The status of the new medium was confirmed by the eagerness with which many writers, composers, critics, and politicians seized the opportunity to speak to a mass audience, as well as by the growth of specialist criticism in newspapers and radio magazines, and the institution of a literary prize for radio drama.

The radio play (*Hörspiel*) was the most obviously appropriate form for radio. There was considerable debate about the nature of this new acoustic genre: the idea that radio drama should be conceived as a theatre of the blind survives in the prestigious 'Hörspielpreis der Kriegsblinden', founded in 1951; others thought that radio drama must give priority to the spoken word; while a third position stressed the whole range of acoustic material which could be exploited.[30] Many prominent literary figures contributed early works to the genre, including Döblin, Toller, Wolf, and Kästner. In contrast, Brecht remained sceptical about the prospects of the new medium: perhaps recalling the days of the 'radio hams', in his *Badener Lehrstück* (1929) he wryly imagined a participatory radio culture in which listeners would discover their *collective* identity.[31] In reality, however,

28 Ernst Jünger, *Der Arbeiter. Herrschaft und Gestalt* (Stuttgart, 1983).
29 Bärbel Schrader and Jürgen Schebera, *The 'Golden' Twenties: Art and Literature in the Weimar Republic* (New Haven, 1990), 119–21.
30 See August Soppe, *Der Streit um das Hörspiel* (Berlin, 1978), 96–117.
31 Brecht, *Werke*, iii. *Der Ozeanflug*.

Brecht realized that the new medium was constrained by the economic conditions of its existence to be little more than 'an acoustic department store'.[32]

The new 'technical media' caused a certain uneasiness. This is still apparent even in one of the greatest satirical exploitations of the photographic image in the whole period, the picture book *Deutschland, Deutschland über alles* (1929), with texts by Kurt Tucholsky written to accompany a selection of photographs and a handful of photomontages by John Heartfield. Tucholsky was a brilliantly prolific and highly successful satirist, but the very format and design of the book produced with Heartfield mark it out as a modern production: unlike Tucholsky's earlier collections, which appeared in uniform octavo editions, bound in linen and set in Gothic type, *Deutschland, Deutschland* is a larger octavo volume with an illustrated photographic cover by Heartfield and is set in roman. This very commitment to the new medium is tempered by an uncertainty about the meaning of photographs. Tucholsky's preface (subtitled 'Die Unmöglichkeit, eine Photographie zu textieren') begins by claiming that the pictures selected for the book are 'more or less characteristic for a class, an estate, a place, a locality' but ends by dwelling on the difficulty of attributing general significance to individual images—the 'private soul that lives in these collective creatures, gets angry'—and calls in a lawyer.[33]

The work is arranged as a picture-book guide to the Weimar Republic. It begins with home-coming soldiers in 1918 and conducts the reader through the class contrasts and class conflicts of the 'new' society. Photographs of the ruling class, whether of the Weimar *grande bourgeoisie* or of the deposed Kaiser and his family, do not in fact attract our sympathy as individuals, while the workers can be seen individually as subject to oppression and exploitation. In this way the work promotes solidarity with the working class, as well as mounting a fierce critique of the political residues of the Empire and of the corruption of the Republic which succeeded it.

Tucholsky's uneasiness about the representative significance of photographs is paralleled, surprisingly enough, by Ernst Jünger's reflections on photography and film in his essay diagnosing the condition of the world after 1918, *Der Arbeiter* (1932). Jünger registers a change in the personal significance of photographs, of which he thinks everyone is aware. Older, nineteenth-century photographic portraits, he claims, reveal more individuality and character than recent ones. But Jünger's conclusion is quite different from Tucholsky's: the meaning of modern photographs is hard to

32 Brecht, *Werke*, xxi. 552.
33 Kurt Tucholsky, *Deutschland, Deutschland über alles* (Berlin, 1929), 11.

Stephen Lamb and Anthony Phelan

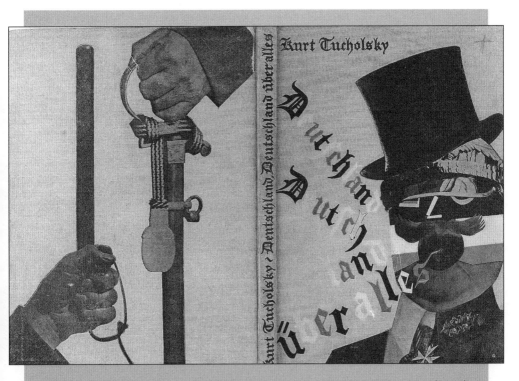

4. Kurt Tucholsky and John Heartfield, *Deutschland, Deutschland über alles* (1929).
John Heartfield (1891–1968) produced photomontages for Kurt Tucholsky in *Deutschland, Deutschland über alles*. In 1916 he changed his name from Helmut Herzfelde in protest against German chauvinism. He used the critical anti-art methods of Dada to mount an attack on the social reality of the Weimar Republic. The cover for *Deutschland, Deutschland* combines the national colours of the Republic, black-red-gold, with those of the Empire, black-white-red. *Weimar* Germany appears as a combination of the military and Imperial past, symbolized by the military helmet, uniform and iron cross, and Wilhelmine moustache, with the financial bourgeoisie's top hat, suit, and tie. The Gothic typeface of the cover contrasts with the aggressive modernity of the montage and the roman type of the text. The back cover parodies a line from the national anthem about fraternal solidarity ('brüderlich zusammenhält') by indicating the unity of military sword and police truncheon.

fix, not because there is a gap between the individual case and the collective truth which it is supposed to illustrate, as Tucholsky thinks, but because photography is the technical genre proper to a new organization of humanity in the epoch of the Worker. This new form and figure (*Gestalt*) informs and gives unequivocal meaning (*Eindeutigkeit*) to a new type (*Typus*), beyond the tensions and contradictions of old thinking in terms of individuality and 'the masses'. In a very important discussion (in section 38 of *Der Arbeiter*) Jünger develops his case by comparing theatre and film as modes of representation. He believes that while the increasingly outmoded theatrical form had demanded that the actor represent a dense and harmonious personality, film requires the representation of a *type* of human being in 'the precise rhythm of a life'.[34] What is seen in films is the mechanized space of modernity in which the epoch of the Worker comes into being: Jünger seems to be thinking of movies like Chaplin's or Buster Keaton's in which the individual is at the mercy of the mechanical and architectural environment. 'Tall buildings are only built so you can fall out of them, it is the point of traffic to run you over, and of motors that they blow you up.'[35]

The differences between this view of a universal typicality which photography reveals and Tucholsky's deep sympathy for the individual as victim of oppression or hero of resistance are evident in the picture books they helped to produce. Jünger worked with two different editors (Edmund Schultz and Ferdinand Buchholz) to put together *Der gefährliche Augenblick* (1931) and *Die veränderte Welt* (1933). To a large extent these volumes simply illustrate central themes of *Der Arbeiter*, which had appeared a year earlier: the meaning of international security, the importance of masks in modern society (whether in welding or cosmetics), the destruction of older ideas of individuality by the spread of mechanization. (This is true even of puzzling details such as the photograph of a Berlin 'school of astrology': compare *Der Arbeiter* section 41!) For Jünger the ruthless honesty of the photograph exposes the falsity of what is merely 'posed' (like older studio photography with a 'backdrop'), and will not tolerate the deception of theatrical representation without leaving a sense of excessive pathos. The immediacy of the camera goes straight for the informing truth. In *Die veränderte Welt*, therefore, a photograph of Mussolini standing on a tractor next to its driver is supposed to reveal the transformation of the peasant into the figure of Worker and the proximity of new-style (fascist) political leadership to the forces of mechanization. Similarly, the captions accompanying the pictures are assertions of what the images ostensibly document. Tucholsky and Heartfield, on the other hand, use images as

34 Jünger, *Der Arbeiter*, 138.
35 Ibid. 139.

Stephen Lamb and Anthony Phelan

part of the whole critical discourse of *Deutschland, Deutschland über alles*. They reveal a society still fissured along class lines and attack it satirically by displaying the unsavoury features of the bourgeoisie, the social consequences of poverty in the working class, and the ludicrous survival of Wilhelmine lifestyles—an overdecorated Berlin *pissoir*, a sign directing servants to a back door, a Hohenzollern coat-of-arms on a Republican government building. The Tucholsky–Heartfield collaboration is successful and entertaining in a way that Jünger's book is not, partly because it is less monolithic and partly because it uses photographs in a more differentiated and inventive way. The underlying principle is montage, a technique of cross-cutting contrasting images as well as image and text, which is much closer to the revolutionary procedures of film-making developed most radically by Eisenstein.

Heartfield had worked on a scissors-and-paste approach to photographic montage ever since the early years of the war and explored the possibilities of sequences of photographs presented on a single page in the 1924 yearbook of the communist Malik Verlag, which he ran with his brother Wieland Herzfelde. The collage techniques employed in Heartfield's greatest photomontages derive from the anti-art or surrealist work of the Dadaists with whom he was associated; but he was careful, especially in his work for the socialist media magnate Willi Münzenberg's *Arbeiter-Illustrierte-Zeitung*, to present his images in an illusionistic space as if they were 'real' photos. They were designed to look puzzlingly realistic because they revealed political aspects of the real world all too clearly.

Heartfield's work with Tucholsky and Jünger's two picture-book collaborations emphasize the growing importance of the visual image in Weimar—but also the extent to which these images were open to conflicting and ultimately political interpretations. As Siegfried Kracauer in an essay on photography in 1927 wryly remarked, 'Never has an age known so much about itself—if knowing means having a picture of things that resembles them in the sense of photography.'[36] Yet he also suggests that, because photography fixes reality in a superficial way, it prevents the viewer from understanding that reality historically or conceptually. For Kracauer the proliferation of printed images in the popular illustrated magazines and newspapers of the Republic actually blocks any understanding of events. In these terms, Heartfield's methods of combination and montage would actively restore the photographic image to its true historical and political context. But in *Deutschland, Deutschland über alles* this rehistoricization of the photographic image goes beyond theoretical debate. The magazine-like format of

36 Kracauer, 'Über Photographie', in *Das Ornament der Masse*, 33.

the book, combining pictures, captions, continuous prose, vignettes, and poems (and even a puzzle-picture), attempts to occupy for the liberal and communist left part of the terrain of popular culture opened up by picture papers and film magazines (such as the *Berliner Illustrirte*, or the *Film-Kurier* and *Kinematograph*).

The Cinema and Brecht's *Kuhle Wampe*

Nowhere was the impact of technology on culture more apparent than in film. With the patenting in 1895 of the *Bioskop*, a camera capable of creating the illusion of permanent movement by taking eight pictures a second, a new form of entertainment was born which gained growing popularity as a side-show at travelling fun-fairs, before acquiring a more permanent home in a rapidly increasing number of cinemas. By 1914 around 13 million regular film-goers were attending some 2,500 cinemas throughout the Reich, and film had outstripped theatre, literature, and the fine arts as a mass medium of popular culture, so that by 1930 over 3,500 cinemas offered Germans the opportunity to indulge in a new, uniquely communal, cultural activity. More than any other single medium, cinema internationalized Weimar culture by enabling Germans to experience vicariously the culture of countries as diverse as France, the United States, and the Soviet Union. Benefiting from the new artistic freedoms guaranteed in the Weimar constitution, Berlin film studios sought to capitalize on the new medium's popularity, with war films, thrillers, historical epics (often celebrating Prussian traditions), westerns, as well as sex-education features and documentaries. While most of the latter were thinly disguised commercial pornography, some directors strove for genuine 'enlightenment'. Richard Oswald's pioneering *Anders als die Anderen* (1919), for instance, pleaded for decriminalization of homosexuality and abolition of Paragraph 175 of the Criminal Code.

Not all Weimar cinema was merely populist. Writers, artists, and stage actors were quick to realize the potential of the new medium, and the 1920s saw a blossoming of works which elevated film to a new art form. Directors enthusiastically seized the opportunity to demonstrate that the cinema was capable of enlightenment as well as entertainment. In many cases, works from these formative years have established their place in the canon of international cinema: Ernst Lubitsch's historical tableau, *Madame Dubarry* (1919); Robert Wiene's anti-realist study of madness, *Das Cabinet des Dr Caligari* (1919); F. W. Murnau's prototype horror film, *Nosferatu*

(1922); his acute observation of frustrated petty-bourgeois aspirations, *Der letzte Mann* (1925); and his populist interpretation of *Faust* (1926); Fritz Lang's fatalistic study of the struggle between good and evil, *Dr Mabuse, der Spieler* (1922); his epic *Nibelungen-Lied* adaptations, *Siegfrieds Tod* and *Kriemhilds Rache* (1923–4); and his futuristic *Metropolis* (1927); and Leontine Sagan's celebration of sisterhood and female sexuality, *Mädchen in Uniform* (1931).

As explained in the previous chapter, the potential of film as a means of influencing public attitudes had already been recognized in 1917, when, in a desperate attempt to boost flagging morale, Germany's military authorities established Ufa (the Universum-Film AG), an organization that dominated film production and distribution in Germany for almost three decades. In 1927 Ufa was acquired by Alfred Hugenberg, leader of the right-wing German National People's Party and owner of a massive media empire, which included a nation-wide chain of publishing houses, newspapers, news and advertising agencies, and the status of film as a major force in German culture had been emphatically confirmed. Increasingly Ufa's considerable resources were devoted to producing nationalistic films, intent on stimulating pride in Germany's military past and challenging the climate of pacifist internationalism created by works such as Pabst's film *Kameradschaft* (1931) and Remarque's bestseller *Im Westen nichts Neues* (1930), the Hollywood film version of which became a *cause célèbre*, debated even in the Reichstag.

Hugenberg's leading role in the 1929 campaign for a referendum against the Young Plan proposals to redraft reparations payments, and his close collaboration with Hitler in 1931 in the Harzburg Front of anti-republican forces, provide further evidence of the extent to which the mass media became a weapon in the political conflicts of Weimar Germany. In many ways this early example of media monopoly prefigured the Axel Springer empire in the Federal Republic, and indeed, more recently, the attempts by Gerhard Frey, the leader of the Deutsche Volks-Union, to harness media power to the new post-1989 ultra-nationalism in Germany and Russia, or Berlusconi's use of his media interests for Forza Italia. As Modris Eksteins has shown, Hugenberg's communications empire was 'a major obstacle to the implantation of democratic, republican ideals amongst the German public'.[37] A significant factor was his indirect control of the predominantly conservative, and therefore anti-republican, provincial press. Its total circulation and influence far outweighed the more republican-minded and commercially independent regional newspapers (such as the *Vossische Zeitung*, the *Frankfurter Zeitung*, and the Berlin-based *Börsen-Courier*, *Tageblatt*,

37 Modris Eksteins, *The Limits of Reason: The German Democratic Press and the Collapse of Weimar Democracy* (Oxford, 1975), 81.

Illustrirte, and *Morgenpost*) published by the Jewish-owned concerns Ullstein, Mosse, and Sonnemann. The fact that none of the national newspapers, with their broadly based reportage of overseas as well as national politics, economics, and culture, ever exceeded a circulation of a million (the highest was the *Berliner Morgenpost* with 600,000 in 1931) contributed in no small measure to the failure of republican and internationalist ideals to gain a firm foothold outside the major urban centres.

A more systematic but ultimately equally unsuccessful challenge to Hugenberg's media monopoly was mounted by Willi Münzenberg, KPD deputy, director of the socialist International Workers' Aid movement (IAH), and publisher of the demotic *Arbeiter-Illustrierte-Zeitung* and the daily *Welt am Abend*. Münzenberg's acute awareness of the political significance of the new media led him in 1925 to issue a call to the left to 'conquer film'. Through his film-production and distribution company Prometheus, Münzenberg sought to counteract the escapism of mainstream cinema's preoccupation with big-budget, Hollywood-style cinema, offering instead films which were socialist in their politics and collectivist in their production values. Between 1926 and 1929 Prometheus produced twelve full-length feature films, including several co-productions with the Soviet film-production company. It also organized the distribution of Soviet films in Germany, including Pudovkin's screen version of Gorki's *The Mother* and Eisenstein's *Ten Days that Shook the World*, *Battleship Potemkin*, and *October*. Eisenstein's impact in Germany was immediate and far-reaching. Soldiers were forbidden to see *Battleship Potemkin* because the military authorities feared they would be infected by the film's positive portrayal of mutiny. But the impact was not just political. Eisenstein's pioneering use of montage inspired a number of film-makers, notably Walter Ruttmann in *Berlin, die Sinfonie einer Großstadt* (1927).

Ironically, given his initial reservations about a medium he regarded as inherently cathartic, Bertolt Brecht was primarily responsible for creating a film—*Kuhle Wampe* (1932)—which, like no other, exemplified the fusion of technical innovation and socio-critical didacticism central to so much of Weimar modernism. By deliberately excluding emotional tension from his closely observed narrative of working-class poverty (each of the four sections is prefaced with an ironic title, such as 'Ein Arbeitsloser weniger' or 'Das schönste Leben vor sich'), Brecht and his collaborators, the novelist Ernst Ottwalt and the young Bulgarian director Slatan Dudow, created an acutely analytical work. They deployed both conventional symbolism, such as shots of bicycle wheels to indicate a furious but

Stephen Lamb and Anthony Phelan

futile search for work, and innovative montage, exemplified in two memorable sequences. In the first, pregnant, unemployed, working-class Anni, walking with her lover Fritz to the tram-stop, is jolted by the sight of a group of schoolchildren into anxious thoughts about the stark realities of motherhood, conveyed in a rapid sequence of images which includes shots of breast-feeding mothers of children 'bouncing with health' in Nestlé adverts for 'natural nourishment', a still of Anni's redundancy notice, and her recollections of the horror of her brother's recent unemployment-induced suicide. The romantic images peddled by the advertising industry are revealed as a tragic illusion. Without material security, the montage suggests, motherhood for many was at best a utopian ideal, at worst a threat to life. The second sequence juxtaposes Anni's father haltingly reading out a newspaper report about Mata Hari ('her perfectly shaped legs rose up like the pillars of a pagoda') with his wife agonizing about the family budget. As well as underlining the discrepancy between male fantasy and female reality, these scenes encapsulate *Kuhle Wampe*'s general concern with the reality of urban working-class life, and form a powerful contrast with the escapist nature of the great majority of German films screened in Weimar cinemas, which sought to emulate Hollywood production values, the most successful undoubtedly being *Der blaue Engel* (1930), where Josef von Sternberg cloaks his misogyny in the guise of a celebration of female sexuality.

Yet Brecht's challenge to the stereotyped screen images of woman as virgin or vamp, which filled Weimar screens and were captured most memorably by Brigitte Helm's two Marias in Lang's *Metropolis*, goes further. Women in Brecht's chronicle of working-class life are given a positive role. Anni's decision to flout the law and abort her child contrasts powerfully with her brother's suicidal act of resignation, and it is a woman whom Brecht has answer the film's climactic question: 'Who will change the world?' Similarly, in the shots in the film's final section, portraying a working-class sports festival celebrating the virtues of collective socialist endeavour, a good deal of screen space is devoted to images of women acting in an autonomous way.

Undoubtedly the film has limitations. The 'Game of the Sexes' scene, in which, after prolonged shots of trees and fields, Anni and her lover disappear into the woods, accompanied by Helene Weigel singing the 'Lied vom Frühjahr' as the camera gradually pans vertically up a tree, verges on kitsch. More seriously, unlike its National Socialist counterpart *Hitlerjunge Quex* (1933), where Communist characters for the most part embody negative stereotypes, *Kuhle Wampe*

5. Slatan Dudow, Bertolt Brecht, and Ernst Ottwalt, *Kuhle Wampe* (1932).
It was Communist Party policy from the mid-1920s to organize regular cultural festivals,
combining sport, theatre, and political discussion. Their aim was to strengthen collective political
and cultural awareness. A lengthy montage of shots in *Kuhle Wampe*'s final section highlights
concerted, non-competitive sporting activity (e.g. rowers and swimmers) at such a festival. The
images are underpinned by Ernst Busch's rendition of Brecht's 'Sportlied' and the repeated
choral incantation of his 'Solidaritätslied'. This still captures a moment from the climax of the
festival, a performance by the agitprop troupe The Red Megaphone ('wir sind das Sprachrohr der
Masse') of a brief single-act play exhorting a working-class family to resist eviction. Involving
some 4,000 'Arbeitersportler', this is quintessential Weimar mass culture: by, for, and about
ordinary people. The initials A I [Z] stand for *Arbeiter-Illustrierte-Zeitung*, Willi Münzenberg's
socialist newspaper. The solitary head turned to camera ironically underlines the scene's
authenticity. A mere extra would have known better!

makes no attempt to engage with (and discredit) its major ideological rival, preferring instead to target the social, economic, and legal iniquities of the Weimar 'system'. Thus the film exemplifies the disastrously misguided nature of the official Communist Party line in the final years of the Republic, when the policy of 'social fascism' identified social democracy and not National Socialism as the main threat to the working class. Nevertheless, *Kuhle Wampe* is both stylistically and thematically a highly innovative work, which exploits to the full the technical potential of the new medium. Through such devices as montage, intertitles, and the occasionally stylized delivery of dialogue, and not least the edgy and strident tones of Hanns Eisler's modernist score, the film deliberately flouts classical narrative conventions in the interests of an analytical approach appealing to rationality rather than the emotions. It thereby challenges the claims of more celebrated screen works, such as *Metropolis* or *Der blaue Engel*, to represent the pinnacle of Weimar cinema.

Weimar Criticized: Three Culture Critics on the Rise and Fall of the Republic

Kuhle Wampe attempted to harness the most modern technical and stylistic developments to the interests of the working class and the Communist Party. The rapid expansion of the cinema in the course of the Republic, along with other developments in photography and printing, constituted the most important changes in the way cultural products were created and distributed in the period. Films, illustrated papers, and magazines were the media in which the whole process of technological modernization made its greatest impact on popular culture, and for a number of important critics this experience of modernity was characteristic of the cultural experience of Weimar as a whole.

In journalism, essays, glosses, and reports, three Jewish critics offered broad accounts—both before and after 1933—of the characteristic phenomena of the Weimar years: Siegfried Kracauer in his regular contributions to the *Frankfurter Zeitung* (including his pioneering socio-psychological study of the petty bourgeoisie, *Die Angestellten*, 1930, which the paper serialized, as well as important film criticism); Ernst Bloch in *Erbschaft dieser Zeit* (1935), which links essays and reviews from the late 1920s and 1930s by further commentary and analysis; and Walter Benjamin in his lecture on the author as a producer at the Paris Institute for the Study of Fascism in 1934 ('Der Autor als Produzent') and in his essay on the work of art ('Das Kunstwerk im Zeitalter seiner technischen Reproduzierbarkeit', 1936). What they have in common is the realization that the technical means by which popular forms of culture are made are profoundly important as part of the broader development of technology and of the economy.

It is hardly surprising that these three figures work along similar lines. They were acquainted, if hardly close friends, and certainly knew of each other's work. Kracauer, who had the most secure job, at the *Frankfurter Zeitung*, put reviews and other freelance work the way of Bloch and of Benjamin, whom he had known from the early and mid-1920s respectively. They corresponded, discussed each other's books, and even reviewed them.

Kracauer took note of *Kuhle Wampe* in a review provoked by the ban imposed on the movie by the Republic's board of film censors. Although he celebrates those aspects of the film's style which are derived from the revolutionary work of Russian directors such as Eisenstein, he is critical of its failure to mount an attack on 'official film production'. This is an important clue to the way in which Kracauer understands the relationship between society and popular culture. One of Benjamin's letters to him paraphrases it as 'the collusion between the imagination of the ruling class and that of the ruled as organized by the film industry'.[38] On this view, film is an adjunct of consumerism and even an instrument of social control; it can guide the imagination and desires of the 'ruled' by providing icons and images for a whole set of values. For Kracauer, anticipating Horkheimer and Adorno's critique of the cinema in their essay on the culture industry, orthodox film production by the German (or American) film industry is also essentially the tool of a capitalist class, designed to draw attention away from the deprivation imposed on factory workers and office workers alike by the ruthless application of methods of mass production. Film is specifically conceived as a form of escapism and already apes the techniques of mass production in its off-the-peg story-lines and repetitive, formulaic editing styles.

Kracauer's method in the series of critical vignettes he wrote for the *Frankfurter Zeitung*, 'Die kleinen Ladenmädchen gehen ins Kino' and 'Der heutige Film und sein Publikum', depends on reading film scenarios as wish-fulfilments on the part of the audience. The capitalist class is supposed to manipulate the imagination of its white- and blue-collar workers, and thus to avoid any direct confrontation with social and industrial reality. Kracauer brilliantly describes the architecture and interior design of 1920s 'picture palaces'

38 Walter Benjamin, *Briefe an Siegfried Kracauer* (Marbach am Neckar, 1987), 41.

Stephen Lamb and Anthony Phelan

as conniving, similarly, at the creation of this synthetic and ultimately insubstantial alternative world of fake experience.

The most everyday experiences—such as the 'look' of a cinema
or, in *Die Angestellten*, the décor of Berlin's large bar complexes—
provide the raw material for his sharp-eyed investigations of the
objects designed to satisfy the fantasy desires of the new middle
class of proletarianized white-collar workers. Kracauer's tight focus,
specially in his 'miniatures'—texts of under a thousand words—is
ideally suited to his journalistic medium and often borders on apho-
rism. (There is a clear parallel between the polished building-blocks
of his journalism, even when put together to provide a broader
view, and the finished individual commodity or the atomic 'partial
function' (*Teilfunktion*) of rationalized labour: the capitalist structure of the press is present even in one of capitalism's most acute
critics.) In its forms, Kracauer's analysis of cultural phenomena
anticipates, in many ways, Roland Barthes's *Mythologies*. Like Barthes,
Kracauer sees the icons of popular culture as ideologically compromised; and popular sports are no more immune to being taken
over for capitalist purposes than is the cinema. (Walter Benjamin
took great pleasure in Kracauer's laconic attack on Brecht's naïve
commitment to proletarian sport, as evidenced in *Kuhle Wampe*!)
For all these reasons, culture criticism, as an analysis of the whole
complex of urban experience, has become the uniquely necessary
tool of left-wing or emancipatory politics.

Like Kracauer, Bloch too focuses his cultural analysis on the role
of the young and specially of the proletarianized middle class.
Benjamin thought Kracauer's work described the 'demise of the
petty bourgeoisie in a remarkable, "loving" account of its bequests';[39]
and this could well summarize Bloch's *Erbschaft dieser Zeit* also.
Bloch's writing, similarly, is built up from miniature *aperçus*, designed to show how the false hopes conjured up in advertising,
magazines, or popular entertainment, for instance, are the symptoms of a desire which the aggressive capitalism of the post-war
years could not satisfy. Bloch sees the years of the Republic as
influenced by a constellation of partly contradictory forces. He seeks
out the ambiguous areas of Weimar's social consciousness, such as
the film-star cult, the defensiveness of the small town, or urban
yearning for 'the country'. In these and many other instances, Bloch
finds symptoms of a social life apparently lived out in the same
historical moment, but in fact split across different phases which
are not really simultaneous at all. The country thus stands for traditional forms of life but also a mode of production in which 'the
process of specialization and division of labour developed more

39 Ibid. 17.

slowly'[40] than in the metropolitan experience of capitalism. Like Kracauer again, this culture criticism addresses the whole problem of modernity as it was experienced in the new and changing popular media, as well as finding expression in art and philosophy. Such manifestations of non-contemporaneity (*Ungleichzeitigkeit*), Bloch believed, could have provided pockets of resistance to capitalist exploitation, but in fact fell under the spell of fascist *ressentiment* as the unsettled middle classes turned for solace and stability to the National Socialists.

The Weimar experience of ruthless modernization was reflected in the multifaceted criticisms of Bloch and Kracauer. Their preference for the miniature form of so-called *Merkprosa* had the shortcoming that it could not readily encompass any larger theory of modernity. The satirist Tucholsky was personally aware of the problem when he wrote in 1933, 'We need either essays with staying power or *facts*.'[41] The crisis for the left occasioned by the Nazi seizure of power forcibly drew attention to the deep ambiguity of modernity and the need for social and political analyses with optimum explanatory force. The work of Benjamin recognized that the technological transformation of production, above all of the means of representation, was a field of dangerous conflicts. It fell subsequently to his associates Horkheimer and Adorno—and to other members of the Frankfurt School—to provide a developed analysis of cultural production from this (quasi-)Marxian point of view.

Benjamin's objection to Bloch's book, expressed in a letter to Kracauer, was that it failed to identify the '*corpus delicti* of the emasculated German intelligentsia'.[42] Benjamin himself focused explicitly on the changes which technology had brought about, and on the ways in which they might be used. In the essay 'Der Autor als Produzent', Benjamin makes the relationship between a cultural object and the means of its production the crucial index of its ideological power. Whatever their intentions may be, artists can only ally themselves with the progressive force of a communist working class by seeing themselves as *producers* supplying material to the production apparatus: publishers, broadcasting organizations, galleries, film companies, etc. The model for Benjamin's cultural producer actively engaged with the means of production is Brecht's reworking of the relations between author, stage, and audience in the theatre. However, his sense that technological development was reconfiguring authorship, audience, and cultural forms is most dramatically evident in his view of the cinema. Film gives the lead, because it shatters the power of tradition and the sense of a historically unique artefact that goes with it. Film *is* reproduction, always

40 See Ernest Mandel, *Late Capitalism* (London, 1978), 378.
41 Kurt Tucholsky, *Ausgewählte Briefe* (Reinbek, 1962), 84.
42 Benjamin, *Briefe an Siegfried Kracauer*, 81.

Stephen Lamb and Anthony Phelan

multiple; and it creates a new—and strikingly self-confident—*collective* audience. Through this popular access to cultural production, so Benjamin hoped, art (in the broadest possible sense) might be made political—that is, democratic and therefore, in his view at the time, communist. And yet, he saw all too clearly the dangers of a fascist appropriation of the same medium which would not grasp that modern and secular possibility, but instead would force it back towards ritual and myth.

Suggested Further Reading

Three volumes provide a wide cross-section of documents relating to the culture and politics of the Weimar Republic:

Kaes, Anton, Jay, Martin, and **Dimendberg, Edward** (eds.), *The Weimar Republic Sourcebook* (Berkeley and London, 1994).

Kunstamt Kreuzberg Berlin and Institut für Theaterwissenschaft der Universität Köln, *Weimarer Republik* (Berlin and Hamburg, 1977).

Reinhardt, Stephan (ed.), *Lesebuch Weimarer Republik: Deutsche Schriftsteller und ihr Staat, 1918–1933* (Berlin, 1982).

The following books aim to uncover the unity and coherence of cultural life in the Republic. John Willett's work offers a comprehensive introduction:

Gay, Peter, *Weimar Culture: The Outsider as Insider* (London, 1969).

Hermand, Jost, and **Trommler, Frank**, *Die Kultur der Weimarer Republik* (Munich, 1978).

Laqueur, Walter, *Weimar: A Cultural History, 1918–1933* (London, 1974).

Peukert, Detlev, *The Weimar Republic: The Crisis of Classical Modernity* (London, 1991).

Sloterdijk, Peter, *Critique of Cynical Reason* (London, 1988).

Willett, John, *The New Sobriety: Art and Politics in the Weimar Period 1917–1933* (London, 1978).

Willett, John, *The Weimar Years: A Culture Cut Short* (London, 1988).

Two collections of essays which discuss the political context of Weimar culture are:

Kershaw, Ian (ed.), *Weimar: Why did German Democracy Fail?* (London, 1990).

Phelan, Anthony (ed.), *The Weimar Dilemma: Intellectuals in the Weimar Republic* (Manchester, 1985).

Critics and theorists writing in and about the Republic have been immensely influential in the subsequent development of cultural studies, including:

Benjamin, Walter, *Illuminationen* (Frankfurt am Main, 1955).

Bloch, Ernst, *Erbschaft dieser Zeit* (Frankfurt am Main, 1962).

Kracauer, Siegfried, *Die Angestellten* (Frankfurt am Main, 1971).

Kracauer, Siegfried, *Das Ornament der Masse* (Frankfurt am Main, 1977).

A number of critical studies set out to relate literary work from the Weimar period to the political and ideological currents of the time:

Bance, Alan (ed.), *Weimar Germany: Writers and Politics* (Edinburgh, 1982).

Bullivant, Keith (ed.), *Culture and Society in the Weimar Republic* (Manchester, 1977).

Dove, Richard, and Lamb, Stephen (eds.), *German Writers and Politics 1918–1939* (Basingstoke, 1992).

Rothe, Wolfgang (ed.), *Die Deutsche Literatur in der Weimarer Republik* (Stuttgart, 1974).

Taylor, Ronald, *Literature and Society in Germany 1918–1945* (Brighton, 1980).

Trommler, Frank, *Sozialistische Literatur in Deutschland* (Stuttgart, 1976).

Kracauer's book on the German cinema is a contentious classic. A number of other studies address issues of politics and gender in the cinema:

Eisner, Lotte, *The Haunted Screen* (London, 1973).

Kracauer, Siegfried, *From Caligari to Hitler: A Psychological History of the German Film* (London, 1947).

Murray, Ben, *Film and the German Left in the Weimar Republic* (Austin, Tex., 1990).

Petro, Patrice, *Joyless Streets: Women and Melodramatic Representation in Weimar Germany* (Princeton, 1989).

Plummer, Thomas (ed.), *Film and Politics in the Weimar Republic* (New York, 1982).

There are a number of anthologies of Weimar radio plays. Müller's Brecht *Arbeitsbuch* gives the context of Brecht's radio theories:

Hammer, Franz (ed.), *Frühe Hörspiele* (Berlin, 1982).

Müller, Klaus-Detlef, 'Brechts Medientheoretische Überlegungen', in *Bertolt Brecht. Epoche–Werk–Wirkung* (Munich, 1985), 162–71.

Piscator described his own theatrical project with great vitality. Other studies examine the changing context of theatrical practice:

Patterson, Michael, *The Revolution in German Theatre 1900–1933* (London, 1981).

Piscator, Erwin, *The Political Theatre*, trans. Hugh Rorrison (London, 1980).

Willett, John, *The Theatre of the Weimar Republic* (New York, 1988).

General accounts of the Weimar Republic, including some listed above, often reproduce important paintings and photographs of Weimar buildings and design. In addition to many specialized studies there are exhibition catalogues of individual artists; the Royal Academy's twentieth-century catalogue also includes a wide range of interpretative essays:

Buchholtz, Ferdinand (ed.), *Der gefährliche Augenblick: Eine Sammlung von Bildern und Berichten* (Berlin, 1931).

Droste, Magdalena, *Bauhaus 1919–1933* (Cologne, 1990).

Ehrlich, Doreen, *The Bauhaus* (Leicester, 1991).

Hartley, Keith, Twohig, Sarah O'Brien, *et al.*, *Otto Dix 1891–1969* (London, 1992).

Joachimides, Christos M., Rosenthal, Norman, and Schmied, Wieland (eds.), *German Art in the 20th Century: Painting and Sculpture 1905–1985* (London, 1985).

Pachnicke, Peter, and Honnef, Klaus, *John Heartfield* (New York, 1992).

Schrader, Bärbel, and Schebera, Jürgen, *The 'Golden' Twenties: Art and Literature in the Weimar Republic* (New Haven, 1988).

Schulz, Edmund (ed.), *Die Veränderte Welt: Eine Bilderfibel unsrer Zeit* (Breslau, 1933).

Steingräber, Erich (ed.), *Deutsche Kunst der 20er und 30er Jahre* (Munich, 1980).

3

Culture and the Organization of National Socialist Ideology 1933 to 1945

WILFRIED
VAN DER WILL

The Fatal Plausibility of Anti-Democratic Rhetoric in 1933

HITLER was nominated Reich Chancellor on 30 January 1933. From the beginning his regime brutally fought and suppressed all racial, ideological, cultural, and party-political pluralism. Politics became the tactical façade of an ideology whose precepts and strategic goals had been set out quite clearly in Hitler's two-volume book *Mein Kampf* (1925 and 1927), and in his earlier occasional writings and his 'second book' (1928) which were both published posthumously.[1] Every kind of cultural expression was soon subjected to some kind of formal or informal ideological approval, from the lyric poem to grand opera, from painting to theatre, from folklore to modern mass entertainment, from cartoons to industrial design, from poster art to architecture. Mass propaganda in all the media was carefully orchestrated by a special ministry so as to ensure the one-sided exposure of the public to Nazi ideology. Departing from it even in thought was classed as resistance and deemed to be treason, as became clear when the members of the politically harmless Kreisau Circle around Count Moltke were sentenced to death despite the judge acknowledging that, unlike Count Stauffenberg, they had not plotted against Hitler. Art was blatantly divested of its independence from the ideology of party or state so that it could be used as a vehicle for National Socialism's Germanocentric symbolic system; even where it was not required to carry explicit ideological

1 Eberhard Jäckel and Axel Kuhn (eds.), *Hitler. Sämtliche Aufzeichnungen 1905–1924* (Stuttgart, 1980); Gerhard L. Weinberg (ed.), *Hitlers zweites Buch: Ein Dokument aus dem Jahr 1928* (Stuttgart, 1961).

messages, it was made to serve the ends of National Socialist cultural politics. Literature and art had to help in the design of a new, supposedly more self-confident, indigenously Germanic lifestyle. While in the eyes of the National Socialists the degenerate art of European modernism had failed, the arts in general were rated highly for they were credited by Hitler with expressing the longings for social unity in Germany at a time of division. In March 1933 he declared before the Reichstag:

> The German, collapsing into himself, divided in spirit, disunited in his purpose, and thus powerless to act, becomes enfeebled in his own existence. He dreams about justice in the heavens and loses ground on earth. . . . As the nation of the bards, poets, and thinkers, they then dreamed of a world in which the others lived. And only after being battered unmercifully by privation and misery, there grew up the longing, perhaps out of the arts, for a renewal, for a new Reich, and thus for a new life.[2]

German grandeur was, of course, Hitler's own obsessive dream, which he believed himself to be divinely chosen to make into political reality. The tragic irony of this passage is that a megalomaniac fantasizer is here accusing the Germans for their lack of realism and practical power politics in which other nations (the British, French, Americans, and Russians) had long been at home. Hitler was determined from the beginning to ignore the status of relative autonomy which the arts (and, for that matter, education, the law, and trade unions) had enjoyed and to use them as tools of National Socialism and as facilitators of his imperial dreams.

It is not merely because of Germany's lapse into dictatorship but because a modern nation, most of its institutions, and its intellectual heritage, including its claims to be a supreme bearer of culture, were instrumentalized for barbarity that the National Socialist period demands ever renewed investigation. Culture and politics were fused into an extremely close symbiosis to the detriment of both. Political pronouncements were saturated with cultural meaning in that the objective of the former was to facilitate the creation of a pure Germanic society. Ideology was not merely a convenient rhetorical arsenal with which to stimulate the masses and sustain their enthusiasm; it was above all the anticipation of a racially nordified (*aufgenordet*) and culturally Germanicized Central Europe. Politics were aestheticized and culture politicized, to modify Walter Benjamin's famous dictum; Nazi politics became the means to realize ideological designs and cultural goals. Consequently the totalitarianism of Nazi government left few spaces for independent expression and only the most cryptic ones for opposition. Once in

2 *Verhandlungen des Reichstags*, cdlvii. 6.

Wilfried van der Will

power German fascism began to persecute its internal enemies with deadly seriousness. Of course, it allowed itself tactical delays and did not immediately, for example, turn its full ferocity on the Jews, in order to give itself an air of respectability and, in particular, to placate President Hindenburg. However, having at its disposal the elaborate machinery of a modern secular state, National Socialism had none of the ambiguities and organizational lapses that persisted both in Italian fascism and Soviet Stalinism. Germany had an efficient bureaucracy which, precisely because it was formally beholden to the authority of the state to the point of suspending all questions about the moral quality of its actions, could be expected to execute the orders of any administration that had merely the semblance of constitutional legitimacy. That was one of the reasons why the main conclusion Hitler drew from his failed *putsch* of 8–9 November 1923 had been that his route to power had to be via the ballot box. And yet, the assumption that Hitler's strategy would bring him success must have bordered on the fanciful to any dispassionate observer of German politics in the stabilization period of the mid-1920s. Only in the eyes of those prepared to believe in the puerile, authoritarian character of the Germans was it inevitable that the most racist, nationalistic, and megalomaniac of party leaders would come to power. In Britain in the 1930s such views were propounded by Robert Gilbert Vansittart, an under-secretary of state in the Foreign Office, who believed the Germans to be endowed with an incorrigible collective psychology. As Noel Annan perceptively remarked, Vansittartism 'resembled the doctrine of original sin. Germans were born bad and grew worse. Had they not started five wars within the space of a century?'[3]

In stark contrast to such generalizing approaches based on a tabloid-type national psychology, we shall attempt to bear with the complexities of German social, political, and cultural history. Hitler would hardly have been able to achieve his aim had he not been aided by a unique constellation of events which drove the German electorate into his arms. The humiliation of Germany through military defeat and, above all, the vengeful Versailles Peace Treaty would not in themselves have been enough to make a sizeable portion of voters turn to Hitler and his National Socialist Party; nor would the hyperinflation of 1923, when large sections of the middle and lower middle class lost their savings. The economic and financial squeeze which set in after Black Friday (1929) and produced mass unemployment on a historically new level (3 million in 1930, 5.4 million by mid-1932, and over 6 million in early 1933) was hardly unique to Germany. Crucially, however, each of these factors acted

3 Noel Annan, 'The Work of the British Control Commission: A Personal View', in Adolf M. Birke and Eva A. Mayring (eds.), *Britische Besatzung in Deutschland* (Deutsches Historisches Institut London, 1992), 7.

as a potent multiplier of the crisis which only in Germany reached such proportions that the middle ground of politics erupted. Most of the fragments scattered to the extreme right, which was tolerated or actively assisted by military, financial, industrial, academic, administrative, and judicial élites that were not so much conservative as reactionary, bemoaning the demise of the German Empire and openly reviling the system of parliamentary democracy.

The long-standing traditions of authoritarianism in Germany, which through the administration of state power and education shaped the character of large sections of the population, culminated in the vote for National Socialism not because this was inevitable but because the economic, parliamentary, and ideological crisis became so acute that it allowed the most negative and anti-democratic characteristics of the nation to become dominant. It was in these specific circumstances that Germans fell under the spell of an orator who, seen from a dispassionate perspective, looked strangely comical. However, he was not a clown and his rhetoric fascinated because it fitted the circumstances. Like no other politician of his time Hitler exploited modern transport, not only supercharged cars and fast trains but also aeroplanes, in order to subject the population to ceaseless demagogy. In its use of modern media, as in its drive for industrial rationalization and technological innovation, National Socialism was emphatically a creature of the twentieth century. Responding to the masses, who were already radicalized politically by their economic misery, and intensifying their mood by the fanaticism of his hypnotic oratory, Hitler concentrated on a limited number of propagandistic fictions and half-truths which were tirelessly repeated: the German army, undefeated on the battlefield, had been 'stabbed in the back'; the German state was suffering under the crippling burdens of reparation payments; the small traders were subjected to the yoke of high-interest payments dictated by 'parasitic international Jewish finance capital'; in short, the German nation was enslaved and a National Socialist revolution was needed to liberate it.

The Shock of Modernism and the Myth of the *Volk*

Applying the sophisticated contemporary methods of voter analysis to the election results of 1932 and 1933 (when the vote for the National Socialists was 17.3 million, i.e. 43.9 per cent) recent research indicates that although the bedrock of support for the Nazi Party (NSDAP) were the mainly Protestant bourgeois and petty-

Wilfried van der Will

bourgeois classes, to a greater or lesser degree all electoral constituencies contributed to Hitler's victory.[4] Nevertheless, within the crisis environment of the early 1930s it was clearly the minutiae of the cultural background which were most important in determining voter preference. This is not surprising if National Socialism, the German variety of fascism, is understood as one of the ideological answers to the disruptions of modern culture. Nowhere had the modernization process occurred with such haste as in Germany. In the space of two generations industrialization, urbanization and mass society, the anonymity of mechanized warfare, the overthrow of the monarchy, the establishment of republican democracy, the advent of ideological pluralism, and the rationalization of large parts of the economy had all followed in rapid succession. Although a late developer Germany in the 1920s made up ground in relation to the politically most advanced nations of Western Europe, Britain and France, in starting on the transition from a traditional authoritarian society to one of democratic pluralism. National Socialism had no chance electorally while the outlines of the modernist utopia—mass affluence in a democratic society generated by applying the benefits of industrial technology—began to appear in the Weimar Republic. If Germany had initially lagged behind in all the major developments which brought about modernity, it made up for lost ground through the intensity of the process of catching up. However, this process exacted a profound psychological price and inflicted on German society traumatic experiences in a crisis where everything that was modern appeared only to spell political and social division, alienation, and proletarianization. The crisis of the late 1920s and early 1930s transformed modernism into an intolerable shock, whose overpowering effects somehow had to be halted. The need for this was felt to be so great that it justified abandoning newly won positions of liberation. A case in point is the changing mood of women who, as 'rebels against emancipation',[5] were ready to submit again to the command of men. Thus it was the profound shock of modernism, transmitted, ironically, with the help of modern media, which removed the emotional and mental barriers to the appeal of Nazi rhetoric, except, that is, where special cultural surroundings or psychological predispositions protected the individual.

As the experience of social and political division in the Weimar Republic grew more widespread, so the chorus swelled of those who saw salvation only in a reinstatement of the close ties of community (*Gemeinschaft*). When the Weimar class compromise was finally broken by the crisis which began to bite in 1930, the disrupting thrust of modernism appeared to be fully revealed and it produced

4 See Jürgen W. Falter, *Hitlers Wähler* (Munich, 1991).

5 Claudia Koonz, 'Nazi Women before 1933: Rebels against Emancipation', *Social Science Quarterly*, 12 (1976), 553–63.

a reaction which made people yearn for the possibility of social reconciliation. It was in this climate that the myth of the undivided *Volk*, the accommodating body politic in which individuals would find integration as parts of a mighty organism, could radiate its appeal. Nothing in this ideology was original, nor was it confined to Germany. All of it was prefigured in the anti-Semitic and pan-German agitation of Georg Ritter von Schönerer in the pre-1914 Viennese parliament; in the occult writings of Lanz von Liebenfels, which Hitler avidly collected when he was still an art student; in the Thule Society and the concoction of ideas, including the so-called *Protocols of the Elders of Zion*, which Gottfried zur Beek published in Berlin in 1919 and Alfred Rosenberg brought to Munich when he began proselytizing for National Socialism there after the end of the First World War; in the fierce nationalistic, racist, and socialistic pamphleteering of Richard Ungewitter; in the Germanocentric, missionary nationalism of Paul de Lagarde (who was anti-Semitic), Wilhelm Marr (who feared the 'victory of Jewry over Teutonism'), Julius Langbehn (who regarded Jews as 'a passing pest and cholera'), and Houston Stewart Chamberlain (who, without being rampantly anti-Semitic, believed in the superior status of the Germanic peoples); and in a score of other, minor ideologues like Otto Weininger, Dietrich Eckart, and Gottfried Feder. Faced with the increasing differentiation and division of society into classes and party-political camps, they all embraced the dream of an integrated, organic national community. Accordingly, the state was conceived neither as a collectivity, as in the Soviet Union, nor as a contractual association of individuals, as in liberal capitalism, but as a wholesome organism stimulating the recovery of those supposedly traditional values which modern civilization had destroyed: the ties of kith and kin, the natural purity and unity of racially identical folk, the ennobling pride of rich and poor alike as members of the finest race, the comradeship of the Germanic tribes in their competitive struggle for expansion and domination. Such notions were common amongst European fascists, particularly the underlying idea of corporatism. Oswald Mosley, founder of the British Union of Fascists, put it most succinctly: 'Our policy is the establishment of a Corporate State. As the name implies, this means a state organized like a human body.'[6] In fact, of course, National Socialism produced a most brutal and heartlessly anonymous form of public administration, but this did not prevent Hitler rejecting the modern state as a cold 'monstrosity of human mechanism',[7] preferring instead the idea of the individual serving as a sacrificial member of the community. Such dedication to the Nazi

6 Oswald Mosley, quoted in R. Osborn, *The Psychology of Reaction* (London, 1938), 60.
7 Adolf Hitler, *Mein Kampf*, trans. Ralph Manheim (London, 1976), 270.

Wilfried van der Will

movement and the nation was the cynical prerequisite in functionalizing the individual as a willing tool in the most colossally destructive war and in a state that, for all its qualities of upholding basic order, was a heinous monstrosity of a criminal mechanism in which the freedom of individual citizenship was annulled and replaced by the collective bondage of race.

The attractions that National Socialism had for the insecure masses were formulated into an effective slogan by Hitler himself after he had combined the two supreme power positions of Reich Chancellor and Reich President into that of *Führer und Reichskanzler*. He then announced at a party rally what the National Socialist 'revolution' had brought about: *Ein Volk, ein Reich, ein Führer*. Joseph Goebbels, the Minister for People's Enlightenment and Propaganda, had spelt out a few months earlier, in his programmatic speech of 15 November 1933, what in his eyes the National Socialist seizure of power had heralded: 'The meaning of the revolution which we have brought about is that we have forged the German nation into one people. . . . The German people, at one time the most divided in the world, atomized by political parties and opinions . . . has achieved a unification which was previously derided and opposed as being in conflict with every experience and teaching of history.'[8] Those who were excluded from that vision were to be enslaved and exterminated, but those included were promised a bright future as a racially pure and culturally harmonious community. Contemporary German artists, amongst them Karl Heinz Dallinger, illustrated this idea in allegorical pictures. In truth, however, German society remained socially divided and it was therefore necessary for the propagandists to supply images of powerful internal and external foes so as to maintain at least the illusion of national identity and integration. Imaginary enemies became even more important than real ones. Hannah Arendt observed that after the real enemies of the totalitarian movement had been driven out or exterminated the much more extensive hunt for imaginary enemies began in earnest.[9] The constant projection of the *Volksgemeinschaft* had a dual function: apart from its ideological value of suggesting the irrelevance of class divisions it ultimately legitimated the establishment of totalitarian domination in a society that, counter to the Nazi myths of being a people's community, a cultic community (*Kultgemeinschaft*), or a community forged by destiny (*Schicksalsgemeinschaft*), obstinately remained divided into social classes and ideological camps.[10]

By concentrating on the lure of the *Volk*, the myth of social unity, and the evocation of an imagined Germanic community,

8 Joseph Goebbels, *Reden*, ed. Helmut Heiber (Düsseldorf, 1971), i. 131–2.
9 See Hannah Arendt, *Elemente und Widersprüche totaler Herrschaft* (Frankfurt am Main, 1962), 581.
10 See Ian Kershaw, *Popular Opinion and Political Dissent in the Third Reich: Bavaria 1933–1945* (Oxford, 1983), 281–330.

6. Karl Heinz Dallinger, Tapestry.
Karl Heinz Dallinger's tapestry for an officers' mess of the Luftwaffe (1938) was one attempt to capture the ideological utopia of National Socialist society. A huge heraldic eagle, spreading its mighty wings and bearing a swastika, heads a squadron of eagles that protectively hover over a community allegorically represented by four figures who face the viewer holding the insignia of their trade: a metalworker, a female farm worker, a woman spinner and cloth maker, and a sword carrier. The banner floating over their heads defiantly carries the legend, 'We are one people and no one can break us; we remain one people and the world cannot ever conquer us.' Knowing the brutal reality of German fascism, the viewer is provoked to conjure up the dystopian reverse of this picture, the cities devastated by war and the grounds of the concentration camps strewn with the corpses of those who were deemed not to belong.

National Socialist demagogy departed from the established party-political divisions of traditional class politics. Significantly, National Socialism was able to exploit and accommodate quite divergent class interests because its rhetoric derived from a *Weltanschauung* anchored in an organic concept of society. This was expressed in symbolic representations of the nation's unity structured by cultural hierarchy. Hence the propaganda, the rallies, and the ideology were characterized by a peculiar mix of political pragmatism, aesthetic self-consciousness, and racial hubris. To unite people from the opposite ends of the class spectrum Hitler had to allay their main fears. With the slogan that there should be a 'surge of the masses, not of wages' (*Massenkonjunktur, nicht Lohnkonjunktur*) Nazi propaganda addressed the fear of unemployment in the working classes. As for the owners of large-scale capital, Hitler offered the best option for swelling their order books in a recessionary market by committing state funds for the improvement of the infrastructure (roads) and the increase in military hardware. The intermediate classes, threatened by the loss of both their business competitiveness and their savings and haunted by the spectre of proletarianization, were driven towards Hitler because his rhetoric appeared in tune with their anxieties and their dreams.

The masses who by their vote enabled Hitler to come to power were motivated by both ideological reasons (nationalism) and basic economic interests (having a job). In terms of conventional class analysis it was the owners of medium-sized and large-scale capital who benefited most under National Socialism as long as their wealth was not consumed by war. Alfred Sohn-Rethel, a sharp-sighted contemporary witness, gives a dramatic account of what drove representatives of different types of capital, irrespective of their personal political predilections, into the arms of National Socialism. The policies promised by Hitler simply appeared to them as their last desperate hope. Bourgeois society was about to go into terminal decline because its economy was fit only to produce deficits. Given its complete dependence on state investment, the exclusive circulation of profit amongst the various monopolistic industries, the need for the absorption of the unemployed by deficit financing, and the necessity for the terroristic disciplining of the labour force,[11] only a fascist state could guarantee that kind of social reconsolidation. It meant, of course, that the monopolies increasingly had to connive in an economy of destruction, that is, in production for war, in order to retain the semblance of profitability. This became clear in the first four-year plan, which favoured the heavy industries, and then in the second four-year plan, which privileged the

11 See Alfred Sohn-Rethel, *Economy and Class Structure of German Fascism* (London, 1978), 128–39.

chemicals, aviation, and electrical industries, with production for an imminent war distinctly scheduled in. The real dynamic of the National Socialist regime was, therefore, its imperial militarism which, in pursuit of the dream of racial superiority and global hegemony, catapulted Germany into a war of unwinnable dimensions.

The mystery of Nazism was that, while in reality serving the long-term interests of no one, it nevertheless enjoyed a broad base of support in Germany. Behind the manipulative culture industry of National Socialism there lurked within the deep structure of its ideology an archetypal pairing of the desire for life and the lust for death. The exaltations about the glory of the 'reawakened' Germany were underpinned with declamations about the readiness for sacrifice. This manifested itself both in the extensive persecution of its perceived enemies and in the self-sacrificing deployment of its troops all over Europe and beyond. Huge monuments to the German dead were planned in Eastern Europe and Africa while the war was still under way. And yet, by no means all Germans fell for the fascinations of fascism and very few of those who did would have believed that it was going to drag them into an orgy of destruction and make them into accomplices of the most murderous racism committed both by the official organs of law and order and by those of the National Socialist Party. The German élites, be they in politics or the military, in the arts, the media, or the universities, in finance or industry, more or less willingly fell in line with National Socialism or withdrew into small conspiratorial or esoteric circles without any chance of influencing events. Those who tried openly to uphold Christian or humanist values got away with it only in exceptional cases, like Count Clemens August von Galen, the Bishop of Münster, who opposed the Nazis' euthanasia policy of killing handicapped children deemed to be 'creatures unworthy of life' (*lebensunwertes Leben*). Nazi propaganda reduced doctrine to a few catch-phrases and tolerated outstanding minds only if they were prepared to collaborate in the manipulation of the masses. There was little room for manoeuvre between ideological conformism and withdrawal into obscurity. In short, the public sphere was claimed by the Nazis as the exclusive stage for their own self-presentation.

The *Gleichschaltung* of the Media and the Reichskulturkammer

There were three acts after Hitler's seizure of power which epitomized the character of his regime: the burning of the books, the

Wilfried van der Will

ideological incorporation or closure of publishing houses, and the foundation of the Reich Chamber of Culture in pursuit of the manipulative organization of all spheres of cultural life.

The reasons for *Gleichschaltung* and its aims were defined in the following way by Bernhard Rust, the Prussian Minister for Culture:

Everybody must recognize that what we are experiencing is not a change of direction but the fundamental fact that the German people is waking up to itself. This movement is progressing relentlessly until one day the whole German people will have been won over to the new cause and will have created for itself its own organizations for politics, the economy, and culture. . . . Our *Gleichschaltung* means that the new German ideology as the only valid one will assume the supreme position over all the others.[12]

Ideological incorporation—the basic meaning of *Gleichschaltung*—was not simply a centrally directed strategy of bringing art, architecture, literature, music, broadcasting, the press, and film into line with the Nazi organization of society; it was also to a large extent a voluntary act of conformism by the individuals and organizations concerned. German society was ready to be thoroughly suffused by Nazi ideology. Except for certain areas of church activity, sections of the army, and some precarious niches in the world of publishing, *Gleichschaltung* rapidly Nazified practically all spheres of life. This was facilitated by the fact that many institutions in the Weimar Republic had been shadowed by National Socialist organizations, whose activists now took control. In some instances traditional institutions were revamped, purged, and given a National Socialist character, as in the case of the Prussian Academy of the Arts, which included the Abteilung für Dichtung (Writers' Section); in other instances newly founded Nazi organizations replaced traditional ones, as in the case of Goebbels's Reichsverband deutscher Schriftsteller (Reich Association of German Writers) supplanting the Schutzverband deutscher Schriftsteller (Association for the Protection of Writers), the Deutsche Arbeitsfront (German Labour Front) taking the place of the free trade unions, and the Nationalsozialistische Frauenschaft (National Socialist Women's League) replacing the Bund Deutscher Frauen (League of German Women), even though, for some years prior to Hitler's seizure of power, that organization had actually played down issues relating to women's emancipation. *Gleichschaltung* brought to an end a policy towards women which at that time 'appeared to be the most progressive in the world'.[13] Other associations concerned with women's emancipation, like the Protestant women's organization, the Socialist women, the League for the Protection of Motherhood,

12 In Joseph Wulf, *Kultur im Dritten Reich,* iv. *Theater und Film* (Frankfurt am Main and Berlin, 1989), 289.
13 Claudia Koonz, *Mothers in the Fatherland: Women, the Family and Nazi Politics* (London, 1987), 30.

and the Sex Reform Movement, were all banned. The fact that the Nazi Kampfbund für Deutsche Kultur (Combat League for German Culture) and its successor formations were allowed to exist side by side with state organizations made for a duplication of power, causing rivalry between its most prominent exponents and differences of opinion about how best to promote the cultural notions of National Socialism; but it certainly did not make for any kind of genuine pluralism. The bickering of the satraps only served to enhance the central dictatorial powers of the leader. While those in opposition to Nazism, like Carl von Ossietzky, Ludwig Renn, Willi Bredel, Kurt Hiller, Erich Mühsam, and others, were incarcerated, *Gleichschaltung* also meant that in the initial phase of establishing totalitarian rule relatively few brutal acts of physical terror were needed. National Socialist activists were operating in a climate where they met with much passive acceptance and tacit consent when they usurped and reorganized the spheres of social and political life which they had infiltrated.

To this extent the burning of the books in a number of university cities in May 1933 was symptomatic of the execution of cultural, ideological, and racial policy under National Socialism. It was an event spontaneously embarked on and overseen by the Deutscher Studentenbund (German Students' League) and actively supported (but not actually conceived) by Goebbels and Rosenberg. Blacklisted authors from Heine and Marx to Freud and the brothers Mann found themselves in an *auto-da-fé* that engulfed a century of German culture in a ritual fire. The list of 'pernicious and undesirable' books comprised in excess of 10,000 titles. The flames of this symbolic holocaust lit not just the ranks of uniformed functionaries but also enthusiastically applauding crowds, ready to accept a tight ideological harness and the dictates of Nazi taste. In both its politics and culture the Third Reich owed its inner stability as much to voluntary consent and the expert manipulation of the masses by propaganda as to the terror and violence perpetrated by the organs of the Party and the state. Moreover, ideological incorporation, which was resented by the more radical elements within the SA (Sturmabteilung), was also a way of integrating critical bourgeois figures whose nationalism prevented them from exhibiting disloyalty to the state and who could be used for the prestige they bestowed on National Socialist Germany.

This policy applied, at least initially, to the Reichskulturkammer and its various sections. Franz Moraller, its chief executive, insisted in a memorandum of 19 June 1935 that the leading positions should not all be filled by National Socialists but were also to include

Wilfried van der Will

'personalities who are critical—not oppositional!—in their attitude to the Reich Chamber, whom we must value and bind to us by giving them responsibilities'.[14] The Reich Chamber of Culture and its six subdivisions (Reichsschrifttumskammer, Reichspressekammer, Reichsrundfunkkammer, Reichstheaterkammer, Reichsmusikkammer, and Reichskammer der bildenden Künste) had been founded with effect from 22 September 1933. There was a further subdivision, for even before this date, on 22 July 1933, the Reichsfilmkammer had been given its basic organizational shape, with ten different departments in its central administration in Berlin and thirty-one regional offices throughout Germany. The reason for such comprehensive restructuring in all spheres of culture was obvious and it was stated quite openly at the time. Describing the Reich Chamber of Culture, a contemporary writer stated:

Its main task is . . . to operate within the cultural professions separating the tares from the wheat, and to decide between the fit and the unfit. . . . to divide by blood and spirit German from alien . . . . What within the new structures will be created is a tremendous leader corps, made up out of all who participate in any way in the process of forming the national will, from the greatest spiritual genius to the most insignificant helper, from the man who does the creative work to the last retailer who hawks literature and journals in the streets and at the railway stations.[15]

In parallel to the Reichskulturkammer which, as a subdivision of the Ministry of Propaganda, was an institution of government, there existed party-political organizations such as the Nationalsozialistische Kulturgemeinde (National Socialist Cultural Community) which was formed in 1934 by Rosenberg amalgamating his Kampfbund für Deutsche Kultur (founded on 19 December 1928 to fight the 'culturally corrosive tendencies of liberalism'[16]), and the Deutsche Bühne which had half a million members. The Nazi 'Cultural Community' was constructed on similar lines to the Party and the Deutsche Arbeitsfront; that is to say, it had a structure of 'cells', 'blocks', and local and regional groups to organize cultural events. Rosenberg, who had been appointed as Hitler's 'trustee' to carry out the 'entire programme of the Party's spiritual and ideological education', naturally wished to retain as much influence as he could in the competition with his arch-rival, Dr Joseph Goebbels, but, not being in charge of a ministry, he was the loser of that particular inner-Party power struggle. Apart from Hitler himself it was Goebbels who staged the big oratorical events and who inaugurated the Reich Chamber of Culture on 16 November 1933 with a speech on 'Die deutsche Kultur vor neuem Anfang'. By their adherence to

14 See Wulf, Kultur im Dritten Reich, ii. Literatur und Dichtung (Frankfurt am Main and Berlin, 1989), 193.
15 Karl Friedrich Schrieber et al., Das Recht der Reichsschrifttumskammer. Sammlung der für den Kulturstand geltenden Gesetze und Verordnungen (Hamburg, 1936), 18.
16 Alfred Rosenberg, quoted in Wulf, Kultur, iv. 65.

traditional professional demarcation lines the various sections of the Reich Chamber of Culture were to ensure the effective control over all spheres of cultural production. To do so they had the right to regulate by decree all conditions of contracts between individuals and institutions in the field of culture. In other words, what they might fail to do by the ideological and racial selection of their members, they could achieve by being able to dictate the economic details of the sale and purchase of cultural artefacts.

As far as the press was concerned, the plethora of different titles of the Weimar years (some 600 of them) representing different ideological orientations and party-political tendencies soon disappeared, just as the political parties themselves were prohibited and dissolved (except, of course, for the NSDAP). Goebbels made cynically clear what the new regime intended to do in order to escape and transform the so-called heritage of decline National Socialism had had to take on. All areas of public life were affected by comprehensive decay, he averred. Hence a purge was necessary. He started with radio, which he considered 'the most modern and the most important instrument for influencing the masses'.[17] By the middle of March 1933 he had dismissed all the leading personnel in broadcasting in order to ensure ideological unison. The 'government of the national revolution' had to tell the people why harsh measures were needed to deal with this situation. Radio and the press must 'not only inform but also instruct'. The media had to be organized in such a delicate fashion that, like the press, they became 'a piano' (Goebbels) in the hands of government on which the rulers could play at will. Wilhelm Röpke has rightly pointed out that it was not possible in Nazi Germany to write with such freedom as Benedetto Croce in his periodical La Critica or Luigi Einaudi in his Rivista di Storia Economica or some authors in Giornale degli Economista in fascist Italy. Gleichschaltung ensured a near-total ideological conformity. Some 2,000 (out of a total of 10,000) journalists lost their jobs early on. Nevertheless, there were several astonishing exceptions, such as the periodical Deutsche Rundschau, which under its courageous editor, Rudolf Pechel, camouflaged criticisms of the regime in historical tales about tyranny. Subversive messages were also to be found in Das Reich, an attempt by more sophisticated National Socialists like Max Amann and Rolf Rienhardt, his influential deputy in the press office of the Ministry of Propaganda, to found a quality weekly, modelled on the English Observer. The reason for this was that by 1937 newspaper reporting was ideologically one-dimensional and monotonous. In particular, the daily Völkischer Beobachter, the chief loud hailer of Nazi propaganda, was

17 Joseph Goebbels in a speech to the directors of broadcasting on 25 Mar. 1933, quoted in Ekkehard Böhm et al. (eds.), Kulturspiegel des 20. Jahrhunderts—1900 bis heute (Stuttgart, 1987), 345.

Wilfried van der Will

felt by the press office to have become too stale to be effective. *Das Reich*, which first appeared on 26 May 1940 and ran until 22 April 1945, was a weekly drawing mainly on the educated middle class for the core of its staff journalists, many of whom were not members of the NSDAP, and it quickly became 'the favoured reading in middle-class houses, in more educated circles of the party, in officers' messes, and in the offices of the intellectually schooled SS'.[18] It was printed in Berlin, Cologne, and Oslo and reached a circulation of 1.4 million copies in 1943. The paper appealed because it was well informed, relatively factual, well written, and sometimes critical of the regime in a barely veiled fashion. This was the case when, in an article on 27 February 1944, Rudolf Sparing, the then chief editor, described the Soviet Union as technically a federal nation based on a constitution but in truth, owing to the fusion of party and government, a centralist and autocratic state. Readers of the article could easily recognize Nazi Germany in this description. Equally, there was no mistaking the critical portrait of Hitler contained in an article by Elisabeth Noelle-Neumann which appeared in June 1941. Here she described Roosevelt basically as a tyrant who could govern all the more easily by crying wolf and instilling in the American people a sense of emergency and imminent war. Goebbels, quite rightly, thought that the author had intended the parallel with Hitler and dismissed her. She survived and after the war founded the Institut für Demoskopie in Allensbach, a well-respected opinion poll organization.

Apart from the exercise of ideological control the Reich Chamber of Culture had the aim of bringing about a unified style which was to be rooted in Germanness and free from the modernist internationalism so characteristic of the Weimar Republic. That period, decried as one of abject decadence and betrayal of what Germany should truly stand for in the eyes of National Socialists, was invoked again and again as the polar opposite of the supposedly bright future that the Nazi regime would deliver in terms of a German, Germanic, or Nordic culture. Hitler himself, in a speech as early as February 1933, had spelt out this pledge for a renaissance of art in terms of a return to traditional German values: 'We want to give back to our people a truly German culture, a German art, a German architecture, a German music, which will restore our soul.'[19]

It was, in particular, the National Socialist Cultural Community which understood itself as the vanguard in an undertaking to evolve a 'National Socialist style' or a 'German style of the twentieth century' that was to be as distinguished and immediately recognizable as Gothic and Renaissance art. One of Rosenberg's band of Nazi

18 John Brech, 'Das Reich—von innen und außen gesehen', *Merkur*, 19 (1965), 288 ff.
19 Adolf Hitler, quoted in Berthold Hinz, *Art in the Third Reich* (Oxford, 1980), 10.

ideologues, Rudolf Ramlow, stressed that the Nationalsozialistische Kulturgemeinde, with its membership of 1.5 million by the end of 1934, had a core of people willing to promote a new culture, who were active in many professional organizations such as the NS Lawyers' League and the NS Doctors' Federation.[20] While Goebbels had emphasized that the mere parading of a National Socialist mentality could not by itself pass for good quality, Rosenberg's Cultural Community, on the contrary, acted first and foremost as an instrument for the dissemination of ideology, not of an artistic style, German or otherwise. Both Goebbels and Rosenberg were wrong in assuming that the manipulative machinery of the state or that of the Party could be used to produce a renaissance of great art conforming to preset ideological norms. National Socialism produced much kitsch in a Wagnerian vein for its public processions and parades, it inspired a macho heroism in sculpture, and it favoured conventional genre painting and neo-Classicist architecture for its official buildings. In other words, just like its ideology the culture of National Socialism was heavily mortgaged to the past, which was at best eclectically exploited with good craftsmanship, at worst distorted into the colossal, but which was hardly ever developed creatively into a style with its own characteristic features. Nevertheless, a fair degree of success and even popularity was achieved, not principally by a revival of old myths, folklore, and customs, but by the strategic orchestration of public life in accordance with ideology through the manipulating agencies of the Reich Chamber of Culture. This strategy often yielded a powerful mass appeal from which, as the staging of the Olympiad in 1936 showed, not even the international community was entirely immune.

The 1936 Olympiad and the *Thingspiel*

The Eleventh Olympic Games were held in Berlin from 1 August to 16 August 1936. It was an occasion used to the full by Nazi Germany as a gigantic international public relations exercise. The manipulation of the media, so expertly directed by Goebbels, had, after all, only been effective inside Germany hitherto. Now it was hoped that the rest of the world might be persuaded to accept a favourable image of the German nation under its new regime. A propaganda coup had to be landed in order to discredit the increasing number of highly critical voices in the Western media that had become especially vociferous since the promulgation of the Nazi race laws (*Gesetz zum Schutze des deutschen Blutes und der deutschen*

20 See Wulf, *Kultur im Dritten Reich*, iii. *Die Bildenden Künste*, 119.

Wilfried van der Will

Ehre) on 15 September 1935. For example, the *Manchester Guardian* had no illusions at all when in a leader article on the opening day, Saturday, 1 August 1936, it stated plainly that the spirit of Baron Pierre de Coubertin had departed from these Olympic Games:

This year at Berlin for the first time we are to see them confessedly exploited not for the peace of the world, not even for the pride of one nation, but as an advertisement for a political party. The conduct of the Games and their setting are to be a demonstration of the excellence of Nazism. Houses in Germany have been whitewashed and there has been other whitewashing as well. German Jews have been given no chance to fit themselves to represent Germany, but a few . . . have been . . . included for the sake of window dressing.

National Socialism was determined to show off the new fascist *grandezza* and to prove to the youth of the world that Germany had been unjustly defamed, and that it was now a land enjoying prosperity under a government which positively supported sport and the arts. Only a totalitarian state was able to organize all the attendant aspects of such an event with the sweeping powers that this required, down to lowering the prices of the hotels, restaurants, and food shops in Berlin. Foreign visitors were allowed up to 60 per cent reductions on journeys by ship, rail, boat, and bus. The theatre season went on without its customary summer break. The *Oresteia* by Aeschylus, an exhibition of German artefacts, with a Gutenberg bible as its centre-piece, concerts, operas, and receptions for the stars of the world of culture all presented a picture of splendour and harmony. Goebbels entertained 2,000 guests on the Pfaueninsel on the River Havel, Göring issued invitations to the opera and laid on an acrobatic air show at Tempelhof, while Hitler threw a reception in the Reich Chancellery for a large number of special diplomatic guests, amongst them Sir Robert Vansittart, Count Jan Szembek, the Polish State Secretary for Foreign Affairs, and Count Baillet-Latour, the President of the International Olympic Committee. The conspicuous display of *Der Stürmer*, the rabidly anti-Semitic and blatantly pornographic Nazi magazine, was forbidden, the Berlin propaganda chief had been instructed to remove all anti-Semitic slogans, and cleanliness was to be the hallmark of Berlin's self-presentation to its many visitors. At the beginning of the Games *Der Angriff*, by that time the organ of the German Labour Front, exhorted its fascist readers—once renowned for their brutality in the pub brawls and street fights before 1933, and now, encouraged by the state, ready for racist vandalism and violence—in the following manner: 'We must be more charming than the Parisians, more light-hearted than the Viennese, more vivacious than the Romans, more cosmopolitan than the Londoners, and more practical than the New Yorkers.'[21] The cosmetic exercise even extended to the point where the authors of the two-volume, numbered edition *Die Olympischen Spiele 1936*, a semi-official publication, could express admiration for the vitality of multiracial America:

Apart from the fact that American university sports arenas with their excellent trainers have acted as breeding-grounds for Olympic champions, the mixture of races in the USA has through its constant rejuvenation with fresh blood remained free of physical degeneration, as can otherwise only be observed amongst primitive peoples who have been spared the disadvantages of civilization.[22]

Beneath the camouflage of civility the international festival of sport was to be functionalized as a spectacle of national grandeur under the special protection of the Führer. Even non-German athletes, notably 'France's proud sons behind the blue, white, and red tricolour',[23] found it opportune to give the Nazi salute when they entered the stadium in the opening ceremony, a ritual which, to a musical accompaniment of fanfares, Wagner, and Handel's 'Hallelujah Chorus', was designed to highlight the pivotal role of the Nazi leader in providing such excellent sports facilities. More specifically, the architecture of the Olympic Games, the mass audiences, the colourful international contingents of sports people, the exhibitions, and festivities were all elements in a grand spectacle ultimately directed by National Socialism in order to present this occasion as a kind of extraordinary world party congress. It was all captured superbly on film by Leni Riefenstahl, who in *Triumph des Willens* (1935) had already proved that she could use the camera to enhance the myth of the Führer and even make the medieval façades of Nuremberg look like the most natural setting for a Germanness which was seemingly represented most clearly by Adolf Hitler and his party. The opening sequence of her two-part film on the 1936 Olympiad (*Fest der Schönheit* and *Fest der Völker*, 1938) is a celebration of the naked body in which Riefenstahl does not conceal her fascination with the physicality of the athletes regardless of their racial origin and yet still manages to convey a thesis about the global centrality of the Germanic races. Even the liberal international press involuntarily carried Nazi messages by concentrating on the sporting events as such and, like the London *Times*, by faithfully reporting on the drama and the splendour of the Games in Berlin without ever mentioning politics. Influential sections of the international community were clearly willing to be fooled, for no

21 Quoted in Uwe Schmitt, 'Der gespielte Friede. Ein Rückblick auf die Spiele der XI. Olympiade 1936 in Berlin. Unter der Tarnkappe der Weltläufigkeit und der Toleranz', *Frankfurter Allgemeine Zeitung* (2 Aug. 1986).
22 Robert Mollenbauer, 'Leichtathletik', in Cigaretten-Bilderdienst Altona-Bahrenfeld (ed.), *Die Olympischen Spiele 1936* (Hamburg, 1936), i. 90.
23 L. C. May, 'Die Weltmelodie erklingt', ibid. ii. 14.

significant protests were voiced over those German athletes who were not allowed to take part because they were Jewish. When the International Olympic Committee expressed its concern about this issue the German National Olympic Committee merely made some insignificant concessions. There were other irregularities. Several American journalists were refused visas and Hitler allowed Baldur von Schirach to attribute the following statement to him: 'The Americans should be ashamed of themselves that they have Ne-groes win medals for them.' The Führer conspicuously refused to shake hands with black athletes. There were rumours that the German secret police, the Gestapo, opened hundreds of letters at the Charlottenburg post office before they were delivered to the Olympic Village. All this became known at the time, but the IOC, far from expressing public criticism, congratulated Germany on its excellent organization and, when Switzerland refused to host the Winter Olympics in 1940, looked to Germany to stage once again a 'grand festival of peace'.

Apart from presenting Berlin to the influx of visitors as a centre of European culture the Olympic Games were also to provide a stage for the nascent Germanic culture which National Socialism wished specifically to promote. This was not possible within the framework of the international art competitions, judged by juries drawn from a number of countries, which were arranged in con-nection with the Games. Significantly, within the section *Dichtung* the prize for dramatic works was not awarded. Yet the Olympic Stadium itself presented the opportunity to stage the type of mass theatre with thousands of participants which in the Weimar Repub-lic had been developed to considerable effect by the Social Demo-cratic worker culture movement. Dr Carl Diem, the General Secretary of the German Olympic Organizing Committee, himself wrote the text for such a play, *Olympische Jugend*. Some 10,000 ac-tors took part when it was performed on the evening of the open-ing day. Their dance movements and choreography were created and rehearsed by Harald Kreutzberg, Mary Wigman, a pupil of Rudolph von Laban and a major exponent of the modern expres-sive dance, and Dorothee Günther, the founder of a school for gymnastics, rhythmical movement, and dance. The links with the Social Democratic mass festivals of the Weimar Republic were direct in that the diction of the spoken verse was clearly influenced by them, as indeed were the techniques of the speech-movement choir and the collective dance, since Mary Wigman had first prac-tised them in the German worker culture movement. Under the searchlights at night five scenic tableaux with music by Carl Orff

7. The Cathedral of Light, Berlin (1936).
The impressive 'dome of light', part of the festivities that concluded the 1936 Olympic Games in Berlin, was a feature borrowed from the Nazi Party rallies, and was designed by Albert Speer, Hitler's chief architect. The deployment of powerful searchlights had for some years before been practised regularly at Nuremberg, the only difference being that on these occasions the beams of light were vertical and parallel to each other rather than forming a luminous pyramid. In other words, the dome of light was a design element which made it plain that in the minds of the Nazi planners the Olympiad was like a world Party congress, another form of 'aestheticized politics', which could therefore be clad in the same secular liturgy as the national Party rallies. Here, too, the Führer was brought to oversee a parade of flags, the dignitaries of the IOC paid homage to him, and Beethoven's hymn 'Die Flamme lodert' introduced an air of sacrificial solemnity before the Olympic bell brought to an end what in the eyes of the Nazi leaders was a charade of international camaraderie.

and Werner Egk were presented, the penultimate one of which, 'Heldenkampf und Totenklage', shows the difference in tone from the class-conscious mass theatre of Social Democracy: 'The sacred meaning of all games is that they are to the glory of the fatherland. The fatherland's highest demand in the hour of need is the sacrifice of death.'[24] Despite this ominous declaration suffused with the spirit of nationalistic militarism the play ended with the all-encompassing appeal of Schiller's 'Ode to Joy', set to music by Beethoven. The ritualization of the Games was not just a Nazi invention. The use of the 'Ode to Joy' for the opening ceremony was originally suggested by Baron Coubertin, who believed that the festival of sports meant 'a religion with a church, dogmas, and a cult' and who had subsequently himself put the accent on the celebration of the fatherland and physical vitality.

However, to demonstrate still further the Nazis' belief that sport, politics, and culture were closely related, an open-air theatre, the Dietrich-Eckart-Bühne, named after one of the founders of the Party, was built into the design of the Reich Sports Field by the architect Werner March. Goebbels, who had asked Eberhard Wolfgang Möller to present him with a number of plots for a *Thingspiel*, selected *Das Frankenburger Würfelspiel*. The historical background of this play was an event in May 1625 when the Governor of Upper Austria, Count Hebersdorf, marshalled the Protestant peasants of Frankenburg on to a field after they had beaten up their newly appointed Catholic priest. The Count, who was supported by 650 troops and who wanted to set an example, demanded to know who were the peasants' leaders. When nobody came forward he selected thirty-six of them, who had to engage in a game of dice. Those who lost, that is half of their number, were hanged from the church spires of Frankenburg, Vöcklamarkt, and Neukirchen. This atrocity led to an uprising during which thousands of peasants were killed and the Catholic faith was restored in Upper Austria. Möller used the *Thingspiel* as a grand choric setting, in which the masses of actors and the audience, numbering some 20,000, were joined together to become a cultic community sitting in judgement on a historical crime. Möller was clearly influenced by the techniques of Bertolt Brecht, Stravinsky's *Oedipus Rex*, the medieval mystery plays, the use of the chorus in Greek classical drama, Max Reinhardt's performances of Hofmannsthal's version of *Everyman*, the plot in Georg Kaiser's *Die Bürger von Calais*, and Ferdinand Bruckner's oratorial drama *Elisabeth von England* (1930), which, like Brecht's writings, was censored after the Nazis came to power. All contemporary accounts agree that the effect of the play, both on 2 August 1936 in

24 Quoted in Henning Eichberg (ed.), *Massenspiele: NS-Thingspiel, Arbeiterweihespiel und olympisches Zeremoniell* (Stuttgart-Bad Cannstatt, 1977), 145.

Berlin and in 1937 in Erfurt, was overwhelming and that the spectators and actors really felt that they were taking part in a kind of
national religious ceremony whose pathos and magic appeal created a feeling of sacred communality for all those present. Theatre,
opera, dance, pantomime, statuesque declamation, chorus, and song
were all combined into a new form of *Gesamtkunstwerk* which ostensibly celebrated the unity of the *Volk*, but in effect was only an
act of state, commissioned by the Minister for People's Enlightenment and Propaganda.

The *Frankenburger Würfelspiel* was the pinnacle of a new, albeit
cursory development in the theatre which, supported by a special
organization under Goebbels's direction, the Reichsbund der
deutschen Freilicht- und Volksschauspiele e.V., for three or four
years was greatly favoured by National Socialism. Möller, with the
benefit of hindsight, believed this kind of play, in which the boundary between drama and opera was blurred, to be an integral part of
a broader stylistic trend in the arts at the time and singled out the
following: Werner Egk's *Columbus*, a pure pantomime, interpreted
and illustrated by soloists with chorus and orchestra in the form of
an oratorio, Lothar Müthel's production of Schiller's *Jungfrau von
Orleans* as a heraldic opera, which Rudolf Wagner-Régeny set to
music in that manner at the same time, and Carl Orff's *Carmina
Burana* and *Triomphi di Aphrodite*.[25] However, to comment only on
these last examples, Orff's operatic musical plays were clearly inspired by the bucolic joys of conviviality and love which he found
in classical and medieval folklore. While the use of such traditions
did not clash with the fascist ideology of the united *Volk*, Orff's
music remained deeply embedded in Bavarian regional custom,
medieval Latin and German poetry, and the Renaissance revival of
the classics. The *Thingspiel* could claim no such provenance. Contemporary programmatic pronouncements about it reveal that it
was conceived as a literary and cultic instrument with which to
revel in the glorified notion of the *Volk* and to deny or diminish the
importance of social class. The spectator is to be divested of all
private reserve and immersed in collective emotion. Under the
editorship of one of the main initiators of this kind of theatre, Otto
Laubinger, *Der neue Weg*, a journal with a long tradition in the
world of theatre, declared:

The *Thingspiele* and the open-air theatre are phenomena which are by no
means new, but they have been rediscovered for us and have become
possible again based on the genuine folk community of blood and soil.
This folk theatre, which involves the audience and, unlike the proscenium
stage of the feudal court, does not separate the public from the action on

25 See Eberhard
Wolfgang Möller in a
letter of 6 Apr. 1965,
quoted by Günther
Rühle, 'Die
Thingspielbewegung',
in Eichberg (ed.),
Massenspiele, 191–2.

Wilfried van der Will

the stage, is the new, decisive form of the theatre, because these plays guarantee a new, overwhelming experience of community. The preliminary stages of this stirring emotion of racial harmony, which almost acquires a mythical and religious character, were the Day of Potsdam, the Party Congress at Nuremberg, and the Sports Festival in Stuttgart.[26]

It is clear from this passage that no fundamental distinction was made by Nazi theorists, and probably also not by the audiences concerned, between the political rally and the *Thingspiel*. They were both occasions of cultic enthusiasm stage-managed by the National Socialist movement to lull the masses into a sense of their own importance. Wolf Braumüller, a functionary who could be quite critical of these plays, thought them indispensable and made a merely formal distinction between the political *Thing* and the cultural *Thing*. The success of both depended on a careful choreography of the participating actors in consonance with the mobilization of the spectators. However, in 1937, by which time over forty new *Thing* amphitheatres had been completed, the whole venture was reined back, basically because the genre had not fulfilled the expectations invested in it. The Nazis lost interest in this kind of theatre; at best it was simply too sentimental and at worst it nourished illusions about the importance of the people's own voice in a system which was clearly steered from a dictatorial centre. 'I can't bear to hear the word *Thing* any more', Goebbels is reputed to have said in the late 1930s.[27] At the same time the attempts to mark the calendar year with a comprehensive set of distinct Nazi festivities in place of the traditional ones, like summer (21 June) and winter solstice (21 December), were largely abandoned, although National Labour Day (1 May), Mothers' Day (a Sunday in May), Harvest Day (the beginning of October), and, of course, Führer's Birthday (20 April) survived throughout the Nazi period, if mostly as matinal celebrations.

Literature and Philosophy in the Nazi Era

The attempts under National Socialism to found a new *volkhafte Dichtung* were basically not much more successful than the *Thing* experiment. One of the chief literary historians writing in the Nazi spirit was Hellmuth Langenbucher, who defined poetic writing as a vital force in the life of the German people and agreed with Paul Ernst that, given the confused state of the great nations of culture, Germany was the only one 'which can bring salvation'.[28] What Langenbucher (and others) termed *volkhafte Dichtung* included all poetic expression which related to the living environment and to

26 *Der neue Weg*, 63 (1934), 120.
27 Reported by Kurt Heynicke in a letter to Claire Sayer, 11 July 1973, in the possession of Wilfried van der Will.
28 Paul Ernst, quoted in Hellmuth Langenbucher, *Die deutsche Gegenwartsdichtung* (Berlin, 1940), 15.

the fate of the 'community of the blood' and which excluded every-thing that was without intrinsic connection to it. It followed from this grounding of literature in an imaginary racial purity that the past had to be rewritten as a striving for racial identity in which the honourable individual acts in the service of the whole nation at all times, fundamentally in line with one of the most topical slogans of the Party, 'You are nothing, the [National Socialist] movement is everything.' The writers who receive special attention in this con-text, apart from Paul Ernst, who died shortly after the Nazis had taken power (May 1933), are Bruno Brehm, Hans Blunck, the Presi-dent of the Reichsschrifttumskammer, Edwin Erich Dwinger and, above all, Erwin Guido Kolbenheyer. Strangely Langenbucher makes no mention of Will Vesper and Mirko Jelusich, who like the others had both written about the legendary Germanic past, ideal leaders, and the ties of the blood. Adolf Bartels, who was one of the first to introduce the racial distinction between Jewish and German authors into literary history, is also omitted. Langenbucher rightly devotes one of the concluding sections of his book to the sung poem as a 'political act'. The enthusiasm of the Hitler Youth was indeed fired by songs like Hans Baumann's 'Siegeslied', which ex-pressed perfectly the nihilistic nonchalance and unbounded imperi-alism of Nazism in the refrain, 'We shall march on even if everything falls to bits. For today we own Germany and tomorrow the whole world.'

The names of these authors are practically forgotten now, unlike those of Ernst Jünger, who by his writings helped to prepare a fascist climate in Germany, and Gottfried Benn, who in a highly prominent manner declared his approval of National Socialism in a radio broadcast on 24 April 1933 under the title 'Der neue Staat und die Intellektuellen'. Jünger, one of a group of intellectuals who have been described as 'conservative revolutionaries' or as proponents of 'reactionary modernism', fetishized the 'community' forged in the trenches of the First World War in his famous masculinist fantasy of a diary In Stahlgewittern (1920). A later influential book of his, Der Arbeiter (1932), placed at the centre of an elaborately technological vision of modern society the figure of the worker-soldier as the archetype of the mobilized masses. Having bemoaned the eclipse of individual valour in mechanized warfare, Jünger nevertheless believed that a new martial nobility ready for collective heroism had been 'hammered, chiselled, and hardened' by this war. The rebirth of barbarism would unleash fresh passions stifled by the decadence of European civilization: 'power, manly courage, heroic community'.[29] Yet National Socialism was perhaps too plebeian for

29 Ernst Jünger, *Der Kampf als inneres Erlebnis* (Berlin, 1922), 13 and 38.

Wilfried van der Will

his liking and in 1933 he declined an invitation to join the Prussian Academy of the Arts. In his *Auf den Marmorklippen* (1939) he shows how a fictitious geographical region is invaded and destroyed by a populist tyrant. This has been interpreted as a critical statement against Nazism, but the story, which was passed for publication by the Party's censors, is too ambiguous to be rated as a document of literary resistance. Jünger still features in Langenbucher's literary history in 1940, while Benn had become a non-person, having by then been thrown out of the Reichsschrifttumskammer (18 March 1938).

When, after his 1933 broadcast, Benn was openly challenged by Klaus Mann to distance himself from the Nazis, he emphatically repeated his declaration of loyalty in another radio talk entitled 'Antwort an die literarischen Emigranten'. In it he proclaimed that the advent of National Socialism meant 'the emergence of a new biological type, history mutates and a nation wants to cultivate itself'.[30] He believed that within a 'final battle of the nations and races' the martial mutation of the nation would help secure Germany's victory and open up a historically new cultural cycle. Social Darwinism, Spengler's theories on the cycles of cultural ascendancy and decline, and Nietzsche's idea of the will to power were fused in an ideological amalgam that bore remarkable resemblance to the views of Hitler and other leading Nazis. But to no avail, for Benn's intellectualism and the unmistakable modernism of his poetry soon brought him into the sights of the SS weekly, *Das schwarze Korps*, which in 1936 denounced him as a cultural bolshevist. By the middle of 1934 he had already begun to revise his attitude to Nazism and he now chose what he called the 'aristocratic form of emigration' by rejoining the German army as a medical orderly. He was forbidden to write and publish during the Nazi era, but at the same time enjoyed the protection of the influential Hanns Johst and even Heinrich Himmler, who in 1937 ordered that there should be no further attacks on Benn by the SS.

Martin Heidegger's inaugural speech as Rector of the University of Freiburg on 27 May 1933 revealed a similarly spectacular case of politically and morally misguided behaviour on the part of a prominent intellectual. As a long-standing Nazi Heidegger wished to make a distinct contribution to the reform of the German universities by bringing students and staff into line with the principle of deference and fealty (*Gefolgschaft*) to the leader. Having long yearned for a return to philosophy's fundamental mission as he saw it, the revelation of true being in general and the knowledge of the nation's essence in particular, Heidegger interpreted the coming to power

30 Gottfried Benn, 'Antwort an die literarischen Emigranten', in *Gesammelte Werke*, ed. Dieter Wellershoff (Munich, 1975), vii. 1698.

of National Socialism as a chance for the re-emergence of philosophical enquiry in the original pre-Socratic spirit. Being was not an
object for definition but was supposed to reveal itself directly to the
philosopher who was in tune with it. This kind of charismatic thinking brooked no contradiction. Heidegger, without doubt one of the
most eminent philosophers of his time, had aspirations to give
National Socialism a proper theoretical grounding and thus to
become the achnowledged philosophical guide of this movement.
Questioning as the basic philosophical attitude is interpreted by
Heidegger not just as a preliminary stage for arriving at answers
but as a journeying forth into the unknown, a deliberate exposure
to insecurity. In other words, it was the philosophical version of
tempting fate, of launching Germany on the search for its essence
the way that the Nazi movement had begun to do. Heidegger
noticed too late that Nazism did not require his guidance. The fact
that, within the context of his philosophical interpretation of history, he rated the Hitler era in the last resort as yet another phase
in humankind's 'oblivion of being' (*Seinsvergessenheit*) and as a further period in the alienation of nations and individuals from their
essence never annulled the considerable credit that the regime
received through his prestigious support.

There were many other thinkers and philosophers who put themselves at the service of National Socialism. Carl Schmitt, Professor
of Law, proposed the friend–foe relationship as a basic category of
politics, predicated on the alternative between self-affirmation and
decline which allegedly faces any nation as a permanent choice.
Alfred Bäumler, through the influence of his book *Nietzsche, der
Philosoph und Politiker* (1931), crucially appropriated that thinker for
German fascism, thus providing it with a valuable quarry of
legitimatory ideas. Apart from his duties as Professor of Education
in Berlin, Bäumler worked for the Amt Wissenschaft under Alfred
Rosenberg (the Führer's official watchdog for the training and education of the Nazi Party), keeping close tabs on university politics.
Erich Rothacker, who held a chair of philosophy at the University
of Bonn, worked in the Ministry of Propaganda for a while. He was
Goebbels's linkman with the German students who organized the
burning of the books in 1933. Later he actively sought to influence
the cultural policy of the Third Reich by evolving a pedagogic concept for the education of Nazism's functional élites. Not recognizing the distinction between civil society and the state, Rothacker
demanded that Germandom, the people, and the state should be a
unified entity and that therefore there could be no separation between the state administration and the intelligentsia. In Rothacker's

logic the latter simply became functionaries in a system which constantly had to organize its own self-acclamation. Unlike the educated bourgeoisie and the socially dislocated intellectuals of the Weimar Republic, who were considered to be traitors to the German cause, the intelligentsia of the 'German awakening' had to teach a fanatical attachment to the essence of Germanness in sharp contradistinction to other ethnicities and in preparation for a future war. The universities had to become the schools for the production of the national leadership in conformity with the achievement expectations of the fascist state. Only in this way could the given human material (*Menschenmaterial*) be fashioned into the desired German subject endowed with a clear, secure national feeling and ready for action. When Rothacker propounded these ideas in his talk on 'Grundlagen und Zielgedanken der nationalsozialistischen Kulturpolitik' at a conference on 'Erziehung im nationalsozia-listischen Staat' held in Munich in August 1933, he received massive applause. No wonder that with teachers like that the German intellectuals who valued their independence of judgement either shut up or left the country.

In the field of belles lettres it has, with few exceptions, not been the literature written within the Third Reich but, rather, that produced outside Germany by the exiles from Nazism which has come to represent the strengths of the German literary tradition. As a result of *Gleichschaltung* many writers, including some of the most prestigious who were members of the Abteilung für Dichtung within the Prussian Academy of the Arts, felt driven out of the new Germany or, like Thomans Mann, simply did not return to it from lecture tours they were undertaking abroad at the time when Hitler was confirmed in office by the March elections in 1933. The decision to emigrate must have been extraordinarily difficult in the case of writers, for they lost contact with their native public. Goebbels's cruel judgement had some truth in it, that the exiles' lifeline had been cut and that they were 'corpses for whom the death-knell was ready to ring out'. Many of them became embittered by the daily struggle for existence, the often hopeless difficulties in procuring vital travel documents or permission for permanent residence, and by their severance from the environment of their mother tongue. Anna Seghers describes these difficulties very convincingly in *Transit* (1944), a novel which is based on her own experience. The number of those who were broken by the burdens of exile and were driven to suicide included Kurt Tucholsky, Ernst Toller, Ernst Weiss, Stefan Zweig, Walter Benjamin, Egon Friedell, and Klaus Mann. Despite this dreadful toll they, and their colleagues who survived, wrote some of their best works in exile. It was perhaps ironic—particularly in the case of bourgeois writers—that, far from being able to uphold the strict division between politics and art, they became intensely politicized. The most famous case in point is Thomas Mann, who, apart from his many lectures and articles on political exile, on freedom, democracy, and socialism, broadcast to Germany for the BBC on a monthly basis from October 1940 until the end of the war. Early on in these broadcasts (e.g. in 'Krieg und Demokratie') he criticized the American policy of neutrality, and his diaries show that he regarded as subversion any attempts to oppose President Roosevelt's cautious approach to entry in the war. In his novel *Doktor Faustus*, published two years after the military defeat of fascism, he attempted to come to terms with the German cultural tradition which appeared to drive the Teutonic genius towards pacts with the devil. Astonishingly the conditions of exile did not prevent the realization of major novel projects like Thomas Mann's tetralogy *Joseph und seine Brüder* (1933–43), Heinrich Mann's *Henri Quatre* (1935–8), and Lion Feuchtwanger's *Josephus-Trilogie* (1932–45). While the focus here is on myth, legend, and history, these novels nevertheless deal with contemporary issues in that the past is used as a means both to stand back from the present and to view it afresh in a historical costume and in the light of idealistically chronicled examples of humanism. Other authors, like Bertolt Brecht, had recourse both to the historical parable, as in his satire on race in *Die Rundköpfe und die Spitzköpfe* (1933–6) or his warning against trying to profiteer from war in *Mutter Courage und ihre Kinder* (1939–41), and to the parable in a contemporary setting as in *Der aufhaltsame Aufstieg des Arturo Ui* (1941), which equates the rise of Hitler with that of the Chicago gangster Al Capone. Untypically, Brecht also resorted to a more conventional realism in the scenic sequence *Furcht und Elend des Dritten Reiches* (1935–8), which, based on eyewitness accounts, arguably achieves greater complexity in its portrayal of National Socialism than the somewhat schematic *Arturo Ui*.

The exodus of writers occurred mainly in the first few months after the Nazis had seized power. It was so massive that German literary centres formed in Zurich, Prague, Paris, Copenhagen, Stockholm, Moscow, London, New York, Los Angeles, and Mexico City. The later military advance of Nazi Germany in Europe obviously meant that the exiles in some European cities had to move on to safer locations, if they could. The publishing houses they founded or refounded outside Germany (Wieland Herzfelde's Malik-Verlag in Prague, Willi Münzenberg's Éditions du Carrefour and Édition

Prométhée in Paris, the Bermann-Fischer-Verlag in Stockholm, the Aurora-Verlag in New York, and El Libro libre in Mexico) were confronted with a precarious economic and/or political existence. Existing publishing houses such as Querido and Allert de Lange in Amsterdam and Oprecht in Zurich provided vital support for German authors. Up until the beginning of the war some of the exile literature found its way back into Nazi Germany, including an extensive anthology, *Deutsch für Deutsche*, in 1935. Despite the dispersal of the exiles and the ideological divisions amongst them they managed to maintain, at least for some years, a number of periodicals such as *Neues Tage-Buch*, which was published by Leopold Schwarzschild in Paris from July 1933 to May 1940; *Die Sammlung* (Querido, Amsterdam, 1933 to 1935), edited by Klaus Mann; *Neue Deutsche Blätter*, edited by Oskar Maria Graf, Wieland Herzfelde, Anna Seghers, and Jan Petersen, and published as a monthly in Prague; *Das Wort*, published under the aegis of Bertolt Brecht, Lion Feuchtwanger, and Willi Bredel in Moscow from July 1936 to March 1939, the periodical in which most of the significant debate about the assessment of German Expressionism and the problem of realism took place; and *Mass und Wert, Zweimonatsschrift für freie Deutsche Kultur* (Oprecht Verlag, Zurich, 1937 to 1940), edited by Thomas Mann and Konrad Falke. The most successful German journal abroad (until October 1938), using the inspired photomontages by John Heartfield together with documentary photography, was Willi Münzenberg's *Arbeiter-Illustrierte-Zeitung* (then titled *AIZ, Das Illustrierte Volksblatt*, later *Die Volks-Illustrierte*) with a print run of 12,000 while it was edited in Prague.

The literature that was written inside Nazi Germany was, of course, cut off from the international literary scene, but this did not mean that all of it was beholden to Nazism. Great efforts were made by some writers, later classed as belonging to the 'inner emigration', to cling on to the values of Western humanism. The term *Innere Emigration* was the title of an open letter by Frank Thieß that tried to defend certain German authors against Thomas Mann's famous, but somewhat simplistic, charge that all literature published during the Third Reich had a 'smell of blood and shame' about it. And yet, the apolitical nature of magical nature poetry by Günter Eich, Peter Huchel, Hermann Kasack, Horst Lange, Elisabeth Langgässer, Wilhelm Lehmann, Oskar Loerke, and Georg von der Vring, influential though it became after the war, was such that its overt or hidden polemic against modern civilization corresponded all too easily with the stereotypes of Nazi anti-modernism. A more convincing attempt at concealed criticism was made by Reinhold

Schneider in his historical narrative *Las Casas vor Karl V. Szenen aus der Konquistadorenzeit* (1938), which allowed a connection to be made between the ruthless enslavement of the Indios and the fascist persecution of the Jews, but naïvely suggested that all that was required was a powerful appeal to the conscience of the dictator. In *Das Reich der Dämonen. Der Roman eines Jahrtausends* (1941) Frank Thieß camouflaged some criticisms of the Nazi regime in a depiction of conflicts between tyrants and the people in ancient Greece, Rome, and Byzantium. However, when the opposition to the regime was too deeply concealed, as in Jochen Klepper's novel *Der Vater* (1937) or Werner Bergengruen's *Der Großtyrann und das Gericht* (1935), National Socialism promoted and praised the work and used it for its own ends. Imbued with ideological ambiguity, these books at best offered the educated German public moments of escapism; at worst they deluded it with authoritarian values in humanist garb. In contrast, Gottfried Benn could only produce texts for the bottom drawer of his desk once he realized that his early praise for Nazism had been an error and that as a committed proponent of modernism creative writing was for him predicated on acknowledging the value-relativism, nihilism, and intellectualism of the time (*Roman des Phänotyp*, 1944, and *Der Ptolemäer*, 1947).

The Aesthetics of Art and Music in Everyday Life

Mussolini held that democracy had made the life of the people all too rational and much too prosaic to allow for any expression of style. Everything that counted within the irrational mentality of the masses had vanished: 'the common direction of behaviour, colour, power, the painterly, the unexpected, the mystical; we play the lyre on all its strings: from violence to religion, from art to politics.'[31] German fascism, too, was intent on projecting itself as a public spectacle and, at the same time, on infiltrating everyday life with its uniforms, its insignia, and its carefully orchestrated media. Life under National Socialism attained a designed quality: the home, the place of work, and the holidays were all subjected to a strategy based on orderliness and beautification. The Volkswagen car was advertised as a *Kraft durch Freude Wagen*, the Strength-through-Joy organization opened up the Mediterranean for educational cruises for the ordinary people, the Amt Schönheit der Arbeit (Office for the Beauty of Labour), founded in November 1933 as a subsection of Kraft durch Freude within the Deutsche Arbeitsfront, saw to it that in the factories there was more light and better air, less industrial

31 Quoted in Ernst Nolte, *Der Faschismus in seiner Epoche* (Munich, 1963), 326.

Wilfried van der Will

noise and grime, as well as healthier food in the canteens. By the end of 1938 some 24,000 changing rooms and washrooms had been constructed, 17,000 landscape gardens had been planted round factories, and 3,000 sports centres had been built by the Office for the Beauty of Labour. Clearly, the aim was to create a work-force with a loyalty to National Socialism (*Betriebsgefolgschaft*) that had learnt to appreciate the beauty not only of the technological environment and its objects (trains, cars, planes, Zeppelins, motorways, bridges, ships, and the whole arsenal of military weapons) but also of art itself. The work-force was to be better motivated and, as far as possible, deproletarianized. It was for this purpose that the Office for the Beauty of Labour signed contracts with the Reich Chamber for the Visual Arts for canteens and social centres for workers to be adorned with wall mosaics. Such projects typified the way in which National Socialism flooded German society with pictures and images in all the available media.

Two forms of artistic expression, painting and sculpture, being chained to the singularity of a particular object in a distinct space, had only been able to reach a wider public since the introduction of new reprographic techniques around the turn of the century. The mass reproduction of images through colour printing, photography, film, and television (for which briefly in the mid-1930s there was a network in Berlin) continued to be one of the most significant areas of technological innovation in the twentieth century and National Socialism privileged these media for the dissemination of both art and politics. Walter Benjamin, by then in exile in Paris, conceptualized this development in his famous essay 'Das Kunstwerk im Zeitalter seiner technischen Reproduzierbarkeit' (1936). While Nazism meant the aestheticization of politics, private publishers promoted beautiful representations of the German historical heritage, the landscape, and current events. Established picture-book series flourished, like *Die Blauen Bücher* with their traditional stress on the photography of German artefacts, landscapes, and towns (e.g. *Die Schöne Heimat. Bilder aus Deutschland* or *Deutsche Dorfkirchen, Deutsche Dome* or *Deutsche Plastik des Mittelalters*, which prominently featured a picture of the *Bamberger Reiter*, the image most frequently reproduced to illustrate the racial features of the Aryan type in Nazi literature). Picture books specifically inspired by the ideas of National Socialism also reached large print runs, like *Auf Deutscher Scholle* (1935) by Hans von der Nordmark, which illustrated life in the different regions of Germany with a large number of colour photographs, or *Deutsche Kulturbilder. Deutsches Leben in 5 Jahrhunderten* (1934), which contained a host of colour prints depicting typical scenes in the cultural development of Germany since 1400, or *Deutschland zwischen Nacht und Tag* (1934) by Friedrich Heiß, a volume of black and white photographs of landscapes, towns, and industry, complete with explanatory text and charts detailing the decline of Germany in the Weimar Republic and contrasting it with the upswing under National Socialism. The traditional *Berliner Illustrirte Zeitung* chronicled events in conformity with the Party's ideas. One of its major pictorial reports in July 1937 was on the first exhibition of German art in the Haus der Deutschen Kunst. Probably the most lavishly and beautifully produced art journal of the time was *Kunst im Dritten Reich*, which had excellent colour reproductions, chiefly of the pictures shown at the mammoth exhibitions of German art in Munich. Traditionalist genre painting or aggressive, masculinist heroization in portraiture were the preferred styles, both of which meant a distinct departure from the international modernism of art in the Weimar Republic in favour of images with proven mass appeal.

Thus the 1937 exhibition of 'degenerate art' (*Entartete Kunst*) held in the Antikenmuseum of the Munich Hofgarten was a coup for the Nazis because it tapped a broad consensus against the distortion of the human figure which allegedly was perpetrated by the madness of modernism. Hitler reviled its protagonists as 'prehistoric art stutterers'.[32] The National Socialist propaganda machine had provided this exhibition with enormous publicity and it was given added curiosity value by the fact that drawings and paintings of mental patients were shown side by side with those by famous German modernists, suggesting that the latter were clearly insane. While this exhibition was taking place Hitler himself inaugurated another one, which ran simultaneously but was less well attended. It showed 'pure' Germanic art in the Haus der Deutschen Kunst. Amongst the 2 million visitors which the 'degenerate art' attracted between July and November in Munich alone there were many who did not want to miss the chance of seeing these exhibits for what they assumed was the last time. This exhibition was subsequently shown in Berlin, Düsseldorf, and Frankfurt. It initiated a ruthless policy of cleansing German art galleries and museums of the modernist avant-garde, whose works were then confiscated by Nazi luminaries like Göring, bought by private collectors, or sold at auction in Lucerne.

The preference for pre-modernist painting and traditional German house styles, which included a ban on flat roofs, did not mean that National Socialism was consistently anti-modernist. The Nazis expunged modernism only in art and literature, while the modernist

32 Adolf Hitler, 'Kunstbolschewismus am Ende', in Peter-Klaus Schuster (ed.), *Nationalsozialismus und 'Entartete Kunst'* (Munich, 1987), 210.

Wilfried van der Will

inspirations of Bauhaus functionalism, now confined to industrial architecture, interior and reprographic design, were allowed to remain alive. Although the Bauhaus had been closed in 1933, prominent members of this institution, like Walter Gropius, Mies van der Rohe, and Oskar Schlemmer, believed in the early years after Hitler's seizure of power that they would be able to develop their ideas and continue to receive commissions for designs. These hopes were not entirely illusory, as the engagement of Gropius for the design of the exhibition 'German People—German Workmanship' in Berlin in 1934 showed. Hitler was an admirer of Henry Ford, probably because of the latter's anti-Semitism but also because Hitler was an enthusiast of technology, notably in his liking for fast cars. The Volkswagen factory in Wolfsburg took its cue from the most rationalized car-production plants in Detroit. However, modernism under the Nazis remained confined to the world of technology, for the use of art in the demonstrations of Party power and in the suffusion of everyday life with Nazi ideology rigorously excluded modernist forms.

The main quarry for the Nazis' 'aestheticization of politics' (Walter Benjamin) was the operatic genre in general and the power and mythical setting of Wagner's music in particular. Musical composition, like all other spheres of culture, had to be Germanicized and musical performance was defined in terms of racial and ideological conformity. The Reichsmusikkammer made sure that this policy of *Gleichschaltung* was carried out. Composers of Jewish descent or of a left-wing persuasion like Paul Dessau, Hanns Eisler, Ernst Krenek, Hermann Scherchen, Arnold Schönberg, Mischa Spoliansky, and Kurt Weill (some 200 of them in all) had to leave to escape ill-treatment and death. Large numbers of musicians lost their jobs because they did not conform to the directive on 'the reinstatement of the professional civil service' or were unable to give satisfactory answers on the questionnaire of the Reich Chamber of Music. A special list of Jewish composers and performers contained the names of 11,000 people.[33]

It suited Nazism to make use of opera because this medium allowed uniquely demonstrative combinations of kitsch and power, sentimentality and death, heroic individualism and collective funereal pomp, repressed drives and megalomaniac fantasy. Given the careful orchestration of public life by the practitioners of fascist propaganda, one is tempted to view the fusion of culture and politics under National Socialism as one enormous operatic *Gesamtkunstwerk*. Music, particularly Wagner's, was used prominently. Hitler had, of

33 Theo Stengel and Herbert Gerigk, *Lexikon der Juden in der Musik. Mit einem Titelverzeichnis jüdischer Werke* (Berlin, 1940).

8. *Reichsparteitag*, Nuremberg (1935).
The Nazi rallies that took place annually on the Zeppelinfeld at Nuremberg were occasions of 'aestheticized politics' typified by the geometry of the marshalled masses. The design was to create an atmosphere of expectation for the arrival of the charismatic leader and to give him a framework of acclamation for his highly charged speeches. Surrounded by the uniformed party faithful, Hitler is seen in this picture of the 1935 *Reichsparteitag* on an elevated rostrum, performing an act of secular liturgy, the consecration of the standards of the various Party districts and the commemoration of those who died fighting for the Nazi cause. The image of the Führer's absolute centrality as an orator and a man of destiny directing the fate of Germany was broadcast to the nation by the weekly cinema newsreels, ensuring that millions of *Volksgenossen* were given some sense of participation and, at the same time, subjected to the mesmeric effects of the occasion.

course, cultivated a connection with the Wagner family in Bayreuth since the early 1920s. Thomas Mann in his essay 'Leiden und Größe Richard Wagners' believed that the master, throughout his life, was a socialist and cultural utopian who desired a classless society freed of the curse of gold and luxury and built on love. The Nazis, however, ruthlessly exploited Wagner for their own political ends. It was particularly the mass chorus 'Wachet auf, es nahet gen den Tag' from *Die Meistersinger* which, according to Goebbels in a broadcast on Wagner in August 1933, had become a symbol for the reawakening of the German people from its 'political narcosis' since November 1918. Wagner's music reflected the 'cultural soul' of the Germans and the composer was thus made into a fascist property. While frequent broadcasts from Bayreuth gave him unprecedented media exposure, his music was also used extensively at the annual Nazi Party rallies. In 1937, for example, the overture from *Rienzi* and the orchestral composition 'Einzug der Götter in Walhall' were played. Other nineteenth-century composers were also much in evidence on appropriate occasions: the finale of Anton Bruckner's Fifth Symphony could be used to suggest greatness, Franz Liszt's 'Siegesfanfare' was featured in the *Deutsche Wochenschau* or as a signature tune for the special newsflashes on Großdeutscher Rundfunk; the themes of Beethoven's *Fidelio* ushered in the National Socialist 'revolution', while those from the 'Eroica' and the Fifth Symphony accompanied the protracted demise of Hitler's Germany. The 'heroic' death of National Socialists, when announced on the radio, was adorned with Wagner's funeral march from *Götterdämmerung*. Thus for brief moments music helped to transform the *Volksgemeinschaft* into a cultic community and prepared it for sacrifice (*Opfergemeinschaft*).

If the nineteenth century, minus its Jewish composers, could be appropriated very successfully for fascist purposes, the twentieth century posed greater difficulties. When the celebrated conductor Wilhelm Furtwängler defended the music of Paul Hindemith, he was dismissed by Goebbels; similarly, when Richard Strauß, who had become President of the Reichsmusikkammer, would not break off relations with his Jewish librettist, Stefan Zweig, he was publicly reprimanded by the Propaganda Minister. Nevertheless, it was one of Strauß's works, the simple love story *Arabella* (with a libretto by Hofmannsthal, a Jewish writer), which was the most frequently performed new opera in the Third Reich.[34] Here, as in cinematic production, entertainment was preferred to hard propaganda although, as we shall see, such diversion could also be made to transmit ideological messages.

34 Hans Günter Klein, *Viel Konformität und wenig Verweigerung: Zur Komposition neuer Opern, 1933–1944* (Frankfurt am Main, 1984), 149.

The Uses of the Cinema under National Socialism

In his famous study *From Caligari to Hitler* (1947) Siegfried Kracauer argues that 'the films of a nation reflect its mentality in a more direct way than other artistic media'[35] because of both the collaborative process of production and the collective nature of reception on the part of the audience. While one may well distrust the general validity of such an assertion, particularly because it gives too little credence to the creative vision of the director, there can be no doubt that in the Third Reich the cinema was a reflection of the mentality of National Socialism and an important vehicle for the dissemination of its ideological myths. These were basically of two kinds: on the one hand, in the bulk of the films life was shown as a series of comic or tragic routines amongst a people released from the cares of unemployment and untroubled by the world of politics; on the other hand, films cultivated the myth of the Führer and of the Nazi movement, addressed particular aspects of its ideology, and lauded certain German figures and events of the past as prototypes of the present. The chief instrument for making films were private production companies like Terra, Tobis, Bavaria, and, biggest of all, Ufa (Universum-Film AG). The majority shareholder in Ufa was Alfred Hugenberg, an anti-democratic right-wing politician who was briefly a member of Hitler's initial cabinet. Although sympathetic to the Nazi movement, he was gradually stripped of his influence, notably by the government itself secretly buying up Ufa shares. By 1942 it had virtually become a government monopoly although it was still officially registered as a limited company. Even before it had established ownership of Ufa and the other film companies, the Nazi government had effective control over the industry through the Reichsfilmkammer. Its policy of ensuring that ideologically and racially undesirable people be purged led to an exodus of famous names (Fritz Lang, Marlene Dietrich, Peter Lorre, Detlev Sierck) to Hollywood, either because they were Jewish or because they preferred not to work for the Nazi film industry. However, there was enough talent left to serve National Socialism.

The Filmkammer developed a system of vetting and subsidizing the production of commercial feature films and of commissioning films relevant to the Nazi movement. It is the latter which, by and large, have received the most analytical attention. There can be little doubt that the brutal face of Nazism is directly revealed in overtly anti-Semitic films like *Der ewige Jude* (directed by Fritz Hippler, 1940), *Jud Süß* (Veit Harlan, 1940), *Die Rothschilds* (Erich Waschnek, 1940), and specially commissioned documentaries like

35 Siegfried Kracauer, *From Caligari to Hitler: A Psychological History of the German Film* (Princeton, 1974), 5.

Wilfried van der Will

Opfer der Vergangenheit (1937) and *Das Erbe* (1937), which plead the case for the necessity of euthanasia. Other types of film with an overtly propagandistic message had the task of converting people to the Nazi cause, for example, Hans Steinhoff's *Hitlerjunge Quex* (1933), or simply celebrating the victory of Nazism, as with Leni Riefenstahl's *Triumpf des Willens* (1935). Steinhoff's film clearly borrowed from the pictorial arsenals of socialist film-makers at the end of the Weimar Republic. It is about a boy who transfers his allegiance from Communism to the Hitler Youth, with the latter becoming a substitute for the family. The boy is killed distributing leaflets for the Nazis in a predominantly Communist district of Berlin, but, of course, the Nazi movement is shown to be triumphant. Riefenstahl, who had been selected by Hitler personally to make the film of the Nuremberg Party rally in 1934, showed how the geometry of the marching masses, the medieval townscape, and even the clouds and the sky could be used by the camera to promote the myth of the charismatic Führer. There were, of course, films that had elements of both propaganda and entertainment in its widest sense. The paradigmatic example of this mix was *Wunschkonzert* (1940), which combines a private love story with the collective epic of the war and interposes newsreel and documentary footage within the fictional narrative. It begins in 1936 when two spectators at the Olympic Games, Inge Wagner (Ilse Werner) and flight lieutenant Herbert Koch (Carl Raddatz), meet, fall in love, and marry within the space of three days. Then Koch is called upon to take part in Operation Condor, a secret mission to help General Franco with the Spanish Civil War, from where he is commandeered for the bombing of Poland. Even after three years, and despite the advances of another suitor, Inge remains faithful to her lieutenant and eventually makes contact with him after listening to a musical request programme for the Wehrmacht. Significantly there is no happy end, for the war goes on and the final shots are of battleships and bomber squadrons headed for England. The film was a resounding success, being seen by an audience of 26 million. The mix of entertainment and propaganda was also in evidence in Wolfgang Liebeneiner's *Ich klage an* (1941), a melodrama about euthanasia that attracted a total audience of 15 million.

The vast majority of films from the Nazi era concealed the fact that fascist politics had transformed the state into an instrument of racial and ideological brutality. On the contrary, the films suggested that life was much as before. Although some 1,150 feature films were made during the Third Reich, only about a sixth of these were concerned with direct political propaganda. The rest were pure entertainment movies, but these too could be used for covert ideological messages in line with Goebbels's sophisticated notion about the dissemination of propaganda amongst the ordinary German people. While Hitler wanted films to be such 'that every cinema-goer knows, today I am going to see a political film',[36] Goebbels, on the contrary, assumed that most people normally did not think in acutely political terms and that even if they did, they wanted to be spared being further bombarded in their leisure time with politics and explicit propaganda (which, in any case, were routinely served up by the accompanying newsreels). Within the highly politicized environment of Nazi Germany merely omitting the fascist salute in entertainment films sufficed to create the impression that ordinary life was still intact and that the idyll of provincial certainties remained unaffected by the Nazi revolution. This did not mean that entertainment films could not be packed with ideological clichés. For example, the precept that a woman who endangers a marriage must lose out in the end informs Veit Harlan's *Die Reise nach Tilsit* (1939) and, even more starkly, his masterpiece of melodramatic kitsch, *Opfergang* (1944). Here Goebbels himself demanded a departure from the original story by Rudolf Binding: since it deals with adultery the film might otherwise have undermined the morale both of the men at the front and the women at home. Kristina Söderbaum plays the vivacious Aels, a rich unattached heiress, who turns out to have both a little daughter and an incurable disease. She wants to live life to the full while it lasts and ensnares Albrecht Froben (Carl Raddatz), a patrician Hamburg explorer, who is about to be married to the reserved, rather statuesque Octavia. This woman displays the all-conquering magnanimity of her love when Aels lies dying, for she sees to it that the rich heiress's little daughter is safe and forgives her husband for his philandering. Being set in a rather refined, high-class social environment in an entirely undamaged Hamburg and shot in remarkably high-quality colours, the film provided a powerful dose of escapism. The educated tranquillity and aristocratic style of the opulent dramatis personae was in stark contrast to the destruction and imminent defeat of Germany. However, there is an obsession with death running through the film, from a declamation of Nietzsche's poem 'Die Sonne sinkt' in a darkened drawing-room to a cholera epidemic threatening the lives of Froben and Aels's daughter, and, finally, to the doomed heroine herself. If the evidence of the films is to be believed, a mood of *Götterdämmerung* hung over the Third Reich right from the beginning. It was captured in 1933 in Gustav Ucicky's *Morgenrot*,

36 Quoted in Erwin Leiser, *Nazi Cinema* (London, 1974), 12.

Wilfried van der Will

where the captain of a stricken U-boat says, 'We Germans may be bad at living but we are certainly superb at dying', and it went through right to the end, when in *Kolberg* (1945) the young commandant of the town, Gneisenau, says just before the last attack by the enemy, 'Now we can die together.'

This final Ufa epic about the resistance of a German town besieged by the French during Napoleon's conquest of Prussia (1806–7) employed 187,000 actors, including real troops as extras, and was Goebbels's ambitious attempt to reverse the tide of war by motivating the German people to fight on against all the odds. The film was begun in 1943 when the Battle of Stalingrad had in the eyes of many decisively altered the course of the war, driving the Wehrmacht into retreat. Veit Harlan now had the task so to fanaticize the home front that the film might become the cinematic equivalent of Goebbels's famous speech about 'total war'. On the day of its first release in Berlin in January 1945 a copy was dropped by parachute into La Rochelle to steel the German soldiers' will against the Allied troops surrounding them. The film amounted to an absurd command to hold out when in reality everything was lost and such an injunction could only lead to further senseless loss of life. In its epic proportions it was consciously modelled on *Gone with the Wind*, just as the Third Reich's film production in general sought to rival Hollywood. Thus the National Socialist film industry even tried to ape one of the most characteristically American genres, the musical. This was done, with some success, in Georg Jacoby's *Die Frau meiner Träume* (1944), where the singing and dancing revue star, Julia Köster (Marika Rökk), falls in love with a construction engineer and marries him. The most interesting aspect of this film—which in other respects invites comparison with the Hollywood musicals featuring Fred Astaire and Ginger Rogers—is that it shows a kind of woman who in many ways has outgrown the earlier Nazi stereotype. In reality, too, women were being reintegrated into the process of industrial production and into public administration mainly as a result of the war effort. Marika Rökk plays a woman who projects a new type of confidence and expects an equal share of responsibilities in her relations with a man. However, inundated as it may be with oblique reminders of the real situation of want and war that characterized the Germany of the mid-1940s, even this film ultimately helped to delude its audiences about a state which could not tolerate the privacy of the individual citizen but instead functionalized everyone for its totalitarian ends.

Culture as Mass Deception

The effectiveness of the propaganda machine proved itself astonishingly well when Germany was opposed by all the major powers and the military defeat of the Nazi regime became inevitable. In spite of the likely destruction of the German Wehrmacht a strong belief was maintained inside Germany that some kind of *Wunder-* or *Vergeltungswaffe*, pilotless bombs (V1) or ballistic missiles (V2), would bring about a decisive turn in the war, and this delusion held until the Allied soldiers had actually overrun the Reich. The physical and moral dissolution of the *Volksgemeinschaft* became glaringly evident at the end of the war, particularly in the large cities that had been reduced to rubble. Elements of civil war broke out and lasciviousness became endemic. Here are the observations of an SS-man on patrol in Berlin just before it fell to the Red Army:

> Here [at Herrmannplatz] German Communists with red armbands were lurking in the rubble and shot at us with machine guns. . . . Numerous Wehrmacht personnel hung around in doorways having discarded their weapons. . . . We also saw soldiers who were blind drunk, swaying about in the streets without paying any heed to grenades or bombs. In one of the house entrances a woman was unashamedly having intercourse with one of the ranks. Opposite an old man and a number of women occupied themselves with tearing large pieces of meat from the swollen carcass of a horse.[37]

Thus ended the Nazi era in which the German people were treated to a deficit-financed economy, steered by the state, and to a centrally organized experiment in cultural direction, carried out by both the organs of the state and those of the Party. German society was enveloped by a systematically deployed propaganda apparatus whose pronouncements were strategically calculated to legitimate the barbarous deeds of National Socialism as an allegedly superior form of culture. That deception was evident in the very name of the institution which perpetrated it, for while one might assume that even convinced National Socialists would be cautious in taking at face value what issued from a ministry overtly committed to propaganda, Goebbels had taken care also to include in its title the notion of people's enlightenment. This helped to create the illusion that propaganda was merely a means of broadcasting to the people what was their due, namely to be told the truth about their government, their Führer, their state, and their strength as a united *Volk*. The philosophy of the eighteenth-century Enlightenment, that individuals should free themselves from subservience and deference

37 Hans Dieter Schäfer (ed.), *Berlin im zweiten Weltkrieg: Der Untergang der Reichshauptstadt in Augenzeugenberichten* (Munich and Zurich, 1991), 315–16.

Wilfried van der Will

to authority, from superstitious creeds, and from their own internalized codes of self-repression, now seemed to be turned on its head: enlightenment meant the enslavement of the masses by state-disseminated falsities and by a centrally organized ideology with mythical and magical ingredients.

It was this observation of the 'dialectic of enlightenment' which inspired Horkheimer and Adorno, the two leading theoreticians of the Frankfurt School then residing in exile in New York and Los Angeles, to collaborate on a book (1944) that was later to be given that title. It contained a substantial chapter which, by its very heading 'Kulturindustrie. Aufklärung als Massenbetrug', made this historic reversal provocatively clear. Unable to sustain either the utopian hopes, so dear to their dead friend Walter Benjamin, of a proletariat freed from the shackles of party dogma or his optimism about a future technology that would not exploit nature as an object but put it in the service of humanity as its partner, Horkheimer and Adorno attempted to uncover the historical dynamic that was driving humankind into a state of unfreedom. The United States, their host country, and fascist Germany, whence they had fled, provided them with their main points of reference. Both societies are seen as the most advanced on the globe, pride of place going to the USA but with the proviso that in some respects it was actually National Socialism that had advanced further down the road to eroding individual autonomy and creativity, the negative goal towards which all modern societies were headed. While the discussion is therefore concentrated primarily on conditions in North America, the focus at times changes quite abruptly to Germany, as though it could without further qualifications be used to illustrate the basic paradigm set by the United States. As a result of such sudden shifts of reference the level of contradiction in the latter society is inevitably underrepresented, so that the USA of the 1940s tendentially appears as proto-fascist. The social structure, politics, and culture of the two countries are seen to be dominated by large-scale capital which in both cases exhibits the relentless logic of making everyone and everything conform to its interests. That is to say, both countries serve to highlight the fusion of economics and politics in advanced capitalism. However, their resultant culture industries are different, the one in Germany being commandeered by politics, while that in the USA is owned by private capital, producing commodities which, as in the case of radio, can appear to the consumer as free gifts. This medium, apart from increasing the power of monopolies since they alone can find the money to advertise coast to coast, uniquely facilitates the omnipresence of a single voice and hence is made for exploitation by dictators. American monopoly capitalism seems logically to require an extension into fascism so that, as in Germany, radio can be used to its full potential and become 'the universal mouthpiece of the Führer'. The political direction that monopoly capitalism demanded as an economic system had in the eyes of Horkheimer and Adorno found its ultimate realization in the ideological structure of fascism, which had seized the new medium as its most appropriate means of expression: 'The National Socialists knew that the wireless gave shape to their cause just as the printing press did to the Reformation.'[38]

What made easy cross-referencing between the USA and Germany possible was Horkheimer and Adorno's perception that in both societies individuals were lured, manipulated, and coerced into conforming to ideological standards set by the powers that be. The room to deviate, disagree, and oppose these powers that had existed in liberal societies was shrinking towards zero. All citizens were engulfed by the uniformity of consumption, which in turn produced a uniformity of attitude in all individuals:

Ironically, man as a member of a species has been made a reality by the culture industry. Now any person signifies only those attributes by which he can replace everybody else: he is interchangeable, a copy. As an individual he is completely expendable and utterly insignificant, and this is just what he finds out when time deprives him of this similarity.[39]

Horkheimer and Adorno were aware of the distinctions between the political systems of the United States and Nazi Germany, but they did not regard them as crucial. The basic categories of their analysis can therefore only be accepted if they are further refined in relation to the different societies to which they are meant to apply. For example, under National Socialism the uniformity of individuals was not restricted to ideological conformity but was additionally defined in racial terms. Nor was that uniformity predominantly achieved through the consumption of commodities via market mechanisms. Rather, it was effected directly by political agitation, propaganda, coercion, and sheer naked terror.

Significantly, the typical vocabulary of the time was constituted by two lexical fields, one which denoted inclusion in and conformity with the body of the *Volk* and the other which referred to the exclusion and administrative utilization of human beings. The first field comprised words like *Volksgenossen, Volkheit, Volkwerdung, Volksgemeinschaft, Volksordnung, Volkssturm, Volksaufklärung, Volksbehandlung, völkisch, volklich, volkhaft, Rassenangehörige, Rassegefühl, Rasseinstinkt, Rasseverfall, Rassenanlage, rassenmäßig,*

38 Max Horkheimer and Theodor W. Adorno, 'The Culture Industry: Enlightenment as Mass Deception', in *Dialectic of Enlightenment*, trans. John Cumming (London, 1973), 159.
39 Ibid. 145–6.

Wilfried van der Will

rassegemäß, rassestark, rassenrein, reinrassig, rassebedingt, arteigen, artfremd, artgemäß, blutmäßig, zersetzend, nordisch, arisch, Aufnordung, hochzüchten; the second field consisted of words like *Säuberung, Säuberungsaktion, Säuberungswelle, Sonderbehandlung, Sonderaktion, Sonderkommando, Sondereinsatz, erfassen, Endlösung, judenrein, lebensunwertes Leben, verarzten* (i.e. murder within an officially sanctioned programme of euthanasia). The vocabulary of this second lexical field was to be found primarily within the world of Nazi administration, while the words of the first were part and parcel of the then dominant Nazi-speak. There was a tendency in all this vocabulary to name a state of affairs with dry clarity and at the same time to veil and to mythicize. The words, while retaining some classificatory innocence, belonged to a barbarous administrative, political, and cultural practice. They were part of the process of representing public life in a formulaic language in which the state's violence against the individual was at once cynically transparent and opaque. The effect of their rhetorical incantation could be so powerful that they even mesmerized their victims; while the cold clarity of such words detached them from rational discourse and reinvested public language with magic. Horkheimer and Adorno observed this pernicious development in verbal usage admirably well:

The demythologization of language . . . is a relapse into magic. . . . When the German Fascists decide one day to launch a word—say, 'intolerable' [*untragbar, unerträglich, unverzichtbar*]—over the loudspeakers, the next day the whole nation is saying 'intolerable'. By the same pattern, the nations against whom the weight of the German 'blitzkrieg' was thrown took the word into their own jargon.[40]

German fascism, which as a phenomenon with mass appeal arose out of an acute economic and political crisis, essentially developed its peculiar allure as a cultural and ideological practice. Without the self-acclamatory rituals of the Party rallies, its symbols, and uniforms and without its twofold mechanism of racial inclusion and racial persecution, of ideological affirmation and ideological exclusion, the Nazi regime could not have hoped to preserve its populist base. Despite a swelling chorus of dissenting voices, this was maintained even through the years of a faltering military campaign against the overwhelmingly more powerful forces of a global alliance. National Socialism was defeated comprehensively in military terms and, in a protracted development of the German political culture after 1945, also psychologically as far as the majority of the German electorate was concerned. Yet neither in Germany nor elsewhere

40 Ibid. 165.

has fascism been entirely divested of its fascination, which derives primarily from its ability to reverse the process of enlightenment and captivate human beings by a return to the brutal rituals of the horde.

Suggested Further Reading

Document collections on the Third Reich and German culture under National Socialism:

Mosse, George Lachmann, *Nazi Culture: Intellectual, Cultural and Social Life in the Third Reich* (New York, 1978).

Poliakov, Léon, and **Wulf, Joseph**, *Das Dritte Reich und seine Denker: Dokumente* (Berlin, 1959); *Das Dritte Reich und die Juden: Dokumente und Aufsätze* (Berlin, 1961).

Wulf, Joseph, *Kultur im Dritten Reich* (Frankfurt am Main and Berlin, 1989), i. *Presse und Funk;* ii. *Literatur und Dichtung;* iii. *Die bildenden Künste:* iv. *Theater und Film;* v. *Musik.*

Zentner, Kurt (ed.), *Illustrierte Geschichte des Dritten Reiches* (Munich, 1965).

General analyses of Nazi culture and its antecedents:

Benjamin, Walter, *Das Kunstwerk im Zeitalter seiner technischen Reproduzierbarkeit* (Frankfurt am Main, 1963).

Bloch, Ernst, *Erbschaft dieser Zeit* (Frankfurt am Main, 1973).

Glaser, Hermann, *The Cultural Roots of National Socialism* (London, 1978).

Hermand, Jost, *Der alte Traum vom neuen Reich: Völkische Utopien und Nationalsozialismus* (Frankfurt am Main, 1988).

Horkheimer, Max, and **Adorno, Theodor W.**, *Dialectic of Enlightenment*, trans. John Cumming (London, 1973).

Mosse, George Lachmann, *The Crisis of German Ideology* (New York, 1981).

Reichel, Peter, *Der schöne Schein des Dritten Reiches: Faszination und Gewalt des Faschismus* (Munich and Vienna, 1991).

Schnell, Ralf (ed.), *Literaturwissenschaft und Sozialwissenschaften 10. Kunst und Kultur im deutschen Faschismus* (Stuttgart, 1978).

Taylor, Brandon, and **van der Will, Wilfried** (eds.), *The Nazification of Art: Art, Design, Music, Architecture and Film in the Third Reich* (Winchester, 1990).

Vondung, Klaus, *Magie und Manipulation: Ideologischer Kult und politische Religion des Nationalsozialismus* (Göttingen, 1971).

Analyses of particular aspects of Nazi culture:

Women:

Gravenhorst, Lerke, and **Tatschmurat Carmen** (eds.), *Töchter-Fragen: NS-Frauen-Geschichte* (Freiburg, 1990).

Koonz, Claudia, *Mothers in the Fatherland: Women, the Family and Nazi Politics* (London, 1987).

Literature, Literary History and Theory:

Eichberg, Henning, *Massenspiele: NS-Thingspiel, Arbeiterweihespiel und olympisches Zeremoniell* (Stuttgart-Bad Cannstatt, 1977).

Gilman, Sander L., *NS-Literaturtheorie: Eine Dokumentation* (Frankfurt am Main, 1971).

Haarmann, Hermann, Huder, Walter, and Siebenhaar, Klaus (eds.), *'Das war ein Vorspiel nur . . .': Bücherverbrennung Deutschland 1933. Voraussetzungen und Folgen* (Berlin and Vienna, 1983).

Ketelsen, Uwe Karsten, *Völkisch-nationale und national-sozialistische Literatur in Deutschland 1890–1945* (Stuttgart, 1987).

Larsen, Stein, Sandberg, Beatrice, and Speirs, Ron, *Fascism and European Literature* (Berne, 1991).

Ritchie, James MacPherson, *German Literature under National Socialism* (Beckenham, 1983).

Stommer, Rainer, *Die inszenierte Volksgemeinschaft: Die 'Thing-Bewegung' im Dritten Reich* (Marburg, 1985).

Intellectuals and Philosophy:

Corino, Karl (ed.), *Intellektuelle im Bann des Nationalsozialismus* (Hamburg, 1980).

Haug, Wolfgang Fritz (ed.), *Deutsche Philosophen 1933* (Hamburg, 1989).

Laugstien, Thomas, *Philosophieverhältnisse im deutschen Faschismus* (Hamburg, 1990).

Art, Architecture, and Design:

Brenner, Hildegard, *Die Kunstpolitik des Nationalsozialismus* (Hamburg, 1963).

Hinz, Berthold, *Art in the Third Reich* (Oxford, 1980).

Nerdinger, Winfried (ed.), *Bauhaus-Moderne im Nationalsozialismus: Zwischen Anbiederung und Verfolgung* (Munich, 1993).

Schuster, Peter-Klaus (ed.), *Nationalsozialismus und 'Entartete Kunst'* (Munich, 1987).

Music:

Heister, Hanns-Werner, and Klein, Hans-Günther (eds.), *Musik und Musikpolitik im faschistischen Deutschland* (Frankfurt am Main, 1984).

Levi, Eric, *Music in the Third Reich* (London, 1994).

Cinema:

Albrecht, Gerd, *Nationalsozialistische Filmpolitik: Eine soziologische Untersuchung über Spielfilme des Dritten Reiches* (Stuttgart, 1969).

Drewniak, Boguslaw, *Der deutsche Film 1938–45: Ein Gesamtüberblick* (Düsseldorf, 1987).

Hull, David Stewart, *Film in the Third Reich: A Study of the German Cinema 1933–45* (Berkeley, 1969).

Kracauer, Siegfried, *From Caligari to Hitler: A Psychological History of the German Film* (Princeton, 1974).

Leiser, Erwin, *Nazi Cinema* (London, 1974).

Language:

Ehlich, Konrad (ed.), *Sprache im Faschismus* (Frankfurt am Main, 1989).

Klemperer, Viktor, *Lingua Tertii Imperii: Notizbuch eines Philologen* (Frankfurt am Main, 1982).

Sternberger, Dolf, and Storz, Gerhard, *Aus dem Wörterbuch des Unmenschen* (Hamburg 1957).

Exile:

Böhne, Edith, and Motzkau-Valeton, Wolfgang (eds.), *Die Künste und die Wissenschaften im Exil 1933–1945* (Gerlingen, 1992).

The Failed Socialist Experiment: Culture in the GDR

AXEL GOODBODY,

DENNIS TATE,

IAN WALLACE

ONE of the least encouraging developments in cultural life in post-unification Germany has been the tendency to belittle the achievements of writers, film-makers, and artists associated with the German Democratic Republic. In the course of the debate which raged through 1990 on Christa Wolf's text *Was bleibt*, the derogatory term *Staatsdichter* was applied in an undiscriminating way to authors who continued to work in the GDR right up to the collapse of the state in the autumn of 1989, while the expression *Gesinnungsästhetik* was revived as a pejorative label to be attached to virtually any cultural product (whether from the GDR or the Federal Republic) of the post-1945 era in which the moral or political concerns of its creator are clearly evident. If these attacks were justified, it might almost seem—in a politically ironic way—as if Horkheimer and Adorno's thesis of the culture industry and its standardizing effects could be applied just as properly to the socialist GDR as to the fascist Third Reich, which served as one of their original models. In the GDR, it might appear, there was an equally concerted attempt by a totalitarian regime to manipulate a whole society into accepting its ideology, with television now at its disposal in addition to radio as a powerful medium of social control. Yet as soon as this superficially tempting hypothesis is exposed to critical scrutiny, its limitations become clear (and not just for the obvious reason that Horkheimer and Adorno derived their model of ideological manipulation from the societies of advanced capitalism). Not only did the new 'technical media' occupy a fairly insignificant position in the GDR's cultural sphere, in terms of their impact on a public far less gullible than the generation of its parents had been; it is also a serious distortion of the facts to use a term like *Staatsdichter* to characterize the role of the intellectuals who opted to work within the manifest constraints of the GDR's *Kulturpolitik*.

A more differentiated approach is needed if we are to do justice to a culture which may have been more homogeneous than its West German counterpart in the years after 1945, but which can in no sense be characterized as a monolithic bloc of party propaganda. The relationship between critical intellectuals in the GDR and the political leadership of the Socialist Unity Party (SED) over the forty-year period of its existence was a complex one, in which periods of conflict far outweighed those in which there was a measure of agreement about the way forward towards a socialist ideal. The growing disenchantment of successive generations of the GDR's creative artists can be charted with reference to the worst acts of repression of the post-war era: the ending of the 'Thaw' of the middle 1950s, the infamous 'Eleventh Plenum' of the SED's Central Committee in 1965, and the range of intimidatory measures which followed the expatriation of Wolf Biermann in 1976. Yet each of these crises was preceded by a surge of creativity across the spectrum of the arts, which indicated the potential of a critical culture driven by the utopian vision of a better society and which produced work much admired beyond the frontiers of the GDR itself.

By the 1980s, the final decade of GDR culture, there were many indications of a mood close to despair which anticipated the final collapse of the GDR, but it was almost invariably accompanied by a determination not to give up a struggle which had now effectively become the *raison d'être* of those who had remained. For many of them the issue was no longer the failure of state socialism, but the way in which this failure was helping to create the new nuclear and ecological threats to the survival of the planet, which now needed to be combated on an international level, in conjunction with their fellow intellectuals in the Federal Republic and further afield. In this sense there was an important process of German cultural convergence occurring well before the demise of the GDR itself. This was evident, too, in the increasing influence of modernism despite the Party's continuing faith in socialist realism. Such details are easily forgotten while the media focus remains firmly fixed on the compromises made by some of the GDR's intellectuals in their dealings with the state, and not least on the extent of their involvement in the disreputable activities of the GDR state security

Axel Goodbody, Dennis Tate, Ian Wallace

police (*Stasi*), but they remain fundamental to the historical assessment of the significance of GDR culture which is our main concern here.

Cultural Renewal and National Aspirations

From today's perspective, the most surprising feature of cultural life during the four years which preceded the creation of the German Democratic Republic in October 1949 is its relative freedom from political control. Even though the plans of the Soviet Military Administration for the reorganization of industry and agriculture in the eastern part of divided Germany, which became its zone of occupation in May 1945, were based on Stalin's model of state socialism, it turned for its cultural strategy to the concept of a broad coalition of democratic forces. This was not a new idea: the need for an anti-fascist Popular Front of this kind to prevent Hitler's rise to power had been widely discussed in the later years of the Weimar Republic, but it had foundered on the rock of the implacable hostility between the Social Democrats and the Communists. It had finally gained the support of the Soviet Union in 1935, and international writers' congresses had been held in Paris (in the same year) and Madrid (in 1937) to highlight the breadth of European cultural opposition to the Third Reich, even if they were by then too late to have any practical effect. The strategy of the Popular Front had now re-emerged from the end-of-war deliberations of the German Communist Party in its Moscow exile, in a blueprint worked out by established writers such as Johannes R. Becher, Marxism's most influential literary theorist, the Hungarian Georg Lukács, and the political leadership, which was already firmly in the hands of Walter Ulbricht, the First Secretary of the SED between 1946 and 1971. It had been endorsed by a Soviet hierarchy which, in 1945, probably saw Germany's medium-term future as a reunified but neutral buffer-state between Eastern and Western Europe, and was therefore primarily concerned with ensuring that the new generation of Germans would be educated according to democratic rather than explicitly socialist values.

This broadly anti-fascist cultural policy suffered from two basic weaknesses. First, it was to be implemented from above, by communist intellectuals whose commitment to the Popular Front of the 1930s had been no more than lukewarm, who had engaged in bitter polemics with fellow Marxists living outside the Soviet Union, like Bertolt Brecht and Anna Seghers, and who had almost certainly compromised themselves by having found a means of surviving the traumatic years of Stalin's purges when so many of their German communist colleagues in Moscow had not. Secondly, it derived from a narrow understanding of culture, which assumed that the traditional literary forms of the novel, drama, and poetry would appeal to a mass audience and have a major role to play in the re-education of the survivors of Hitler's Germany. The obvious virtues this policy of privileging literature offered amidst the chaos of 1945 were the speed with which it could be implemented and the coherence of its immediate objectives. Once established, however, these assumptions regarding the hierarchy of cultural forms became an integral part of SED thinking, and East German intellectuals could not afford to lose sight of this reality. This, in turn, helps to explain why literary texts have to be given an exceptionally high profile in any discussion of culture in the GDR context.

The first proof of the short-term effectiveness of this cultural policy was the launching of the Kulturbund zur demokratischen Erneuerung Deutschlands (Cultural Alliance for German Democratic Renewal) in Berlin, only a matter of weeks after the end of the war, on 4 July 1945. Its manifesto expressed a clear commitment to German unity and to a cultural revival based on 'Germany's great culture' and 'the true German cultural values' exemplified in the work of Goethe, Schiller, and Lessing. It was to be above party politics and to establish a forum for intellectuals in all parts of Germany. Although Johannes R. Becher was duly elected president, the appointment of an 'inner émigré', Bernhard Kellermann, as its vice-president and the presence of only a minority of communists on its executive were seen as evidence of a genuine determination to initiate a close collaboration between the cultural exiles and those who had remained in Hitler's Germany on a broad programme of anti-fascism and anti-militarism. The Kulturbund met an obvious need: by the time of its first all-German congress in May 1947 it had gained 93,000 members in 580 branches scattered across the whole country, even though the bulk of these were based in the Soviet Zone. Under its aegis the literary life of the new Germany was powerfully stimulated, and immediate progress was made towards the Kulturbund's aim of restoring Berlin to the status it had enjoyed in the 1920s as a cultural metropolis. In August 1945 a major publishing house, the Aufbau Verlag, was established in East Berlin and, despite all the material shortages of the time, it managed to produce more than a hundred volumes with a combined print-run of 2.5 million copies in its first two years. Its bestsellers included

Axel Goodbody, Dennis Tate, Ian Wallace

Theodor Plievier's war novel *Stalingrad* (1945), Anna Seghers's *Das siebte Kreuz* (originally in English, 1942), and Becher's autobiographical novel *Abschied* (first published in Moscow, 1940), exemplifying its general commitment to the creative writing of the exile generation. In September 1945 the first issue of the Kulturbund's new monthly journal, also entitled *Aufbau*, appeared, to be followed in 1946 by a weekly, *Sonntag*. Between them they provided a broad platform for genuine debate on international issues of the day, such as existentialism, the nature of literary realism, or the impact of psychoanalysis on creative techniques, and for the publication of new writing by German authors as well as their more controversial foreign contemporaries like Hemingway and Cocteau.

Although all of this activity reflected the primacy accorded by the Kulturbund to literature and to traditional forms of intellectual debate, it was accompanied by a similarly open-minded spirit of renewal in other spheres of culture. The Soviet Military Administration facilitated the rapid reopening of theatres throughout Berlin, and the Renaissance-Theater won the race back to normality, albeit with an unedifying farce, *Der Raub der Sabinerinnen*, performed just three weeks after the end of the war. By September 1945 another famous Berlin location, the Deutsches Theater, was initiating the revival of the classical national repertoire with its performance of Lessing's famous plea for tolerance, *Nathan der Weise*, which, as another indicator of the mood of the period, was to be played more than 400 times on the major stages of the Soviet Zone by 1949. The Soviet-funded radio station, the Berliner Rundfunk, quickly gained a reputation for the quality and range of its cultural coverage which derived at least partly from the curious fact that its studios were located in the British sector. The existing radio station taken over by the Soviet administration for this purpose was in an area of central Berlin which was transferred to British control in July 1945 following a revision of the zonal boundaries, and it was not until 1952 that the studios were moved back into the Soviet sector.

Relaunching the film industry was a technically more daunting task than the resumption of broadcasting in this pre-television era, but an impressive start was also made here. The Ufa studios in Berlin, where many of Germany's internationally acclaimed films of the Weimar Republic had been made, were in 1946 placed in the hands of a small collective of film-makers who renamed their organization the Deutsche Film-Aktiengesellschaft (German Joint Stock Film Company; DEFA). By October of the same year DEFA's first production, Wolfgang Staudte's grim contemporary account of the pursuit of a war criminal, *Die Mörder sind unter uns*, was enjoying a widely praised première in Berlin. Meanwhile Dresden was asserting its claim ᵗo be the centre of the visual and plastic arts in the Soviet Zone with the first post-war Exhibition of German Art (September–October 1946), which was primarily a retrospective display of the modernist 'degenerate art' banned by the Nazis and gave special posthumous recognition to the work of Ernst Barlach.

There were therefore solid grounds for hoping that a new era of partnership between creative intellectuals and political leaders (*Geist* and *Macht* in Heinrich Mann's much quoted terms) had been initiated, in which culture would be actively promoted as a force supporting the regime's broad anti-fascist objectives. The problematic nature of the proposed renewal of the cultural heritage of German classicism—its élitist and patriarchal historical context and the idea that great works of the past provided models to be uncritically imitated—was not yet evident. This helps to explain the attractiveness of the Soviet Zone in the later 1940s to the initially sceptical intellectuals who had spent their years of exile from Hitler's Germany in the West. The new state offered them material advantages and positions of influence as well as optimal working conditions. Anna Seghers returned from Mexico in 1947 and was later to become president of the GDR Writers' Union; Bertolt Brecht came back from the United States the following year to establish his own theatre, the Berliner Ensemble; Arnold Zweig was tempted back from Palestine in 1948 and became the first president of the GDR's Academy of the Arts in 1950, after the plan to give this position to Heinrich Mann had been thwarted by the latter's death. Leading academics too benefited: the literary scholar Hans Mayer and the philosopher Ernst Bloch both returned to professorships at Leipzig, in the expectation that the democratization of the education system, heralded by the introduction of the comprehensive *Einheitsschule* in 1945, would be accompanied by a commitment to establish the highest international standards of teaching and research at university level. But the climate rapidly worsened as divided Germany became the cockpit of the Cold War and the dream of a nation reunited under broadly socialist principles began to fade. The first German Writers' Congress in October 1947 was also to be the last all-German gathering of its kind, as Johannes R. Becher's plea for continued collaboration in the task of rebuilding the nation was drowned by the mutual recriminations of American and Soviet guests expressing the hardline views of their respective governments.

Cold War Constraints

The years between 1947 and the mid-1950s were marked by an extended struggle about the nature of a socialist cultural policy between these intellectual figureheads and what was now an overtly Stalinist regime. The SED, which had been created in 1946 from a merger of the Communists and Social Democrats, now sought to impose Soviet-style socialist realist principles on every aspect of a culture which had set out to evolve its own distinctively German identity. Dogmatic cultural functionaries such as the Politburo member Alexander Abusch began to insist that art forms now had to become the servants of ideology. According to these *Kulturpolitiker* the prime task of artists was to find the appropriate formal means to convey simplistic messages about the successful construction of socialism in what was, from October 1949, the German Democratic Republic. Catchwords like 'formalism' and 'decadence' were used to condemn all manifestations of modernism in the arts, which included the Expressionist movement from which Becher's generation of poets and artists had emerged and innovations in German drama such as Brecht's epic theatre. Hostility to all things American, to what Abusch called 'Coca-Cola culture', led to sweeping dismissals of popular fiction, jazz and the beginnings of rock music, abstract art, and any portrayal of sex, an attitude which showed no understanding of the potential impact of new media on traditional conceptions of culture.

The GDR's press showed all the worst features of this doctrinaire regime. Right from 1945 it had never enjoyed the degree of latitude which literary culture had been given and had been organized under strict Leninist principles as the mouthpiece of the Party's Department of Agitation and Propaganda, in order to provide a regular diet of socialist success stories and nightmarish depictions of life in the capitalist world. As the sole source of information was the state-run Allgemeiner Deutscher Nachrichtendienst (ADN-General German News Service), the impression of choice provided by the range of newspapers published was largely illusory. Apart from the main SED newspaper, *Neues Deutschland*, there was a daily aimed at the members of each of the other parties in the GDR's permanent ruling coalition (such as *Neue Zeit* for the Christian Democrats and the *National-Zeitung* for the reformed Nazis who made up the National Democratic Party); the Free German Federation of Trade Unions (FDGB) had its own newspaper (*Tribüne*), as did the Free German Youth (FDJ—*Junge Welt*) and the German

Gymnastics and Sports Council (*Deutsches Sportecho*); there were regional dailies like the *Leipziger Volkszeitung* and the *Sächsische Zeitung* in Dresden: but the 'news' they each provided was simply a differently flavoured version of the truth as determined by the SED's propagandists. In broadcasting the same degree of centralized control became evident once the Berliner Rundfunk had been properly established in East Berlin. While it continued to target Berlin as a whole, Radio DDR was directed at the domestic audience and the Deutschland-Sender led the propaganda assault on the Federal Republic, in what was envisaged as a neat division of labour.

The newly reformed education system inevitably also suffered under these ideological constraints. On the surface the emphasis still appeared to be on the process of democratization, with the constitution of 1949 promising equal rights to education for all citizens of the GDR. In the comprehensive *Einheitsschule* the first steps were being taken to ensure that the vocational needs of the younger generation were being met, on the road to what would later be called the *allgemeinbildende polytechnische Oberschule*; in the universities *Arbeiter- und Bauernfakultäten* were instituted to give previously underprivileged sectors of the population accelerated access to degree courses. But all aspects of education were now becoming subject to rigid Marxist-Leninist control, with the new school subject of *Gegenwartskunde* (current affairs), renamed *Staatsbürgerkunde* (civics) in the late 1950s, as the focus of an intensifying process of indoctrination. Scarcely had the new socialist openness of higher education been proclaimed than it became subject to new forms of selectivity based on social background and political loyalty, which had the disastrous effect of encouraging outwardly conformist behaviour among the intelligentsia of the future at this sensitive stage in the GDR's development.

The realization that the arts were now also expected to play a purely conformist role in GDR society rapidly removed the gloss from the regime's generous funding of the arts and individual artists. In purely material terms the series of annual National Prizes, inaugurated in 1950 and worth between 25,000 and 100,000 marks to their recipients, far surpassed anything available in the free market of the Federal Republic, and they were only one element in an extensive system of financial support which maintained established artists and encouraged young talent. It was not long before the high price exacted by the SED for this support began to manifest itself both in the broken lives and in the mediocre creative work of many of the beneficiaries.

The apparatus of censorship was effectively put into place in

Axel Goodbody, Dennis Tate, Ian Wallace

1951 with the creation of the Amt für Literatur und Verlagswesen (Bureau for Literature and Publishing) and the Staatliche Kommission für Kunstangelegenheiten (State Commission for Artistic Matters), with powers to reject manuscripts, control the allocation of paper to publishers, and order the withdrawal of unwelcome plays, concerts, and art exhibitions. A number of test cases followed, exposing the narrowness of the SED's *Kulturpolitik*: the DEFA film of Arnold Zweig's novel *Das Beil von Wandsbek* was banned because the characterization of the negative figure of a fascist executioner played too prominent a part; Hanns Eisler's libretto *Johann Faustus*, although published by Aufbau, was so heavily criticized for its portrayal of Goethe's hero (as a bourgeois humanist unwilling to support the revolutionary actions needed to turn his ideas into social reality) that Eisler abandoned his musical score; and an exhibition of Ernst Barlach's drawings and sculptures in Berlin, just five years after his work had been given pride of place in Dresden, was obliged to close prematurely, despite an intervention by Brecht, because it contained, in the words of *Neues Deutschland*, 'nothing which points the way forward'.

The public responses of *Geist* to these manifestations of decidedly old-style *Macht* were ambivalent. To have adopted an overtly oppositional stance might have seemed like a betrayal of the fledgling GDR at a time when its political and economic survival hung in the balance and it faced the Adenauer government's unrelenting hostility. The limits of West German tolerance of the Kulturbund's Popular Front strategy were also already threateningly apparent: the organization had been banned in the Western zones since the débâcle of the 1947 Writers' Congress; Western pressure had brought about the division of the German section of the international writers' association, the PEN-Club, into two mutually hostile halves by 1951; publishers in the Federal Republic had begun the boycott of virtually all works by intellectuals associated with the SED regime which—with the notable exception of Brecht's work—was to continue until the 1960s; the occasional initiatives to hold cross-border cultural debates in the West under the slogan 'Germans at one table' tended to be thwarted by police action; and the availability in the Federal Republic of books and journals published in the GDR was to be further curtailed by a blanket ban on their import imposed in 1954 by Bonn's Ministry of Posts and Telegraphs.

It was in this increasingly hostile context that the GDR's older generation of creative intellectuals sought to find a way of reconciling their socialist commitment with their goal of a reunified German culture. The hope that they might simultaneously modify the SED's crudely utilitarian attitude to the arts and appeal over the heads of the Adenauer government to a West German audience looked more and more futile, yet they saw no alternative to persisting with the broad outlines of their post-1945 strategy. The celebrations in 1949 of the two-hundredth anniversary of Goethe's birth had already illustrated their predicament. As the political process moved inexorably towards the creation of the two German states, Thomas Mann's visit to Weimar was greeted as a symbol of the indestructible unity of German culture and Becher spoke emotionally, but unconvincingly, about the survival of the 'Reich called Goethe'.

There were, nevertheless, tangible successes to be recorded. A major new cultural journal, *Sinn und Form*, was launched in 1949 under the editorship of another inner émigré, Peter Huchel, who had proved a very effective advocate of the Popular Front policy in his previous work for the Berliner Rundfunk. As well as making *Sinn und Form* a forum for the revitalization of German cultural traditions, Huchel underlined the need for openness to international influences, especially those of the modernist era, through his policy of introducing authors like Mayakovsky, Lorca, Aragon, and József to his readership with the help of high-quality translations produced by the GDR's leading poets. In 1950 *Sinn und Form* became the cultural flagship of the newly created Academy of the Arts, whose twenty-three founder members, including Becher, Brecht, Zweig, Seghers, and Eisler, could with some justification claim to represent the élite of the cultural exiles who had returned to Germany after the war.

Even within the Academy, however, there were tensions. Becher in particular was dangerously unpredictable, siding with the SED's political leadership in rejecting the image of Faust conveyed by Eisler in his libretto and at times making unscrupulous use of his special relationship with Walter Ulbricht to protect his creative reputation from increasingly justified criticism. He was at his most embarrassing in 1953, after the death of the Soviet leader Joseph Stalin, when he wrote a commemorative poem, 'Danksagung', which depicted Stalin as a godlike figure in a socialist heaven, stimulating growth in all parts of Germany and willing its unification:

> Mit Marx und Engels geht er durch Stralsund,
> Bei Rostock überprüft er die Traktoren,
> Und über einen dunklen Wiesengrund
> Blickt in die Weite er, wie traumverloren.
>
> Er geht durch die Betriebe an der Ruhr,
> Und auf den Feldern tritt er zu den Bauern,

Die Panzerfurche—eine Leidensspur.
Und Stalin sagt: 'Es wird nicht lang mehr dauern.'[1]

(He walks with Marx and Engels through Stralsund, | Near Rostock he checks over all the tractors, | And turning now beyond a darkened meadow | He looks into the distance, lost in dreams. | | He's moving through the factories on the Ruhr, | And in the fields goes over to the peasants, | The tank tracks just a trace of suffering past. | And Stalin says: 'It won't be too long now.')

The Academy was, however, sufficiently in accord in the aftermath of the workers' uprising of 17 June 1953 to push strongly for the abolition of the Party's control mechanisms and for the liberalization of a cultural policy focused on the production of industrial novels, plays, and paintings depicting the GDR's heroic progress to success. It was grimly appropriate that the protests of 17 June against the regime's economic policies were initiated by the building workers on Berlin's most pretentious architectural project, the Stalinallee, a neo-classical boulevard of flats, shops, and restaurants symbolically linking the city centre with its main working-class suburbs, which had been the subject of much of this self-congratulatory art and literature.

Brecht was in the forefront of the GDR's internal reform process, publishing poems which attacked the faceless bureaucrats in the Kunstkommission and the Amt für Literatur, but remaining sufficiently wary of garnering the 'deafening thunder of applause | From beyond the sector boundary' to withhold his most biting comments from the readership of the day. Only after his death did his cycle of poems, *Buckower Elegien*, appear in full and receive recognition as one of the very few lasting literary achievements of the GDR's early years. The cycle includes the much-quoted poem 'Die Lösung', which exposes the absurdity of the complaint by the Writers' Union secretary, Kurt Barthel (known as KuBa), that the people had 'betrayed the trust' which their (unelected) government had placed in them by taking part in the uprising: 'Would it not be easier | In that case for the government | To dissolve the people | And elect another?' It also provides in the poem 'Böser Morgen' one of the first examples of self-criticism by a GDR author in acknowledging his remoteness from the underprivileged majority of the populace:

Die Silberpappel, eine ortsbekannte Schönheit
Heut eine alte Vettel. Der See
Eine Lache Abwaschwasser, nicht rühren!
Die Fuchsien unter dem Löwenmaul billig und eitel.
Warum?

1 Quoted in full in Manfred Jäger, *Kultur und Politik in der DDR* (Cologne, 1995), 70.

Heut nacht im Traum sah ich Finger, auf mich deutend
Wie auf einen Aussätzigen. Sie waren zerarbeitet und
Sie waren gebrochen.

Unwissende! schrie ich
Schuldbewußt.[2]

(The silver poplar, a celebrated local beauty | Today an old harridan. The lake | A puddle of dish water, don't touch! | The fuchsias among the snapdragon cheap and vain. | Why? | Last night in a dream I saw fingers pointing at me | As at a leper. They were worn with toil and | They were broken. | | You don't know! I shrieked | Conscience-stricken.)

An example of how this remoteness might be overcome was provided in the same year by a newly arrived author, Stefan Heym, who had successfully combined the activities of a popular journalist and a bestselling novelist before his belated return from the USA in 1952. As one of the youngest of the exiles, who had only established his literary career after leaving Hitler's Germany, Heym had a much broader view of his cultural role in his new environment. He relished the opportunity given to him by the *Berliner Zeitung* to write a weekly column on current affairs, with an unprecedented degree of editorial independence. From 1953 to 1957 he engaged in vigorous debate with his readers, identifying with the frustrations of ordinary workers and showing a willingness to criticize SED bureaucracy or the journalistic style of newspapers like *Neues Deutschland*, thereby providing almost the only example in the GDR's history of a regular open dialogue conducted in the press.

It is no coincidence that the four-year period when Heym's populist approach was tolerated also gave GDR culture as a whole its best opportunity during the Cold War era to fulfil the expectations raised by the high status it had been formally given by the regime. In the aftermath of 17 June 1953 Becher's plan for a Ministry of Culture to protect the interests of artists at government level became a reality, and its creation in 1954 (with Becher as the first Minister) coincided encouragingly with the demise of the discredited Kunstkommission. (When the Amt für Literatur was replaced in 1956 by a less threateningly titled Hauptverwaltung Verlage und Buchhandel (Central Administration for Publishers and the Book Trade) it briefly—but misleadingly—suggested the complete scrapping of the SED's original censorship apparatus.) The GDR Writers' Union, which had been under tight Party control after being separated from the Kulturbund in 1952, also began to display a healthy degree of independence. Its monthly journal, *Neue deutsche Literatur*, recovered impressively from a disastrous start in 1953 to

2 See 'Not what was meant', 'The Solution', and 'Nasty Morning', in Bertolt Brecht, *Poems 1913–1956*, ed. John Willett (London, 1976), 437–40. The originals are in Brecht's *Gesammelte Werke* (Frankfurt am Main, 1967), x. 1008–10.

Axel Goodbody, Dennis Tate, Ian Wallace

become a forum for the younger German authors from East and West who were not yet sufficiently established to have serious hopes of being published in *Sinn und Form*. By the mid-1950s it was playing an important role for this generation, the young soldiers and civilians of Hitler's world war, in publishing its literary depictions of this experience and thereby encouraging the crucial process of *Vergangenheitsbewältigung* (coming to terms with the past) after the interruption created by the SED's insistence on a literature exclusively focused on industrial reconstruction. Like *Sinn und Form*, *Neue deutsche Literatur* saw itself as meeting a national cultural need in the face of West German obstructiveness, and authors like Böll and Nossack were, for a time, treated seriously alongside their GDR counterparts.

The Achievements of the 'Thaw' Years

This post-Stalin relaxation of cultural control was not unique to the GDR. It was part of the general Eastern European 'Thaw' which accompanied Khrushchev's rise to power in the Soviet Union and provided a first hint of how socialist culture might develop—in terms of the cinema in Poland or poetry in Czechoslovakia, for example— if the producers were given room to experiment. In the GDR, the urge to debate the potential of this newly liberated culture reached an impressive culmination at the Writers' Congress of January 1956, addressed by all the figureheads of the exile years—Becher, Brecht, Seghers, and the guest of honour, Georg Lukács—who reiterated their shared commitment to creating a new *Nationalliteratur*. But there was still little evidence in the work of the older generation of the quality this term implied. The 'Thaw' had provided an opportunity for Brecht to tour Western Europe with the Berliner Ensemble and confirm his international status with his own productions of earlier works like *Mutter Courage* and *Der kaukasische Kreidekreis*, but the GDR had not stimulated him into new dramatic writing of any significance. Becher's aesthetic deliberations of the mid-1950s, the *Bemühungen* which appeared in four volumes, showed him striving to reinstate sounder qualitative criteria for his own writing, but there was little evidence of this in his poetry of 1955–7. Seghers, too, still had years of uninspired effort ahead of her before she completed a major novel, *Die Entscheidung* (1959).

In creative terms it was the GDR's younger authors who benefited most from the opportunity the 'Thaw' provided to display their talents and appeal to a wider national audience. Those who had uncritically supported the SED's propaganda campaigns of the early 1950s and risen to dubious prominence as *Staatsdichter*, such as Franz Fühmann, had rapidly recognized the disastrous effects of these pressures on the quality of their published work and now sought to make amends. After three years dominated by the production of the instant poetic responses to political events which he later dismissed as 'the cheapest kind of doggerel', Fühmann devoted his main creative energies in the period between 1953 and 1955 to a single short prose narrative, *Kameraden*, based on his war experience. The end-product not only marked a personal breakthrough to literary significance, but had a remarkable galvanizing effect on his fellow writers, as well as helping to revive film-production in the GDR.

The key to this success was Fühmann's tight narrative focus on an authentic psychological portrayal of young German soldiers on the eve of Hitler's invasion of the Soviet Union in June 1941. Defying the conventions of socialist realism, he left his text open-ended, without ideologically reassuring pointers to the dawning of a better era for these misguided children of the Third Reich. Indeed, the central moral theme of *Kameraden*, the exploitation of youthful idealism which occurs when abstract values such as 'comradeship', 'honour', and 'loyalty' are abused for political ends, could have been taken as having a continuing relevance beyond the Hitler years. And although Fühmann was not yet confident enough to write autobiographically about his Nazi past, he captured the contradictions inherent in his own experience very effectively in the tensions between his two young protagonists, the intellectually convinced fascist Josef and the morally anguished Thomas, after they are involved in the accidental killing of their commanding officer's daughter.

The reception of Fühmann's story after it appeared in the autumn of 1955 was predictably controversial, but it was instrumental in stimulating a wave of realistic war stories which changed the nature of GDR literature. *Kameraden* was also seized upon by DEFA as the basis of a feature film which in turn helped to liberate it from its predominantly propagandist role of the period up to the 'Thaw'. After its première in March 1957, under the title *Betrogen bis zum jüngsten Tag* , the film version of Fühmann's story (directed by Kurt Jung-Alsen) became DEFA's first production to be shown at the Cannes film festival. Even though it was excluded for political reasons from consideration for an award at the festival, it received very positive reviews from French and British critics, including the director Lindsay Anderson, and was later released in the English-speaking world as *Duped till Doomsday*.

Kameraden was a rare case, even in the relatively enlightened period of the 'Thaw', of a creative breakthrough which received appropriate public recognition from the GDR's cultural politicians. The impressive list of works produced during the same period which met with a less sympathetic response shows what a missed opportunity this was for the GDR to foster a culture which could have greatly strengthened its international credibility as a state prepared to engage in serious debate about its future development. Heiner Müller's play *Der Lohndrücker* (1957), for example, showed how much more could be achieved with the industrial subject-matter which was always at the heart of the SED's idea of popular culture by an author prepared to offer a credibly complex view of working life. He set out to expose the superficiality of the cliché of the proletarian hero by placing the most celebrated industrial success story of the GDR's early years in its proper historical context. The feat of the Berlin bricklayer Hans Garbe in the winter of 1948–9—repairing part of a damaged blast furnace while its other chambers continued to operate at their full 1000°C temperature—had been heralded by the SED as a shining example of the potential of the new working class and had provided the focus for the best of the GDR's mediocre crop of 'novels of reconstruction', Eduard Claudius's *Menschen an unsrer Seite* (1951). Müller, the most gifted of the young dramatists who had worked with Brecht at the Berliner Ensemble, set out to undermine the propagandist assumption that industrial activists like Garbe should automatically be regarded as 'positive heroes'.

His protagonist Balke is a mass of unresolved contradictions. He is a workaholic without clear political convictions, who might earlier have denounced fellow workers attempting to sabotage the Nazi war machine, a loner who benefits disproportionately from his productivity bonuses while his colleagues suffer extreme economic hardship and who generates hostility rather than inspiring others to follow his example. Even more provocative is Müller's wider portrayal of working life as the newly created GDR struggles for its economic survival. The majority of his characters have been so deeply scarred, morally and politically, by their involvement with fascism that an overnight conversion to an alternative ideology is unthinkable, while the SED is seen to have made too many mistakes and to include too many opportunists or dogmatists to merit uncritical support. If the damaged furnace is successfully repaired— and the play ends before the outcome is clear—then it will be the result of a sober collaboration between mutually suspicious workers responding to the economic need to survive rather than a heroic contribution to the future of socialism. As Müller's Brechtian prologue makes clear, the 'struggle between the old and the new' is still far from resolved and will only be decided in the future by the actions of 'the new public' watching the play. There is even a scene—which would inevitably have evoked memories of 17 June 1953 in the minds of any East German audience—where the need for a workers' strike against increased productivity requirements is passionately debated, with convincing arguments on both sides, before a majority gives its grudging support to Balke and the local SED leadership. More important to Müller, though, was the point— echoed, as already noted, in Stefan Heym's combative journalism of the mid-1950s—that only through forceful open debate might the SED hope to win the respect of the GDR's work-force in the longer term.

Der Lohndrücker came close to making a similar impact to Fühmann's war stories. It was published in *Neue deutsche Literatur* in May 1957, was actually performed in Leipzig, Berlin, and Potsdam in 1958–9, and Müller was nominated for the prestigious literary prize of the GDR's Federation of Trade Unions in 1959, only to fall foul of a Party campaign against what was confusingly termed 'didactic drama', in a cultural climate which was by then much more hostile. As a result, *Der Lohndrücker* virtually disappeared from public view in the GDR, whether in book form or on the stage, until 1988, when Müller directed an adapted version of his play at the Deutsches Theater in Berlin, an outstanding production which included other elements from his historical and satirical writing in its montage of scenes but came too late for its political message to have any significant effect.

Another new talent of the 'Thaw' years who failed entirely to persuade the GDR's publishing houses, from the Aufbau Verlag downwards, to take him seriously was Uwe Johnson. His sensitive account of teenage life amidst the repressive atmosphere of the early 1950s, *Ingrid Babendererde*, only saw the light of day in 1985, after Johnson's suicide had put an end to his long period of exile from both German states. In the GDR's film industry it was basically the same story, with *Betrogen bis zum jüngsten Tag* remaining a rare exception of a significant new film allowed to enjoy the public success it deserved. Konrad Wolf's *Sonnensucher* (1957) had something in common with *Der Lohndrücker* in the harsh perspective it adopted on the GDR's early years, focused in this case on the aggressive lifestyle of the workers in the Wismut uranium mines, but it was withdrawn on the day of its première because of Soviet sensitivities to the evidence it provided of their early commitment to developing the atomic bomb. The influence of the neo-realism

Axel Goodbody, Dennis Tate, Ian Wallace

of post-war Italian cinema was also evident in Wolfgang Kohlhaase's *Berlin—Ecke Schönhauser* (1957), a gripping contemporary study of juvenile delinquency in the socialist sector of the still open city, which was also rapidly withdrawn following criticisms of its incompatibility with socialist realism.

Less obvious, but even more serious, was the retarding effect the SED's blinkered view of socialist culture had on the emergence of distinctive creative work by women in the GDR's first decade. The promise enshrined in the constitution of 1949 that women would enjoy equal rights and equal opportunities to fulfil their potential meant little in reality in the cultural sphere. Even though some of the younger generation of female intellectuals were able to establish a career in this arena, most notably Christa Wolf, who was a major contributor to, and eventually the chief editor of, *Neue deutsche Literatur* in its early years, there seemed little scope for them to make headway as creative artists when the GDR's cultural policy prescribed its central themes, and especially that of industrial reconstruction, in terms which assumed they were predominantly male preserves. Surprisingly, perhaps, the most prominent role model for aspiring women authors, Anna Seghers, had ruthlessly excluded her subjective experience from her creative writing: the principal female character in the only novel of hers to appear during her first decade in East Germany, *Die Toten bleiben jung* (1949), is a self-sacrificing proletarian mother who devotes her life to the welfare of the son of her lover murdered during the attempted German revolution of 1918–19. Where the theme of the emancipatory effect of economic independence was treated, as in Elfriede Brüning's *Regine Haberkorn* (1955), there was a counter-productive propagandist tendency to suggest there were few serious problems in the way of the harmonious reconciliation of working and domestic life.

The career of one of the GDR's most talented younger authors, Brigitte Reimann, reflects the frustrations of a long apprenticeship producing commissioned work in line with the priorities of cultural policy. In her first decade as a full-time writer she dutifully wrote three works of fiction: *Der Tod der schönen Helena* (1955), an 'adventure story' about Greek partisans for what must have been the least attractive of the GDR's publishing houses, the Verlag des Ministeriums des Innern; *Die Frau am Pranger* (1956), which describes a wartime love affair between a German woman and a Russian prisoner of war; and *Ankunft im Alltag* (1961), a novel officially praised for its portrayal of a young woman's successful integration into working life, but which Reimann herself viewed as an unexciting 'hard slog'.[3] Only then did she feel sufficiently self-confident to

3 Reimann's own account of these years, even in the much censored volume *Brigitte Reimann in ihren Briefen und Tagebüchern*, ed. Elisabeth Elten-Krause and Walter Lewerenz (Berlin/GDR, 1983), is very revealing: see esp. pp. 29–95.

develop the subjective style which characterizes her novel about the disintegration of a family during the Berlin Wall crisis, *Die Geschwister* (1963), and her outstanding account of the barriers to female self-fulfilment in the GDR, *Franziska Linkerhand* (1974), which had to be published in its unfinished form after her death from cancer at the age of 39. In the struggle for the GDR's cultural identity which dominated the mid-1950s, the absence of the authentic narrative voice of female authors like Reimann and Christa Wolf was a serious deficiency.

Repression in the Guise of 'Cultural Revolution'

The limited progress which had been achieved by some of the GDR's younger male authors was forcibly halted in the repressive aftermath of the Hungarian uprising of October 1956, which affected cultural developments throughout Eastern Europe. The death of Brecht in August 1956, just before events in Hungary reached their bloody climax, had in any case been a body-blow to the reform process, but the SED now rapidly set about undermining the protective presence of the Academy of the Arts and the authority of the Ministry of Culture. Although Becher nominally retained his ministerial post until his death in 1958, he was effectively deprived of his powers, on the grounds that he had allowed the debate to get out of control and because of his association with Georg Lukács, who had come close to being executed after taking up a similar ministerial role in Hungary's provisional government during the uprising.

The GDR's cultural world then experienced its only Stalinist show trials, where the main victims were theoreticians (Wolfgang Harich) and administrators (Walter Janka, the head of the Aufbau Verlag, and Gustav Just, the deputy editor of *Sonntag*) rather than creative artists (although one young author, Erich Loest, also received a prison sentence). Yet because the alleged conspiracy of the so-called *Harich-Gruppe* to subvert the state originated in discussions with sympathetic West German intellectuals about initiating a 'third way' to German reunification between the ideologies of the two states, the show trials of 1957 also represented a final blow to the all-German cultural aspirations of Becher's generation of artists, since they made it politically unacceptable to persist with any hopes of restoring cultural unity between East and West. The foundations on which GDR intellectuals had built their original claim to cultural distinctiveness, as the true heirs of the Weimar Classicists, had been destroyed. This produced a fundamental identity crisis and it was to take several years before the younger generation of artists became confident of the potential of the alternative option, an autonomous GDR culture.

The later 1950s were as a result an arid period for creative endeavour, dominated by the pronouncements of SED spokesmen about the need for a 'cultural revolution' according to their own prescriptions. The tone was set in October 1957 at a conference organized by the SED's Central Committee, where Alexander Abusch, who was soon to succeed Becher as Minister of Culture, launched a general attack on writers and artists, whose 'political vacillations' of 1956–7 were contrasted with the 'resolute and principled policy of our Party leadership'. A succession of these supposedly irresolute intellectuals, who had individually been subjected to enormous pressure in the run-up to this conference, then went through the ritual of public self-criticism required by the SED leadership. By the time of the Party conference in July 1958 Walter Ulbricht was defining the goal of the GDR's forthcoming cultural revolution as that of overcoming 'the still unbridged gulf between art and life, the alienation between the artist and the people', and thereby heralding the promotion of an alternative workers' culture. Whatever fruits this campaign was to bear by the early 1960s as a result of the opening up of new areas of everyday life in the GDR to creative exploration (see the discussion of the *Bitterfelder Weg* below), its origins as a crude means of disciplining the cultural élite for their alleged errors during the 'Thaw' were unmistakable.

This change of policy brought about some absurd contradictions in the evaluation of individual artists. The award of a National Prize to Franz Fühmann for his war stories early in October 1957 did not prevent him from undergoing humiliating criticism during the crack-down which followed only a few weeks later. When the new collection of war stories he had written since *Kameraden* finally appeared in 1959 in book form under the title *Stürzende Schatten*, he was attacked for his failure to give them a present-day perspective which would show how the fascist past had already been overcome in the GDR. It was not until he had written his stock-taking autobiographical volume *Zweiundzwanzig Tage oder Die Hälfte des Lebens* (1973) that Fühmann felt he had worked through the effects of the crisis induced by this attack on his creative integrity.

The most noteworthy cultural event of the late 1950s was curiously unaffected by this widespread repression. Bruno Apitz's novel about life in the Buchenwald concentration camp, *Nackt unter Wölfen* (1958), the GDR's first genuine bestseller, which by the early 1970s had sold over a million copies in the GDR alone (whose total population was only 17 million) as well as being translated into twenty-five languages, was a late addition to the war literature of the 'Thaw' years. It was evidently tolerated by the SED because it culminated in the communist-led revolt of the surviving inmates in April 1945 against the camp authorities, yet its attraction to many GDR readers was the way it showed the iron discipline of the underground communist leadership in the camp being modified in the face of a basic humanitarian dilemma. The involvement of some members of the underground committee in protecting a 3-year-old child previously smuggled into Buchenwald exposes them, and the liberation plan, to risks which some of the communist hardliners regard as unacceptable, yet these feelings are seen to triumph over the need for total discipline. In the happy ending, which is one of the few obviously socialist realist aspects of a grippingly factual narrative, the child survives while the liberation is achieved, but the underlying message of Apitz's text posed a challenge to the nature of post-1957 SED authority. When DEFA finally gained permission to produce a film version of *Nackt unter Wölfen* (directed by Frank Beyer, 1963), it was an early sign of its re-emergence from the ideological clampdown on its activities since the end of the 'Thaw', as well as being one of its most popular productions ever.

No reassessment of GDR culture in the period up to the building of the Berlin Wall would be complete without an acknowledgement of the fact that the most innovative and convincing depiction of the GDR of the 1950s is to be found in another novel which was never deemed suitable for publication in the GDR's lifetime, Uwe Johnson's *Mutmaßungen über Jakob* (1959). After his failure to have *Ingrid Babendererde* accepted in 1956–7, when the cultural climate was at its most favourable, Johnson went straight to the Suhrkamp Verlag in Frankfurt with his second work of fiction (even though they too had rejected its predecessor), assuming that its publication would compel his emigration from the GDR. *Mutmaßungen über Jakob* stands out against other literature of the 1950s written in the GDR in three essential aspects. Johnson's historical context, the autumn of 1956, marked by a major crisis for both world ideologies (the Suez affair alongside the Hungarian uprising), was the vital one for any assessment of the GDR's future prospects. His narrative structure, based on the efforts of the group of individuals closest to the recently deceased protagonist, Jakob Abs, to reconstruct the circumstances which led to his death, highlighted the elusive nature of individual identity in the darkest hour of the Cold War and thereby exposed the superficiality of ideological constructs like

Axel Goodbody, Dennis Tate, Ian Wallace

the 'positive hero'. And with his constellation of memorably portrayed characters—a wavering intellectual, an agent of the *Stasi*, an émigrée now working reluctantly for NATO, as well as the eponymous hero, a worker with the skills and sensitivity the GDR would have needed to utilize to the full in order to make a success of its socialist experiment—Johnson captured the complexity of the era in a remarkably perspicacious way. In each of these respects, *Mutmaßungen über Jakob* established a yardstick by which the authenticity of work subsequently published in the GDR itself could be judged and became an unacknowledged influence on its subsequent development.

The Emergence of a Distinctive GDR Culture

Sealing off West Berlin from the rest of the city on 13 August 1961 completed the division of Germany and ushered in a decade of divergence between the GDR and the Federal Republic. Despite its official justification as an 'anti-fascist protective fortification', the Berlin Wall was a humiliating restriction for GDR citizens and a practical admission that the SED's version of socialism could not survive on the basis of the voluntary participation of a population which could choose to leave for the West. At the same time, however, the Wall ended the flight of predominantly skilled, educated citizens the economy could ill afford to lose, thus providing the basis for an economic upturn and a new phase of cultural activity focused on internal problems.

The next few years were characterized by a comparative relaxation of state control in social and cultural spheres. Under these circumstances a generation of writers and artists participated with genuine enthusiasm in the official programme for the creation of a 'socialist national culture', which now definitively replaced the older concept of a unified German culture and helped to stabilize GDR identity. The 1960s and early 1970s consequently witnessed the emergence of a distinctive GDR culture, which was beginning to make an impact on the international scene before it was undermined by the exodus of writers and artists to the West after 1976. The identification of the literary and artistic intelligentsia with the state, their commitment to socialism, and the earnest debate in which they engaged with their readers on the advancement of society, even after the political and cultural climate had hardened in the mid-1960s, distinguished GDR culture from its contemporary West German counterpart.

That support for state cultural policy was accompanied by demands for a new openness and insistence on individual integrity is nowhere clearer than in the writing of Christa Wolf. Her breakthrough came with *Der geteilte Himmel* (1963), which succeeded in combining a realistic presentation of the tensions and conflicts of life in the GDR with popular appeal (after serialization in the student magazine *Forum* the first book edition sold out before reaching the bookshops) and in satisfying the ideological demands of the censor. Seen by West German critics as the first work of genuine literary merit to come out of the GDR, it was widely read in the Federal Republic, translated into English, French, and other languages, and filmed by DEFA in 1964 (directed by Konrad Wolf).

The central issue in the book is the national, ideological, and (as Wolf argues) moral choice with which East Germans were confronted, namely whether they were prepared to commit themselves to socialism in the GDR and to renounce the temptation to pursue individual aims in the West. But the focus is on the problems which have to be overcome in building up socialism. Manfred, Rita's middle-class fiancé, represents the generation which had grown up in the Third Reich. His initially sceptical attitude towards socialism deepens to cynicism in the course of the 1950s, and he leaves for the West shortly before the Wall is built. While his action is unequivocally condemned, for the first time in a novel published in the GDR such a figure is presented as deserving the reader's understanding. Rita, younger than Manfred and of simple rural origins, develops through her experience of collective responsibility in a factory towards clear socialist commitment and opts to stay in the GDR. However, the painful consequences for her private happiness are made clear by Wolf: after the Wall has sealed her separation from Manfred, Rita suffers a breakdown and attempts suicide. Her slow recuperation suggests the difficult return to normality of the East German population, and Wolf insists on the right of the people to the whole truth from the authorities in the future.

Although Wolf's loyalty to the state and the Party and the moral earnestness of her dedication to socialism won her novel official approval, her sombre, almost pessimistic presentation of life in the GDR did not escape criticism. Wolf was described as 'an as yet ambivalent author' in a polemical article, and though the charge was not typical in the public debate conducted in the press, radio, and literary journals over subsequent months,[4] the weakness of the 'positive' figures and the absence of clear authorial support for the Party line in discussions on the nature of man or the achievements of socialism were greeted cautiously.

4 See Martin Reso (ed.), *'Der geteilte Himmel' und seine Kritiker: Dokumentation* (Halle, 1965).

Axel Goodbody, Dennis Tate, Ian Wallace

The space devoted to the affairs of the factory where Rita gains industrial experience reveals *Der geteilte Himmel*'s link with what was probably the most ambitious, and potentially the most exciting experiment in GDR cultural policy, the *Bitterfelder Weg*. This attempt to bridge the gap between high and popular culture began with a conference held in April 1959 in the Bitterfeld chemical works by the Mitteldeutscher Verlag, which specialized in publishing young writers. Walter Ulbricht had already launched a stirring call to workers to take writing into their own hands the previous year: 'In politics and the economy the working class is already in control in the GDR. Now it must also storm the heights of culture and take possession of them.' As indicated above, in the *Bitterfelder Weg* a genuine desire to promote workers' culture was coupled awkwardly with the aims of the SED to bring the arts further into line with Party policy and to promote forms of culture which would stimulate material productivity. A policy was formulated urging writers and artists to spend time in factories and on collective farms, to gain the necessary experience with a team of a dozen or so workers (a *Brigade*) to be able to treat themes relevant to their lives, while the workers themselves were to take up their pens and document their everyday struggles and advances in productivity. Amateur art circles were also to be established. Under the slogan 'Reach for your pen, mate, the socialist national culture needs you!' hundreds of circles were formed in factories, offices, and schools, in which amateur writers wrote in what was intended to be the supportively critical environment of the group. Between 1960 and 1964 a series of anthologies were published, the *Brigadetagebuch* or work team diary (a form adapted from the Weimar worker correspondent movement) emerging as a new literary genre incorporating reportage and commentary, satire, portraits of individuals, and poems.

A second Bitterfeld Conference was held in 1964, at which the aims of the movement were modified in line with the principles of the New Economic System of Planning and Management introduced the previous year, placing the emphasis on the depiction of planners and managers rather than factory-floor workers. But by then this potential development of a mass culture as a genuine self-expression of the working class had effectively been stifled by ideological restrictions, unrealistic didactic demands, and inappropriate aesthetic expectations. From the start there had been little attraction for writers to become involved in industry, since their writing was clearly expected to be affirmative regardless of the nature of their actual experience. Christa Wolf and Franz Fühmann (the latter's refreshingly frank and critical reportage *Kabelkran und Blauer Peter*

(1961), researched in a shipyard in Warnemünde, resists any tendency to idealize) formed the exception rather than the rule. Nevertheless, the *Bitterfelder Weg* remains an experiment particularly appropriate to what after all called itself a 'Workers' and Peasants' State', whose achievements invite comparison, in literary terms and as a source of sociological information, with the contemporary novels and stories of the Gruppe 61 and the later reportage and documentary novels of the Werkkreis Literatur der Arbeitswelt in the West.

One of the most significant novels associated with the *Bitterfelder Weg* was Erwin Strittmatter's *Ole Bienkopp* (1963). Strittmatter had been one of the many labourers who had been given a farm of their own in the land reform of 1945 before turning to writing. Despite weaknesses in characterization and structure and a somewhat wooden style, *Ole Bienkopp* is a lively, honest, and humorous account of agricultural life in the 1940s and 1950s. Strittmatter fascinated readers with the psychological complexity of his protagonist, the independent-minded Bienkopp, whose down-to-earth character and optimism gained their sympathy. Initially indifferent to politics, Bienkopp is jolted into action by the murder of his friend, the local Party Secretary, and founds the first agricultural co-operative in the GDR. Caught between conservative farmers bent on resisting change, opportunists, and ignorance, inefficiency, and corruption in the Party, he literally works himself to death rather than compromise and conform. Though Bienkopp's end is due as much to his own stubbornness as to circumstances, it occupied the media for months, with its implication that the state was letting some of its best citizens go by the board.

Parallel to these developments in prose, the early 1960s saw the emergence of a group of poets in their late twenties and early thirties. Their mentors were Georg Maurer, who taught poetry at the Johannes R. Becher Institute for creative writing in Leipzig, Gerhard Wolf (Christa Wolf's husband), who published anthologies and critical essays on contemporary literature, and Stephan Hermlin. Hermlin, who had been responsible for literature at the Academy of the Arts since 1961, organized a reading of unpublished work by young poets in the Academy in December 1962. Among the poems he chose to present were texts by Sarah and Rainer Kirsch, Volker Braun, and Wolf Biermann. Though an article in the press the next day praised Braun's 'creative impatience' and spoke of Biermann as an original young poet who had earned the loudest applause singing to his guitar, the event was later sharply criticized by the Party and Hermlin was relieved of his Academy post.

Braun's poem 'Kommt uns nicht mit Fertigem', one of those read by Hermlin, expresses the feeling of a generation flexing its muscles to take on lingering aspects of Stalinism in the GDR. Biermann, too, insists on the right to find his own way to socialism, in 'Antrittsrede des Sängers', 'Rücksichtslose Schimpferei', and, most directly, in 'An die alten Genossen':

> Seht mich an, Genossen
> Mit euren müden Augen
> Mit euren verhärteten Augen
> Den gütigen
> Seht mich unzufrieden mit der Zeit
> Die ihr mir übergebt.
>
> Ihr sprecht mit alten Worten
> Von den blutigen Siegen unsrer Klasse
> Ihr zeigt mit alten Händen auf das Arsenal
> Der blutigen Schlachten . . .
>
> *Die Gegenwart*, euch
> Süßes Ziel all jener bittren Jahre
> Ist mir der bittre Anfang nur, schreit
> Nach Veränderung. . . .
>
> Drum seid mit meiner Ungeduld
> Nicht ungeduldig, ihr alten Männer; . . .
> *Setzt eurem Werk ein gutes Ende*
> *Indem ihr uns*
> *Den neuen Anfang laßt!*[5]

(Look at me, comrades | With your tired eyes | With your hardened eyes | Your kind eyes | See I am unsatisfied with the times | Which you are passing on to me. | | You speak using old words | Of the bloody victories of our class | You point with old hands at the armoury | Of the bloody battles . . . | | *The present*, for you | The sweet goal of all those bitter years | Is only the bitter beginning for me, calls out | For change. . . . | | Therefore do not be impatient | With my impatience, you old men; . . . *Give your work a good ending | By leaving to us | The new beginning!*)

Biermann, who succeeds in fusing his iconoclastic attacks on authoritarianism, bureaucracy, and militarism with infectious enthusiasm and pathos, making effective use of humour, blunt language, and simple imagery, founded the tradition of *Liedermacher*, or political song writers and performers, in the GDR, to which Gerulf Pannach and Christian Kunert (members of the Klaus-Renft-Kombo, which performed Rhythm and Blues with critical texts in the early 1970s), Bettina Wegner, and Katharina Thalheim belonged. These singers, whose texts touched on sensitive political issues, had a

5 Wolf Biermann, *Nachlaß 1* (Cologne, 1977), 75–6.

significant following in the GDR, though they were often subjected to restrictions and more often than not ended up in the West.

The GDR's conflicting needs for stabilization and innovation in the period after 1961 made for contradictory developments in all spheres of culture in the first half of the decade. The sculptor Fritz Cremer (best known for his moving memorials to the victims of fascism at the former concentration camps Auschwitz, Buchenwald, Mauthausen, and Ravensbrück) mounted an exhibition of paintings by young artists in the Academy of the Arts in September 1961 which included not only establishment painters such as Günther Brendel, Karl-Heinz Jakob, and Konrad Knebel, and other officially accepted artists such as Harald Metzkes and Willi Sitte, whose painting was more innovative, but also an artist who was never to achieve recognition in the GDR, A. R. Penck (pseudonym of Ralf Winkler), later famous for his stick figures and calligraphic art. At the opening of the exhibition viewers were surprised to find Alfred Kurella, a member of the Central Committee and a doctrinaire critic of the arts, taking down off the wall pictures he disapproved of, and the exhibition was attacked in the press because the pictures presented GDR society in too negative a light and aped 'decadent' Western artists. This did not prevent the exhibition and others organized privately by Cremer from providing a stimulus to innovative young artists. The 1960s witnessed far-reaching developments in GDR art, with painters such as Werner Tübke, Willi Sitte, Bernhard Heisig, and Wolfgang Mattheuer increasingly eroding the significance of socialist realism by introducing elements of modernism.

The Eleventh Plenum and Repressive Cultural Policies in the Second Half of the 1960s

Meanwhile, in the literary sphere, the holding up of publication and banning of performance of plays by Heiner Müller, Peter Hacks, and Volker Braun, together with Peter Huchel's removal as editor of *Sinn und Form* in 1962, were reminders of the Party's essentially dirigiste policy, and after Khrushchev's fall in October 1964 there were increasing indications of a drift towards greater ideological control. The tentative democratic reforms initiated since 1963 were terminated abruptly in a reinstatement of bureaucratic centralism at the Eleventh Plenum of the Central Committee of the SED in December 1965. The previous month, in what amounted to a dry run of the arguments and accusations to follow, Ulbricht attributed recent rioting by young people in Leipzig to the corrupting influence

Axel Goodbody, Dennis Tate, Ian Wallace

9. Fritz Cremer, Buchenwald memorial sculpture (1958).
One of the best examples of socialist realist art in the GDR,
Cremer's representation (in bronze) of the liberation of
Buchenwald, achieved by the prisoners themselves in April 1945,
forms part of the memorial which stands outside the former
concentration camp. Each figure in the sculpture is endowed with
symbolical significance in this ideologically orthodox
interpretation of the event. The dominant characters are the
communists: the self-sacrificing victim in the foreground,
followed by the central group of determined comrades whose
courage inspires both the waverers (on the right) and the younger
generation (on the left). Part of its function was thus to
legitimize the GDR's claim to be the rightful heir to this anti-
fascist legacy. The publication of Bruno Apitz's novel *Nackt unter
Wölfen*, which culminates in an account of the same event, was
carefully timed to coincide with the formal opening of the
memorial in September 1958.

of certain GDR television programmes, films, and literary works. At the Plenum itself, writers, film directors, publishers, and cultural officials were disciplined where they were seen to have dwelt on the shortcomings of everyday life in the GDR and expressed doubt as to the Party's ability to lead. Wolf Biermann, only recently returned from a successful tour in the Federal Republic, where he had been hailed as *the* leading young poet of the GDR, was now denounced as a 'watch-dog of reactionary forces' and refused permission to perform in public. The ban was to last for more than ten years. Practically the only person to speak out in protest after Erich Honecker's lengthy report for the Politburo, which repeated and added to Ulbricht's accusations the month before, was Christa Wolf. Stung by the assertion that the Writers' Union had acted as a 'Petöfi Club' (the group of Hungarian intellectuals whose debates paved the way for the October Uprising in 1956), Wolf spoke with considerable personal courage on behalf of GDR writers and film directors, appealing for the clock not to be turned back on the liberal developments of the last few years.

In fact, film and literature were pawns in an ultimately more serious game. The New Economic System had introduced a degree of economic decentralization. In the short run this led to unsettling price increases, and the Eleventh Plenum coincided with an unfavourable trade agreement with the Soviet Union and generally worrying prospects for the economy. The so-called Second Phase of the NES announced at the Plenum (actually the beginning of its dismantling) indicated the Party's decision to reinstate its control over the economy. Ulbricht's cultural clamp-down served to divert public attention from the far-reaching political implications of this move.

As in the literary and economic spheres, the Eleventh Plenum marked a return to restriction in youth policy. The Youth Commission, established in 1963, had organized youth clubs, had contributed to major events such as the all-German youth festival *Deutschlandtreffen der Jugend* in May 1964, the first opportunity for young people from both parts of Germany to meet since the building of the Wall, and had assisted in the setting up of the radio programme 'DT64', which broadcast pop music. The 'Regulation on Programmes of Entertainment and Dance Music' of January 1958 had laid down that in order to protect socialist cultural life from 'manifestations of decadence', at all public events at least 60 per cent of works were to be by GDR or socialist composers, but the 60 : 40 ratio was not always strictly adhered to. None the less, 'Beat' (a term used indiscriminately by the GDR authorities to cover everything from the

Axel Goodbody, Dennis Tate, Ian Wallace

music of British groups to rock 'n' roll, blues, and other more traditional forms of Western pop music) and the associated youth
culture, as expressed in dance forms, dress, and hair-style, were
regarded with suspicion by the Party as atavistic, immoral, and
potentially criminal. The Youth Law of 1964 had allowed dance
styles such as Jive and Twist, but a media campaign against Beat
was launched in the summer of 1965, after attempts to control the
wave of enthusiasm for the Beatles and the Rolling Stones which
had swept over the GDR had failed. In a historic misjudgement,
Ulbricht fulminated at the Eleventh Plenum: 'Are we really dependent on the monotonous Western pop songs and dances? . . . The
unending monotony of their "yeah, yeah, yeah" is both stupefying
and ridiculous.' Well-known groups such as the Butlers in Leipzig
were banned, others forced to conform by adapting their repertoire
and style. The most productive effort to counter Western influence
lay in the *Singebewegung*. This revived a 1950s initiative to promote
anti-fascist songs and folklore in an attempt to foster and raise standards in GDR entertainment culture. Groups were now encouraged
to develop a repertoire including original lyrics, German and international folk-songs, numbers with texts by progressive writers of
previous generations such as Heine and Tucholsky, and American
anti-nuclear and anti-Vietnam protest songs. The Party's efforts to
encourage rock groups to stop copying Western bands and write
their own songs were to lead to the GDR becoming the birthplace
of *Deutschrock* in the late 1960s.

Ulbricht's closing speech at the Plenum singled out for attack
what he called 'the Havemann–Heym–Biermann circle'. The physi-
cist Robert Havemann, a communist since 1932, imprisoned and
condemned to death as a member of the resistance in the Third
Reich, was appointed director of the Kaiser Wilhelm Institute in
West Berlin but dismissed for political reasons in 1950. Subsequently
Professor of Physical Chemistry at the Humboldt University and
long-serving member of the GDR Volkskammer (People's Chamber, or parliament), he was relieved of his academic post and excluded from the Party after delivering a course of political lectures
in 1963/4 (published in the West under the title *Dialektik ohne
Dogma*). Havemann was a proponent of 'third-way' Marxism, an
outspoken critic of dogmatism and bureaucracy, arguing for a combination of economic liberalism and democratic socialism. Because
of the potential popular appeal of his political views and his personal example of integrity and courage, he was denied a public
platform after 1965 and remained an isolated figure. The only period
in which a dissident milieu might have consolidated in the GDR

was that between 1961, when the border to West Germany was closed, and 1976, after which intellectuals were in constant danger of being expelled from the country. The clamp-down in 1965 was a major factor in preventing the formation of dissident groups, and organized opposition comparable to that in Poland or the Czech 'Charter 77' did not emerge until the late 1980s.

The artistic medium most immediately and drastically affected by the restrictions emerging from the Eleventh Plenum was film. Two films were explicitly condemned: *Denk bloß nicht, ich heule* (1965), directed by Frank Vogel, and Kurt Maetzig's *Das Kaninchen bin ich* (1965). By autumn 1966 a further ten DEFA productions had been banned or discontinued. Eight of these 'rabbit'-films as they became known—Horst Sindermann's term of abuse was *Kaninchen-Filme*—were recovered and shown at the Fortieth Berlin Film Festival in 1990. They addressed social problems in the GDR frankly and realistically, though they did not challenge the political system. *Das Kaninchen bin ich* is typical in the sense that the central character, a 19-year-old waitress in a Berlin night-club, encounters misunderstanding and rejection from those approached for help. Everyday life in the GDR is presented from her point of view, and careerism and dishonesty in the legal system are revealed when she has an affair with a lawyer, who, as it turns out, has been responsible for sending her brother to prison.

The fate of the lively film *Spur der Steine* (directed by Frank Beyer, based on Erik Neutsch's industrial novel of 1964) is symptomatic. Filming started in April 1965, editing discussions took place with senior Party members, and the film was accepted by the Film Advisory Committee and billed for nation-wide showing. After the première in June 1966 at the Workers' Cultural Festival in Potsdam it was praised in the press. However, the Politburo decided to release the film for one week's showing only in selected cinemas, and some of these removed it prematurely from their programmes after organized disturbances had forced the interruption of the film screening.

If television emerged from the Eleventh Plenum relatively un-scathed, this was because it was practically insignificant as a channel for social criticism. Broadcasting had begun officially in 1956 with a programme of two hours daily, when there were a mere 70,000 registered TV sets to receive it. By 1965 there were over 3 million. Just as radio listeners in the GDR tended to tune in to Western stations, GDR television effectively broadcast in competition with ARD and ZDF, which could be received (sometimes only with elaborate aerials) in most parts of the GDR except the extreme

Axel Goodbody, Dennis Tate, Ian Wallace

south-east, which consequently became known as the 'valley of the clueless'. Watching Western programmes was officially frowned upon—aerials directed towards the West were removed in an FDJ campaign in the 1960s—but not actually illegal, and became accepted in the 1970s. Many viewers turned to Western programmes for entertainment and to fill in the gaps in GDR news reporting. To counter this, 'Der schwarze Kanal', a long-running half-hour weekly programme, presented extracts from the week's West German television accompanied by a political commentary, but it was too obviously concerned with putting across the Party standpoint to gain credibility with viewers. Perhaps the most critical programme in the 1960s, 'Prisma', dispatched teams to investigate social grievances and political abuses, taking those responsible (including Party officials) to task personally in a way quite untypical of the GDR. Efforts to improve the attractiveness of GDR television after 1971 included increasing the proportion of entertainment programmes, better sports coverage, and the showing of Western feature films.

The Eleventh Plenum was a traumatic experience for Christa Wolf which resulted in months of depression. The bitterness of her disillusionment regarding the possibility of reform is reflected in her next novel, *Nachdenken über Christa T.* (1969). Based on the life of her student friend Christa Tabbert, who died from leukaemia aged 35, this work pursues the search for self-realization present in *Der geteilte Himmel* with a new rigour and aesthetic radicalism. Against a background of GDR society as one in which socialist conviction has given way to calculation, craftiness, and conformity, the central figure's terminal illness acquires symbolic character. *Christa T.* is a passionate statement of the individual's right to self-determination, of the indispensable nature of imagination and individual conscience, and amounts to a diatribe against the role model of dynamic but ultimately unthinking activity: 'The new world of people without imagination gives me the shudders. Factual people. Up-and-doing people.'[6]

Christa Wolf's novel played a central role in furthering three important trends in GDR prose: greater realism in the presentation of society, increased subjectivity, and aesthetic modernism. 'Subjective authenticity', a term coined by Wolf in an interview of 1973 with Hans Kaufmann, precludes the omniscient narrator and presumes personal narrators unreliable, situating the truth rather in a network of varying viewpoints. The complex narrative structure and modernist techniques introduced tentatively in *Der geteilte Himmel* (conceived in part as a response to Uwe Johnson's *Mutmaßungen über Jakob*), such as interior monologue and symbolic presentation

6 Quoted from *The Quest for Christa T.*, trans. Christopher Middleton (London, 1982), 51.

of Rita's situation in dreams, had by now become acceptable in the GDR so long as they were not used to suggest alienation or present social reality as incomprehensible. *Christa T.*, in which the traditional story-line is replaced by a montage of memories and essayistic reflection, broadly following a chronological development, but using leitmotifs and associative links between different periods in the protagonist's life, demanded a new degree of sophistication from the GDR reader.

The only other uncompromisingly modernist work written in these years was Fritz Rudolf Fries's *Der Weg nach Oobliadooh* (1966). This cosmopolitan and irreverent picaresque novel recounts the amorous and musical, literary and political adventures of two young jazz fans in the GDR in the late 1950s, modern-day equivalents of Don Quixote and Sancho Panza. Tired of life in Leipzig, they leave for West Berlin, which they associate with the dreamland of Oobliadooh from Dizzy Gillespie's song. However, they take a dislike to the Allied reception camp and return, homesick, telling the GDR authorities a cock-and-bull story of having been kidnapped, in order to obtain replacements for the identity cards they had surrendered in the West. The narrative breaks off some months later with them drying out in a sanatorium after an alcoholic binge. The plot is reminiscent of Johnson's and Wolf's novels on the division of Germany, but Fries has none of their ideological seriousness, and the satirical asides on GDR society show provocative disregard for official political sensibilities and expectations of the writer.

In the climate after the Eleventh Plenum *Der Weg nach Oobliadooh* stood no chance of publication in the GDR. (It appeared in the West in 1966.) Christa Wolf's special position as author of *Der geteilte Himmel* and as Candidate Member of the Central Committee of the SED enabled her to succeed where Fries had failed. However, she encountered numerous obstacles between completion of the manuscript of *Christa T.* in March 1967 and release of the book in late spring 1969.[7] Her refusal to come out in unequivocal support of the GDR's participation in the invasion of Czechoslovakia in August 1968 almost put an end to prospects of publication. Wolf was subject to sustained attack at the Writers' Congress in May 1969, and when the book eventually appeared (in a ridiculously small edition), the authorities suppressed discussion of it and refused to reprint.

The second half of the 1960s was a bleak period for writers and artists in the GDR. Christa Wolf was, as we now know, recruited by the *Stasi* in March 1959 and provided them with information irregularly (and apparently largely unwittingly) over the next three

7 See Angela Drescher (ed.), *Dokumentation zu Christa Wolf 'Nachdenken über Christa T.'* (Hamburg and Zurich, 1991).

Axel Goodbody, Dennis Tate, Ian Wallace

and a half years, only to be dropped when it became clear that she was not prepared to denounce colleagues. From the Eleventh Plenum on she was herself regarded by the *Stasi* with increasing suspicion, and in 1968 she and her husband Gerhard became the focus of an intensive observation operation. They were to remain under surveillance until the end of the GDR.

No Taboos?

The deepening gloom in the cultural sphere in the late 1960s was, however, to be alleviated by political change at the beginning of the new decade. The Brandt/Scheel *Ostpolitik* launched in 1969, which led in 1972 to the Basic Treaty between the two German states, gave the GDR international recognition, prestige, and stability, as well as facilitating the adoption of more liberal domestic policies. Erich Honecker, who replaced Ulbricht as First Secretary of the SED in 1971, intensified the production of consumer goods, which led to a rise in living standards in the following years, and introduced a broader concept of culture, extending state support to expressions of mass and entertainment culture, leisure activities, and sports. In sport more than any other sphere the GDR's consolidation of national identity and growing self-confidence became apparent. Gifted sportsmen and -women were promoted as national heroes to stimulate pride in the country, from the cyclist Täve Schur in the 1950s (portrayed as 'Achim' in Uwe Johnson's novel *Das dritte Buch über Achim* (1961)) to the ice-skater Katarina Witt in the 1980s. (Sigmund Jähn similarly became a popular hero in 1978 as the first GDR cosmonaut and, incidentally, the first German from either state to travel in space.) Representatives from the GDR had brought home Olympic medals since 1956, but in an all-German team. It was only at the Munich Olympics in 1972 that a GDR national team could appear with their flag and national anthem. The economic success of the GDR in the late 1960s and early 1970s, when figures seemed to indicate that it had climbed into the top ten industrial nations (a position undermined by the energy crisis in 1973 and subsequent modernization in the Western economies), was paralleled by remarkable sporting achievements. In 1974 the GDR beat its arch-rival West Germany in a preliminary round of the football World Cup (although its team was later eliminated and West Germany went on to win the cup), and throughout the 1970s and 1980s it ranked consistently only behind the USA and the USSR in terms of Olympic medals.

The relatively liberal climate from 1971 on permitted an explosion in the number of discotheques and rock groups, and though this led to official restrictions in 1973, when things were deemed to have got out of hand, there was no longer any serious attempt to exclude Western influence in music or dress. Indeed, one of the first liberalizing measures taken in 1971 was to ensure an adequate supply of jeans in the shops. In art the trend towards a pluralism of styles continued with collage, abstraction, Pop and Action Art becoming accepted by the end of the decade, when GDR works began to arouse interest at international exhibitions. Although a number of important artists (Gerhard Altenbourg, Peter Graf, Carlfriedrich Claus) were not members of the Artists' Union and had an uneasy relationship with the state, pictures such as Wolfgang Mattheuer's *Die Ausgezeichnete* (1974) reveal the change which had taken place in official expectations.

Honecker called for a frank, objective, creative debate on literary matters, a broadening of the topics which writers and artists could treat beyond those obviously useful to socialist society, and new forms. His 'no taboos' speech at the Central Committee Plenum in December 1971 was followed by a rich literary harvest. However, this was at least in part because what had been suppressed in the second half of the 1960s was now able to re-emerge. Ulrich Plenzdorf's *Die neuen Leiden des jungen W.*, Volker Braun's *Das ungezwungne Leben Kasts*, and Christa Wolf's essay volume *Lesen und Schreiben* were all published now, but had been conceived earlier. Hitherto banned plays of Braun's and Müller's could now be staged. On the other hand, the limitations of the new licence granted to the arts were apparent in the continued exclusion of Biermann from cultural life. Stefan Heym's *König David Bericht*, a thinly disguised satire on GDR bureaucracy and opportunistic historiography, was published in 1973, but not *Der Tag X*, his moderately critical account of the events of June 1953 (which appeared in revised form in the West in 1974 under the title *5 Tage im Juni*).

The continued failure of GDR journalism and the media to investigate social grievances meant it again fell to literature to stimulate public debate and challenge traditional attitudes on social and political issues. Among the most prominent of these issues in the early 1970s were the role of women and the alienation of the individual in socialism. In *Christa T.* Wolf had described the process of self-discovery in gender-neutral terms as the 'attempt to be oneself'. It is none the less no accident that Christa T. is a woman. The book stands half-way between *Der geteilte Himmel*, the most questionable aspect of which was arguably Rita's development from

10. Wolfgang Mattheuer, *Die Ausgezeichnete* (1974).

Die Ausgezeichnete reflects the liberalization of cultural policy after Honecker's replacement of Ulbricht as First Secretary of the SED in 1971. Mattheuer caused a stir in the second half of the 1960s with powerful, ambiguous symbolic canvases which often featured decaying industry and environmental damage. Here he portrays an elderly woman receiving an award (perhaps for years of loyal service), sitting alone behind a table bare but for a bunch of limp tulips, motionless, her eyes closed in exhaustion. The complete absence of heroic idealization of the worker in this figure, who appears to be patiently enduring the carefully chosen, but routine words of praise of some speaker, contrasts sharply with the rose-tinted view of workers and their leisure occupations in the paintings of Walter Womacka, representative artist of the 1960s and a favourite of both Ulbricht and Honecker.

female spontaneity and sensitivity to an acceptance of her allotted place in a male-dominated world, and later feminist works such as *Kassandra* (1983). *Christa T.* includes a number of critical passages on women's role in socialist society and integrates fragments of diary and letters, traditionally regarded as forms of women's writing.

A work more directly concerned with the paradoxes and contradictions of women's lives in the GDR was Irmtraud Morgner's *Leben und Abenteuer der Trobadora Beatriz nach Zeugnissen ihrer Spielfrau Laura* (1974). Morgner's novel marked the emergence of a women's literature in the GDR which set out to combat male repression, armed with the weapons of fantasy and myth. The main narrative strand in this montage of short prose chapters tells the story of the medieval Provençal woman troubadour Beatriz de Dia, who awakens (in an ironic echo of the fairy-tale of Sleeping Beauty) after having chosen to sleep an enchanted sleep of 800 years in the hope that when she wakes up it will be in a world of equality between men and women. After devastating initial experiences she is attracted to the GDR as the 'promised land' in which exploitation of women has been (theoretically) abolished together with capitalist exploitation of the worker. This allows Morgner to present a satirical panorama of manifestations of male dominance in the GDR.

In the 1960s women's emancipation had been regarded in the GDR primarily as a matter of participation in the production process on an equal footing with men. To facilitate the employment of women, a series of laws were passed addressing inequalities between men and women. The Family Statute Book of 1965 declared all matters of communal life (care and education of children, housework, etc.) as joint rights and duties of both partners and confirmed women's right to work. In 1968 laws provided for special training programmes and positive discrimination, and by the 1970s provision for maternity leave and child care in crèches and nurseries was among the best in the world. This led to an ever increasing percentage of women going out to work: by 1984 50 per cent of the workforce was female, compared with 39 per cent in West Germany. (Measures taken in the 1970s to stem the declining birth-rate which accompanied this rise in women's employment included the extension of maternity leave—from 1984 a full year on full pay!—and special incentives to have more than one child.)

By the end of the 1960s the relative legal, social, and economic position of GDR women was undoubtedly better than that of most women in the West. Abortion on demand in the first twelve weeks of pregnancy was introduced in 1972, an event greeted in *Trobadora Beatriz* as a significant step towards the end of male control over female sexuality. Women's expectations of life were changing. However, equality in the key areas of work and household duties was not achieved in practice. Women continued to work in predominantly lower-paid and lower-status jobs. In 1978 some 66 per cent of teachers were women, but only 20 per cent of heads of schools. Though there were more women in the Volkskammer than in the West German Bundestag or the House of Commons, women also remained poorly represented in high Party office. Moreover, old attitudes about family life died hard. Surveys showed that women still did 80 per cent of household chores and that the average married man enjoyed 40 per cent more leisure time than his wife.

In Morgner's novel the *trobadora* befriends the single parent Laura Salman in Berlin. Laura, a partly autobiographical figure, suffers from her dual roles as mother and working woman. The story of her life gives the lie to official notions of equality between the sexes and is a moving indictment of the treatment of women in the GDR in the 1950s and 1960s. When she becomes pregnant as a student, Laura experiences only chauvinist attitudes among doctors and aborts the child herself, endangering her life in the process. Marriage to a dull but safe young man enables her to complete her studies and take up a post at university. However, when she has a baby, she ends up doing all the housework and looking after the child (who spends the day in a crèche), with no help from her husband. Her work suffers and she is unable to devote sufficient time to her daughter, who dies of pneumonia barely a year old. Laura resigns from her academic post and takes a job as a train-driver. She later divorces her husband, who has not shown understanding of her problems at any stage.

Trobadora Beatriz, whose publication signalled the emergence of feminist consciousness in GDR culture, was widely discussed both in the GDR and in West Germany (where it appeared in 1976). The major debate of these years was, however, the one sparked off by Plenzdorf's *Die neuen Leiden des jungen W.*, whose impact has been compared with that of Zola's *J'accuse* in late nineteenth-century France or Lawrence's *Lady Chatterley's Lover* in the UK in the 1960s. Plenzdorf's story (originally a DEFA film scenario, which had been rejected in 1969) was published in *Sinn und Form* in spring 1972. A theatre adaptation followed in the summer which was so successful (particularly with teenage audiences) that it was eventually staged in twenty GDR theatres. This tale of the problems in the way of a young man's integration in GDR society attracted a positive response in academic circles (a series of contributions on the work appeared in *Sinn und Form*), but equally met with disgusted condemnation from conservative quarters. Plenzdorf was accused of providing a negative model who would mislead young people, of encouraging individualism, and of desecrating the cultural heritage. While loyal to the fundamentals of socialism, his book (published in 1973) champions authenticity and spontaneity in a world of petty-bourgeois respectability and lack of imagination. In his perspective on life in the GDR, Plenzdorf is indebted as much to Salinger's *Catcher in the Rye* as to Goethe's *Die Leiden des jungen Werthers*. The 17-year-old Edgar Wibeau, who starts off as a model apprentice, rebels against pressure to conform in a society where people apparently only live to work, leaves home for Berlin, and becomes a virtual drop-out, living in a building due for demolition. Eager to impress the *Brigade* of decorators he has joined with the invention of a new paint-spray machine, he dies in an explosion of his equipment. Though this is probably an accident rather than a repetition of Werther's suicide, Plenzdorf is careful to leave open the question of responsibility for Edgar's death. He broke new ground with his convincing presentation of young people, their needs, and their subculture. The Americanisms, vulgarisms, hyperbole, and paradoxes of his 'jeans' language, reflecting GDR teenage group identity, are skilfully contrasted with extracts from *Werther*, the standard language of adults, and the ideological distortions of the truth in the official media. Despite indirect censure from Honecker himself in 1973, the stage version of *Die neuen Leiden* was not banned and the book was repeatedly reprinted. Plenzdorf's work also met with considerable success outside the GDR. It became a bestseller in the Federal Republic and was soon included in West German school curricula and filmed for television, while the theatre version was staged in some sixty theatres in West Germany, Austria, and Switzerland, and the book was translated into fifteen languages.

Die neuen Leiden struck a chord with a generation of young readers. A survey in *Forum* revealed 40 per cent of young people shared Edgar's frustration with a monolithic, authoritarian society, and over 60 per cent could imagine having him as a friend. Edgar's experience at school, and in particular a scene in which he vividly expresses his disgust with the task he has been set in a practical work experience class (laboriously filing down a piece of metal to size by hand, where the job could be done by machine in seconds) exemplify the development of education in the GDR. Access to industry for young people, a central aspect of the polytechnical principle aiming at a harmonious unity between practical and academic knowledge, had been introduced to the curriculum as *Werkunterricht*

Axel Goodbody, Dennis Tate, Ian Wallace

in the Education Acts of 1959 and 1965. However, by the 1970s a tendency to overqualification of the work-force in relation to the jobs actually performed at work and the unattractiveness of many jobs dictated a limitation of the numbers going on to higher education and a restrictive pattern of vocational guidance and selection, frustrating individual career aspirations. In the comprehensive *Polytechnische Oberschule*, which virtually all children attended, with its rigid curricula, stress on learning achievement, and almost military discipline in teacher-centred classes, increasing numbers became resigned, apathetic, or even dropped out like Edgar Wibeau. Community activities with the FDJ or other organizations were similarly regarded by the younger generation merely as irksome demands they had to comply with in order to get a job or a place at university.

A work which went deeper than Plenzdorf in its analysis of GDR society and confronted such issues as the infringement of the individual's rights and press censorship was Volker Braun's *Unvollendete Geschichte*, published (again in *Sinn und Form*) in 1975. The central theme of this story is the state's lack of trust in its citizens and the alienation of the individual prevalent in GDR society. Braun presents the political and ideological situation as one resulting in widespread insecurity and mistrust. The young electrician Frank is falsely suspected of intending to defect to the West, and his girlfriend Karin, daughter of a Party functionary, is warned not to have anything to do with him, but not told why. Karin, brought up to identify with the authorities both intellectually and emotionally, has her eyes opened by a suicide attempt of Frank's. She falls out with her parents and, after encountering the gulf between social reality and harmonious gloss working in a newspaper office, loses her job.

These works on the situation of young people in the GDR illustrate a changing relationship with the German cultural heritage. The idealized conception of Weimar Classicism as the embodiment of the principles of humanity, freedom, and democracy, to be read and passed down untrammelled to future generations as a bulwark against the decadence of modern writing, was increasingly challenged by writers such as Braun and Müller, who appropriated and reinterpreted the classics, using them to shed light on contemporary reality. In the course of the 1970s, writers such as Christa and Gerhard Wolf, Stephan Hermlin, Franz Fühmann, Günter Kunert, Günter de Bruyn, Volker Braun, and Heinz Czechowski began in any case to identify (in prose and poetic portrait, essay, and radio play) not with the harmonious balance and optimistic vision of the classics, but rather with an alternative canon of outsiders in literary tradition, Hölderlin, Kleist, and Karoline von Günderrode, Jean Paul, Büchner, and the Romantics. The integrity of these nonconformists in a post-revolutionary situation of social stagnation and alienation was seen as relevant in the 1970s, while the importance they attached to the imagination and their open-ended forms provided welcome alternative models at a time when guidance from an omniscient narrator, rational argument, and predictable endings were expected.

In *Die neuen Leiden* Plenzdorf chooses the young *Sturm und Drang* Goethe rather than the wise classicist as his point of reference. Edgar Wibeau finds a copy of *Werther* on the lavatory, where he uses the cover and the editor's introduction (!) before discovering his affinity with passages on the self-realization of the individual in society. *Unvollendete Geschichte* is both richer and more subtle in its literary references, alluding to a series of works on alienation, social conflict, love, and suicide which include Büchner's *Lenz*, *Der geteilte Himmel*, and *Die neuen Leiden*. We find Karin reading *Die neuen Leiden*, but dismissing Plenzdorf's dichotomy of individual and society as superficial, where what is needed is a work reflecting the complexity of political reality and the rifts within the individual. Büchner reminiscences play a central role in Braun's story, serving to suggest the social situation in the GDR is no better than in the presocialist era (though Braun hints things can change for the better) and to associate Karin's situation with one of German literature's best-known accounts of personal anguish and shattered identity.

By the mid-1970s, then, GDR writers and artists had established an appreciable degree of autonomy from the state and were achieving increasing recognition outside the country with their treatment of themes of international relevance, such as the alienation of the individual and women's struggle to achieve equality in a male-dominated society. However, there were also indications of the impending return to repressive state policies. Ever wary of destabilization, the authorities felt Braun's *Unvollendete Geschichte* had gone too far: unsold copies of the issue of *Sinn und Form* the story appeared in were withdrawn and, though a West German book edition came out in 1977, the work was not to be available again in the GDR until 1988.

The Biermann Affair and the 'Lex Heym'

In the autumn of 1976 the more liberal cultural policy introduced by Honecker in 1971 was abruptly abandoned. Despite the great hopes originally invested in it, there had been clear signs virtually from its inception that the policy was not leading to the high degree of harmonious co-operation which the Party had hoped for from writers and artists. Indeed, the latter seemed far more interested in removing any restrictions on their creative work than in adopting what an increasingly impatient Party saw as a responsible (self-limiting) approach in the interests of socialism. In October 1976 the Party therefore decided to act swiftly when Reiner Kunze published in the West a collection of short prose texts, *Die wunderbaren Jahre*, which were highly critical of everyday life in the GDR. Kunze's membership of the Writers' Union of the GDR was rescinded. Three weeks later, probably encouraged by the muted reaction to this event, the Party expatriated perhaps the GDR's most celebrated dissident, Wolf Biermann, while he was in the Federal Republic on an officially approved concert tour. The SED's leadership had evidently decided to confront and sideline those who were intent on challenging its authority in the cultural sphere.

Reaction to Biermann's expatriation was swift and unprecedented, however. Twelve leading writers published in the Western press a letter of protest which, while moderate in tone and careful not to identify itself with Biermann's every word and deed, clearly called on the Party to reconsider its decision. They were joined in the days that followed by a succession of noted GDR intellectuals, so that the Party suddenly and unexpectedly found itself under attack across a broad front. Paradoxically, this development was a tribute to the greater (but not unlimited) freedoms introduced by Honecker's new cultural policy, since a revolt of this kind, however muted, would have been unimaginable under the much more fierce regime of Ulbricht.

Such considerations had little appeal to startled Party leaders, however. They interpreted the mildly worded letter of protest not as an opportunity to reach a compromise (which would have been in the declared spirit of Honecker's cultural policy) but as an open challenge to their authority. Their response was therefore inevitably a determined attempt to regain the initiative. *Neues Deutschland* published declarations of support from a wide spectrum of the Party faithful. Pressure was applied to signatories of the protest letter, persuading some to withdraw or qualify their support. Those who were Party members were subjected to the Party's disciplinary procedures, suffering varying degrees of punishment, from an official reprimand to withdrawal of membership.

Although the Party in this way regained control of the situation, it is equally clear that it forfeited any confidence in the idea that

11. Wolf Biermann and friends (1965).

The poet and singer Wolf Biermann moved as a 17-year-old from the Federal Republic to the GDR in 1953. His uncompromisingly critical songs and poetry led in 1965 to a long period of exclusion from the GDR's officially promoted culture, but he continued to write, perform, and even record his songs at his home in East Berlin's Chausseestraße. His apartment became the meeting-place for critical writers and thinkers, and the photograph shows him there (with guitar) together with friends, including the poets Helga Novak and Sarah Kirsch, the prominent dissident Robert Havemann (clasped hands), the poet and essayist Rainer Kirsch, the poet Kurt Bartsch, and the novelist Fritz Rudolf Fries (front). In 1976 Biermann was expatriated during an officially approved concert tour in the Federal Republic. The unusual degree of unrest which this produced among GDR intellectuals led many to leave the GDR for the West, among them Sarah Kirsch and Kurt Bartsch.

complete trust and unity of purpose was henceforth possible between Party and cultural intelligentsia. The Biermann affair also showed that solidarity among critical, reform-minded members of the intelligentsia could be achieved, although, unlike in other Eastern-bloc states such as Poland and Czechoslovakia, this proved disappointingly short-lived and in fact hardly outlasted the 1970s.

Much more durable than such solidarity was the polarizing split which from now on divided those writers who had rallied to the Party and those who had supported Biermann's cause. This became apparent in 1979 when it was the turn of Stefan Heym to incur the wrath of the Party. Heym had been a source of considerable irritation for a number of years despite his partial rehabilitation at the beginning of the Honecker era. He added to the anger provoked by the appearance of *5 Tage im Juni* in 1974 by publishing his novel *Collin* in the West in 1979. *Collin* is by no means his best work of fiction but one in which he deals boldly with the theme of the corrupting influence of Stalinism in the GDR of the 1950s. The Party concluded that punishment was called for and, in the dispute which followed, public support for Heym was limited to a relatively small but courageous group of colleagues while numerous fellow writers attacked him, sometimes in very crude terms.

On this occasion the Party's approach was not to expatriate the offender but to criminalize him. Like Robert Havemann, Heym had published in the West without first soliciting the written permission of the GDR's Copyright Office, as was officially required. Instead of prosecuting both Heym and Havemann on these grounds, however, it was decided to charge them with having in effect stolen from the public purse by paying no taxes on their hard-currency earnings from sales abroad. Heym was subsequently fined 9,000 marks and Havemann 10,000 marks. But both refused to be silenced, with Heym declaring that what was at issue was not the violation of currency laws but freedom of speech. This was underpinned in an open letter of support from eight colleagues, who insisted that criminal proceedings were not an appropriate way of dealing with problems in cultural policy.

Once again the Party's attempt to bully rebellious members of its cultural intelligentsia into toeing the line had succeeded only in emphasizing the depth of division. Its next ploy was to stage-manage the expulsion from the Berlin section of the Writers' Union of Heym himself, three colleagues who had spoken up for him, and those of the letter's signatories who were members of the section, on the grounds that they had defamed the Party's cultural policy. The fact that approximately sixty dissenting votes were registered and that a number of respected writers protested in letters addressed to the Union leadership showed that, yet again, strong-arm tactics had failed to have the desired effect.

A much more threatening development came on 28 June 1979 when the Volkskammer rubber-stamped changes to the Criminal Code making it illegal to disseminate abroad any materials which might 'damage the interests of the German Democratic Republic' and raising the maximum sentence for being part of an illegal organization or 'any other group of persons' from two to five years. This 'Lex Heym' came into force on 1 August 1979 and, although the Party continued in other ways to hold out an olive branch to those it threatened, there is no doubt that what seemed the very real prospect of eventual imprisonment led many, like the novelist Jurek Becker, to leave for the West when they saw an opportunity to do so.

The consistent attacks on Heym's literary reputation and moral integrity contrasted sharply with the Party's parallel efforts to promote Harry Thürk's novel *Der Gaukler* (1978). This is a thinly disguised attack on Alexander Solzhenitsyn and, through him, on all critical intellectuals in the Soviet Union and in the socialist world generally. With all the subtlety of a sledgehammer the novel smashes home the message that the central character, the writer Wetrow, is a vain, unprincipled, and philandering egotist with absolutely no redeeming features. In the view of Wadja Shagin, a writer of children's stories who functions as the novel's positive hero, Wetrow is moreover a fascist. He is interested in only two things: taking his revenge on Soviet society for the years he spent in prison and then in a labour camp, and making as much hard currency as possible out of his reputation in the West before leaving the Soviet Union for a life of easy luxury. Thürk works hard to suggest that his thirst for revenge is unreasonable, contrasting it unfavourably with the manly resolve of Gorbatschewski and Shagin. Both had suffered a similar injustice but had come to regard it as only an aberration in the inexorable progress of Soviet society. Wetrow owes his fame entirely to the CIA, who see him as a useful means of discrediting the Soviet Union. Presenting him as a worthy successor to Tolstoy and Dostoevsky and as a heroic dissident determined to reveal the terrible truth about the Soviets, they even arrange for him to receive the Nobel Prize for Literature.

The fact that a work of such poor literary quality, and one which in intellectual terms represented a descent to the level of the most primitive Cold War tracts of the 1950s, should in effect become the Party's standard-bearer in the late 1970s was a sure indication of how cultural policy had gone into reverse gear. In view of the novel's attack on the CIA's manipulation of public opinion, there was an unpleasant irony in the way GDR newspapers orchestrated a campaign of praise for the novel in 1979. In *Sonntag*, Heym's work was described as 'anti-communist trash' and *Der Gaukler*, in contrast, as a 'valid analysis of social mechanisms'. In the newspaper *BZ am Abend* Heym and the other writers expelled from the Writers' Union were dismissed as 'little Wetrows'. It came as no surprise when Thürk (twice a winner of the National Prize for Literature) was given, jointly with Dieter Noll, the annual literary award sponsored by the Free German Federation of Trade Unions.

Clearly alarmed at these developments, an increasingly large segment of the cultural intelligentsia chose to take advantage of the Party's decision to allow critical intellectuals simply to leave the country. The preferred method was now not expatriation but the granting of a visa to move West. Striving to give the impression that this was part of a carefully considered policy rather than a somewhat panic-stricken attempt to restore peace on the cultural front by exporting the crisis, the Party ensured that the conditions attaching to a visa varied considerably from case to case. The calculation may have been that, once their visas had expired, some at least of those who had left would wish to return to the GDR, perhaps even chastened by their experience of life in the West. In the event, no one chose this course of action. The loss of over a hundred of the GDR's leading creative artists, the majority of them writers, represented a serious undermining of the country's cultural energies from which it was never fully to recover. This was exacerbated by the fact that even many of those who eventually decided to stay frequently agonized long and hard in private about the wisdom of doing so. Perhaps just as seriously, the stream of those leaving the GDR represented a corresponding enrichment of the cultural environment in the Federal Republic, a possibility which the Party certainly underestimated in arriving at its new policy.

There is no doubt, however, that most of those who moved to the Federal Republic initially found it much more difficult to adapt to their new surroundings than they may have originally anticipated. They found in the West a new set of often disorienting assumptions about their role in society, for instance, or about the requirements of a free market economy. Any idea that a shared language and history would make the process of integration a short one and the interruption of creative work equally brief proved generally unfounded. Hans Joachim Schädlich, for instance, confidently predicted not long after his move to the Federal Republic that this would not affect his work in any material sense. In fact, he underwent a severe creative crisis which reduced him to virtual silence for five years. Similarly, the novelist Karl-Heinz Jakobs quickly discovered that the adjective *deutsch* was not sufficient to promote an unproblematic identification with the Federal Republic and to offset the long years of socialization in the GDR. Even Erich Loest, who adapted more readily than most and rapidly established himself as a significant presence on the West German cultural scene, fretted that the experience of the GDR on which his work as a novelist continued to feed would become increasingly remote and, ultimately, unproductive. Although the émigrés were, in time, remarkably successful in meeting the challenge posed by their move to the West, the difficulties that they encountered in doing so demonstrated that, notwithstanding the history of struggle between politicians and cultural intelligentsia in the GDR, the latter had developed and internalized a sufficiently distinctive cultural identity to make it difficult for them to continue their creative work under the very different conditions prevailing in the West.

One consequence of the exodus to the Federal Republic was that, despite the Party's policy of *Abgrenzung* (demarcation) with its insistence on the GDR's complete sovereignty and separate identity, it became difficult to define precisely what was meant by a 'literature of the GDR'. Were those writers who had left on temporary visas still part of that literature? Or was residence in the GDR a prerequisite? If so, how were those to be regarded who, whether by choice or because they saw no other option, regularly published in the West and used the Western media, thereby undermining the policy of demarcation? The Party's strong-arm tactics in the late 1970s, which the Politburo's cultural spokesman, Kurt Hager, had described at the time as no more than a storm to clear the air, had in fact produced not clarity but only conflict and confusion. Moreover, the years that followed gave the impression of an inconsistent strategy, with some critical works being banned while others were approved without explanation. Not even the conclusion of a Cultural Treaty with the Federal Republic in 1986, with its clear implication that the political division of Germany was now recognized in the very cultural sphere which had hitherto been regarded as the best testimony to Germany's continuing unity as a single *Kulturnation*, could restore the self-confidence and sense of direction to a policy increasingly uncertain of its bearings.

The cultural crisis which overwhelmed the GDR after Biermann's expatriation had clearly demonstrated the failure of cultural policy and the final breakdown of the belief that Party and cultural practitioners could ever be equal partners in pursuit of shared goals. It revealed too that, despite all its attempts to cut itself off from the Western world and particularly from West Germany—most notably by building the Berlin Wall in 1961 and by its policy of demarcation in the 1970s—the GDR could not divorce itself from global problems such as the threat to the environment and the danger of war.

The Threat to Peace and the Environment

NATO's plan to station Cruise and Pershing II missiles in Western Europe and the Soviet Union's deployment of SS 20 missiles within the Eastern bloc brought both German states to the sobering realization that they faced virtually certain and total destruction if a nuclear war in Europe, even of the allegedly 'limited' kind commonly referred to by American strategists, should ever break out. In the GDR this gave added impetus to the autonomous, unofficial peace movement which had begun to emerge in the late 1970s, not least as a response to the state's introduction of Defence (i.e. Military) Studies into the school curriculum. Its main concerns were all sensitive issues within the GDR's peace debate: the search for an acceptable alternative to military service and for ways of reducing the militarization of daily life, and the protection of human rights and civil liberties. Finding in the Protestant churches the space which it needed in order to function (the church was the only organization in the GDR which was not under the direct control of the Party), the movement attracted many young people with its appeal to turn 'swords into ploughshares'.

The same concern for peace led the writers' unions in both the Federal Republic and the GDR to take the uniquely important step in August 1981 of jointly sponsoring an 'Appeal of European Writers' warning against the consequences of nuclear war for Europe and calling for progressive disarmament. Such unusual collaboration was rapidly followed in December 1981 by a conference in East Berlin, initiated by Stephan Hermlin and surprisingly approved by the GDR authorities, at which representatives of the cultural intelligentsia of both states and other guests from each side of the Iron Curtain engaged in debate on the threat of war, with the specific purpose of building up trust and mutual understanding and thereby promoting the interests of peace. Despite the evident ideological differences between the two sides (which were articulated even more sharply in a follow-up conference in West Berlin sixteen months later), the meeting did show that dialogue was possible when the participants followed Hermlin's request to temper frankness with moderation in their exchanges.

Even more significantly, the conference highlighted the elements of a shared culture which the GDR was otherwise concerned to play down. Apart from the not unimportant fact that the conference language was German, all the participants were linked by a very German conviction that, as members of the cultural intelligentsia, they had a particular responsibility to guide the states in which they lived towards a better future. Moreover, the idea that all Germans bear a special responsibility to ensure that war never again begins on German soil was expressed by representatives of both sides.

In her contribution to the debate Christa Wolf relativized even further any difference between culture in the GDR and that in the Federal Republic by including both in a single Western culture which, having brought the world to the brink of nuclear destruction, perhaps did not even deserve to survive. An industrial civilization, she averred, which obeyed only the laws of economic efficiency and growth whatever the human cost could only be called sick. In addition to responding as a European to this crisis, Wolf also responded as a German (rather than an East German), asking whether Hitler had now returned to haunt the European civilization which he had once set out to destroy. But she also spoke as a woman, rejecting a civilization which she saw exclusively as the work of men, a civilization which, ever since the destruction of the matriarchy in Minoan culture and its replacement three thousand years ago by an aggressive patriarchy, had quite deliberately excluded women from positions of power and influence. In renouncing this cultural tradition and seeking an alternative rooted in more feminine qualities (she referred to friendliness, graciousness, trust, spontaneity, dignity, and poetry, for example), Wolf was clearly also turning her back on the culture and cultural policy of the GDR.

These ideas are developed more fully in Wolf's *Kassandra* (1983), which, when taken together with the four lectures which accompanied it, constitutes a brilliant and complex investigation of the cultural processes which in Wolf's view have pushed Western, patriarchal civilization ever closer to self-annihilation. While it is true that allusions to the GDR can be identified (the figure of Eumelos, for example, may be seen as a reference to the *Stasi* and the insidious growth of its power), *Kassandra* clearly transcends any parochial concern with GDR-specific issues, focusing instead on what

Wolf sees as the crucial events which gave birth to the cultural crisis threatening to overwhelm all Western civilization. Like Irmtraud Morgner's *Amanda* (1983), to which in its major concerns and even in some matters of detail it bears an often striking resemblance, *Kassandra* suggests that it is women, with their particular gifts of insight and empathy, who can show how the disaster towards which the blind and unfeeling rationalism of men is inexorably pushing humankind can be averted. Wolf was typical of her generation of GDR writers in insisting that a clear (socialist) alternative did exist to the suicidal destructiveness of patriarchal culture, an alternative represented here by the utopian, non-hierarchical community of (mainly) women who share a life of friendship and self-discovery in the caves of Mount Ida.

As regards environmental criticism, this was articulated by GDR writers as early as the 1960s, but it was in the 1980s that such criticism became particularly pronounced. Over this period there was evidence—in, for example, Jurij Brezan's *Krabat oder Die Verwandlung der Welt* (1976) and Franz Fühmann's *Saiäns-Fiktschen* (1981)—of an increasing erosion of confidence in technology and science as the instruments of social progress and growing concern about the impersonal, alienating rationalism which was seen as the guiding force behind them. Without explicitly denying the real and potential achievements of science and technology, writers called for a radical reassessment of the ways in which their innovations had been arrived at and applied, usually without sufficient consideration of their social and human consequences. In an acrimonious exchange of views with Wilhelm Girnus, the editor of *Sinn und Form*, the poet Günter Kunert insisted as early as 1979 on an essential symmetry between ecological developments in the East and those in the West, but the idea that the devastating ecological effects of an increasingly industrialized civilization did not stop at the border between East and West proved a bitter pill to swallow for those who clung to the idea that, in socialism, technology and science served only the cause of progress.[8]

The same observation could be made of the publication by *Neue deutsche Literatur* in April 1981 of an extract from Hanns Cibulka's *Swantow*. This work, which takes the form of a diary produced by the fictional writer Andreas Flemming during an extended stay on the Baltic island of Rügen, highlights the evidence he finds there of the existential threat facing man towards the close of the twentieth century and leads him to ask whether mankind is now staring into the abyss.[9] The extract in *Neue deutsche Literatur* contained critical passages on atomic energy and on the potential ecological dangers

8 'Anläßlich Ritsos. Ein Briefwechsel zwischen Günter Kunert und Wilhelm Girnus', *Sinn und Form*, 4 (1979), 850–64.
9 Hanns Cibulka, *Swantow* (Halle and Leipzig, 1982), 107.

of oil and coal, provoking the Deputy Minister of Culture, Klaus Höpcke, to a defensive reaction. These passages were removed from the book version (1982), which also showed a shift in focus from criticism of conditions specific to the GDR towards a global view of environmental problems, with the USA predictably serving as a particular target of criticism.

Despite this shift of focus from the local to the global, a significant number of works did concentrate on the destructive effects in the GDR itself of an industrialized civilization. The mining of lignite, a particularly dirty form of fuel on which the GDR relied for most of its energy needs and as a source of chemical products, led to the brutal disfigurement of large parts of the southern GDR. Monika Maron's largely autobiographical novel *Flugasche* (published in 1981, but only in the West) presents a harrowing picture both of the terrible air pollution which the burning of lignite produces in the industrial town of B. (clearly intended as a reference to Bitterfeld) and of the way in which such information is suppressed. The destructive impact of lignite-mining on the daily life of the Sorbs living in the Lausitz area was a particularly sensitive issue. The GDR had always made much of its commitment to respecting and promoting the rights of the Sorbs, the only significant minority (Slavic) group within the borders of the GDR. Now Sorbian writers drew attention to the threat to their culture represented, for instance, by the death of a village which fell victim to the encroaching mines (Kito Lorenc's poem 'Dorfbegräbnis') or by a plan to flood an entire valley in the Lausitz regardless of the impact on the daily lives of ordinary people (Jurij Koch, *Der Kirschbaum*, 1984).

Environmental disfigurement of another kind was an unfortunate consequence of Honecker's otherwise laudable promise to build enough homes to ensure that every family had its own accommodation. The prefabricated, largely anonymous housing which rapidly sprang up across the country, often with inadequate social amenities and with little thought given to the need for proper landscaping, tended to destroy established communities without creating the conditions required to allow new ones to develop. Given the prestige which the Party had invested in its building programme, this was an issue which writers approached with caution. Benno Pludra was one who did so in his story for children, *Insel der Schwäne* (1980). Focusing on the life of a teenager, Stefan, who is torn away from an idyllic existence in the country when his family moves to a new estate in Berlin, it had to be reworked several times in order to take the sting out of its criticism before it could be published. This *Kinderbuch*—a genre which was much favoured by official policy and undoubtedly represents one of its major achievements in the cultural field—was in any case likely to have minimal public impact, given its intended readership.

The same could not be said of the film script which Ulrich Plenzdorf based on Pludra's story. This was initially found acceptable by the authorities, but after the film had been made under the direction of Hermann Zschoche a list of twenty required changes was produced. As a result, when the film was finally released in 1982, parts of it had been rendered unintelligible. Nevertheless, it is evident that Plenzdorf focuses more sharply than Pludra on the social and environmental problems produced by a massive housing estate. Unlike Pludra, he locates this not near the centre but at the very edge of Berlin, thus emphasizing that it is an organic part neither of the city nor of the rural surroundings from which it is being torn. It is effectively still a building site across which children must make their way to and from school. Although Stefan is aware of the creature comforts offered by modern housing, he clearly feels out of place on the fourteenth floor of a twenty-storey skyscraper in which people can live together without getting to know each other. There is no play area for the children and, when one is at last built, it is simply an unimaginative concrete rectangle which takes no account of their own ideas and wishes. Inevitably, their spontaneous protest, during which they effectively occupy the play area by racing back and forth across the still wet concrete and covering it with their playthings, proves exciting but short-lived.

Stefan's conflict with the youth known as Windjacke, whose bullying aggression appears completely unmotivated—probably as a result of the cuts imposed on the film—is of a kind found in any society, but Plenzdorf suggests it is made more dangerous by this environment. The final scene takes the form of a confrontation between the two boys in the unfinished shell of a new building, which culminates in Stefan struggling to pull Windjacke up by the finger-tips from the edge of the lift-shaft to which he is clinging for his life. Characteristically, the censors insisted on a positive ending showing Stefan rescuing Windjacke, but Plenzdorf's script has the film frozen and cut precisely at the point where Stefan's struggle is at its most intense and the outcome is still open.

The Limits of Female Emancipation

Solo Sunny, completed in 1979 and the last film made by the GDR's most celebrated director, Konrad Wolf, presented an equally challenging picture of everyday reality in the GDR when it had its première in 1980. Within three months it had been seen by over half a million people across the country. A lively public debate took place in newspapers and journals of a kind not seen since the appearance of Plenzdorf's *Neue Leiden des jungen W.* The film also enjoyed great success at West Berlin's annual film festival in 1980, with Renate Krössner being awarded the prize as best actress for her performance as Sunny, a young singer striving against the odds both to achieve public recognition and to overcome the loneliness and sense of rejection she has felt since childhood. Despite her many setbacks and disappointments, culminating in a failed suicide attempt, she refuses to give up the struggle, thereby encouraging the belief that it is possible for ordinary people to dream of breaking free of everyday constraints and achieving a unique personal identity.

Wolf's film was only one of a number of works of this period to have a woman's life as its central focus. Indeed, the number of women writers publishing on similar themes increased significantly from the second half of the 1970s. By the mid-1980s it was estimated that women made up a quarter of all GDR writers. This development bore testimony to the increased self-confidence of women in a society which placed the emancipation of women high on the political agenda and which Irmtraud Morgner, as already noted, had consequently celebrated in *Trobadora Beatriz* as 'the promised land'. But, paradoxically, it was also above all evidence of women's dissatisfaction with the limitations of such emancipation. A particular landmark was the appearance in 1977 of Maxie Wander's *Guten Morgen, du Schöne*, a volume containing nineteen interviews with a variety of GDR women. Breaking with the clichés of official discourse, it presents a remarkably frank picture of the women's experiences, including a strong sense of dissatisfaction with many aspects of life and not least their relationships with men. Although based on a series of recorded interviews, the book is more than a documentary, for Wander edits, rearranges, and, in part, even invents her texts in order to heighten their impact. Like this volume, the fictional works of the period show a perceptible shift in interest from the officially promoted view of women's role (especially in the world of work) to an exploration of particular episodes from women's daily experience—as mothers, housewives, lovers, or victims of the 'double bind' of combining family life with the demands of a profession. They have a strongly autobiographical, even confessional flavour, depicting women who are suffering stress or unhappiness and who are therefore generally very different from

Axel Goodbody, Dennis Tate, Ian Wallace

the energetic, purposeful heroines favoured by socialist realism. There is an undercurrent of frustration and even despair in this which is underpinned by the striking use of fantastic elements to show, for example, that only a woman who can live two separate lives simultaneously or one who can transform herself into a man (a theme explored by a number of writers) is able to achieve self-fulfilment while satisfying society's demands.

Morgner was not alone in seeing such fantastic elements as an essential ingredient of a specifically female mode of writing, reflecting women's receptiveness to non-rational, imaginative thinking. Another was a preference for short texts, whether published separately or, as already discussed in the classic case of Morgner's *Trobadora Beatriz*, as a carefully constructed montage. Again, this preference is seen to derive from the writers' specifically female experience, where domestic and other duties usually mean that extended periods of uninterrupted time are simply not available for the production of longer texts. In *Kein Ort. Nirgends* (1979), *Kassandra*, and the essays and lectures which accompanied them, Christa Wolf made a major contribution both to a reconstruction of the history of women writers and to a critique of female modes of writing. Like Morgner, she sees these as grounded in the fact that women experience a very different reality from men, the reality of the ruled rather than that of the rulers. At the same time, she rejects the kind of militant feminism which regards every man as an enemy, seeing a like-minded ally in anyone, regardless of gender, who seeks an autonomous alternative to the dominant culture.

Modernism and the Challenge to Official Culture

As already noted, the SED's espousal of socialist realism as the indispensable foundation on which socialist culture had to be erected led it to view modernism as a dangerous rival which (after a brief honeymoon period immediately following the war) had to be vigorously opposed at every turn. Learning from the example of the Soviet Union, where modernism had been outlawed in the 1930s, the GDR's Stalinists had no wish to grant to the aesthetic sphere the autonomy which it enjoyed in the West. Since all art had to be instrumentalized for political purposes, it was in a sense not so much modernism itself as *any* form of independent artistic activity which had to be ruled out of court.

Particular charges against modernist art were that it was élitist and esoteric and therefore excluded the masses, that it was nihilistic because it offered no positive historical and social perspective, that it was formalistic in that it merely dressed up old themes in new forms, and that it was cosmopolitan since it ignored or negated national traditions in the cultural sphere. Such terminology seemed to offer no grounds for hope that modernism might eventually be absorbed into acceptable cultural practice.

However, a long process of emancipation from the stranglehold of socialist realism, stretching back (as we have seen) to the work of Uwe Johnson and marked by the appearance of Christa Wolf's novel *Nachdenken über Christa T.* in 1968 and by the publication in the 1970s and 1980s of such modernist authors as Benn, Joyce, Beckett, Eliot, Rimbaud, and Valéry, eventually led the SED to admit openly in 1985 that the unqualified rejection of modernism as 'decadent' or 'formalistic' had proved unproductive and ill-advised. A major element in this volte-face was undoubtedly the fact that, from the late 1960s, the GDR's leading writers simply began to learn from and use the literary strategies of modernism. Stephan Hermlin and Franz Fühmann consistently argued for a positive reception of modernism in the GDR, and work in this spirit by the GDR's literary scholars could also not be overlooked. Honecker's initially more liberal cultural policy, together with the adoption of a less restricted understanding of what could legitimately count as part of the socialist cultural heritage, encouraged this development, as did the increasing contacts with the West which détente and diplomatic recognition of the GDR had brought about.

The GDR's cultural functionaries may also have realized that the real danger to their brand of socialism did not after all come from a literature moulded in the modernist image (which could be expected to appeal to a limited public) but from relatively straightforward, even conventional texts with mass appeal such as those by Biermann, Kunze, and Heym. This may in part explain why they seemed prepared in the 1980s largely to ignore attempts by young artists and writers in the Prenzlauer Berg district of East Berlin to turn their back on establishment culture and, indeed, on the mass public which that culture sought to engage. The experience of these artists and writers was restricted to life in the GDR and other Eastern-bloc states, so that their encounter with modernism in its various guises became for them an adventure, a way of breaking out of the restrictive environment within which they felt trapped and to which they felt no commitment of a political or ideological nature. The counter-culture which they consciously nourished coincided with and in many ways mirrored the alternative punk culture which made its appearance in the late 1970s, most

Axel Goodbody, Dennis Tate, Ian Wallace

visibly among the disaffected younger generation living in the run-down housing of Prenzlauer Berg. The arrival of punk was accompanied in the 1980s by a dramatic increase in the number of amateur rock and pop groups and discos across the GDR. Once officially rejected and suppressed as a particularly pernicious and corrupting Western influence, such popular music continued to face obstacles from officialdom but nevertheless became, as in the West, a factor of increasing importance in the daily lives of young people.

In pursuit of creative autonomy, members of this counter-culture were prepared to accept menial jobs which paid just enough to keep body and soul together and prevented the authorities from harassing them as work-shy or anti-social elements. Generally shunning any link with official cultural institutions such as the Writers' Union and publishing houses, they disseminated their work in home-made, illegal journals of a technically primitive kind. Wishing to avoid the usual fate of the nonconformist artist whose work remains unseen or unread because it is denied an official outlet, they organized readings and exhibitions in their own rooms or in church buildings, producing audio- and video-cassette recordings of these and similar events. In all these endeavours their aim was to establish their own autonomous public sphere at the edges of GDR society. Turning away from official cultural discourse and the desiccated rhetoric of socialist 'progress' and 'utopia', they experimented with language, colour, and abstraction, and reflected on their practice in theoretical writings of considerable sophistication.

The break with official culture had never been total, however. Poems by Uwe Kolbe and Frank-Wolf Matthies appeared in the journal *Sinn und Form* as early as 1976, while Kolbe's first volume of poetry, *Hineingeboren*, was published by Aufbau in 1980. But such concessions by the authorities remained insignificant in scale until the late 1980s, when Aufbau began to publish the work of the Prenzlauer Berg poets in a series entitled *Außer der Reihe*. What would have seemed a major policy breakthrough only a few years earlier was now seen as merely a belated attempt to swim with the tide of inevitable change and in this sense was of no more than symbolic value.

A similar development was apparent in the fine arts, where the late 1970s and the 1980s gave birth to a vigorous 'alternative' art scene in the GDR. This was characterized by a rich plurality of styles and by a determined struggle for acceptance of abstract art and of multimedia action art of a kind which cannot be fixed in a frame or set on a pedestal. Voices began to be heard in favour of seeing abstract art as a complement rather than a rival to socialist realism, and the Eighth Art Exhibition in Dresden (1977–8), at which over a million visitors were able to view approximately 3,000 exhibits, included for the first time a few abstract works such as had effectively been banned hitherto. However, the old guard continued to resist innovation so effectively that many artists chose to leave the GDR for the West. A notable loss in August 1980 was A. R. Penck, who was then followed by other young painters, especially after the First Leipzig Autumn Salon in November 1984. This was the first independently organized and self-financed exhibition to be held in an 'official' building in the GDR and was the brainchild of young creative artists committed to multimedia action art. By working in some secrecy and even misleading the authorities where necessary, they managed to trick their way into putting on the exhibition in an attempt to force public recognition of their (in GDR terms) unconventional work. The Party vowed the event would never be repeated, however, so that the exodus of much of the GDR's best creative talent to the West continued.

The Final Crisis

The artists who remained were not all blind to the GDR's growing crisis. Mattheuer's remarkable painting *Geh' aus deinem Kasten* (1985), for instance, is dominated by the figure of a naked man fleeing from a dark, windowless room which has burst into flames, leaving the observer with the sense that the need to escape from impending catastrophe is urgent. But the authorities were much more interested in the kind of officially commissioned, monumental art represented by Werner Tübke's enormous fresco-like painting on the revolt of 1525 in Germany. Housed in its own circular building in Bad Frankenhausen, the painting is 123 metres long and 14 metres high. It was completed in 1987 after over ten years' work and officially unveiled in 1989 to mark the 500th anniversary of Thomas Müntzer's birth. In Berlin, Lew Kerbel's gigantic statue of Ernst Thälmann in Berlin's newly opened Thälmann Park (1986) and Ludwig Engelhardt's uninspired Marx-Engels Monument behind the Palast der Republik (1986) were expressions of the conventional socialist realism favoured by the authorities. They were part, too, of a conscious attempt to refurbish East Berlin by 1987 in time for the 750th anniversary celebrations of the founding of Berlin. Although such reconstruction was overdue, the cost was crippling and caused some resentment in disadvantaged areas outside of the capital. There was also no hiding the fact that the relatively cheap,

Axel Goodbody, Dennis Tate, Ian Wallace

mass-produced blocks of flats which had mushroomed across the country during the Honecker era were more representative of the country's recent achievements in the field of architecture than the reconstruction of, say, the Nikolaiviertel or the Schauspielhaus in the capital.

The final years of the GDR were dominated by the impact of Gorbachev's accession to power in the Soviet Union in 1985. His policy of 'new thinking', embodied in the twin concepts of *glasnost* and *perestroika*, alarmed the SED and gave courage to those in the cultural sphere who favoured radical change. At the Tenth Writers' Congress held in November 1987 in Berlin, Christoph Hein and Günter de Bruyn called for the abolition of the system of censorship which, despite previous official denials that it even existed, had seriously hampered the work of writers and other creative artists throughout the history of the GDR. As the country slid into ever deeper crisis and the calls for reform grew louder, there were demands from rock musicians and others for an opening of the media to genuine dialogue. The leading role taken by the cultural intelligentsia in preparing the ground for and then pushing through radical change gave rise to the impression that they spoke and acted for the GDR population as a whole. The mass demonstration which writers and artists organized on Berlin's Alexanderplatz on 4 November 1989 and which was attended by an estimated half a million people appeared to confirm this view. The conviction seemed widespread that, once the chains of the old Stalinist system had been thrown off, true socialism and a genuinely socialist culture would at last flourish.

The rapid transformation of the demonstration's characteristic slogan 'We are the people' into 'We are one people'—the switch, that is, from the call for a non-Stalinist form of democracy to a demand for unification with West Germany—revealed that this was an illusion. With the GDR's demise in October 1990 and its absorption by the Federal Republic, GDR culture as a distinctive entity officially ceased to exist, leaving behind an often impassioned argument about what, if anything, it would pass on as a permanent bequest to the new Germany. The sense of loss felt by critical intellectuals who had pushed for reform in the hope of realizing a truly democratic, socialist culture only to see their country taken over by Western capitalism is memorably expressed in Volker Braun's poem 'Das Eigentum':[10]

> Da bin ich noch: mein Land geht in den Westen.
> KRIEG DEN HÜTTEN FRIEDE DEN PALÄSTEN.

10 Volker Braun, 'Das Eigentum', in *Die Zickzackbrücke: Ein Abrißkalender* (Halle, 1992), 84.

Ich selber habe ihm den Tritt versetzt.
Es wirft sich weg und seine magre Zierde.
Dem Winter folgt der Sommer der Begierde.
Und ich kann *bleiben wo der Pfeffer wächst.*
Und unverständlich wird mein ganzer Text
Was ich niemals besaß wird mir entrissen.
Was ich nicht lebte, werd ich ewig missen.
Die Hoffnung lag im Weg wie eine Falle.
Mein Eigentum, jetzt habt ihrs auf der Kralle.
Wann sag ich wieder *mein* und meine alle.

(Here I am still: my country has gone west. | WAR ON THE HUTS PEACE TO
THE PALACES. | I was the one who kicked it down the road. | It's thrown
itself and its meagre charms away. | Winter is followed by the summer of
desire. | And I can *go and take a running jump.* | And my whole text has
become incomprehensible | What I never possessed is torn from me. |
What I never lived I shall forever miss. | Hope lay like a trap in my path. |
What I owned you now have in your claws. | When shall I again say *mine*
and mean us all?)

Braun captures the bitter disappointment of those who had invested
their hopes and energies in the idea of achieving a distinctive socialist culture in the GDR. It was a disappointment made all the more
bitter by incontrovertible evidence that prominent members of the
cultural intelligentsia had for years worked as agents of the *Stasi*.
The accusation made in some quarters, however, that this was
tantamount to the moral disqualification of the GDR's entire cultural intelligentsia does not stand up to dispassionate examination.
Nevertheless, as more sources of previously inaccessible information become available, there will clearly be a continuing need to
reassess and refine our understanding of a cultural experiment which
failed.

Suggested Further Reading

Agde, Günter (ed.), *Kahlschlag: Das 11. Plenum des ZK der SED 1965* (Berlin,
1991).
A collection of essays and documents, including excerpts from the SED's
secret tape-recording of the Central Committee meeting, which heralded one of the worst periods of repression in GDR cultural history.
Böthig, Peter, and **Michael, Klaus**, (eds.), *MachtSpiele: Literatur und Staats-
sicherheit* (Leipzig, 1993).
This volume focuses on the shocking extent of the *Stasi*'s infiltration of
the supposedly autonomous and alternative (i.e. non-official) cultural
scene in the Prenzlauer Berg district of East Berlin. Excellent choice of
documents with a helpful introduction by the editors.

Damus, Martin, *Malerei in der DDR: Funktionen der bildenden Kunst im Realen Sozialismus* (Reinbek, 1991).

A comprehensive and up-to-date account of the development of painting in the GDR, with over a hundred illustrations and a useful index.

Drescher, Angela (ed.), *Dokumentation zu Christa Wolfs 'Nachdenken über Christa T.'* (Hamburg and Zurich, 1991).

An exemplary case-study of the behind-the-scenes struggle which preceded the publication of one of the GDR's most important works of literature, and of the controversy which followed.

Emmerich, Wolfgang, *Kleine Literaturgeschichte der DDR: Erweiterte Ausgabe* (Frankfurt am Main, 1989).

Although written before the *Wende*, this is the standard guide to the history of GDR literature. Indispensable.

Gaskill, Howard, McPherson, Karin, and **Barker, Andrew** (eds.), *Neue Ansichten: The Reception of Romanticism in the Literature of the GDR* (Amsterdam, 1990).

A collection of informative essays on the struggle to redefine the GDR's cultural heritage in the 1970s and 1980s.

Gerber, Margy (ed.), *Studies in GDR Culture and Society* (Lanham and New York, 1981–) [annual volumes].

Since the late 1970s the annual conference on the GDR which takes place in New Hampshire (USA) has been a major forum for scholars of all specialisms engaged in research on the GDR. These volumes make available some of the most valuable papers presented at the conferences.

Gersch, Wolfgang, 'Film in der DDR: Die verlorene Alternative', in Wolfgang Jacobsen, Anton Kaes, and Hans Helmut Prinzler (eds.), *Geschichte des deutschen Films* (Stuttgart, 1993), 323–64.

A concise history of cinema in the GDR, helpfully illustrated with stills from important films and statistics indicating their public impact.

Glaeßner, Gert-Joachim, and **Wallace, Ian** (eds.), *The German Revolution of 1989: Causes and Consequences* (Oxford and New York, 1992).

A wide-ranging analysis of the events of 1989 and their aftermath.

Goodbody, Axel, and **Tate, Dennis** (eds.), *Geist und Macht: Writers and the State in the GDR* (Amsterdam, 1992).

A reassessment of the relationship between writers and politics in the GDR, and of the achievements of GDR literature. Contains suggestions for a new theoretical framework for the study of GDR literature as well as contributions on individual writers.

Hutchinson, Peter, *Stefan Heym: The Perpetual Dissident* (Cambridge, 1992).

A perceptive and readable study of the work and influence of the GDR's 'first, one of its most popular, and certainly one of its most successful dissidents', the writer Stefan Heym.

Jäger, Manfred, *Kultur und Politik in der DDR 1945–1990* (Cologne, 1995).

A reliable overview of the relationship between culture and politics which provides a broad view of culture in the GDR context.

Janka, Walter, *Schwierigkeiten mit der Wahrheit* (Reinbek, 1989).

A fascinating memoir by a prominent victim of the show-trials of 1957 which casts some of the leading figures of GDR cultural life in a critical light, notably Anna Seghers and Johannes R. Becher.

Kane, Martin (ed.), *Socialism and the Literary Imagination: Essays on East German Writers* (Oxford and New York, 1991).

A volume of essays on major GDR authors which argues the case for their international significance in terms of the literary quality of their writing.

Klier, Freya, *Lüg Vaterland. Erziehung in der DDR* (Munich, 1990).

A critical personal reckoning with the GDR's education system by a dissident theatre director expatriated in 1988.

Kuhn, Anna, *Christa Wolf's Utopian Vision: From Marxism to Feminism* (Cambridge, 1988).

The standard work in English on Wolf's development over the lifetime of the GDR towards self-awareness as a feminist author in a wider international context.

Labroisse, Gerd, and **Wallace, Ian** (eds.), *DDR-Schriftsteller sprechen in der Zeit* (Amsterdam, 1991).

This volume contains interviews with twenty-five GDR writers, which were conducted between 1976 and 1991.

Leitner, Olaf, *Rockszene DDR: Aspekte einer Massenkultur im Sozialismus* (Reinbek, 1983).

A lively account of popular music in the GDR from the 1960s to the early 1980s. Still the most comprehensive book available on the subject. Has a good reference section.

Reid, James H., *Writing without Taboos: The New East German Literature* (Oxford and New York, 1990).

An authoritative study of the literature of the Honecker era. The focus is on prose fiction against the background of cultural policy, examining developments in narrative technique and analysing central thematic complexes.

Riedel, Heide (ed.), *'Mit uns zieht die neue Zeit . . .'—40 Jahre DDR-Medien* (Berlin, 1993).

A volume of essays and panel discussions on many aspects of the neglected field of radio and television in the GDR.

Tate, Dennis, *Franz Fühmann: Innovation and Authenticity* (Amsterdam, 1995).

A study of the career of an author of equal stature to Heym and Wolf whose achievements have so far been less widely appreciated outside the GDR.

Wallace, Ian (ed.), *GDR (German) Monitor* (Dundee, Loughborough, and Amsterdam, 1979–).

Founded in 1979, the journal *GDR Monitor* was renamed *German Monitor* in 1991 as a consequence of German unification. The principal focus is on GDR literature, but a number of issues have also been devoted to other themes, such as the Church in the GDR (no. 28) and Women and the 'Wende' (no. 31).

Walther, Joachim (ed.), *Protokoll eines Tribunals: Die Ausschlüsse aus dem DDR-Schriftstellerverband 1979* (Reinbek, 1991).

A documentation of the infamous meeting of the Berlin branch of the Writers' Union at which nine critical writers, including Stefan Heym, were deprived of their membership.

Wichner, Ernst, and **Wiesner, Herbert** (eds.), *Zensur in der DDR: Geschichte, Praxis und 'Ästhetik' der Behinderung der Literatur* (Berlin, 1991).

Published in conjunction with an exhibition on literary censorship in the GDR. Contains fascinating examples of texts and material from private and public archives documenting the practice of censorship from the 1950s through to 1989.

Williams, Arthur, Parkes, Stuart, and **Smith, Roland** (eds.), *German Literature at a Time of Change 1989–1990: German Unity and German Identity in Literary Perspective* (Berne, Frankfurt am Main, and New York, 1991). Focuses on the interplay of unity and divergence in the relationship between East and West German literatures, with further contributions on writers' responses to the *Wende* and reflections on the social role of the writer.

Williams, Rhys, Parker, Stephen, and **Riordan, Colin** (eds.), *German Writers and the Cold War* (Manchester and New York, 1992). A comparative volume casting fresh light on the period of post-1945 history which has suffered most from ideological distortion on both sides.

5

Reconstruction and Integration: The Culture of West German Stabilization 1945 to 1968

KEITH BULLIVANT

C. JANE RICE

1945: Germany's Zero Hour?

THE capitulation of the German High Command on 8 May 1945 brought to an end (in Europe) a war that had wrought destruction on a scale unique in human history. While the First World War had been an essentially stationary battlefield conflict, the extensive and intensive use of bombing by the Allies, especially in the later stages, together with the highly mobile nature of the armed conflict on the ground, had devastated German cities; initial estimates calculated it would take fifty years to rebuild the country. Some 3.7 million German soldiers were killed or missing, there had been almost as many civilian casualties, between 6 and 7 million soldiers were prisoners of war, 12 million Germans had been displaced, there were 3 million homeless and 2 million war-wounded; over 2 million homes had been destroyed. The extreme privation of the first year, when most Germans survived on around 900 calories a day, was slowly eased somewhat by the arrival during 1946 of millions of *Carepakete* from the United States, each containing 40,000 calories in the form of canned meats, fats, preserves, and other staple foods. The rigours of life in the ruined cities, exacerbated by the vast numbers of refugees who had fled from the east, produced appalling living conditions of unimaginable proportions: only with the aid of the cinema, through Roberto Rossellini's *Germany Year Zero* (1948) and Rainer Werner Fassbinder's *Die Ehe der Maria Braun*

(1978), can we get some idea of life in Germany in the immediate aftermath of the war.

The victorious Allies quickly imposed military administration on Germany, having already confirmed at the Yalta Conference (4–11 February 1945) decisions taken as early as 1943 (in Tehran) for dealing with the post-war situation: on 5 June the country was divided into four zones of occupation, with Berlin being given special status and administered by all four powers. These early actions, together with important political decisions soon taken by the Allies, were to have lasting consequences for Germany. On 7 July 1945 the Saarland was made an autonomous French protectorate (not becoming part of the Federal Republic until 1957). The Potsdam Conference (17 July–2 August 1945) placed Königsberg and the northern part of East Prussia under the control of the USSR, the rest of Germany east of the line formed by the Rivers Oder and Neisse under Polish administration (in both cases until a peace treaty with Germany was signed). It was agreed in addition that Germans could be expelled from Poland, Hungary, and Czechoslovakia, but not from the eastern territories. Arrangements were made for the war-crimes trial in Nuremberg of the leading surviving Nazis (beginning on 20 November 1945 and concluding on 1 October 1946) and in March 1946 laws were passed requiring the 'denazification' of those born before 1919. Closely linked to these measures and stemming from the Allied concept of the 'collective guilt' of the Germans for the Nazi atrocities was the programme of 're-education' for the country, particularly in the Western zones. Various schemes were also put forward to ensure that Germany would never again endanger world peace: the US Minister of Agriculture Morgenthau had even proposed the total de-industrialization of the country and, although this idea in its totality was soon dropped, hundreds of industrial concerns were stripped of their plant, while others were split up into smaller units. In a speech of 29 April 1946 US Secretary of State James Byrnes was arguing that, despite these various measures, it would be necessary to keep Germany completely demilitarized and occupied by Allied forces for the next quarter of a century. Against this background the rise of West Germany to economic prosperity, together with its complete political and military integration into the alliance of Western nations, was truly astounding.

The efforts of the Western Allies to re-educate the Germans into an inherently democratic people and the encouragement of socialist and communist developments that went on in the Soviet Zone constituted but one aspect of the sense of a fundamental need for

Keith Bullivant and C. Jane Rice

change in Germany after 1945: it was also a topic of intense debate amongst Germans themselves. A most important forum for such debate was the periodical *Der Ruf*, founded in April 1946 by Hans Werner Richter and Alfred Andersch, to which they and others who had been in American POW camps contributed. There, as Richter's first novel *Die Geschlagenen* (1949) brought out, they had first been confronted with the inflexibility of American notions of German collective guilt; their opposition to this, and consequent criticism of the policies of the occupying forces, was to lead to the periodical being banned by the US military government after just twelve months. *Der Ruf* was viewed by Andersch as the mouthpiece of the 'young generation' (understood as those aged between 18 and 35), who were marked by 'their non-responsibility for Hitler'.[1] Rejecting 'the alleged incorrigibility of the German people', Andersch stressed that each German should deal individually with his or her guilt over the past; the 'transformation' thereby attained would form the starting-point of national renewal. Here Andersch wrote in terms akin to those of the philosopher Karl Jaspers, whose *Die Schuldfrage* (1946) also stressed the necessity of an individual, rather than collective, coming to terms with guilt. Hans Werner Richter, describing life in the Western zones in 1945 as being one 'behind the Chinese Wall of collective guilt', called the effectiveness of Allied policies radically into question, arguing that the imposition of the role of penitent on the Germans in their collective captivity was hardly likely to induce an appreciation of the advantages of democracy (although it has to be pointed out that an important part of his thinking was the crucial role allocated to people like himself as members of a regenerative élite). Again and again the stifling constraints of a 'military dictatorship' designed to bring about a democratic consciousness were attacked in *Der Ruf*.

This was not the only fundamental disagreement between Germans in the Western zones and the occupying forces. The essential thrust of the 'educational' policies of the Western Allies, led by the Americans, was to demonstrate the virtues of the 'American Way of Life', that is, of a political democracy identified as coterminous 'with a capitalist market economy based on the private ownership of the means of production' (Otto Brenner). Among Germans, on the other hand, there was a broadly based rejection of capitalism; not only was it seen as having produced National Socialism, but humankind had now reached a stage in its development, argued Alfred Andersch, when 'the private ownership of the means of production seems just as absurd as slavery did 2,000 years ago'.[2] This 'democratic socialism' or 'socialist humanism', as Andersch

1 Alfred Andersch, 'Das junge Europa formt sein Gesicht' (15 August 1946). Reprinted in Hans Schwab-Felisch (ed.), *Der Ruf: Eine deutsche Nachkriegszeitschrift* (Munich, 1962), 25.
2 Ibid. 22.

called this 'third way' between the extremes of capitalism and communism, commanded considerable support: in December 1946 a plebiscite in Hesse produced a 72 per cent majority in favour of nationalizing key industries, whereupon the American military government declared the election invalid, and in 1947 the Ahlen Programme of the conservative Christian Democratic Party (CDU) provided what can now only be seen as staggering support for socio-economic change radically different from that foreseen by the Allies. Concluding that 'the capitalist system has not been appropriate to the national and social interests of the German people', it went on to maintain that the 'goal of a new social and economic order can no longer be the profit and power motive of capitalism; it has to be, rather, the welfare of the people'.[3] Through consistent blocking in the British and American zones of efforts by trade unions to work towards these ends and, above all, through the shifts in the policy of the Western Allies, such ideas were rapidly thwarted. In 1966 Karl Jaspers published a controversial examination of the state, *Wohin treibt die Bundesrepublik?*, in which he maintained that it was entirely a creation of the Western Allies, while as late as 1977 Heinrich Böll spoke bitterly of Germany being 'raped' at this time by 'the decision in favour of such a crassly capitalist economic system'.[4] After the failure in December 1947 at the conference of foreign ministers of the former wartime Allies to agree on the future of Germany, the European Recovery (i.e. Marshall) Plan was enacted in the West in April 1948; the Russians countered with the Berlin Blockade, which lasted 322 days (until 12 May 1949), during which time the city was supplied by the now famous 'air bridge'. The introduction of the Marshall Plan was followed on 20 May 1948 by the Currency Reform: each person received forty of the new Deutschmarks and, two months later, a further twenty. Swiftly the West German economy started moving and the success of the Currency Reform in turn determined the political path of the zones of Western occupation. On 23 May 1949 the *Grundgesetz* (Basic Law) was proclaimed as the constitution of the new Federal Republic of Germany and in September of that year Theodor Heuss was elected the state's first President, with Konrad Adenauer as Chancellor. With the matching in the East of each of these stages of the establishment of the state, the division of Germany, inevitable since 1947, was constitutionally sealed by October 1949.

Konrad Adenauer, whose Economics Minister, Ludwig Erhard, was to become the embodiment of the West German 'Economic Miracle', claimed that his election victory of 1949 was a clear rejection by the electorate of a socialist economy. The success of a

3 Quoted in Karl D. Bracher, *Nach 25 Jahren: Eine Deutschland-Bilanz* (Munich, 1970), 85.
4 Karl Jaspers, *Wohin treibt die Bundesrepublik?* (Munich, 1966), 175; Heinrich Böll, *Querschnitte* (Cologne, 1977), 141.

Keith Bullivant and C. Jane Rice

free market economy was to be, he maintained, the ultimate basis of all social policies pursued by his governing coalition of the CDU and its Bavarian sister party, the Christian Social Union (CSU). The coming to power of Adenauer, from 1917 to 1933 Lord Mayor of Cologne, was widely felt in those circles that had hoped for radical change to represent 'a phase of social restoration'. While Adenauer himself had undoubtedly kept his distance from the Nazis, his lack of concern about facing up to the problems of the National Socialist past was demonstrated by the inclusion in his government of former Party members such as Hans Globke, who had formulated the Nuremberg Race Laws. Adenauer's insensitivity to the issue was compounded by the decision taken as early as August 1947 by General Lucius Clay, commander of US occupying forces, that the denazification process was to end by 31 March 1948, which had the effect of leaving many major offenders unpunished (their more complex cases having initially been put on one side) and enabling them quickly to resume positions of power; as late as 1968 both the Federal President, Heinrich Lübke, and the Chancellor, Kurt Georg Kiesinger, were former members of the Nazi Party, as were many prominent men in various important walks of life. Not a single West German obituary made mention in 1977 of the fact that Hanns-Martin Schleyer, chairman of the (West) German Confederation of Employers and victim of a terrorist attack, had made his fortune as the Nazi commander of a slave-labour factory in the eastern territories. Critical intellectuals were quick to realize that their 'dream of the regeneration of Germany [was] at an end', as Alfred Kantorowicz ruefully noted in October 1949.[5] Looking back in 1966, Karl Jaspers argued that the Western Allies had 'de facto forced upon us those old politicians who were responsible for the Germans submitting to the Hitler regime'; as a result, he claimed, 'the moral and political obligation' Germans had in 1945 to create a completely new state had still not been met.[6]

Women and Post-War Reconstruction

Photographs and newsreels of *Trümmerfrauen*, crews of women clearing away mountains of rubble in bombed-out cities all over Germany, have provided one of the best-known portrayals of German women at the close of the war. While this image of women lifting and stacking stones from devastated buildings has been idealized, it was indeed women on whom the burden of beginning the process of recovery primarily fell. Some 65 per cent of the

5 Alfred Kantorowicz, *Deutsches Tagebuch*, i (Berlin, 1978), 647.
6 Jaspers, *Wohin treibt die Bundesrepublik?*, 176.

German population in 1945 was female; millions of men were dead, missing, or still in captivity, and many of those who had survived the war were severely injured or otherwise disabled; in addition, someone had to replace the forced labourers and prisoners of war who had done much of the agricultural work and physically demanding jobs during the later war years. Since there was a great shortage of workers in heavy industry and construction, women took up jobs even in these traditionally male industries, as laws protecting them from heavy labour were temporarily relaxed. But women had to confront more than just the shortage of male workers; shortages of food, shelter, fuel, and other basic commodities made the very task of survival arduous and exhausting. Because women were generally responsible for keeping the household functioning, even in those households that included a man, they queued for hours to obtain insufficient rations and then had to search for additional food by foraging, producing it themselves, bartering, or buying on the black market. Water had to be carried, often several kilometres, and heating material had to be collected from the rubble or nearby woods. So-called hamster trips (*Hamsterfahrten*), excursions from cities into the countryside to obtain food and other goods, were common, in spite of attempts by the occupation authorities to put a stop to them.

Yet another difficulty that women faced was the danger of being raped by members of the Allied forces, which reportedly occurred especially frequently in the French and Russian zones. Since the late 1970s, a number of West German film-makers have problematized the issue of widespread rape at the end of the war, including Edgar Reitz in *Die Stunde Null* (1977), Helma Sanders-Brahms in *Deutschland, bleiche Mutter* (1979), and, most recently and explicitly, Helke Sander in her documentary film *BeFreier und BeFreite* (1992), in which women who lived through that time describe their experiences. Although there was little attention paid to this issue before the 1970s, one contemporary account of the constant threat of rape in 1945 appeared in the book *Eine Frau in Berlin* (1954 abroad; 1959 in Germany), a personal diary in which a woman recorded her strategies for surviving the breakdown of civil order at the close of the war. She describes her deliberate decision, after having been raped numerous times within a few days, to find herself 'a wolf to protect [her] from the wolves', a sexual relationship with a Russian officer who would provide protection from other soldiers as well as food.[7] The distinction between rape and prostitution became blurred in many instances during this period of social upheaval and existential desperation. Some women and girls supported their families with

7 Anonymous, *A Woman in Berlin*, trans. James Stern (New York, 1954), 88.

Keith Bullivant and C. Jane Rice

the food, cigarettes, and other goods that they obtained from liaisons with members of the occupation forces. For many women, the battle for survival only intensified in 1945; yet in shouldering the burden of recovery and surviving the hardships, many developed an independence and self-reliance that contrasted sharply with the restricted role that had been prescribed to them under National Socialism.

As the millions of prisoners of war gradually returned home and millions more expellees and refugees arrived from the areas to the east, unemployment began to rise again, reaching almost 13 per cent by March 1950. As a result, many women were forced out of their jobs to make room for men, especially those women in traditionally male jobs, but even civil service employees lost their jobs, as administrators took advantage of a law that allowed them to dismiss female employees if they married. Although there was resistance and in certain instances public protests against such practices, most married women willingly relinquished their employment in order to take up the role of full-time home-maker. Attempts in recent years on the part of feminists and others to understand and explain the readiness of so many German women in the 1950s to abandon their new-found independence and self-reliance and to return to the dependent position of housewife have focused on a variety of factors responsible for this apparent step backwards in women's equality and autonomy. Most women were employed on a temporary basis as unskilled or semi-skilled workers, without career prospects or opportunity for professional training; the legendary *Trümmerfrauen*, for example, were among the very lowest paid of workers in jobs that were by their very nature temporary. Women's wages were so low that, until the Currency Reform in 1948, those who spent their day foraging and bartering were generally better off than those who had jobs; women's wages averaged only 60 per cent of men's during the 1940s, and they received less pay for the same work—a problem that was ameliorated only partially by a Federal Labour Court ruling in 1955 that at least officially prohibited such policies. Some women (and men) took jobs initially only because they were compelled to do so by the occupation authorities; in most areas, women between the ages of 16 and 45 who had no children younger than 14 were required, along with adult men, to register for 'work duty' and could then be called up for compulsory employment. Not working continued to be a sign of affluence and social privilege, just as it had been during the war, when only wealthy women or those with important Nazi connections were able to avoid compulsory menial and low-paid work. Moreover, women's significant contributions to rebuilding the country received relatively little recognition. By retreating to the private sphere, women were in many instances fleeing unrewarding toil and hardship for the Christian ideal of marriage and family that promised them security, protection, and stability.

After the establishment of the Federal Republic in 1949, the CDU-led government put great pressure on women not only to leave the work-force but also to have large families, especially after 1953 when the CDU/CSU coalition controlled half of the votes in the Bundestag and government policies began to shift further to the right. In 1953 Chancellor Adenauer established a Ministry for Family Policy and appointed as its head the strict Catholic Franz-Josef Wuermeling, who served in that capacity for nearly a decade. Wuermeling, who declared himself the 'protective patron of the family', viewed large families as the ideal and not only opposed abortion and public child-care facilities, but also called for laws making divorce more difficult, the abolition of civil marriage, the prevention of birth control, and strong incentives to deter housewives from working outside the home. One of many financial incentives instituted to encourage large or 'children-rich' (kinderreich) families was the introduction in 1954 of Kindergeld, a monthly subsidy to families for each child they had after the second.

Another measure intended to strengthen families was a law passed in 1961 making divorce more difficult, in that it could no longer be granted against the will of the 'guiltless' party. This and other policies purportedly designed to protect women and families were encouraged by the churches (especially the Catholic Church) and endorsed by numerous newly established family organizations, as well as by conservative politicians who supported a hierarchical structure of marriage and the family (the authority of parents over children and the pre-eminence of the father) and the revival of the traditional role of women as housewives and mothers. In addition, prominent sociologists like Helmut Schelsky argued that the family should be the focus of West German social policy and that families should be strengthened by making it possible for women to follow their 'natural inclinations' and stay at home to nurture children. Adenauer and other politicians also justified the promotion of large families in terms of population policy, as they invoked the Cold War spectre of hostile countries to the east, where large families were much more common. In spite of the fact that the population of the area that made up the Federal Republic had increased by 18 per cent from 1939 to 1950, Adenauer argued that the only defence against the threat from the East was to strengthen the 'will for children' among West Germans. The family politics of the Adenauer era, which were ostensibly aimed at protecting the family, thereby providing a bulwark against communism, in fact perpetuated many features of National Socialist policy, such as pronatalist sentiments, the glorification of motherhood, the preservation of patriarchal authority, and a biological determination of women's lives.

The news and entertainment media also encouraged 'family-friendly' policies. The women's magazine *Constanze*, for example, in its early years of publication (from 1948 to the mid-1950s) included articles on such political topics as equal rights, problems of discrimination against single women, and the importance of political involvement, but then gradually dropped references to political issues altogether and concentrated increasingly on advice for finding a husband, becoming a perfect wife, running an efficient household, as well as tips on interior decoration, fashion, and beauty, along with more and more advertising. Popular films reinforced the ideal of wife and home-maker as the ultimate career goal for women and depicted marriage and motherhood as the only means for achieving true fulfilment. In spite of these social norms and policies designed to encourage women to stay out of the work-force, the number of women working nevertheless increased during the 1950s and was higher at the end of the Adenauer era than at any previous time in the post-war period.

When the Parliamentary Council, the body responsible for drawing up the constitution, discussed the issue of equal rights for women from September 1948 to January 1949, the representatives from all of the parties (with the exception of the two Communist delegates) voiced reservations and proposed initially the limitation of equality to the issue of political rights. Only after a storm of protest, in the form of petitions, letters, and resolutions from women who believed that they had earned equal rights in their contributions to rebuilding Germany, did the Parliamentary Council adopt Elisabeth Selbert's petition to extend women's equality to all spheres and it became part of Article 3 of the Basic Law in her simple, unqualified formulation: 'Men and women have equal rights.' Article 117 further stipulated that existing laws in the Civil Code (dating from the beginning of the century) that were not in agreement with this Equal Rights Article had to be brought into conformity by 31 March 1953. In fact, the Bundestag failed to revise the laws in question until five years past the deadline stipulated in the constitution and, when the changes finally became law in 1958, they reinforced a hierarchical, patriarchal family structure and women's economic dependence on men. The new law stipulated that in marriage the wife was responsible for the household and that she could only take employment if it did not hinder her in carrying out her duties to her husband and her responsibilities to her family. She was obliged to seek employment, on the other hand, if her husband was unable to earn an adequate living, but this would not absolve her from her household duties. In addition, the father retained the right of final decision in all matters relating to his children and the sole right to represent them, but the Federal Constitutional Court struck down this provision in 1959. One of the improvements for women in this so-called Equal Rights Law was that property acquired during marriage was no longer considered the sole property of the husband, but rather joint property, and a woman had a right to half of it if her husband died or they divorced.

The lives of women in West Germany after 1945 were characterized by stark contradictions: independence and dependence, equality and inequality, strength and weakness, special status and subordinate position. The simultaneous power and powerlessness of post-war German women was rooted primarily in the traditional dual character of women's work, which remained unaltered by the social upheaval of post-war German society, as well as in the fact that patriarchy, although severely discredited by German fascism, remained very much alive at the end of the war. The typical conflict between paid employment and housework, between production and reproduction, rather than being suspended, was dramatically heightened by the struggle for survival in the aftermath of the war. The exacerbation of their double burden had pushed women to breaking-point by the economic and social crisis of 1947, and many found the price for their new independence too high. These contradictions deriving from traditional role definitions became anchored in the constitution, which granted women equal rights in Article 3 but guaranteed mothers the 'right to protection and care by the community' in Article 6. In addition to Article 6, the Law for the Protection of Mothers, which was enacted in 1952, placed women in a separate category of workers who were disadvantaged by their special physiology and the necessity of working a double shift. The law purportedly protected pregnant women from unfair dismissal; in fact, however, women who were married to men with an income sufficient to support the entire family were in practice frequently not granted protection under this law. This legislation, like many other laws and policies of the Adenauer era, protected the sexual division of labour, the economic dependence of women, and

Keith Bullivant and C. Jane Rice

a conception of sexual difference that strongly characterized the self-understanding of West German women until the 1970s.

The Culture of Restoration: The Mass Media, Literature, and the Cinema

The tendency for an older generation to be restored to positions of authority was by no means confined to politics and business; it was also true of literature and the arts in general. After the Currency Reform many of the periodicals and theatre groups founded by younger artists had been forced to close, while many positions in established ventures were taken over by those of an older generation, freshly rehabilitated by the Western Allies. The one positive legacy of the occupying forces, one that was to be of great importance in subsequent decades, concerned the media. Among the first actions by the occupying Allied forces was the creation of news-sheets to get important information over to the German population. This was quickly followed by the issuing of licences to publish newspapers to individuals, rather than to political groupings and trade unions, as had been the case in the Weimar Republic. By and large the Allies succeeded in creating a politically independent press after certain early problems caused by the proximity of the *Frankfurter Rundschau* to the Communist Party in the American Zone and by a number of clashes between the British and left-wing editors in the Rhineland and the Ruhr. Despite a brief upsurge of new newspapers after the abolition of the licensing system in 1949, the period of Allied control of the press was decisive in shaping the longer-term pattern of West German press holdings up to the present day. The bulk of the newspapers were regional in content, with no publication at this time acquiring the influential national circulation of major British papers. Nevertheless, this period saw the establishment of the *Süddeutsche Zeitung*, the *Frankfurter Rundschau*, and *Die Welt*, West Germany's 'quality' national dailies. The last-named is something of an oddity in that it remained under British control until 1953. The period of Allied occupation also witnessed the licensing of the liberal weeklies *Die Zeit* (1946) and *Der Spiegel* (1947) and the beginnings of the Gruner + Jahr and Springer press empires. Axel Springer acquired a licence to produce the influential evening paper the *Hamburger Abendblatt* and the weekly radio (and later TV) programme magazine, *Hör zu!* (still Germany's largest-selling magazine) at this time. In 1952 he launched the tabloid *Bild-Zeitung*, which

DIE ZEIT

Frankfurter Rundschau

Süddeutsche Zeitung

Frankfurter Allgemeine

Aids-Alarm Blut-Konserven verseucht

Bild

Die Woche

Das Schock-Programm der SPD

12. Press in the Federal Republic.

Daily press	Circulation figures ('000)			
(Founded)	1947	1970	1980	1990
Frankfurter Rundschau				
(July 1945)	154	147	184	196
Süddeutsche Zeitung				
(October 1945)	260	259	331	383
Die Welt				
(April 1946)	600	226	204	228
Frankfurter Allgemeine Zeitung				
(November 1949)	—	255	312	386
Bild-Zeitung				
(June 1952)	—	3,391	4,710	4,339

Until unification *Die Zeit* (founded 1946), the left-liberal 80-page weekly with a circulation in 1990 of 487,000, had no serious rival. But February 1993 saw the launch of two competitors in the weeklies market: *Die Woche*, a tabloid published by Hoffmann & Campe and boasting ultra-modern design techniques, and Gruner + Jahr's *Wochenpost*, formerly the GDR's premier weekly with a circulation of over a million (but down to just over 100,000 by 1993).

quickly established itself as Germany's largest and only true national daily. With the acquisition of *Die Welt* from the British in 1953 the basis of Springer's newspaper empire was laid, and was consolidated in the 1950s by the purchase of a number of regional newspapers. It came to constitute the largest press concentration in the world. As economic pressures forced the closure of many smaller enterprises and the sales of the *Bild-Zeitung* soared, the size of Springer's press empire became a worrisome problem in the 1960s, when two public commissions addressed the issue and the Extra-Parliamentary Opposition of the latter part of the decade came to view the Springer empire as a particularly potent anti-democratic centre of power.

A very similar initial situation pertained in the area of radio, the other significant means used by the Allies to disseminate information. In 1945 special units of the American Psychological Warfare Division took over radio stations in Frankfurt, Munich, and Stuttgart, with stations in the other zones also being requisitioned by the French and the British. Here again the pattern was a regional one that was to shape the future of the West German media in subsequent decades. Although sovereign control of the radio was not officially granted to West Germany until 1955, the transfer of the regional radio stations to Germans was completed by 1949 and made subject to the legal control of the individual *Länder*. This important cultural autonomy of the states (*Kulturhoheit der Länder*), which was, and still is, also true of a number of major areas of the media and the arts, led to the growth of a vibrant and uniquely decentralized cultural scene in West Germany and, as Gottfried Benn and others lamented, to a paucity of national culture. Although the regional radio stations came together under the umbrella organization of the Committee for the Public Broadcasting Corporations of the Federal Republic of Germany (ARD) in 1950, the pattern of essentially regional programming was unaffected. It was, indeed, then replicated when the regional ARD members began television broadcasting in 1954; a national evening television news was not introduced until 1956, but this did little to alter the regional structure that is still in place today. Although composition of the commissions supervising the ARD stations was undoubtedly more strongly exposed to greater political influence over the years, their autonomy was clear, much to the annoyance of Chancellor Adenauer. During the 1950s he and his party made a number of unsuccessful attempts to challenge that autonomy and he was determined to ensure central control of the proposed new second television channel. When the ARD applied to the Post Office in 1957 for the allocation of the frequencies necessary for such a service, it was turned down. In the mean time a private company, Freies Fernsehen GmbH, was set up to establish a commercial TV service and even entrusted with this task by the Government Press and Information Office. In 1960 the Chancellor and his Minister of Justice, having had a proposal for the creation of a public corporation called Deutschland Fernsehen rejected by the Upper House of Parliament (Bundesrat), which is essentially controlled by representatiuves of the *Länder*, set up a private company called Deutschland-Fernsehen-GmbH. There was a public outcry as to the legality of all this, with the *Länder* taking the matter to the Federal Constitutional Court in Karlsruhe, which in February 1961 pronounced in their favour. They then quickly reached agreement on the setting up of Second German Television (ZDF), separate from ARD and to be concerned only with television. Based in Mainz, it began transmitting in 1963. Despite its separate identity, ZDF was and is very similar to ARD in having from the beginning a very regional character. Only with the introduction of commercial channels and, in particular, commercial satellite television aimed at a broad European market at the end of the 1980s did channels without a regional component become accessible.

As far as West German literature of this period is concerned, there is a danger here of the picture being distorted by later constructions of the canon of major authors, with a concomitant exaggeration as to their status in the 1940s and 1950s. Another problem is created by the rather comforting myths about the development of West German literature in those early years that were encouraged by literary historians and semi-official organizations. The impression was given that just as the foundation of the Federal Republic supposedly constituted a radical break with the Nazi past—a break facilitated by the so-called zero hour of 1945—so too did post-war literature mark a new beginning. Thus a new generation of writers, essentially those we associate with *Der Ruf*, was said to have set about cleansing the German language of its corruption by the Nazis; this was, in the term coined by Wolfgang Weyrauch, the *Kahlschlag*, the clearing away of the dead wood. Closely linked to this was the supposed discovery of hitherto unknown American realist writers like Hemingway, Dos Passos, and Saroyan, whose work provided the stylistic basis for a new critical, humanitarian realism, the major theme of which was a reckoning with the Nazi past. Both *Kahlschlag* and this new realism were associated, in turn, with Gruppe 47, a literary circle founded by Hans Werner Richter after the banning of *Der Ruf*.

It was not until the 1960s that studies exposed this reading of the

Keith Bullivant and C. Jane Rice

immediate post-war situation as myth. Not only had no real linguistic break taken place, but the claims made for the type of writing produced and for the stature in the 1940s and 1950s of the writers named was greatly exaggerated. Above all, though, such a view ignored the prominent role played in those first two decades by an older generation of writers, conservative critics, and scholars.

The war was hardly over before those who had stayed in Germany were proclaiming their 'inner emigration', as they termed it, to have been a form of resistance to National Socialism. Thus in the autumn of 1945 Walter von Molo and Frank Thieß, two such writers, urged Thomas Mann to return to Germany, but stressed at the same time the inherent superiority of the writing of 'inner emigration' over exile writing. Mann's critical response led to a public leave-taking by Thieß of the 'American citizen of the world', as he dismissively termed him. Mann did return to Germany for the two-hundredth anniversary of Goethe's birth in 1949, but his visit to Weimar (as well as Frankfurt) led to his being labelled 'a defendant of the Eastern world of torture' by the *Frankfurter Allgemeine Zeitung*. Not surprisingly, Mann did not return to live in Germany, instead moving in 1952 from the USA to Switzerland, where he died in 1955.

Astonishingly, much the same sort of case was made by the ex-Communist Alfred Andersch in 'Deutsche Literatur in der Entscheidung', a paper read to Gruppe 47, in which he expressed a marked preference for writers like Ernst Jünger over the exiles Mann and Alfred Döblin. Here a clear contradiction between the claims made for the programme of the group and the views of important major members became apparent. A final indication of the strength of support for the older generation of conservative writers is afforded by Hans Egon Holthusen, the major West German literary critic of the period, who in 1948 declared Hermann Hesse, Ernst Jünger, and Gottfried Benn to be the most important writers of the age for the way in which they endeavoured 'to restore old truths in new language', rather than addressing the immediate social and political concerns of the day.[8] Here, as elsewhere, the role played by the Western Allies in their over-hasty rehabilitation of members of the older generation was of significance: Jünger and Benn (who had briefly declared his support for the Nazis), as well as Walter von Molo and Friedrich Sieburg, the influential conservative literary editor of the *Frankfurter Allgemeine Zeitung* in the 1950s, had all been on the 'black list' of banned artists, a list that was quickly scrapped as the process of general denazification was terminated in 1948.

8 Hans Egon Holthusen, *Der unbehauste Mensch* (Munich, 1951), 33.

Despite the importance later literary historians now rightly attach to early works—dealing with the war experience—such as Walter Kolbenhoff's *Von unserem Fleisch und Blut* (1947), Hans Werner Richter's *Die Geschlagenen* (1949), and Heinrich Böll's *Der Zug war pünktlich* (1949) and *Wo warst du, Adam?* (1951), the type of writing that received the most favourable critical attention in the late 1940s, apart from the older writers mentioned, was not by such critical realists, but was, rather, in the 'magical realist' style of the 'inner emigrants' of the 1930s. The most important of these, Hermann Kasack's *Die Stadt hinter dem Strom* (1947), is typical of a series of such works in the way in which the aftermath of the war was portrayed in entirely allegorical terms, with questions of guilt or historical specificity being ignored—indeed, this is precisely why the novel was so widely praised. The award of the Fontane Prize to Kasack for this work in 1949 was a clear indication of the preferences of the conservative literary establishment that so successfully continued its role after 1945, as, more generally, was the overall pattern of the distribution of literary prizes (in the nominating committees of which that establishment held complete control) up to the end of the 1950s: the names that recur are Rudolf Alexander Schröder, Wilhelm Lehmann, Ina Seidel, and other writers of 'inner emigration', together with those younger authors following in their footsteps, such as Kasack, Ilse Aichinger, and Gerd Gaiser. The success of Gaiser's *œuvre* at this time, permeated by the cultural pessimism of Martin Heidegger and Oswald Spengler, both of whom were enjoying a considerable renaissance, and with its affinities to the work of Ernst Jünger, tells us much about the structure of feeling of the decade. Nor was the situation fundamentally different in Gruppe 47 until the latter half of the 1950s. Despite the bold words of the founding fathers, the central importance of critical realism, as demonstrated by Böll, Richter, and Kolbenhoff, was soon challenged and displaced. Günter Eich received the group's own prize in 1950 for 'Fränkisch-Tibetanischer Kirschgarten', a timeless nature poem far removed from his famous earlier 'Inventur', the classic example of *Kahlschlag*, and Ilse Aichinger the group's prize for 1952. The so-called autonomous poetry of Eich and Ingeborg Bachmann, together with their many radio plays of an equally symbolic or allegorical nature, constituted the most prominent and representative works emanating from Gruppe 47 in the 1950s, with Böll ploughing a lonely furrow until the arrival on the scene of a younger generation (Hans Magnus Enzensberger, Martin Walser, and Günter Grass, in particular) towards the end of the decade. Recent research has demonstrated that in the case of Eich

Keith Bullivant and C. Jane Rice

there was, anyway, no real stylistic break between his post-war publications and those produced in the 1930s (and in certain instances they had actually been written in the earlier period).

The restoration indicated by the types of writer awarded literary prizes in the 1950s was further reflected in the recommendations of the major literary critics of the day—Hans Egon Holthusen, Friedrich Sieburg, Günter Blöcker, and Karl August Horst, all of whom had been active writers before 1945. It was therefore not surprising to discover, in a survey of West German students in 1959, that the most popular German authors for them were all either dead or of an older generation—Thomas Mann, Brecht, Goethe, Hesse, Musil, Bergengruen, Kafka, Zweig, and Benn. Despite Brecht's second place, the predominance of conservative authors is apparent. Of post-war writers Böll was the most popular—coming tenth, immediately after Benn.

Looking back on the writing of Gruppe 47 between 1947 and 1962, Fritz J. Raddatz observed that by and large (and Böll would again have to be cited as an exception) 'matters of general public concern' did not feature in the work of the group;[9] much the same sort of thing could be said about the West German cinema of the period. Whilst films made before the Currency Reform—notably Wolfgang Staudte's *Die Mörder sind unter uns* (1946), Helmut Käutner's *In jenen Tagen* (1947), and Josef von Baky's *Und über uns der Himmel* (1947)—were directly concerned with the problems posed by the legacy of the Nazi past and/or of life in the ruins, the films of the 1950s were set in a totally depoliticized world of pretence, much in the manner of so many Nazi films. The film industry favoured regional films (*Heimatfilme*) set in what was portrayed as a timeless world of unchanged social order, as exemplified by Hans Deppe's *Das Schwarzwaldmädel* (1950) and *Grün ist die Heide* (1951), and later by a string of similar Austrian 'Sissi' films starring Romy Schneider. The same affirmation of traditional order in a timeless, and frequently kitschy, German world was to be observed in the historical films of the time; Alfred Braun's *Stresemann* (1957), in particular, was notable for its total (mis-)representation of the Weimar chancellor as a 'grand old man' akin to Konrad Adenauer. The decade also saw a substantial number of war films such as Alfred Weidenmann's *Der Stern von Afrika* (1957) and *U47 Kapitänleutnant Prien* (1958) which, though often posing as being against war, tended to accentuate the glamour of military deeds of valour, rather than examining critically the Nazi regime, or, as with Helmut Käutner's film of Carl Zuckmayer's successful stage drama of 1946, *Des Teufels General* (1954), and Weidenmann's *Canaris* (1955),

9 Fritz J. Raddatz, 'Die ausgehaltene Realität', in Hans Werner Richter (ed.), *Almanach der Gruppe 47 1947–62* (Reinbek, 1962), 55.

merely reinforced the myth of the soldier as the decent citizen misused by the evil Nazis. Only Bernhard Wicki's unambiguously anti-war film *Die Brücke* (1959) was felt by reviewers to mark a significant exception. Other films of note were Kurt Hoffmann's *Wir Wunderkinder* (1958) and Wolfgang Staudte's *Rosen für den Staatsanwalt* (1959), both of which deal with the restoration to power and prestige of former Nazis, and Rolf Thiele's biting critique of the fetishes of the German 'Economic Miracle', *Das Mädchen Rosemarie* (1958), based on a highly successful novel by Erich Kuby (also 1958).

The generally lamentable state of the West German cinema at this time, as most critical commentators perceived it, was compounded by the emergence during the late 1950s of romantic musicals featuring the stars of German 'schmalz' Freddy Quinn, Peter Krauss, Conny Froboess, and Caterina Valente. In frustration, a group of young directors got together during the Oberhausen festival of 'shorts' in 1962 to sign a manifesto that declared its intention to change things. While it might be argued that even more decisive was the establishment in 1965 of the 'Curatorium for the New German Film', which made interest-free loans available to young directors, the subsequent productions by Volker Schlöndorff (*Der junge Törless*, 1965), Alexander Kluge (*Abschied von gestern*, 1966, and *Die Artisten in der Zirkuskuppel: ratlos*, 1968), Werner Herzog (*Lebenszeichen*, 1967), and others from the mid-1960s onwards did indeed turn the tide as far as innovative cinema was concerned. Subsequent films by these directors, together with the astonishing output of Rainer Werner Fassbinder between 1969 and his death in 1982, made the 'New German Film' of the 1970s one of the most productive national cinemas in the Western world. At the same time it has to be conceded, though, that the West German commercial cinema did not change greatly, continuing to be dominated by Hollywood, musicals, and a successful series of Karl May Westerns, starring Lex Barker, and of Edgar Wallace thrillers, both produced by Herbert Wendlandt in the 1960s. The 1970s saw the start of the highly profitable West German 'soft porno' industry.

Women in the Cultural Life of the Adenauer Era

In cultural life, as in other spheres of West German society, the restoration of a conservative ideology perpetuated the setbacks that women had experienced under National Socialism, particularly in the field of literature, one area in which they had made significant gains during the Weimar Republic. Virtually none of the successful

Keith Bullivant and C. Jane Rice

13. Bernhard Wicki, *Die Brücke* (1959).

In a small southern German town in the very last days of the war, seven schoolboys are conscripted and given but rudimentary weapon training before being set to defend a bridge against the advancing American troops. In the ensuing clash all but one of them are killed, although, as the closing shot (above) emphasizes, even he will still be severely scarred psychologically. Some audiences at the time responded enthusiastically to the heroic last-ditch stand of the youths, feeling that the course of the war might have been different if all had behaved like them. Yet clearly Wicki's intention was to attack the criminal senselessness of the action: absurdly the Germans themselves want the bridge destroyed (to delay the Allied advance) and, as the closing titles relate, the events, though true, were deemed too insignificant to be recorded in any reports of the Wehrmacht. Both in its anti-militarist subject-matter and harrowingly (neo-)realist style *Die Brücke* recalls one of the classics of Weimar cinema, G. W. Pabst's *Westfront 1918* (1930).

women writers of the 1920s found recognition from the conservative West German literary establishment. West German critics ignored the work of Nelly Sachs, Irmgard Keun, and Gertrud Kolmar until the mid-1960s or even later; theatres rejected the plays of Maria Lazar, Christa Winsloe, Hilde Rubinstein, and, with a few minor exceptions, Ilse Langner, all of whom had seen their works performed during the Weimar Republic. Women who had established themselves as writers during the 1920s were disregarded by the literary establishment of the Federal Republic; most works by women from the Weimar period had been eliminated from the officially sanctioned German literature by the National Socialists and continued to be excluded in the Federal Republic for at least two decades after the end of the Third Reich. The women writers who did achieve some critical attention during the early post-war years had, in most cases, begun writing during the Nazi era and represented a humanistic, Christian, usually conservative world view; such were Elisabeth Langgässer, Gertrud von le Fort, and Luise Rinser. Unlike their male counterparts women very frequently wrote about the immediate past, including such topics as daily life under fascism, resistance efforts, the civilian war experience, the persecution of Jews, and concentration camps.

One of the first literary works published after the war was the novel *Das unauslöschliche Siegel* (1946) by Elisabeth Langgässer, who had been designated a 'half-Jew' by the Nazis and prohibited from publishing in 1936. In this work of 'inner emigration' the forces of good finally win out over the forces of evil in the life of Lazarus Belfontaine, a Jew who converted to Catholicism at the time of his marriage and whose life is unexpectedly transformed by the 'indelible seal' of baptism. In this and other works Langgässer used highly metaphorical language in her explorations of Christian themes, avoiding historical specificity and incorporating elements from mythology and antiquity. Her work is thus typical of the early post-war writers who received critical acclaim, and it is not surprising that she was the best-known woman writer in West Germany until the mid-1950s. Another of the earliest works published after the war, Luise Rinser's *Gefängnis-Tagebuch* (1946), was less typical. In it she recounted her own experiences and those of other inmates in the women's prison in Traunstein, where she had been incarcerated in 1944 for 'high treason and undermining military morale'. This was one of very few autobiographical works until the 1970s to treat the personal experience of fascism, but in her fiction Rinser repeatedly dealt with aspects of life under National Socialism, even in very early works, such as the story *Jan Lobel aus Warschau* (1948).

Keith Bullivant and C. Jane Rice

Of the almost one hundred writers invited to read their works at the meetings of the Gruppe 47, only ten were women writers, and the group bestowed its coveted literary prize on only two women, both of them Austrian: Ilse Aichinger in 1952 and Ingeborg Bachmann in 1953. Bachmann, in particular, represents an exception to the general predominance of men among the West German writers who were favoured by critics. She was the most celebrated poet of the early 1950s and *Der Spiegel* even devoted a cover story to her in 1954. Her lyric poetry was praised for its 'timeless', 'classic' beauty, but her popularity was due not only to the beauty of her verse, but also, ironically, to the fact that critics of the 1950s generally overlooked the way in which many of the poems in her highly acclaimed first volume of poetry, *Die gestundete Zeit* (1953), dealt with the National Socialist past. Indeed, readers often failed to recognize the social and political content of her poetry because of the complexity and ambiguity of the images and the frequent use of mythology. The publication of *Das dreißigste Jahr*, a collection of short prose works, marked Bachmann's return from writing poetry back to prose, in which the themes of fascism and of male–female relationships were more explicit, but critics dismissed these more obviously socially critical works as inferior to her poetry, until feminist critics 'discovered' them in the late 1970s.

The question of a specifically feminine aesthetic, which was to become a subject of intense discussion in the 1970s, was rarely addressed explicitly during the Adenauer era, not surprisingly perhaps, given the overwhelming predominance of men in West German cultural life. One noteworthy exception was a panel of three writers (Marie Luise Kaschnitz, Ilse Langner, and Oda Schaefer) who expounded their position on the particularity of women's literature at a conference of the German Academy for Language and Literature in Darmstadt in the autumn of 1957. All three of these prominent writers presented traditional views of women's writing, linking it with emotion and nature and men's writing with abstraction and logic. In addition, Kaschnitz claimed for women an affinity to the world of dreams, the unconscious, and irrationality, while Schaefer identified the patient, suffering, passive character of women as the determining element in their literary work ('the female nature seeks the harbour and protection . . . while the male intellect plunges into the unknown and adventure'). Langner, the only playwright of the three, claimed that the drama in women's daily lives, particularly the act of childbirth, makes them uninterested in pursuing it in writing, and she described the epic theatre of Brecht negatively as a feminization of drama (since it includes epic elements), which she saw as a parallel to the equally negative masculinization of women in society. Although a somewhat different discussion might have emerged with other participants, the positions of the panel were representative of the understanding on the part of most West German women in the 1950s of what it meant to be female. This view that women and men were polar opposites, differing substantially and fundamentally in all aspects of their lives, was another remnant of National Socialism that persisted well into the post-war era. Only Langner's characterization of art as androgynous contradicted that polar opposition; her explanation for the lack of women dramatists, on the other hand, reflected a biological determinism, which was widely accepted by women and men alike and which pervaded every sphere of society, from the Law for the Protection of Mothers to popular films to sociological theories.

Although women writers did not belong to the literary élite, for the most part they were highly productive during the Adenauer era and saw a large number of their works published. In other fields, however, such as theatre, film, and the visual arts, men's domination of cultural institutions was much more complete. There were virtually no women directors in the film industry or the theatre; accomplished visual artists, such as Irmgard Wessel-Zumloh and Ida Kerkovius, received scant recognition, and even prominent artists of the 1920s, such as Hannah Höch and Meret Oppenheim, were forgotten. The widespread resistance to women's participation in cultural and intellectual life was reflected in a survey of faculty members at West German universities in 1960, which found that 64 per cent of respondents were opposed to allowing women even to attend university, 4 per cent were neutral on the subject, and 32 per cent stood somewhere between neutrality and opposition; in addition 79 per cent objected to the idea of hiring women at lecturer level or above.[10] Nor did the majority of women aspire to participate publicly in cultural life, but instead accepted the role of homemaker, which was still their legal responsibility even after the Equal Rights Law came into effect in 1958.

The Affluent Society and West German Politics

10 Reported in Gisela Kaplan, *Contemporary Western European Feminism* (New York, 1992), 106–7; and Harry G. Shaffer, *Women in the Two Germanies* (New York, 1981), 129.

The general intellectual and cultural stagnation of the Federal Republic in the 1950s was in stark contrast with the economic and political development of the country. In 1949 it joined the Organization of European Economic Co-operation, this being the first step towards increasing integration into Western Europe, with the

Keith Bullivant and C. Jane Rice

changing of a long-established antagonistic relationship with France being of particular importance. West Germany became a founder-member of the European Economic Community (EEC, later EC and EU) in 1957, a move which facilitated even greater growth of an economy that was by now the most powerful in Europe. A crucial tenet in the philosophy of the 'social market economy' was the notion that wealth generated should be used in part to compensate the less well-off. In keeping with this, a real achievement of the 1950s was the expansion of a welfare state, actually initiated in the late nineteenth century by Bismarck, that offered all citizens generous old-age pensions, health and accident insurance, unemployment benefits, family allowance, and student grants, creating an outstanding network of social care. Another concomitant of material prosperity was the way in which the transition to a consumer society during the 1950s, coming on the heels of the breaking down of many old social barriers in the aftermath of the war, created a 'levelled-in middle-class society' (to use the term coined by the sociologist Helmut Schelsky) that increasingly defined itself according to material criteria, rather than traditional political consciousness. This gave rise to a political climate very different from that of other European industrial countries and rapidly eroded the traditional political base of the Social Democratic Party (SPD). As a result the 1950s saw a campaign within the party, led by Erich Ollenhauer, Carlo Schmidt, and Herbert Wehner, to shed the 'ballast' from its programme (i.e. its essentially Marxian components). The new Godesberg Programme of 1959, which established the SPD as an essentially centrist, pragmatic party, eliminated a radical alternative voice from mainstream political discourse, moving politics closer to the American model some twenty-five years before the British Labour Party under Neil Kinnock adopted similar policy changes.

This shift in the programme of the SPD, which was to be of consequence in the 1960s and beyond, finally tolled the knell for one important part of the 'young generation's' immediate post-war vision as to the nature of a renewed Germany, namely 'democratic socialism', as Alfred Andersch called it. The dream of the 'other Germany' following the 'third way', which was shared by so many intellectuals at that time (and which was to surface again in 1989–90 during debates about the future course of Germany after the collapse of the GDR), also envisaged the country being undivided, demilitarized, and neutral, so that it could in future be 'the free bridge between the divergent powers' that would prevent war, rather than causing it.[11] The events of 1948 and 1949 (the Currency Reform, the Berlin Blockade, and the foundation of the two German

11 Alfred Andersch, 'Grundlage einer deutschen Opposition', Der Ruf (1 Dec. 1946), 96.

states) also seemed to spell an end to hopes of neutrality and reunification, particularly as the Adenauer government, with the encouragement of the Western Allies after the outbreak of the Korean War (1950), pursued a policy of integration into the Western sphere of influence. Offers were in fact made by the GDR in 1951 and by the Soviet Union in 1952 to open discussions on German unification, and as late as 1958 Adenauer rejected a Soviet suggestion that a German Federation be formed as the first step towards unification. The stumbling-block, both for the Western Allies and Adenauer, was Soviet insistence on German neutrality and disarmament. As early as 1950 the issue of West German rearmament was on the agenda in Bonn. An attempt to force a referendum on the matter, in which writers were prominent, was banned by the government the following year, while in 1953 the Federal Republic, which had been granted limited sovereignty by the Western Allies in 1952, indicated its intention to join the proposed European Defence Union. In the autumn of 1954 West Germany was admitted in principle to NATO, joining on 9 May 1955. The first units of the Federal Army (Bundeswehr) were formed in 1956, when general male conscription was also introduced.

The controversy over rearmament led to considerable public protests, with a large-scale demonstration in Essen on 11 May 1952 costing the life of Philipp Müller at the hands of the police. *Frau und Frieden*, a monthly publication of the West German Women's Peace Movement, dealt with the role that women, particularly mothers, could play in the fight for peace; and the women's magazine *Constanze* even carried an article in 1950 advocating a general strike by women at home and at work, should any military conflict involving the Federal Republic take place. The debate, which also formed an important part of Wolfgang Koeppen's novel *Das Treibhaus* (1953) about the restorative nature of West German politics at this time, was joined by Thomas Mann (in an article for *L'Express* in autumn 1954) and by a large number of writers and intellectuals within the Paulskirche movement. Their manifesto of 29 January 1955 deplored in general the increase in East–West tension that would result from rearmament and stressed in particular the need for the claim to German unification to have precedence over the creation of military power-blocs. In 1956 Hans Werner Richter was one of the organizers of the Grünwald Circle, formed to combat a perceived growth in militarism. The initiation of the debate in the Bundestag about equipping the Bundeswehr with tactical nuclear weapons significantly increased public concern. In

1957 eighteen prominent scientists, including Otto Hahn and three other Nobel Prize winners, signed the 'Göttingen Declaration', opposing such a step. Their action was undoubtedly a significant factor in protests against nuclear warfare in the following two or three years: various resolutions were signed by the vast majority of leading writers and intellectuals, across the generations, in protest actions organized by the 'Fight Atomic Death' campaign and the Committee against Atomic Armament. In 1960, following the British example of the Aldermaston Marches, the first Easter March against the nuclear threat took place. The Bundestag actually approved the arming of German troops with nuclear field weapons in 1958, but the Western Allies eventually had second thoughts on the matter. Nevertheless, the East–West tension brought about by the building of the Berlin Wall and the Cuban Crisis of 1962, soon to be followed by the Vietnam War, ensured the continued activity of the peace movement throughout the 1960s, culminating in 300,000 demonstrators taking part in the 1968 Easter March.

While their resistance to the major drift of the agenda of the Adenauer government was unambiguous, there is a danger here of overemphasizing the status of writers and intellectuals in the 1950s. The contempt with which Konrad Adenauer reacted to the 'Göttingen Declaration' was a clear indication of the marginality of such intellectuals. While the extra-parliamentary nature of the protests by intellectuals and writers, which prefigured a key feature of the 1960s, tells us a lot about the centrist nature of Bonn politics even at this time, it is also indicative of their distrust of the world of party politics. Born or having grown up in the age of National Socialism and confronted before or after the war with the excesses of Stalinism and with the black-and-white ideological simplicities of the Cold War, they had good reason to be suspicious of ideology, and their writing of this time, as Hans Mayer persuasively demonstrated, was characterized precisely by that suspicion. The imaginative works of Koeppen, Andersch, and Böll of the 1950s, as well as much of the poetry and many of the radio plays of the decade, were highly resigned. This was in turn a reflection of their self-perceived role as 'court jesters' having little influence on practical matters. Martin Walser, whose own first novel, *Ehen in Philippsburg* (1957), was equally resigned in the way in which Hans Beumann abandons all his early ideals in order to enter the smart set of Philippsburg, was one of the first publicly to give voice to a collective sense of guilty ineffectuality and to a determination to change things.[12]

12 Martin Walser, 'Skizze zu einem Vorwurf', in Wolfgang Weyrauch (ed.), *Ich lebe in der Bundesrepublik* (Munich, n.d. [1960]), 110–14.

14. *Kampf dem Atomtod*, Berlin (1958).

The 1950s was a decade rich in protest against militarism and rearmament, culminating in the 'Fight Atomic Death' campaign opposing plans to equip the Bundeswehr with tactical nuclear weapons. While the brunt of the organization was borne by the SPD, trade unions, and religious groups, the public esteem the campaign enjoyed derived largely from the massive backing it received from West Germany's critical intelligentsia: scientists, including the eighteen distinguished physicists who published the 'Göttingen Declaration', theologians like Martin Niemöller and Helmut Gollwitzer, writers such as Heinrich Böll and Hans Werner Richter, as well as artists and publishers like Otto Dix and Ernst Rowohlt. In Berlin, symbol of the East–West divide and presumed epicentre of the dreaded conflagration, many a silent march of protest would, like the one shown here, converge on the Kaiser-Wilhelm-Gedächtniskirche, whose ruined shell was a constant reminder of the horrendous destructiveness of war.

The Politicization of West German Culture and the Rise of the Extra-Parliamentary Opposition

A number of literary historians have argued persuasively that 1959–60 marked a decisive turning-point in West German literature, with the appearance of a number of major novels, including Günter Grass's *Die Blechtrommel*, Heinrich Böll's *Billard um halbzehn*, Uwe Johnson's *Mutmaßungen über Jakob* (all 1959), and Martin Walser's *Halbzeit* (1960); while all of these novels were notable for their formal innovation, the works by Grass and Böll were also significantly new in their critical examination of the Nazi past. Instead of the allegorical treatment of National Socialism that characterized the novel of the 1940s or the narrow focus on the war experience of the ordinary soldier in the early works of Kolbenhoff, Richter, and Böll himself, *Billard um halbzehn* offered a critical, essentially historical view of National Socialism located within the wider spectrum of German militarism in the twentieth century. Böll's later *Ansichten eines Clowns* (1963) was a bitter but acutely perceptive study of the restorative nature of post-war West German society, focusing through the eyes of the critical clown on the smooth transition of former Nazis into the affluent world of the Federal Republic. Grass's first novel not only, in its second part, put forward a jaundiced critique of the post-war affluent and increasingly pluralistic society, but also, in its treatment of the Matzerath family, offered a reading of the German petty bourgeoisie's propensity for certain aspects of National Socialism that predated similar findings by social scientists and historians. At the same time, and despite the dwarf Oscar's essential rejection of compliance with the values of established society, the likelihood of anyone of his generation succumbing to some extent to National Socialism—a recurrent theme with Grass that was born of his own experience—is demonstrated by Oscar's involvement in a theatrical group entertaining the troops on the western front. *Die Blechtrommel* was also the most significant of a spate of socio-critical picaresque novels that appeared around this time, including—some critics would argue—Walser's *Halbzeit*, where the life of Anselm Kristlein constitutes the basis of a radical critique of the affluent society. All of these novels were, in turn, concerned with the problem of identity in modern society, with Walser and Johnson reflecting the increasing fragmentation of the individual by means of formally radical prose-writing that set the tone for a number of major novels in the following decades.

There are equally good arguments for seeing 1960 as marking a decisive shift in terms of the attitude of writers and intellectuals to the state. The initial stimuli were events that took place outside Germany: Israeli agents arrested Adolf Eichmann, a former high-ranking officer with a real responsibility for the mass exterminations in the Auschwitz death-camp, and the subsequent trial of the 'man in the glass booth' inevitably brought the issue of the Nazi past back centre-stage. In the same year 121 French intellectuals issued a manifesto against the war in Algeria, calling on those drafted to refuse to serve. A small group of West German writers signed a public letter of support for the position of their French colleagues, while the vast majority of liberal writers signed a declaration sponsored by, amongst others, Hans Werner Richter and Hans Magnus Enzensberger, in which they declared it their 'duty to take up a political stance as and when necessary and with the same determination as our French colleagues have shown. We will not acknowledge any law that attempts to deny us this right'.[13] The erection of the Berlin Wall on 13 August 1961 was another issue that sparked off united action on the part of writers, with Günter Grass and Wolfdietrich Schnurre organizing public protests against this 'threat to world peace' in letters to the Writers' Union of the GDR and to the President of the United Nations and with Hans Werner Richter editing a special volume of critical statements by leading writers. Perhaps the most unambiguous sign of a determination on the part of literary intellectuals to bring their socio-critical marginality to an end was the decision by much the same group of writers to pronounce publicly their support in the federal elections of 1961 for the SPD, despite 'all our scruples, various misgivings, criticisms, qualms of conscience, fears, and foreboding' and whilst stressing that this action was taken 'only because no better ally is available'.[14] Martin Walser, the editor of the election special that was produced, was at pains to emphasize the need for writers to mount the 'borrowed rostrum' of political involvement precisely because the compromises made by the SPD made such an inherently unnatural step necessary.

Although some sort of alliance between critical writers and the SPD, particularly in federal elections, was to continue into the 1980s and reached a high point of intensity during the government of Willy Brandt (1969–74), the increased involvement in affairs of the day remained an essentially extra-parliamentary one. The most striking example of this—and, arguably, the instance when the impact of a public stance by writers and liberal journalists was beyond dispute—came with the so-called *Spiegel* Affair of autumn 1962. After the magazine had published an article on a NATO manœuvre on 10 October (an act Konrad Adenauer was to describe

13 Quoted in Klaus Wagenbach *et al.* (eds.), *Vaterland, Muttersprache: Deutsche Schriftsteller und ihr Staat seit 1945* (Berlin, 1994), 176.
14 Peter Rühmkorf, 'Passionseinheit', in Martin Walser (ed.), *Die Alternative oder Brauchen wir eine neue Regierung?* (Reinbek, 1961), 49–50.

as representing 'the depths of treason'), its offices were occupied by police and federal lawyers in a dawn raid on 27 October, the editor Rudolf Augstein was imprisoned (for over two months), and vast quantities of materials from the files were impounded. Gruppe 47, which happened to be meeting in West Berlin at the time, published a manifesto on behalf of *Der Spiegel* the day after the incident, which explicitly called for the resignation of the Defence Minister, Franz Josef Strauß. The manifesto, supported by public telegrams from others to Adenauer and the Federal President, had an extraordinary impact and led to the resignation of Strauß (a blow to his political career from which he never fully recovered) and the ultimate exoneration (in 1965) of Augstein.

The theatre in the first half of the 1960s also succeeded in focusing attention on an important matter of public concern, in this case one that had been essentially suppressed in the push for economic renewal: the legacy of the Nazi past. West German theatre had been vigorous in the short time before the Currency Reform, but after the truncating of the denazification process it was quickly taken over again by the old establishment that had dominated it during the Third Reich; here, as in other areas of West German culture, the émigrés were frozen out. The significant exception was Carl Zuckmayer, attached to the American occupying forces, whose *Des Teufels General* (1946) was the theatre 'hit' of the immediate post-war years. It was, to say the least, a play with a politically unfortunate message: the central character Harras, an air-force 'ace', realizing the way that he has been duped by the Nazis, honourably commits suicide in an unsafe plane—thus confirming the myth of the decent and valiant warrior misused by the evil, scheming Nazis. It went right against ideas of collective guilt and was initially banned by the Allies, but was cleared for performance in the following year. Zuckmayer was, however, the significant exception to a pattern of restoration that saw even the best-known theatre director of the Nazi period, Gustav Gründgens—whose successful career in the Third Reich was the subject of *Mephisto* (1936), Klaus Mann's *roman à clef*—able to obtain appointment as theatre director to the city of Düsseldorf as early as 1947; he quickly re-established himself as the most influential director in the country and retained this status throughout the next decade. The West German theatre of the 1950s was highly conservative in repertoire and style, with only foreign plays and, in German, the work of the Swiss dramatists Max Frisch and Friedrich Dürrenmatt and (towards the end of the decade) the great exile plays of Bertolt Brecht marking significant exceptions to the rule. Suddenly, stimulated by the revelations during the trial of Adolf Eichmann in Jerusalem and the Frankfurt Auschwitz Trials of 1962–4, a series of documentary dramas shook up the West German theatre and, in turn, provoked a public controversy over the Nazi past and the question of responsibility for its atrocities.

It was significant that Erwin Piscator, one of the great directors of the Weimar period denied a directorship on return from exile, was the only person prepared to risk producing the first of these plays, Rolf Hochhuth's *Der Stellvertreter* (1962). Its most sensational aspect was Hochhuth's charge that the Roman Catholic Church, in the person of Pope Pius XII (the 'representative' of the title), was not devoid of blame for the extermination of the Jews, but the range of characters in the play—from the military, industrial, medical, and academic worlds—made the point that Hochhuth's focus was a much wider one. Heinar Kipphardt's *Joel Brand* (1965), based on testimony given by Brand in Eichmann's trial about the trade between Eichmann and groups attempting to save the lives of Jews, brought out the machine-like nature of the military bureaucracy administering the 'final solution' and in the process suggested certain uncomfortable similarities with aspects of the Vietnam War. The most compelling work of this group, Peter Weiss's verse 'oratorio' *Die Ermittlung* (1965), based on the Frankfurt trials, was also the most wide-ranging. Weiss resisted the temptation to recreate either Auschwitz or the drama of the court-room on the stage. Instead he depersonalized his players—they are simply called Witness 1 or Defendant 3 etc.—and thus avoided the danger of looking only at individual guilt, asking through his selection of material awkward and far-reaching questions of wider relevance and pleading for the critical self-examination of the attitude of West German society to the Holocaust. A statement made by Defendant 1, in particular, summed up and in turn held up to critical examination the attitude to the Nazi past that had prevailed in the Adenauer era: 'Today | now that our nation | has once again worked its way up | to a leading position | we should be concerned with other things | than with recriminations | These should long ago | have been banished from the law books | by the Statute of Limitations.'[15] The 'influence of these plays on public opinion' (Peter Rühmkorf) was, however, such that the Bundestag found itself having to extend the Statute of Limitations in March 1965.

The public stance of West German intellectuals on the *Spiegel* Affair and on its country's 'inability to mourn'[16] for the victims of the Nazi regime were the first indications of a politicization of the cultural life of the Federal Republic that gained intensity during the 1960s. Exploiting an ease of access to the whole range of the media

15 Peter Weiss, *The Investigation*, trans. Alexander Gross (London, 1966), 203.
16 The reference here is to the study of the West German suppression of the Nazi past by Alexander and Margarethe Mitscherlich, *Die Unfähigkeit zu trauern* (Munich, 1967).

Keith Bullivant and C. Jane Rice

not found in other democratic societies, a broad front of writers, artists of various kinds, academics, and liberal journalists drew public attention to worrying aspects of government policy and other matters of concern, both internal and external. One important issue that was addressed throughout most of the decade was the attempt by the various CDU chancellors to pass Emergency Laws giving the government sweeping powers free of parliamentary control in the event not only of war or a nuclear disaster, for example, but also in a situation of 'threatened emergency'. Given historical examples of the abuse of uncontrolled government power in Germany—the examples cited were most commonly the suppression of the Munich Soviet Republic in 1919 and the use made by the Nazis of their Enabling Law of 1933 to suppress opposition—such legislation evoked widespread suspicion. Originally put forward in 1959, but rejected by the Bundesrat in 1960, the Emergency Laws remained part of the declared programme of the Adenauer and Erhard (1963–6) governments. The publication of Karl Jaspers's *Wohin treibt die Bundesrepublik?* in 1966, which quickly became a bestseller, stirred up a vigorous public debate about this bill. Jaspers viewed the Federal Republic as having degenerated into a state dominated by a party oligarchy that ignored the interests of the people. The power of that oligarchy was such, argued Jaspers, that a gradual shift to an authoritarian state, then to dictatorship and with a subsequent war likely to follow, was harrowingly plausible. One indication of the intolerance towards independent criticism of government was represented for him by the *Spiegel* Affair, but of greatest concern were the movement towards a Grand Coalition, which he perceptively anticipated, and the sweeping powers of the proposed Emergency Laws. In this situation it was crucial, he concluded, for citizens to challenge directly the growing might of the party oligarchy. An intensified lobby for this legislation towards the end of Erhard's chancellorship led to the formation in 1966 of the oppositional group 'Crisis of Democracy'—much in the manner that Jaspers recommended—which in October of that year organized a mass rally in Frankfurt, with Hans Magnus Enzensberger and the philosophers Ernst Bloch and Jürgen Habermas among the major speakers. The formation of the Grand Coalition of the CDU/CSU and the SPD in December 1966, which eradicated any effective opposition in the Bundestag, inevitably further heightened anxiety about the erosion of democratic principles in the Federal Republic. Despite a strenuous extra-parliamentary campaign, the Emergency Laws were passed by the Bundestag with the support of the SPD on 30 May 1968.

Another issue which generated emotional energy throughout the 1960s and where, yet again, there was a gulf between parliament and a significant popular lobby, was the American involvement in Vietnam. One important component part of the widespread protest against the escalation of the war, especially against saturation bombing and the use of napalm, was represented by the peace movement that had criticized the militarization of the Federal Republic in the 1950s and which, since 1960, had been addressing in the annual Easter Marches the danger to world peace represented by the increased military build-up of the superpowers. The American military involvement in Vietnam was viewed as yet another extension—the first being the Cuban crisis of 1962—of the ideological conflict into the Third World; it was of particular concern to many West Germans, in that, whether they liked it or not, their country's membership of the Western alliance meant that the Federal Republic was involved in the growing US presence in South-East Asia. The main composers of the songs that were an important part of the culture of the Easter Marches of the early 1960s were Gerd Semmer, Fasia Jansen, and Dieter Süverkrüp, who were just a few years later prominent with anti-Vietnam songs. Much in the way that singers like Pete Seeger, Joan Baez, and Odetta influenced the civil rights movement in the USA, songs by these artists and later by others, such as Franz Josef Degenhardt, Wolf Brannasky, and Reinhold Conrad, played an important part in the many demonstrations against the escalation of the war.

A further important forum of protest against the Vietnam War was provided by the same sort of loose coalition of artists, academics, and journalists that opposed the Emergency Laws. The strength of that stance is apparent from the fact that, in both cases, it is difficult to find the name of any prominent artist or intellectual of the time missing from the lists of participants in demonstrations of all kinds and signatories of numerous public statements. The first major public pronouncement criticizing the war, by Gruppe 47 in 1965 and 'signed by almost all members', distanced itself from Chancellor Erhard's assurance to President Johnson that the country fully supported US policy in Vietnam, viewing the 'scorched-earth' tactics as being tantamount to genocide, and further criticizing the use of napalm and other chemical weapons, as well as the treatment of the civilian population. A large public protest meeting against the war took place in September 1966 and was addressed by Martin Walser, who spoke of the necessity for protest against the 'man-hunt in Vietnam'; later in the same year he spoke of the need to form an organization to co-ordinate and inform protest action against the war. On 2 June 1967 a demonstration took place in West Berlin against the visit of the Shah of Persia, another undemocratic ruler supported by the United States, which led to the shooting of the student Benno Ohnesorg. This was an event that not only intensified the campaign against the Vietnam War in particular, but was of more general significance in the growth at that time of the *Außerparlamentarische Opposition* (APO–Extra-Parliamentary Opposition), within which the criticism of the war was a central issue. In February 1968 the APO organized an international conference on Vietnam, in which major West German writers and intellectuals, as well as representatives from Britain and Italy, took part. Its composition foreshadowed the founding of the Russell Tribunals that were to continue to hammer away at the Vietnam issue.

One important dimension of this campaign was the designation of the Vietnam War as a manifestation of neo-imperialism, that is, as an aggressive form of capitalism that was also to be observed in other parts of the Third World. This identification with the poor and oppressed of such regions, expressed most vividly in the cult of Che Guevara, the revolutionary who had fought with Fidel Castro in Cuba and was later killed fighting with the guerrillas in Bolivia, was an important integral part of the utopian socialism of the 1960s and also led to hopes of solidarity with the working class and of subsequent change towards a socialist society. This was one aspect of what Herbert Marcuse termed the 'Great Refusal' of the time, namely the widespread questioning by those born in the 1930s and later of the status quo in the Federal Republic, as defined by their parents' generation. Gathering pace in the course of the 1960s as a result of the issues examined here, this resistance to the given received further impetus in December 1966 with the formation of the Grand Coalition. A state now headed by an ex-Nazi President, Heinrich Lübke, and an ex-Nazi Chancellor, Kurt Georg Kiesinger, with a government made up of the CDU/CSU and the SPD and thus devoid of any effective opposition, was felt to be anything but democratic. The similarities detected between the planned Emergency Laws and the Nazi Enabling Law provided further confirmation for many of the restorative nature of the Federal Republic, as did a number of scandals exposing the Nazi past of certain prominent persons. To this increasingly ideological rejection of the institutions of the state was added not only a rejection of the material values that defined the older generation, but also the feeling that in industry, as in politics, the same people were in charge as before the war, making money whatever the political climate. This was a dominant theme in the early, increasingly popular chansons of Franz Josef Degenhardt, with his 'Horsti Schmandhoff', 'Im Innern des Landes', and 'Wenn der Senator erzählt' being particularly forceful examples here. This highly sceptical view of the development of the German economy after 1945 was enhanced by the first recession of 1966–7, one that hit older heavy industries especially hard: now earlier notions of class society began to re-emerge. Strikes and demonstrations by miners and steelworkers, often supported by songs and agitprop plays, brought about in the centres of heavy industry a climate redolent of the 1920s and at variance with the policies of compromise and consensus followed by West German trade unions since 1949.

The shooting of Benno Ohnesorg also quickly gave significant impetus to the perhaps most important grouping within the *Außerparlamentarische Opposition*, namely the student movement, centred on the Sozialistischer Deutscher Studentenbund (SDS—Socialist League of German Students). Their criticism of the structure of West German universities in particular and society in general, previously given little attention outside their own circles, was quickly embraced by a much wider group of students after 2 June 1967. While a significant section of the membership of the SDS, schooled in classical Marxist-Leninist texts, took a rigidly communist political line (in the so-called *K-Gruppen* of the later 1960s), a much larger group, including students outside the SDS, was influenced by the utopian ideas in Karl Marx's earlier writings—especially *The German Ideology* and the *Economic and Philosophical Manuscripts* of 1844—and the *Grundrisse*, all of which were discovered by a new generation during the decade. Closely linked to this aspect of Marx's work were ideas stemming from the Frankfurt School (Max Horkheimer, Theodor Adorno, Herbert Marcuse, Erich Fromm, and Jürgen Habermas). The critique of the mass media in modern society in Horkheimer and Adorno's *Dialektik der Aufklärung*, for example, influenced student criticism of the ideological power of the Springer press empire and the campaign demanding its breakup (under the slogan 'Expropriate Springer') in 1967 and 1968. There is little doubt, however, that the most significant influence on the political thinking of young people in the 1960s was that of the German philosopher Herbert Marcuse (then living in San Diego, California). Marcuse's *One-Dimensional Man* (1964) and *An Essay on Liberation* (1969) provided a thoroughgoing critique of advanced modern societies—not just capitalist ones—as being dominated by a dehumanizing and all-pervading technological rationality. Whereas early industrial societies contained within them the possibility of social

Keith Bullivant and C. Jane Rice

and political change, advanced modern affluent society had eroded completely any political opposition, with the bulk of its members content with the pleasures derived from the false liberation of contemporary humankind, as represented by a world free of material shortages and the traditional constraints of taboos on human behaviour. In these two works Marcuse took the line that a humanizing liberation from this new form of enslavement could only be achieved through a 'Great Refusal' co-ordinated by those outside the system within a loosely constituted 'New Left'. Although Marcuse, basing his analysis on his observation of the American civil rights movement and the activities of the hippie generation in the USA, did not include students within the new alliance for change, the appropriation of his ideas by West German students and younger intellectuals clearly signified that they ascribed themselves to such a grouping within the West German context, as did the swift publication of the German translation of Marcuse's *An Essay on Liberation*.

Working-Class Culture and the Emergence of a Counter-Culture

The new anti-capitalism of the 1960s quickly transformed a feature of cultural life that had emerged with gathering momentum during the early years of the decade. In 1961 a group of—initially—local writers from the Ruhrgebiet met in Dortmund to form Gruppe 61; the organizers were Fritz Hüser, a city librarian, and Max von der Grün, a miner with literary ambitions. From its inception there was a fundamental disagreement amongst the membership as to whether it was writing as workers for fellow workers, drawing on a long-established local tradition, or whether it was to broaden the narrow base of West German literature along the lines of what had happened in Sweden and Britain in the 1950s. Max von der Grün's novels— *Männer in zweifacher Nacht* (1962) and *Irrlicht und Feuer* (1963)— were important in breaking new ground, with the latter in particular addressing for the first time in the modern German novel the existential problems of the industrial worker exploited by management and inadequately represented by his trade union in the workplace, whose free time was being increasingly encroached upon by the emergent consumer society of the early 1960s. At the same time *Irrlicht und Feuer* reflected some of the group's uncertainty as to its aims, being critical of working conditions and of the compliance of union officials, but also, in von der Grün's predilection for metaphors, archaizing the miners' relationship to work.

Much of the early work of Gruppe 61 was severely criticized by the literary establishment for its use of outmoded literary forms and clichéed imagery. However, an anthology published in 1966, by which time a number of younger writers had joined the group, not only contained impressive short stories by von der Grün, Matthias Mander, and Angelika Mechtel, but also a reportage by Günter Wallraff, describing his experiences working on the production line in Ford's Cologne plant and exposing the huge discrepancy between the image of the work-place given by Ford's publicity office and the harsh reality. Wallraff's emergence played a major part in the intense politicization of much of West German literature—not merely that dealing with the industrial world—in the 1960s, with his and similar documentary writing continuing to have an important role to play in subsequent decades. Wallraff's collection *Wir brauchen Dich* (1966, reissued in paperback as *Industriereportagen* in 1969) was one of the publishing successes of the decade, to be followed by his *13 unerwünschte Reportagen* (1969). The anti-capitalist critiques of the first volume and the more widely ranging exposés of the second led to court cases and vigorous public discussion, demonstrating in the process the power of an investigative journalism that, with the significant exception of *Der Spiegel*, had been missing from a West German society in which the popular press was dominated by the right-wing Springer concern's *Bild*. This success, together with the growing influence within Gruppe 61 of Erika Runge, editor of the socio-critical *Bottroper Protokolle* (1968), and a number of left-wing critics, led in 1968 to the creation within the group of an informal 'Workshop for Literature of the Industrial World', which launched a competition for reportages from workers. After considerable internal controversy the group decided in 1969 not to recognize this development and in the following year the independent Werkkreis 70 was set up not as a literary organization, but as 'a broadly based democratic movement with unquestionably socialist aims'.[17] Literature such as this was to be of increasing significance during the next two decades.

The documentary prose exposés of Wallraff represented an important, but by no means the only, aspect of a widespread challenge to established ideas about the nature and function of literature, which in turn had consequences for what was considered its appropriate form. The path had, of course, been charted by the documentary plays of Hochhuth, Kipphardt, and Weiss, discussed earlier, and the case of Weiss is particularly illuminating for the

17 Erasmus Schäfer, in the opening speech of the 1970 conference of the new group, *Info*, 5 (1970), 3.

interrelationship between increasing ideological certainty and literary practice at this time. While his famous *Marat/Sade* (1964) does indeed draw on documentary material, it is an essentially fictional work that reflects the—publicly admitted—lack of clarity in Weiss's political thinking at this time. By 1966, however, he had become so firm in his views that he was attacking Enzensberger over the latter's unclear position *vis-à-vis* Vietnam.[18] His agitprop play *Gesang vom Lusitanischen Popanz* (1967) indicting Portuguese colonialism, the play *Vietnam-Diskurs* (1968), and the prose work *Notizen zum kulturellen Leben in der Demokratischen Republik Viet Nam* (1969)—the last two being purely documentary works—all testify in the sharpness of the focus to Weiss's determination now to attack 'capitalism and imperialism on the broadest front'. A related work was Enzensberger's documentary drama *Das Verhör von Habana* (1970), a critique of capitalism focusing on a model situation outside Western Europe, in this case Cuba at the time of the Bay of Pigs invasion (1961), which, the author argued, enabled him the better to make his critical analysis of the nature of international capitalism. Wallraff's 'scenic documentation' *Nachspiele* (1968) attacked the class-based nature of injustice in the Federal Republic in general, with the final part ('Social Partners or the Overcoming of the Class Struggle') being a specific attack on capitalism, much in the manner of the 'street theatre' of the Cologne group Interpol, or of Johannes Schenk and Peter Schütt. Not unrelated to these dramas was F. C. Delius's verse text *Wir Unternehmer* (1966), which like them critically exposed the language of those with economic power; in this case Delius took the proceedings of the Economics Conference of the CDU/CSU in Düsseldorf in 1965 and, by breaking up the flow of the original syntax, showed how apparently high-flown ideals masked a position of self-interest.

Martin Walser's political development during the 1960s was in many ways similar to that of Peter Weiss, in that it was the Vietnam War that induced a move to what became a more or less socialist position. Walser's two major novels of the decade, *Halbzeit* and *Das Einhorn* (1966), both constituted resigned critiques of the negative impact of the affluent society on the individual personality and on human relationships. It was not surprising, therefore, to find Walser claiming that 'bourgeois' literature had lost the 'emancipatory' element it had had in the eighteenth century and had by now degenerated into nothing but 'pure language games'. The reinterpretation of literature by Walser, as with Weiss, led to his opting for the documentary form; Walser, however, took the decision to stop writing and devoted himself from 1967 to 1970 to

18 Cf. 'Peter Weiss und Hans Magnus Enzensberger. Eine Kontroverse', *Kursbuch*, 6 (1966), 165–76.

securing the publication of what Reinhard Baumgart called 'the literature of the non-authors'. He encouraged Erika Runge's *Bottroper Protokolle*, to which he also wrote the preface, as he did to Ursula Trauberg's *Vorleben* (1968) and Wolfgang Werner's *Vom Waisenhaus ins Zuchthaus* (1969). These works, together with Rosalie Rother's *Rosalka oder Wie es eben so ist* (1969), were all derived from tape-recorded interviews with victims of society. For Walser they represented a return of the emancipatory to literature and, at the same time, the adaptation of a more down-to-earth narrative style. The texts themselves are not unproblematical, but in these views Walser was by no means alone: it was highly significant that in his famous—and frequently misunderstood—pronouncement of 'the end of literature' in 1968 Enzensberger, naming Wallraff as one outstanding example, declared the immediate future to belong to documentary literature.

While the publication of *Kursbuch 15* in 1968, in which Enzensberger's polemic was contained, is rightly seen as the rhetorical high point in the debate about literature in the latter half of the decade, documentary literature was only one part, although arguably the most important, of the complex that was the radical questioning of established literature at this time. One strand of this was the criticism made by Peter Hamm, Walter Boehlich, and Karl Markus Michel of the *Großkritiker*; Hamm specifically attacked the Zurich Germanist Emil Staiger as exemplifying the authoritarian emphasis on 'timeless values' in the evaluation of art and the total ignoring of its material context, but it was also true of the critics writing for the conservative press, especially in the *Frankfurter Allgemeine Zeitung*. In the universities similar charges were made against *Germanistik*, which was criticized for the close connection with National Socialism of some of its best-known practitioners in the past and for not having changed after 1945; it was seen as conservative and authoritarian, resisting change, and even, it was argued in some quarters, serving the capitalist system. One response to this unease was the founding, in the course of the 1960s, of a number of expressly left-wing journals, such as *Das Argument*, *kürbiskern*, *konkret*, and, most importantly, *Kursbuch* (meaning literally 'train timetable'). The latter was founded by Hans Magnus Enzensberger in 1966 and rapidly became the foremost journal of the APO. Another thrust, drawing on Walter Benjamin's essay 'Der Autor als Produzent' (1934), was the attempt to desublimate the writer, enlisting him/her in the service of the working class and, in the process, changing the social function of literature. This applied to ideas being developed within Gruppe 61, but notions of taking

Keith Bullivant and C. Jane Rice

publishing outlets away from 'alien capitalist control', put forward in the late 1960s, also fitted in here.

Another butt of increasing criticism was Gruppe 47, which was now felt by many to have attained establishment status. Heinrich Böll expressed concern that the group was by now effectively 'in absurd conformity with society' and, together with other prominent members, stopped attending its meetings;[19] for Martin Walser and some others the decision to hold the group's 1966 meeting in the United States led to their staying away as a protest against the Vietnam War. The next and, as it turned out, final meeting of the group was picketed by students who urged it to take a stance against the power of the Axel Springer newspaper empire. This it duly did, but the voting pattern over this issue brought out the extent of internal rifts in the group, and the criticism of Springer failed to change the perception of Gruppe 47 within the student movement as being 'in complicity with the ruling class'.[20] There is a clear generational aspect to this, as Peter Handke's attack on Gruppe 47 at its 1966 meeting in Princeton and the criticism of it in the (then) student periodical konkret made clear. The campaigns against the Emergency Laws and the Vietnam War, important component parts of the APO, were heavily dependent on the prestige stemming from the involvement of Heinrich Böll, Hans Magnus Enzensberger, Erich Fried, Rolf Hochhuth, Walter Jens, Reinhard Lettau, and Martin Walser, but this was essentially to be understood as the individual participation of members of Gruppe 47 who had, during the 1960s, been politicized in a way that brought them ever closer to the student movement than to their former colleagues in the group. A significant exception here was Günter Grass, a target of sharp criticism at this time; his unease about the APO was at the heart of his 1969 novel Örtlich betäubt, the dramatic version of that text, Davor (1969), and his documentary novel Aus dem Tagebuch einer Schnecke (1972).

The mocking by Peter Handke of the 'descriptive impotence' of the established members of Gruppe 47 was only in part a challenge of disrespectful youth. The controversy also represented a symbolic clash of more or less traditional writing and a radically different alternative that had its origins in Handke's native Austria. The experimental writing of the Wiener Gruppe, notably of H. C. Artmann, Eugen Gomringer, Ernst Jandl, and Gerhard Rühm, drew its inspiration from the ideas on language of the philosopher Ludwig Wittgenstein and from the example of Dada. At a first glance much of this writing appears to be nothing more than entertaining linguistic play, but to Rühm and Helmut Heißenbüttel, who were

19 Heinrich Böll, 'Wer hat Angst vor der Gruppe 47?', in Reinhard Lettau (ed.), Die Gruppe 47: Bericht, Kritik, Polemik (Neuwied and Berlin, 1967), 400.
20 Ulrike Meinhof, konkret (Oct. 1967), 3.

responsible for introducing the work of the Wiener Gruppe to West Germany in the 1960s, it had much greater significance. Rühm claimed that it rejected the 'hierarchical principle of the sentence', while Heißenbüttel said that Gomringer's texts 'broke the impact of authority in society' by the way in which they ceased to be a 'bearer of ideas' for established social values.[21] Handke made much the same point in the most famous of his speech-plays of the late 1960s, *Kaspar* (1968). Drawing on the story of the foundling Kaspar Hauser, Handke suggests through the way Kaspar is made to speak that language pre-shapes experience and forces him to submit to its authority, robbing him in the process of his individuality. Somewhat similar to this was the claim made by Dieter Wellershoff in his essays of the late 1960s that conventional styles of writing constantly reproduce a known world and thereby serve to confirm it, at the same time suppressing untapped human potential in individuals essentially crippled by social norms.

This challenge to the authority or aura of established notions of literature was similar to the basic stance behind the pop art of Andy Warhol, Roy Lichtenstein, and other American artists who emerged around this time, and whose work was immediately made accessible to the West German 'scene' in 1969 in two much-discussed anthologies edited by Rolf Dieter Brinkmann, *ACID* and *Silverscreen*. Something very similar was also at the heart of much West German avant-garde writing in the 1960s that effectively tried to desublimate both the work of art and the writer, as perceived by 'bourgeois' culture. One method of doing this practised by Heißenbüttel, Franz Mon, and a number of other writers was the use of literary collage, in the creation of which the writer was reduced from 'creative personality' to compiler and organizer of 'ready-mades'. Whereas, in a conventional text, 'it is the intention behind a given meaning that directs the selection and structuring of the linguistic material, in the case of collage the meaning is retrospectively fashioned by the reader', argued Franz Mon.[22] In Ror Wolf's *Pilzer und Pelzer* (1967) the author attempted to produce a book 'that you can take off the shelf, open at random, begin to read at any page';[23] in Peter O. Chotjewitz's novel *Die Insel* (1968) the reader was at one point invited to alter it in any way if it were not to his or her taste and in *Der Postversand-Roman* (1970) by Peter Faecke and Wolf Vostell the readers had to arrange the material according to their own preferences. Others, notably Rolf Dieter Brinkmann, tried to destroy the aura of the writer as creative personality by emphasizing the instant nature of their work; there were, Brinkmann maintained,

21 Gerhard Rühm, introduction to Gerhard Rühm (ed.), *Die Wiener Gruppe* (Reinbek, 1967); and Helmut Heißenbüttel, introduction to Eugen Gomringer, *worte sind schatten* (Reinbek, 1969).
22 Franz Mon, *prinzip collage* (Neuwied and Berlin, 1968), 50.
23 Quoted in Lothar Baier (ed.), *Über Ror Wolf* (Frankfurt am Main, 1972), 154–5.

better things to do than 'fiddle away at a poem for a long time—walking around town, reading the paper, going to the cinema, picking one's nose, listening to records, chatting to people about this and that'.[24]

The challenge of a generation, marked by its thoroughgoing anti-authoritarian position *vis-à-vis* concepts of art perceived as élitist and thus outdated, received public support in a lecture given by the American critic Leslie Fiedler at the University of Freiburg in 1968. Rapidly translated into German, 'The Case for Postmodernism' evoked strong support from younger writers and anxious criticism from those with more conservative tastes. The basic thesis of Fiedler's lecture was that literature in the modern age should subvert established values by focusing on those embodied by the new anti-heroes of pop culture:

The notion of one art for the 'cultured' and a sub-art for the 'uncultured' represents the last survival in mass industrial societies of an invidious distinction proper only to a class-structured community. Precisely because it carries on a war against that anachronistic survival, pop art is, whatever its overt politics, subversive, a threat to all hierarchies in so far as it is hostile to order.[25]

Given the strength of anti-American feeling because of the Vietnam War, it was ironic that the real inspiration forces for the new pop literature should have come from America. They included, apart from Leslie Fiedler, Frank O'Hara's *Lunch Poems* (translated by Brinkmann in 1969), a large number of texts from the 'dirty speech' movement and 'Fuck you' magazines, the comics of Robert Crumb, the Hollywood cinema, and the world of pop. Here Janis Joplin and Jimi Hendrix in particular were allocated significant status as the embodiments of what Herbert Marcuse, emphasizing much the same agenda as Fiedler, called the 'New Sensibility' in his influential *An Essay on Liberation*. In the whole range of manifestations of the West German 'underground' or 'subculture' scene of the late 1960s we find a blend of certain ideas of the early Marx on alienation fused with a radically anti-bourgeois lifestyle that included drug-taking and the breaking down of sexual taboos. The result was that—in stark contrast to the unmitigated seriousness of the strictly political agenda of the SDS—the change that seemed to be within reach in 1968 was essentially defined, much in the terms of Timothy Leary's notion of the 'Politics of Ecstasy', as 'a revolution with guitars and sex and pot and giving up and refusing and laughing'.[26]

24 Rolf Dieter Brinkmann, 'Anmerkungen zu meinem Gedicht "Vanille"', *März-Texte 1* (Darmstadt, 1969), 141–4.

25 Published in English under the title 'close the border, cross the gap', *Playboy* (Dec. 1989), 230. It appeared in German as 'Das Zeitalter der neuen Literatur' (in two parts) in the weekly *Christ und Welt* on 13 and 20 Sept. 1968.

26 Helmut Salzinger, 'Das lange Gedicht', in Vasilis Tsakaridis (ed.), *Super Garde* (Düsseldorf, 1969), 167–91.

1968: The Year of Revolution

The main impetus of the 'Great Refusal' that we have been tracing through the second half of the 1960s culminated in the events of 1968, a year in which the USA, France, and Germany were hit by a wave of social turmoil. The international Vietnam Conference in West Berlin in February 1968 was quickly followed by the attempted assassination of the SDS leader Rudi Dutschke in Berlin on 11 April. The latter event immediately sparked off a series of nation-wide demonstrations against the Springer press, which had been vociferous in its denunciation of all protest and had already been the object of criticism by liberal writers concerned at the power wielded by a media empire controlling well over 30 per cent of the German press. That year's Easter March, which took place soon after the attack on Dutschke, attracted over 300,000 participants, largely as a result of the escalation of the Vietnam War, which in May of that year took a significant turn for the worse with the MyLai massacre. These events, fuelled by the events in Paris in that same month—when students seemed to obtain significant conces-sions from the authorities—provoked constant demonstrations in the streets of major cities and on university campuses, where the student movement was demanding radical reform of the archaic West German system of higher education. Moreover, the over-reaction of the police and other authorities further increased appre-hension about the consequences of the possible misuse of the Emergency Laws, which were finally passed at the end of that month. The excitement generated by the 'Prague Spring' of 1968 and the subsequent disillusionment as troops from the Warsaw Pact invaded Czechoslovakia in August of that year coexisted with the sense of the necessity for a 'cultural revolution' along the lines of the Chinese model. The International Song Festival in Essen in September, following on the fifth such festival at Burg Waldeck (Hunsrück) in May, was testimony to the international nature of revolutionary events and to the cultural breadth of the agenda for change. In October of that year there were extensive protests—where yet again the police were called in—at the annual Frankfurt Book Fair against the way in which the big literary houses such as Suhrkamp and Rowohlt made money out of the left-wing move-ment. At the same time there were attempts made by the editors in a number of publishing houses to 'democratize' the production of literature, and Enzenberger's *Kursbuch*, the prototypical journal of the New Left, moved from Suhrkamp to Wagenbach, in turn the

Keith Bullivant and C. Jane Rice

example *par excellence* of the new sort of venture that was felt to be needed. Perhaps the fullest realization of these aspirations came in 1973, with the founding of the 'AutorenEdition' as a writing and publishing collective, in which manuscripts were evaluated by an editorial board made up of colleagues elected by their fellow writers.

Many new trends began and a younger generation of writers-to-be came to the fore at this time who were going to be of importance in the 1970s and beyond. Taken together, these various aspects of the multifaceted year of revolution represented the apogee of the APO, which was in the following year rendered redundant in its then form by the election victory of Willy Brandt and the end of the Grand Coalition. The turbulent events and focal issues of the year, recorded so graphically in the pages of *Kursbuch* and other left-wing journals on the one hand, and the 'bourgeois' press on the other, brought out just to what extent the Federal Republic was now locked in an essentially generational conflict, with the student generation seeing the state in all its manifestations as restoratively authoritarian and, indeed, inherently fascist. And one particular protest—the placing of small fire-bombs in a Frankfurt department store in March 1968 by Andreas Baader, Gudrun Ennslin, and others, in protest against the Vietnam War—not only led to severe punitive action by the courts in October, but also marked the start of a campaign of terrorism, based on an extreme radicalization of the agenda of 1968, that was to dominate the life of the Federal Republic for years to come.

While 1968 was perhaps not a 'year of revolution' for women, it did mark a turning-point in many respects. In that year, the West German women's movement began to take shape, with the founding of the Action Committee for the Liberation of Women in Berlin and its protest at the national conference of the SDS in Frankfurt against the male leadership, as well as the establishment of the Women's Council (Weiberrat) in Frankfurt. The late 1960s also brought a political engagement and feminist interest to women's literature, but the striking changes of the end of the decade were preceded by a number of more subtle shifts.

By the early 1960s, the lives of a large number of women had also begun to change. With more women in the work-force than at any previous time in the post-war period, women began to gain greater economic independence, and the rigidly defined gender roles of the early post-war period began to blur slightly. The rising divorce-rate and the declining marriage- and birth-rates reflected the fact that women were less inclined to define themselves solely as housewives and mothers. According to a series in the magazine *stern* in 1960 and 1961, approximately 1 million abortions were performed in West Germany each year, in spite of the fact that abortion remained illegal; and the introduction of the birth-control pill in the 1960s, by further diminishing the connection between having sex and having children, also contributed to a shift in male–female relationships. The 'sexual revolution' of the mid-1960s, which included attempts to overcome sexual taboos and seek freedom from repressive norms, likewise led to a rethinking of gender relations. When the generation of women born after the war came of age in the mid-1960s, they were less willing to tolerate the double burden of housework and career and the other negative repercussions of the conservative West German family policy; in fact, the Action Committee for the Liberation of Women grew out of efforts by young women of the left to organize day-care centres. Finally, the emancipatory impulse of the anti-authoritarian student movement served to heighten the mounting discontent among a wide variety of women over their role in society and their personal relationships with men, which spawned the feminist movement of the following decade.

While some cultural and political analysts were arguing as early as 1971 that all hope of change in West German society had dissipated (others opted for 1973 or even 1982, the year of the SPD leaving power), the long-term effects of the APO are not to be underestimated—indeed, some have even claimed that it ultimately brought about a thorough modernization and Westernization of the country. Taking stock of the situation in 1969 Jürgen Habermas criticized the naïve analysis of the APO and the inappropriateness of its 'pseudo-revolutionary tactics', urging instead 'a campaign of mass enlightenment'. That particular lesson seemed to have been well learned: a whole range of citizens' initiatives and, in particular, the emergence of the Green Party as a sort of synthesis of many of these in the early 1980s were testimony to this and helped to shape the commendably lively forum of public debate that developed in West Germany after 1969. A less visible, but none the less important part of German public life after that time was the relative success of the 'long march through the institutions' that was recommended to the students and others as the APO (in its then form) came to an end. The political parties—and not just the Greens—at national and regional levels, the professions, the civil service, and the media were all increasingly influenced by the generation of 1968 and that impact seemed likely to grow in the 1990s and beyond.

Keith Bullivant and C. Jane Rice

One particularly striking example here was in the area of town-planning and architecture. In the 1950s, as the serious rebuilding of the cities was embarked upon, the dominant style adopted was a modern internationalism, understood as indicative of West German 'progress', but used indiscriminately, without regard to the tradition and the ambience within which projects were contextualized. Two striking examples from Berlin illustrated this especially clearly: between 1957 and 1959 the *Hansaviertel*, a previously lively neighbourhood on the edge of the Tiergarten, was cleared for the *Interbau* exposition; it resulted in a soulless potpourri of then current modernist styles and the total destruction of the social infrastructure that had given the area its pre-war vitality. Similarly, the modern building located within the shell of the Kaiser Wilhelm Memorial Church (1962) demonstrated vividly the clash of old and new, rather than harmonious coexistence, that marked much urban rebuilding of the 1950s. Other cities were blighted by the priority given at this time to the motor car, leading to the soulless vehicular jungle that still characterizes, for example, Cologne, Frankfurt, and, above all, Hanover, the supreme monument to the planning obsessions of the day. Against that has to be noted the way in which so many city councils during the 1970s and beyond were concerned with re-establishing the neighbourliness of their cities, creating pedestrian areas and 'drive slow' zones, children's playgrounds and pleasant green areas, while encouraging local markets in the city centres that returned the communal feel to many previously barren urban centres. All this is unimaginable without the environmental concerns expressed and addressed by the generation of 1968, a generation which, as the following chapter argues, helped bring about a sea change in the political culture of the Federal Republic.

Suggested Further Reading

The following studies trace developments in the political and social history of the Federal Republic since 1945:

Benz, Wolfgang (ed.), *Die Geschichte der Bundesrepublik Deutschland*, i. *Politik*; iii. *Gesellschaft* (Frankfurt am Main, 1989).

Bracher, Karl D., *Nach 25 Jahren: Eine Deutschland-Bilanz* (Munich, 1970).

Childs, David, and **Johnson, Jeffrey**, *West Germany: Politics and Society* (London, 1981).

Greiffenhagen, Martin, and **Greiffenhagen, Sylvia,** *Ein schwieriges Vaterland: Zur politischen Kultur im vereinigten Deutschland* (Munich and Leipzig, 1993).

Smith, Gordon, *Democracy in Western Germany: Parties and Politics in the Federal Republic* (London, 1978).

The general surveys listed below provide detailed histories of culture in West Germany since 1945:

Benz, Wolfgang (ed.) *Die Geschichte der Bundesrepublik Deutschland*, iv. *Kultur* (Frankfurt am Main, 1989).

Glaser, Hermann, *Die Kulturgeschichte der Bundesrepublik Deutschland*, i. *Zwischen Kapitulation und Währungsreform 1945–1948*; ii. *Zwischen Grundgesetz und Großer Koalition 1949–1967* (Frankfurt am Main, 1990).

Hermand, Jost, *Kultur im Wiederaufbau: Die Bundesrepublik Deutschland 1945–1965* (Munich, 1986).

The following discuss the social and cultural position of women:

Brinkler-Gabler, Gisela (ed.), *Deutsche Literatur von Frauen* (Munich, 1988).

Delille, Angela, and Grohn, Andrea, *Blick zurück aufs Glück: Frauenleben und Familienpolitik in den 50er Jahren* (Berlin, 1985).

Delille, Angela, and Crohn, Andrea, *Perlonzeit: Wie die Frauen ihr Wirtschaftswunder erlebten*[3] (Berlin, 1988).

Freier, Anna-Elisabeth, and Kuhn, Annette (eds.), *'Das Schicksal Deutschlands liegt in der Hand seiner Frauen': Frauen in der deutschen Nachkriegsgeschichte* (Düsseldorf, 1984).

Kolinsky, Eva, *Women in West Germany: Life, Work and Politics* (Oxford, 1989).

Moeller, Robert G., 'Reconstructing the Family in Reconstruction Germany: Women and Social Policy in the Federal Republic, 1945–1955', *Feminist Studies*, 1 (1989), 137–69.

Ruhl, Klaus-Jörg (ed.), *Frauen in der Nachkriegszeit: 1945–1963* (Munich, 1988).

The following books are concerned with the education system in the Federal Republic and the anti-authoritarian student movement of the 1960s:

Fichter, Tilman, and Lönnendonker, Siegward, *Kleine Geschichte des SDS* (Berlin, 1977).

Hearnden, Arthur, *Education in the Two Germanies* (Oxford, 1974).

Hearnden, Arthur, *Education, Culture and Politics in West Germany* (Oxford, 1976).

Hearnden, Arthur, *The British in Germany: Education Reconstruction after 1945* (London, 1978).

Lüdke, Martin, *Literatur und Studentenbewegung* (Opladen, 1977).

The following volumes provide collections of important primary material relating to West German writers and their involvement in politics:

Lettau, Reinhard (ed.), *Die Gruppe 47: Bericht, Kritik, Polemik* (Neuwied and Berlin, 1967).

Richter, Hans Werner (ed.), *Almanach der Gruppe 47 1947–1962* (Reinbek, 1962).

Schwab-Felisch, Hans (ed.), *Der Ruf: Eine deutsche Nachkriegsgeschichte* (Munich, 1962).

Wagenbach, Klaus, *et al.* (eds.), *Vaterland, Muttersprache: Deutsche Schriftsteller und ihr Staat seit 1945* (Berlin, 1994).

The following studies provide detailed analyses of developments in literature and the theatre:

Bullivant, Keith, *The Future of German Literature* (Oxford, 1994).

Hermand, Jost, Peitsch, Helmut, and **Scherpe, Klaus**, *Nachkriegsliteratur in Deutschland 1945–49* (2 vols; Berlin, 1982–3).

Mayer, Hans, *Deutsche Literatur seit Thomas Mann* (Reinbek, 1967).

Thomas, Richard Hinton, and **Bullivant, Keith**, *Literature in Upheaval* (Manchester, 1974).

Thomas, Richard Hinton, and **van der Will, Wilfried**, *The German Novel and the Affluent Society* (Manchester, 1968).

The following may be consulted for information on particular aspects of the mass media:

Humphreys, Peter J., *Media and Media Policy in Germany: The Press and Broadcasting since 1945* (Oxford, 1994).

Sandford, John, *The Mass Media of the German-Speaking Countries* (London, 1976).

Sandford, John, *The New German Cinema* (London, 1980).

Schmieding, Walter, *Kunst oder Kasse—Der Ärger mit dem deutschen Film* (Hamburg, 1961).

Vosz, Manfred (ed.), *Songbuch* (Munich, 1968).

Williams, Arthur, *Broadcasting and Democracy in Germany* (Bradford, 1976).

6

The Federal Republic 1968 to 1990: From the Industrial Society to the Culture Society

ROB BURNS

WILFRIED
VAN DER WILL

THE central feature of the period to be dealt with in this chapter is German society's increasing preoccupation with the quality of life, even though this theme informed neither the political battles and social tensions at the beginning of that period nor, for that matter, the breathtaking process of national unification which concluded it. Initially, it was the most traditional problem of capitalism that appeared to confront West German society. By the late 1960s the 'social partnership' characteristic of the Adenauer era threatened to give way to a renewed class antagonism: 1968 was the high-water mark of the anti-authoritarian student movement and the APO, while the following year saw the eruption of mass wildcat strikes by the metalworkers. Just as the students questioned the legitimacy of West Germany's class-based society and its capitalist foundations, so sections of the labour movement displayed a new militancy that seemed to herald the resurgence of class conflict. Additionally, the early 1970s witnessed the emergence of small gangs of political terrorists, whose atrocities were committed in the name of class warfare. Yet the hallmark of the period under review here was not in fact the reinstatement of class politics but the determination on the part of West German citizens to shape the political agenda and inject it with new themes.

The achievements of the previous period—the restoration of a competitive market economy, the establishment of a consumer society, the economic, political, and military integration of the

Federal Republic within the Western world—began to be queried. In particular, the obsession with economic growth and purely materialist notions of progress were increasingly called into question. What now seized the social and political imagination of West Germans were the following issues: How could an increase in active political participation be attained in order that the processes of planning and decision-making become more transparent to the people affected by them? How were the social provisions of the state to be expanded and educational opportunities to be extended to economically less privileged sections of society? How might the quality of urban life be improved? How could industrial growth be structurally transformed so as not to destroy the natural environment? These concerns indicated a redirection of social and political energy away from pure economic achievement and towards the qualitative improvement of the physical and cultural environment. In the 1970s and 1980s, then, a new political agenda was established which included the expansion of culture at all levels and allowed the vision of a 'culture society' to edge towards the centre-stage of politics.

The Emergence of the *Kulturgesellschaft* as a Political Programme

At the beginning of the 1970s the head of the cultural department in the German Foreign Office, Hans Georg Steltzer, strongly advocated a definition of culture which both went far beyond the narrow confines of high culture and dispensed with a particular German twist in this concept. Uniquely, German traditional education had insisted on a strict separation between the values of civil society, such as the conduct of politics or the shaping of the environment (*Zivilisation*), and those of the individual, such as the cultivation of the spirit, character, and intellect (*Kultur*). This idiosyncrasy had to be ended, Steltzer urged: 'Culture and civilization must be one, the entire environment which human beings have created for themselves must be encompassed by the modern conception of culture.'[1] In the same year, 1971, the Foreign Minister, Walter Scheel, argued forcefully that culture must be socially inclusive and extend to questions of the physical environment: 'Culture is no longer a privilege for the few but should be accessible to everyone. We should no longer sit in awe of Dürer, Bach, and Beethoven; we must arouse interest in the burning problems of the present day, including adult education, opening up educational opportunities, the reform of the school system, and problems of the environment.'[2]

1 Quoted in Wolfgang Mangenbucher, Ralf Rytlewski, and Bernd Weyergraf (eds.), *Kulturpolitisches Wörterbuch: Bundesrepublik Deutschland/DDR im Vergleich* (Stuttgart, 1983), 383.
2 Ibid.

Rob Burns and Wilfried van der Will

Increasingly there was talk of fashioning the Federal Republic as a *Kulturstaat*. The Minister of the Interior, Gerhart Baum, stated in 1976 that while the creation of art was the responsibility of the individual artist and must remain free of any interventions by the state, all the relevant state institutions should conceive of themselves as organs of a *Kulturstaat* and give every possible financial support to the arts. The big towns, with their vast budgets for theatres, opera houses, libraries, museums, and their many artistic prizes, began to compete against each other with respect to the quality of life and diversity of culture they were able to offer, in order to attract and retain a sophisticated labour force. In a speech at the beginning of the 1980s, setting out the priorities that had crucially informed town-planning in the 1970s, the cultural secretary of the Council of German Cities and Towns, Jürgen Grabbe, identified with admirable clarity the vital interconnections between culture and the economy:

It is the diversity of its cultural assets and resources which constitutes the attractiveness of a town. . . . The high value placed by a town on its provisions for living space and leisure—essentially predicated on the quality of its cultural life—determines the attractiveness of employment in that town and hence represents an important factor in its efforts to attract new trade and industry; it is decisive for the creation of jobs. . . . Investing in culture, therefore, means investing in the future.[3]

In other words, towns in the Federal Republic realized that their image depended substantially on their ratings as centres of culture.

In the 1980s culture became the object of parliamentary debates in Germany. The first of these, held in 1983, was still astonishingly vague, amounting to little more than an affirmation of pride in the liberality of the arts this side of the Iron Curtain. The manipulative attempts of the East German regime to give that state an identity as a socialist *Kulturnation* were matched at that time by the lip-service the Bundestag paid to cultural freedom. Four years later, however, the government struck an altogether more visionary note. In his inaugural address to the German parliament following the federal elections of 1987 the Chancellor, Helmut Kohl, stated with amazing boldness:

We are simultaneously an industrial society and a culture society (*Kulturgesellschaft*). At a time which both demands and encompasses a new sense of responsibility, an acute sensitivity for values as well as fresh ideas on how to shape all spheres of life in an increasingly humane fashion, culture acquires a leading role. The federal government will, therefore, as far as is feasible, give particular stress to the development of our culture state (*Kulturstaat*).[4]

3 Quoted in Karla Fohrbeck and Andreas Wiesand, *Von der Industriegesellschaft zur Kulturgesellschaft* (Munich, 1989), 78.
4 Quoted ibid. 145.

He then went on to announce—no doubt mindful of the ambitious cultural plans being pursued in Paris—a number of German prestige projects, like the House of History of the Federal Republic, the German Historical Museum, and the Cultural Foundation of the Federal States. Under close scrutiny Kohl's statements revealed the conceptual difficulty of positing the 'culture society' as a political goal. On the one hand, culture was recognized, along with industry, as the chief pillar of German society; on the other hand, in his specific proposals culture was still essentially seen as a decorative, prestige-giving adjunct to politics restricted to the privileged social strata that benefited from high culture.

The inclusion of the 'culture society' in his speech was by no means an entirely original initiative on the Chancellor's part. Shortly before, at its conference in 1986, the Christian Democratic Union (CDU) had issued a 'Manifesto for the Future' in which it was acknowledged that German society derived its identity as much from its status as a 'culture society' as from its economic and social achievements. The Manifesto envisaged that both urban and rural environments were gradually to be developed as spaces for cultural experience; a plurality of lifestyles was to be encouraged and politics had to respect the autonomy of decentralized, community-based cultural initiatives. The Free Democrats, too, approved a strategy paper in 1986 in which they declared that culture as the fulfilment of diverse spiritual and intellectual needs was to be accorded at least equal status with the economy. Arguably, however, it was the Social Democrats who advanced the most sophisticated and comprehensive elaboration of the concept of the 'culture society'. Their deliberations, also initially formulated in 1986, culminated in the SPD's new Basic Programme of 1989, with its centre-piece, Section IV, pleading for 'a new culture of mutual toleration and collaboration'. The projected 'culture society' was to engage in responsible interaction with nature, enhance the quality of labour, and evolve a political culture which thrived on adversarial debate (*Streitkultur*) rooted in a basic social consensus. Culture, once thought of by socialists as part of an ideological superstructure that was subject to economic determinations, now became defined as the basic social environment which channelled, and gave meaning to, economic activity. In other words, the *Kulturgesellschaft* was clearly seen by the SPD as a project in which society was to be endowed with its cohesion and purpose through the transformative impetus of culture.

It is a striking coincidence that all the various parties set out their programmes for the development of the 'culture society' literally at the same time, in the one year, 1986. Moreover, they evidently

Rob Burns and Wilfried van der Will

believed that they were each individually pioneering an entirely new and distinctive vision. In truth they merely responded, within a framework of democratic federalism, to well-established social and cultural changes which they perceived in much the same way. Hence the remarkable consensus that emerged from their programmatic statements. Their emphasis on decentralization and autonomy derived from a long-held conception of culture as an area of legislation which constitutionally devolved upon the individual federal states (their oft proclaimed 'cultural sovereignty'). This was itself a reaction against the manipulative cultural centralism of the Third Reich. At the same time, and more significantly, the CDU/CSU, the FDP, and the SPD were reacting to a variety of demands and pressures largely generated by grass-roots movements in the 1970s. These were flanked by the Greens in the 1980s, but ultimately cut across all party-political divides. The projection of the 'culture society', therefore, could not remain the preserve of any one political organization and became a central plank in the platforms of all the major parties of the Federal Republic. However, it is equally striking that these programmes were formulated relatively late, especially since, as we have seen, a number of voices in the social-liberal government had already advocated the importance of a broader, socially differentiated understanding of culture in the early and mid-1970s. It is true that the debate on culture was not always in the foreground of politics, owing to more pressing and conventional themes occupying the political agenda: the oil crisis and its ramifications for the economy, the containment of terrorism, and the resurgence of the Cold War. However, the topicality of these issues in the 1970s and early 1980s did not, of course, mean that the process of change which had initially inspired some representatives of government to seek a discourse on culture had in fact been halted. We propose to address that process of change in order to show the transition from a society chiefly preoccupied with economic growth to one in which cultural concerns came to attain paramount importance.

Social Change and the Increasing Importance of Culture

While we need to focus attention on lifestyles, changes in social values, and the diversification of cultural environments, the fact remains that progress towards the 'culture society' was crucially dependent on the maintenance of material affluence. Net earnings per capita had risen from DM4,301 per annum in 1960 to DM8,790 in 1970, increasing further to DM16,281 in 1978. That is to say, after making allowance for inflation, West Germans achieved an average real growth of income per annum of 2.9 per cent. The average net income per family in 1980 was an annual DM37,920. In 1981 out of every hundred middle-income families 97 possessed a television set, 96 a camera, 90 a telephone, 84 a car, 83 a refrigerator, 80 a radio and an automatic washing machine, 65 a deep freeze, 35 a hi-fi, 28 a dishwasher, and 18 a steam press. Consumer durables of this type either were labour-saving devices freeing time for cultural activities in a broad sense or themselves directly facilitated certain kinds of cultural consumption. While in 1967 52.8 per cent of the average disposable income was spent on food, clothing, and housing, this figure had dropped to 39.5 per cent in 1985, with 60 per cent being set aside for savings, travel, and leisure activities.

The importance of the latter was significantly enhanced by an appreciable reduction in labour time. By the end of 1974 some 90 per cent of employees in commerce and industry had achieved a 40-hour or five-day week without any loss of earnings. In 1984 the metalworkers, after a protracted strike, negotiated a 38.5-hour week, which was further reduced to 37.5 in 1987, with paradigmatic effects for other industries. By 1982 no fewer than 150 days of the year, including official holidays, weekends, and holiday entitlements, were work-free for most employees. The German obsession with work had become transformed into an obsession with leisure. For example, the membership of clubs and associations affiliated to the German Sports Federation shot up from 5.3 million in 1960 to 10.1 million in 1970, 16.9 million in 1980, and 20 million in 1987. Expenditure on leisure and holidays stood at DM220 billion in 1986 (10 per cent of GDP), with two-thirds of the population going on holiday, mainly in their private cars. Suffice it to say, the vastly increased significance of leisure within contemporary German society was attested to by the establishment of leisure studies as an academic discipline and by the institutionalization of the politics of leisure at all levels of public administration from the early 1970s onwards.

In addition to the increase in affluence and leisure, the third factor in the heightened importance of culture was the expansion of the education sector. Between 1970 and 1980 the number of students staying on at school until the age of 16 grew by 69 per cent, from 273,000 to 461,000, while the sixth-form population nearly doubled. Several new universities and polytechnics (*Fachhochschulen*) were established and the total number of students in higher education rose from 471,000 to 1,120,000. Within this expansion of the student body there was a disproportional acceleration in the number

Rob Burns and Wilfried van der Will

of women (from 25 per cent in 1960 to 38 per cent in 1987) and of students from working-class backgrounds (from 4 per cent in 1960 to 13.5 per cent in 1987), although in the traditional universities the percentage of the latter, after an initial increase in the mid-1970s, was less notable, and indeed declined again during the 1980s.

Some analysts, clinging to a traditional Marxist approach, interpreted the expansion of education and the modernization of the curricula in the schools and universities merely as a function of the increased pressures of rationalization exerted by the capitalist market. In other words, these analysts were still centrally concerned with a discussion of German society purely as a market economy. Yet, as we have shown, it was precisely because of the successful functioning of the German economy that the spheres of education, leisure, and the media could assume a weightier and relatively independent status. It was, of course, still possible to apply to German society the analytical categories of classical political economy and describe it as fundamentally divided between a class of wage-earners and one of owners of capital, or, alternatively, as a 'two-thirds society', with the majority actively involved in consumption and civic affairs, and one-third ascribed to the status of a politically and economically marginalized 'underclass'. However, for the purposes of cultural analysis these approaches lacked differentiation. Contemporary research into the sociology of industrial society, though not specifically focused on Germany, is more helpful, in particular the studies of 'post-industrial society' written in the early 1970s by Daniel Bell and Alain Touraine. These highlighted the long-term shifts in occupational patterns, social composition, and levels of affluence which could be found in all advanced Western nations. Although talk of a post-industrial society may be exaggerated in view of the persistence of industrial manufacturing, there can be no doubting the massive expansion of the service industries in the second half of the twentieth century. This tertiary sector (trade, finance, transport, health, recreation, research, education, and government administration) gave rise to a vast, politically and culturally diffuse service class which swelled to around three-fifths of the population, basically at the expense of agricultural and blue-collar labour. It was within the context of these far-reaching social changes that cultural sociology focused on the increasing pluralization of lifestyles in the 1970s and 1980s. Such studies were guided by the perception that social groups acquired their identity less through their location in the production process than through differences in the patterns of consumption. As a consequence of the progressive reduction in working hours, the continued expansion of white-collar labour, and the recomposition of the work-force in terms of education and skills, most people now typically defined their identity by their choice of distinctive lifestyles that were played out in discrete social milieux. These were determined as much by taste and moral preferences as by differences in income.

Studies undertaken from the mid-1970s onwards by the German market research organization SINUS Institut produced statistics which, while based on other analytical categories, nevertheless seemed to corroborate the findings of post-industrial sociology. SINUS originally identified eight distinct classes of consumption in different material and cultural environments. This differentiation is highly relevant in our context because the milieux indicate varieties of lifestyle, social behaviour, ethos, and taste; they thus point to differences in cultural consumption and creativity. It is striking that the milieux could be divided into two basic groups: those which were traditional and generic, and those which formed as a result of recent modernization processes. The first group comprised the 'upper conservative milieu' (9 per cent; traditional educated upper class), the 'petty-bourgeois milieu' (25 per cent; traders, artisans, and the self-employed), and the 'traditional working-class milieu' (8 per cent; manual labourers with an ethos of hard work, family values, and collective solidarity). The second group was constituted by the 'technocratic-liberal milieu' (10 per cent; managers, civil servants, and the professions), the 'upwardly mobile working class' (24 per cent; skilled workers and white-collar labour), the 'non-traditional working class' (10 per cent; dedicated to the immediate consumption of their income and dismissive of collective solidarity), the 'hedonistic milieu' (11 per cent; predominantly young people, dependent for their income on parents and occasional jobs), and the 'alternative milieu' (3 per cent; sections of the student population, some part-time workers, and freelance artists, living in collective households). Within the Federal Republic pre-1989 the first group comprised 42 per cent and was decreasing, the second, 58 per cent and expanding. Just as individuals in the latter group were characterized by a certain lack of traditional ties (with regard to family, neighbourhood, region, work-place, religion, or politics), by the same token they typically proved socially and/or intellectually mobile and hence showed a greater readiness to embrace innovation, changes in lifestyle, and new values. The milieux exhibiting avant-garde—and, to many, provocative—characteristics were the 'hedonistic' and 'alternative' ones. Reluctant to accept authority as a matter of blind deference, respectful of the cultural heritage but unwilling to rely on the unquestioned certainty of tradition, the

Rob Burns and Wilfried van der Will

members of these milieux were dependent on articulate communication and public debate for the formation of their attitudes. It is they who most clearly represented 'post-materialist' values stressing cultural creativity, the importance of public ethics, and the need for civic involvement in preference to the fixation on economic well-being and compliance with authority. Rejecting the notion that standards of living could simply be measured in terms of material consumption, the members of the alternative scene championed the 'quality of life' as the most fundamental of social values. Such attitudes, however, were not without their internal contradictions in that, as we shall see in the context of our discussion of postmodernism, they could also give rise to anti-rationalism and a somewhat nostalgic revival of tradition.

The new social differentiation based on lifestyles and cultural milieux was complemented by a similar process of diversification with regard to the cultural institutions and agencies engaged in promoting culture. The first are the public ones: the municipalities, the regional governments, and, to a far lesser extent, the federal government. In 1975 total public expenditure on culture amounted to DM3.5 billion. In response to demands for new initiatives that figure had risen by 1980 to DM5.9 billion and by the end of the 1980s to DM9.7 billion (an increase of 177 per cent). The largest portion of this money was raised by the municipalities (57.9 per cent in 1989) which were thus spending DM169 per head of population on culture (compared with DM117 in 1981). A significant feature of this expansion was the contribution rendered by the relatively small municipalities (i.e. those with a population of between 20,000 and 50,000). Throughout the 1980s these provided between 13 and 16 per cent of the total figure, with the largest municipalities (of 500,000 inhabitants or more) contributing only just over one-third of the overall budget. The various headings under which it was disbursed were the following: theatre and music (DM3,898 million in 1989), museums (DM1,441 million), monuments (DM445 million), art academies (DM390 million), adult education (DM1,141 million), libraries (DM829 million), and other cultural areas (DM1,573 million).[5]

In no other country of the Western world was the number of state-supported theatres and opera houses greater than in the Federal Republic. By 1980 the cost of a ticket for one of the eighty-five municipal and state theatres was being subsidized to the tune of DM72 (double the figure for the early 1970s). Quite simply, without such subsidies virtually none of these theatres would have been able to survive, notwithstanding the fact that audiences were on

5 Statistics taken from *Öffentliche Ausgaben für Kunst und Kulturpflege, Kunsthochschulen, Erwachsenenbildung und Bibliothekswesen* (Ergebnisse der Finanzstatistik des Statistischen Bundesamtes, Dokumentationsdienst Bildung und Kultur, Veröffentlichung der Kultusministerkonferenz, Sonderheft 59; Neuwied, 1992), 1418.

average about 70 per cent of capacity. Nor was it merely the big cities like (West) Berlin, Munich, and Hamburg which could boast prestige theatres, for at various times the reputation of the latter was rivalled by those in Frankfurt, Bochum, Stuttgart, Kassel, and Bremen, which were able to engage directors of international repute such as Hans Neuenfels, Peter Palitzsch, Claus Peymann, Peter Stein, and Peter Zadek. Another way of gaining cultural prestige was by awarding prizes. In their title these prizes often associated a famous person with a particular locality, for example, the Büchner Prize (Darmstadt), the Heinrich Böll Prize (Cologne), and the Hölderin Prize (Bad Homburg) for literature, the Max Ophüls Prize (Saarbrücken) for film, the Lovis Corinth Prize (Esslingen) and the Lucas Cranach Prize (Kronach) for painting, to name but a few. There were hundreds of such prizes which, as this list illustrates, were awarded not only by the metropolitan centres but often by quite minor towns.

By the end of the 1980s there were some 2,300 museums in the Federal Republic, almost three-fifths of which were run by the *Länder* and the municipalities. Here too the principle of cultural federalism obviously applied, so that the boom in new museums was to the benefit of all regions in the Federal Republic and not just the internationally renowned cultural centres of Munich and Berlin. To cite but three examples: within a period of ten years cultural facilities in Frankfurt—which allocated a greater proportion of its total budget to culture than any other city in Europe (10.2 per cent) —had been ambitiously expanded to include a German Film Museum (1976), a Museum of Modern Art (1978), a Museum of Architecture (1979), the Museum of Arts and Crafts (1985), and the Schirn Hall of Art (1986). The largest municipal collection of art was to be found in the city of Cologne with its eight public museums and galleries, including the most extensive exhibition complex to be built since 1945, the Wallraf-Richartz/Ludwig Museum for modern and medieval art (1986). Cologne also developed into one of the most important European trading centres for art through the annual 'Art Cologne Fair'. Internationally the otherwise little-known town of Kassel became a byword for modern art on account of the *Documenta* displays that have been taking place there every four or five years since 1955. In recent times the *Documenta* reached such a scale that their enormous costs have had to be borne jointly by the town, the state of Hesse, and the federal budget. In parallel with this growth of museums attendance figures surged in equally spectacular fashion. Whereas in 1975 some 22 million visitors had been recorded,

Rob Burns and Wilfried van der Will

within six years that figure had more than doubled to 54 million and by 1987 it stood at 66.3 million.

These statistics, of course, pale into insignificance when set beside the audience figures for television since the mid-1960s. In 1964 there were 8 million television sets registered in the Federal Republic, a figure which by 1988 had all but trebled to reach virtual saturation point where 96.4 per cent of households possessed a TV (and 97.5 per cent a radio). This expansion of the audience was matched by a diversification in the system of broadcasting that was effected in two distinct phases. The first occurred in the mid-1960s with the founding of the second national television channel (ZDF) in 1963, the establishing from 1964 onwards of regional third programmes, and the introduction of colour in 1967. The second phase was ushered in by the replacement of the social-liberal coalition in 1982 by a conservative-led government that was committed to removing the broadcasting monopoly enjoyed by the public service corporations. One by one, throughout the 1980s, the federal states introduced changes in their broadcasting legislation so as to allow the development of commercial radio and television. In November 1986, the Federal Constitutional Court completed the legal steps necessary for the establishment of a 'dual system' of public and private broadcasting, but stipulated nevertheless that the public service corporations were to retain the responsibility for the 'basic provision' of broadcasting and were to be guaranteed funding appropriate to that task.

Thus, in the second half of the 1980s television in Germany entered an expansionary phase, at least with regard to the number of channels which households could now receive via terrestrial broadcasts or satellite (and later via cable). In 1987 the federal states agreed on four new satellite channels, two each for the private and public sectors. By the end of 1989 there were in fact four public-sector channels broadcasting nationally (two terrestrial ones, ARD and ZDF, and two via satellite or cable, Eins Plus and 3sat), flanked by four private channels (RTL Plus, SAT.1, PRO 7, and Tele 5). It was clear from their initial programme design that the commercial channels wanted to attract viewers mainly by light entertainment, although they also did so by the snappier style of their news presentation. But this was not the only innovative feature. In 1988 the Development Company for Television Producers, an association founded by Alexander Kluge, persuaded the commercial television stations to allocate it a number of 'independent windows' in their schedules. Within this framework the magazines *stern* and *Der Spiegel* established regular broadcasting slots in which they presented documentaries based on a type of research journalism that did not shy away from controversial issues. In this way the private channels served as a platform for established news publishers and independent film-makers, thus enhancing the diversity of broadcasting output. In other respects, however, programme variety was diminished as public service television, trying to hold on to its audiences, began to compete with the commercial channels by offering more light entertainment in the form of quiz shows, sports programmes, and American-style talk shows, soap operas, and detective series. Nevertheless, German television did continue its support for the domestic film industry, without which the development of the New German Cinema since the mid-1960s would have been unthinkable. In accordance with the General Agreement of 1974 the German broadcasting corporations undertook to resource co-productions with independent film-makers. Such films were to be shown first in the cinema, before they were screened on television after a period of two years. Apart from considerable financial support television thus provided the German film industry with mass audiences.

The appearance of new television channels was symptomatic of the growth of the media in general. For example, the largest private television company, RTL Plus, which in terms of audience figures soon came to rival ARD and ZDF, was 40 per cent owned by the Bertelsmann Group, a vast multimedia concern with over 40,000 employees, whose interests in electronic media accounted for a mere 2 per cent of its total turnover of more than DM12 billion in 1988–9. This was mainly achieved by the Group's five other internationally operating divisions: book club (22.7 per cent), publishing firms (13.8 per cent), printing, paper-making, and communications technology firms (15.1 per cent), sound recording and video industry (22.7 per cent), and glossy magazine publication (23.7 per cent). Other large media concerns were Axel Springer Verlag, Gruner + Jahr (basically controlled by Bertelsmann), the Heinrich Bauer Publishers, the Burda Group, and Georg von Holtzbrinck GmbH. Between them they acquired a considerable market share in daily newspapers and glossy weeklies. Springer's *Bild-Zeitung* (with a circulation of 4,339,000 in 1990) constituted one-fifth of the daily-newspaper market but without being able to alter the extraordinary variety of newspaper choice which was basically predicated on the regional orientation and the multiplicity of production centres of the German press. As far as the glossy weeklies were concerned the market share of the large companies was more considerable, 66.1 per cent, representing 48.8 million copies. However, none of these

Rob Burns and Wilfried van der Will

companies attained a monopoly position, nor had they between them a restrictive and homogenizing effect on cultural production. While the bulk of the turnover of these large firms was targeted at the mass market, minority audience groups were also accommodated by virtue of the fact that the multimedia concerns encompassed smaller publishing firms (there were 16,970 registered publishing houses in 1984) with distinctive book-production programmes competing with an immense number of independent publishers. Bertelsmann, for example, owned thirty-five publishing houses world-wide at the end of the 1980s. Inside Germany their publishing activities covered the entire range from literary works to all areas of non-fiction, including reference books, lexical works, theology, philosophy, architecture, and science publications, with some seventy periodicals in these fields. Given the complexity of this output it would be difficult to maintain that they were all under some unifying ideological control. The main purpose of preserving such variety was clearly to cater for a plurality of tastes and preferences, including minority ones. The same was true of the music industry, where a similar pattern could be discerned: over one thousand firms were dominated by six companies (amongst them Deutsche Grammophon, EMI-Electrola, and Ariola, the latter being a subsidiary of Bertelsmann) which, at the beginning of the 1980s, accounted for almost three-quarters of the record and cassette market. As in book production, all consumer niches were accommodated, including classical and avant-garde music which, mainly for prestige reasons, was produced by the larger companies even when it had to be subsidized by profits from the mass market.

In the light of such cultural diversity special interests could gain prominence only if supported by massive material resources. Given the upsurge of left-wing politics at the beginning of the 1970s and given the wealth of the German trade union movement, one might perhaps have expected the Deutscher Gewerkschaftsbund (DGB) to support the development of a class-based culture. The German trade unions and the Social Democratic Party, apart from having their own publishing houses (Bund Verlag, EVA, Büchergilde Gutenberg), possessed considerable real estate where they could organize cultural and educational programmes for their members. However, these activities, like the more spectacular *Ruhr Festspiele* and art exhibitions in Recklinghausen, both of them held annually as trade-union sponsored events, were not conceived in the spirit of class warfare. Reflecting the general policy of the the DGB and the SPD, they were designed to compensate for the educational disadvantages suffered by those from working-class backgrounds. Guided by the general idea that the individual must be given optimal chances for personal development, the cultural policy of the trade unions was based on the educational advancement of the individual and not on the concept of a collective class culture such as had existed in the Weimar Republic. The spirit of the worker culture movement was, however, revived in the early 1970s with the so-called *Arbeiterfilme* (workers' films) produced by the school of directors that formed in Berlin around Christian Ziewer, Klaus Wiese, Marianne Lüdke, and Ingo Kratisch and with the foundation of the Werkkreis Literatur der Arbeitswelt, a national network of worker writer workshops. Through an agreement with a distinguished publisher, Fischer Verlag, the Werkkreis had many of its writings printed in easily accessible paperbacks throughout the 1970s and early 1980s.

The breadth of the secular culture in Germany was further extended by the churches. In contradistinction to practically all other Western nations there was in the Federal Republic a close interlocking of church and state as far as the finance of the former was concerned. Quite unusually the German states shared their right to levy taxes with those churches (basically Catholic or Protestant) which were officially recognized as public service corporations. Every taxpayer who had not officially renounced the Christian faith was deemed liable to a church tax, which amounted to between 8 and 10 per cent of income tax. As a result of this the German churches were (and still are) amongst the richest in the world, with their income from such taxes alone rising from DM3.98 billion in 1970 to DM13.88 billion in 1988. These figures go a long way to explaining why the churches were able to make a considerable contribution to the economic and cultural life of both urban and rural communities. Not only did they provide a boost for traditional skills (such as organ construction, stone masonry, gilding, wood-carving, and other trades connected with the preservation of the cultural heritage), they also acted as patrons for modern and restoration architecture, musical composition and performance, painting, and interior design.

Despite their integration in the political establishment the churches as agents in the preservation and production of culture were located at the intersection of an officially subsidized and administered culture and a legion of cultural initiatives which emanated from the protesting margins of society. Young people brought up in the Christian faith and eager to translate their moral commitment into action introduced into the life of the parishes idioms and forms of expression from the discourse of protest—songs, sketches, festivals,

Rob Burns and Wilfried van der Will

exhibitions, workshops—thus incorporating into contemporary Christianity concerns for world peace, the Third World, and the environment. It was, however, within what became known as the alternative cultural scene that these themes elicited their most creative response. From the 1960s onwards an avant-garde and popular subcultural creativity began to make itself felt, initially subversive situationists, Provos, Hippies, and Yippies. These later merged into the counter-cultural manifestations of the anti-authoritarian movement and its offshoots in the 1970s. This alternative culture, also referred to as a 'second culture' or a counter-culture, was not only meant to challenge the established one, but sought to discredit and replace it. Based on post-materialist, anti-competitive values, this culture encompassed a myriad of local intitiatives in the urban centres, with its protagonists typically inhabiting large old housing stock, redundant factories, and warehouse floors or moving into old farms in and around the conurbations. Materially, the alternative scene was parasitic on the discarded capital of the dominant culture: furniture and machines, if not constructed on a do-it-yourself basis, were collected from the bulk rubbish (*Sperrmüll*) in the streets, while condemned houses and shops were occupied by permanent squats and refurbished. Within this decentred spontaneity, networks of creative projects arose: anti-authoritarian nurseries, alternative book and newspaper presses, crafts workshops, Third World shops, alternative bookshops, bakeries, and clothes shops, cinemas, cafés, pubs, and other venues for theatre and music groups. Although these ventures jealously defended their creative autonomy, they nevertheless shared roots in the anti-authoritarian movement and thus pursued common cultural and political aims whose co-ordination was felt to be a marked need in the latter half of the 1970s.

Accordingly a national daily newspaper, blandly called *die tageszeitung* (taz), was established in 1979, which not only gave alternative views of current affairs but also acted as a central reporter on the development of protests by local, regional, and national citizens' initiatives, the women's movement, the peace campaigners, and Green organizations. The women's movement had periodicals like *Courage* (which folded in the 1980s) and *Emma* (which survived). By the beginning of the 1980s there were hundreds of local papers, such as *Pflasterstrand* (based in Frankfurt), *Szene Hamburg*, and *Stuttgart live*, which bore the hallmark of their metropolitan origins in their titles. In the course of the 1980s the alternative scene successfully invaded the urban centres and made its presence felt in the pedestrianized precincts and central squares as well as

15. Political magazines.

Though much expanded in size (the inaugural edition of 4 January 1947 contained 26 pages compared with the current average of over 200) Rudolf Augstein's news magazine *Der Spiegel* has essentially retained the structure of the original: then as now its four main sections were 'Germany', 'Foreign News', 'Economics', and 'Culture'. With its consistently rising circulation (890,000 in 1970, 948,000 in 1980, and 1,087,000 in 1990) the left-liberal *Spiegel* had a monopoly in the weekly current affairs market until the arrival in January 1993 of *Focus*, a centre-right magazine modelled on *Newsweek* and launched at a cost of DM160 million by one of the big four German publishers, Burda Verlag. At the other end of the spectrum Germany's flourishing alternative press is exemplified by Alice Schwarzer's feminist monthly *Emma*, which at its peak in the 1980s sold 120,000 copies (though it now appears bimonthly with half that circulation), and *Titanic*, the German equivalent of *Private Eye*, which, within five years of its début in 1979, could boast monthly sales of well over 100,000.

outside the town halls and in underground rail stations, which all became the stage for the performance of music, drama, literary readings, political sketches, and dance. Having emerged from its subcultural niches and gained political representation through the entry of the Greens into the Bundestag (in 1983), the alternative culture had by its now considerable social presence gained a degree of acceptability. It was meanwhile even subsidized by certain local councils. In other words, it was no longer alternative in the sense of implying a wholesale displacement of the established culture. Hilmar Hoffmann, the pioneering head of Frankfurt's Department of Culture, had already declared at the end of the 1970s: 'Alternative culture is neither a substitute for traditional culture nor just a bridge to it. Alternative and traditional culture should not be mutually exclusive but should address the public in such a fashion that it can profit alternately from both spheres as from one culture.'[6] Hoffmann was clearly envisaging an expanded spectrum of cultural expression in which the alternative culture would not be permanently marginalized but accommodated as a properly acknowledged constituent of a truly pluralist culture. It could, then, still provide elements of spontaneity, be an antidote to the pap provided by the mass entertainment industries, and cater for minority tastes, while also attempting to gain popularity amongst wider audiences, encourage their active participation, and help revive the importance of locality.

The Culture Industry and the Critical Intelligentsia

The tacit assumption behind these developments of a cultural praxis was, of course, that the relentlessly negative critique of modern culture advanced by Horkheimer and Adorno in their essay 'Kulturindustrie. Aufklärung als Massenbetrug' was no longer valid. The crux of their argument was that culture in late capitalism, far from providing some space for opposition and encouraging critical reflection pointing beyond the status quo, had deteriorated into mere commodity, affirmation of the given, and stereotypical sameness: 'Culture now impresses the same stamp on everything. Films, radio, and magazines make up a system which is uniform as a whole and in every part.'[7] Culture was made exclusively for profit, was therefore incapable of suggesting any transcendence of this system, and hence lulled its consumers into conformity through entertainment. This thesis, developed in the mid-1940s on the basis of the mass culture of German fascism and American capitalism,

6 Hilmar Hoffmann, *Kultur für alle* (Frankfurt am Main, 1979), 261.
7 Max Horkheimer and Theodor W. Adorno, 'The Culture Industry: Enlightenment as Mass Deception', in *Dialectic of Enlightenment*, trans. John Cumming (London, 1973), 120.

was reaffirmed by Adorno in a 1963 radio talk. Here he insisted once again that the culture industry was a prime instrument for the delusion of the masses that left no room for the critical emancipation of the individual:

The overall effect of the culture industry is that of anti-enlightenment. It turns enlightenment into a practice of mass deception, into an instrument for the enfetterment of awareness. The culture industry prevents the development of autonomous individuals capable of making independent judgements and conscious decisions. These, however, are the prerequisites of a democratic society which can only flourish amongst citizens who have truly come of age politically.[8]

However, the dialectical fate of Adorno's negative vision about the effects of the culture industry was that, initially with the help of the young university intelligentsia, it was stood on its head. For in the course of the 1970s and 1980s a new political culture arose as the citizens of the Federal Republic developed a range of political practices which were not aligned with either the established political parties or their revolutionary opponents, the anti-authoritarian students. Ironically, this process began when, in the second half of the 1960s, Horkheimer and Adorno's analysis of the culture industry began to attract adherents. The anti-authoritarian student movement in particular lapped up this thesis because it could be used to explain why the mass of the working class, instead of recognizing the necessity to overthrow the capitalist exploiters, appeared to connive in its own oppression. The students wished to wrench West German society out of its smug bourgeois torpor, free the working class of its false consciousness, and reinstate it as a revolutionary subject. Singularly unsuccessful though they were in attaining these particular objectives, they did manage to advance key elements of critical theory within education and the media and to establish the habit of public protest in an all too conformist society. It is in this sense that the late 1960s could be seen as a watershed in the history of the Federal Republic, marking the beginning of a period when the assumptions and values prevailing during the 1950s and 1960s were increasingly called into question and revised. Paradoxically, then, the very thesis which denied the possibility of critical citizenship itself helped trigger developments that led to a quantum leap in the advancement of an active, participative democracy.

Not surprisingly it was the older, conservative politicians and commentators who were most unsettled by the direction of events, signalling, as they did, a sea change in the political culture. Karl Carstens, the President of the Federal Republic in the 1980s, while

8 Theodor W. Adorno, 'Résumé über Kulturindustrie', in *Ohne Leitbild. Parva Aesthetica* (Frankfurt am Main, 1967), 69.

Rob Burns and Wilfried van der Will

alert to the significance of this historical shift, could describe it only in terms of an irretrievable loss: 'In my opinion a deep rupture occurred at the end of the 1960s and in the 1970s. Before that time diligence, individual achievement, and the fulfilment of duty were standard values and generally recognized as virtues. After this a different phase set in: the scene was dominated by protest and these virtues were derided and accorded a secondary status.'[9] Carstens was, of course, reflecting a situation in which the manipulative power of the culture industry could no longer be presumed to invert this change in values. Indeed, the citadels of the media, notably the liberal press, public service television, and radio had themselves been infused to some extent with the anti-authoritarian spirit. Not only did they provide the critical thought of the young intelligentsia in the universities with the oxygen of publicity, but they also promoted the discourse about Germany's Nazi past and the limits of democratic tolerance.

It was particularly Heinrich Böll who, exploiting his fame as a literary author, used the media as a platform from which to intervene in these debates. He was the most prominent post-war German writer in a loose alliance of distinguished journalists, philosophers, psychologists, and sociologists, commonly referred to as *die Intellektuellen*. In engaging in political debate Böll and other intellectuals (Grass, Frisch, Walser, Enzensberger, Weiss, Habermas, Mitscherlich, etc.) were privileged in the extensive exposure they received, but were also able for their part to open up opportunities for critical reflection within the media which might otherwise have been foreclosed by the workings of the culture industry. For these intellectuals writing, addressing audiences, and broadcasting were different ways of subverting widely accepted versions of reality. In other words, they were, to some extent, themselves capable of manipulating the instruments of manipulation for the purposes of fostering a broad, critically informed awareness. They thus created a distinctive role for themselves as self-appointed public prosecutors in matters of fundamental democratic concern. In thrall to no particular political lobby, social class, or ideology, they could be regarded as intellectual nonconformists who spoke in their own right as prominent advocates of a pluralist culture. The danger was— and Böll in particular was aware of it—that they might themselves be reduced to a media image, that of being 'the conscience of the nation'. Plainly, they were afraid that as such they could be used by the representatives of the state, both internally and externally, as advertisements for a society that now prided itself on its democratic credentials. Moreover, they feared that the general public, instead

9 Quoted in *Der Spiegel*, 41 (5 Jan. 1987), 28.

of actively exploring practical forms of critical citizenship, might be lulled into complacency by the belief that a vociferous intelligentsia in itself sufficed to guarantee the well-being of democracy.

Not surprisingly, perhaps, the intellectuals reacted with equanimity to the slanderous labels which irritated politicians and commentators attached to them—'rats and blowflies', 'armchair terrorists', 'sympathizers of left-wing fascism', etc.—for these denunciations implicitly acknowledged the influence of the intelligentsia on public opinion and only succeeded in enhancing its high profile. This was further attested to by the fact that intellectuals now became the subject of special sociological scrutiny. They seemed to enjoy a dual status, being regarded, on the one hand, as notorious troublemakers and, on the other, as internationally respected representatives of German culture. This paradox motivated the conservative social scientist Helmut Schelsky to mount a sustained polemical attack on them. In his much-discussed book *Die Arbeit tun die anderen: Klassenkampf und Priesterherrschaft der Intellektuellen* (1975), Schelsky took issue with what he judged to be the overwhelmingly powerful hold the critical intelligentsia had on the mind of the general public, enforced through its influential role in the media. In stark contrast to Horkheimer and Adorno's analysis, which assigned critical intellectuals a position of impotence, Schelsky averred that they were dangerously undermining Germany's social market economy. This argument rested on his thesis that they had successfully constituted themselves as a class, comprising a 'priesthood' of freelance opinion-makers working in alliance with a corps of opinion-disseminators. He cited Heinrich Böll as the most prominent example of the former and Rudolf Augstein, editor of *Der Spiegel*, as a model of the latter. Between them, Schelsky held, they had usurped the real governorship of society, with the elected political representatives increasingly marginalized or, willy-nilly, acting within the conceptual framework set by the intelligentsia. Amongst the values preached by the latter was liberation from the obsession with ever increasing material productivity, a cause Böll certainly supported, for he cherished a 'utopia of boycotting the work ethic' where 'human beings were to work only for the reproduction of their real needs'.[10] The danger of such subversive views gaining ground in society was, in Schelsky's eyes, all the more acute since the relentless process of modernization was accelerating the emergence of a new intellectualist élite ever more susceptible to arguments in favour of a radical downgrading of the work ethic.

Böll's reaction was a mixture of satire, astonishment, and qualified acceptance. He flatly contradicted Schelsky's description of him

10 Heinrich Böll and Christian Linder, *Drei Tage im März* (Cologne, 1975), 91.

Rob Burns and Wilfried van der Will

as the 'cardinal' of some new religion of social redemption: no one had conferred any authority on him, he lacked assistants to execute his will, and his only weapons were a typewriter and a telephone. Moreover, the real reasons why writers like himself had become moral authorities had not been analysed. Schelsky had, indeed, ignored the fact that the extraordinary significance of the intellectuals had only come about because of the lack of democratic spirit amongst ordinary German citizens in the post-war years. Böll insisted that his prominent position in public life was not something he had actively sought, but was merely a symptom of the 'vacuousness of public morals'.

The Culture of the 'German Autumn'

In Böll's view, as in that of his fellow combatants, the mass of the population still had much to learn in terms of participative citizenship. The intellectuals considered themselves a poor substitute for a critical public, which they could at best help to create by setting an example of democratic commitment. This was especially necessary in a situation where the state, reacting to the urban terrorism of the Baader–Meinhof group, resorted to methods of surveillance and prosecution which threatened to undermine the democratic guarantees of the constitution. The scaremongering rhetoric of politicians and political commentators stoked the fear that, confronted by the anti-authoritarian convictions shared by many young people and the strategy of urban terrorism pursued by a few, the state was not doing enough to defend law and order. Equally, however, there was concern in some quarters that it was doing far too much. Branded as terrorism's sympathizers, the intellectuals felt called upon to come to the defence of democracy. As Böll put it, 'it is time to declare a state of national emergency, the state of emergency of public awareness'.[11] This clarion call from 'the conscience of the nation' was echoed in a remarkably broad spectrum of cultural responses which embraced essays, fictional and documentary prose, drama, poetry, popular song, and film. Three problems in particular were addressed in the course of the 1970s: the mass manipulation perpetrated by sections of the media, the fear that the law might be reduced to an instrument of arbitrary state power, and the perversion of democratic society into a surveillance state.

The critical engagement of German intellectuals with the right-wing press, specifically with the media empire of Axel Springer, in

11 Heinrich Böll, 'Will Ulrike Meinhof Gnade oder freies Geleit?' (originally pub. in Der Spiegel, 10 Jan. 1972), in Heinrich Böll, Ende der Bescheidenheit: Schriften und Reden 1969–1972 (Munich, 1985), 226.

fact predated the 1970s. In October 1967 some 106 writers of the Gruppe 47 had signed a statement condemning the quasi-monopoly position commanded by the Springer publications as a serious restriction on the freedom of opinion. This warning was accompanied by a pledge, renewed in the mid-1980s, not to collaborate in any way with the Springer press. Undoubtedly, however, the most dramatic intervention in its affairs came not from a group of writers but from the documentarist Günter Wallraff. Working under a pseudonym, Wallraff had infiltrated the staff of the *Bild-Zeitung* in Hanover and in his book *Der Aufmacher* (1977) he exposed the murky practices and cynical attitudes he had encountered there. In two sequels (*Zeugen der Anklage*, 1979, and *BILD-Handbuch bis zum Bildausfall*, 1981) Wallraff then revealed the many personal tragedies *Bild* had caused with its ruthless sensationalism. The Springer press brought litigation against Wallraff which, ironically, only succeeded in providing him with free publicity and a further sales boost. When all else failed *Bild* tried to discredit Wallraff as a terrorist sympathizer.

As early as 1972 the force of this accusation had been directed against Heinrich Böll. In an article in *Der Spiegel* he had warned that the measures taken by society against terrorism should be commensurate with the threat which a small group of deluded individuals actually posed and that there should be no witch-hunt by the entire populace as advocated by the *Bild-Zeitung*. Even terrorist suspects, Böll pleaded, were, like any other citizens, entitled to be considered innocent until proven guilty in the proper courts. His reward for attempting to inject a note of calm into the debate was that he, in turn, became the object of a sustained campaign of vilification in the press and on television. The reaction to Böll's intervention showed that he had by no means overstated the power of sections of the media to whip up a climate of panic, in which all critical citizens might be intimidated into silence by the McCarthyite suggestion that they were merely the socially respectable accomplices of terrorism. Böll exacted his revenge in the form of a bestseller, his story *Die verlorene Ehre der Katharina Blum* (1974), in which he showed how a web of collusion between the police, industrialists, and the gutter press could envelop an ordinary citizen and induce her to commit physical violence. As the book's subtitle indicates, the narrative is centrally concerned with 'how violence can arise and where it can lead to'. In other words, Böll attempted a fundamentally new appraisal of the theme of violence, relegating that of terrorism to the margins and focusing instead on the brutality inherent in and generated by the manipulation of public opinion.

Rob Burns and Wilfried van der Will

Although Böll was routinely denounced for advocating violence, he never ceased, in fact, to reject the methods of the Red Army Faction (RAF, as the Baader–Meinhof group now called itself). While in his view such urban guerrilla tactics might conceivably be appropriate in the context of the liberation struggles in South America, they were wholly counter-productive in the Federal Republic. His fear that the strategy of the terrorists played straight into the hands of the most reactionary and anti-democratic forces in West Germany was borne out by developments in the legal sphere. It was entirely predictable that writers and intellectuals should unite in opposition to new legislative measures whose primary target appeared to be none other than the intelligentsia itself. Such was the case with Article 88a of the Basic Law which, allowing a wide range of interpretations, made it an offence to advocate in print any kind of violence that could be construed as undermining the constitutional order. Even before this legislation had parliamentary approval it was used to justify the seizure of *Wie alles anfing* (1975) by Bommi Baumann, a self-critical account of his experiences as a terrorist. In an overt challenge to the authorities this book was then brought out again two years later under the imprint of various publishers, thus effectively pre-empting prosecution. The law was, in fact, revoked in 1980 when saner counsels prevailed. However, for much of the 1970s the old German tradition of the *Obrigkeitsstaat* (that is to say, rule by an administrative apparatus that brooked no opposition) appeared to be reasserting itself in the eyes of critical observers. In his novel *Die erdabgewandte Seite der Geschichte* (1976) Nicolas Born allows his first-person narrator to articulate this very position: 'The state incessantly passed laws for its own protection, until its very protectiveness prevented us from breathing.'[12] In a poem entitled 'Vorschlag zur Strafrechtsreform', published in 1970, Hans Magnus Enzensberger heavily ironized the jargon of the Criminal Code and intimated that all but the most deferential forms of behaviour would be punished, to wit: 'Whosoever tempts a woman into permitting intercourse or | stimulates any other impropriety in her . . . | Whosoever on a railway station by severance diminishes an important | member of an official . . . | Whosoever after careful examination of his conscience | belittles the authorities.'[13]

Enzensberger's poem, of course, amounted to a satirical postulation of a negative utopia. There was, however, one particular piece of legislation in the early 1970s whose negative effects were sadly all too real, namely the Decree on Extremists of January 1972. It was justified by the government as a necessary measure for the defence of the state against terrorism. But since it was directed at

12 Nicolas Born, *Die erdabgewandte Seite der Geschichte* (Reinbek, 1979), 188.
13 Hans Magnus Enzensberger, *Gedichte 1955–1970* (Frankfurt am Main, 1971), 143.

those already working in or applying for positions of employment in the state sector, it was clearly the so-called sympathizers, largely the participants in the anti-authoritarian student movement, who were the immediate targets. The state plainly feared that their plans to infiltrate the professions, more specifically their threatened 'long march through the institutions', might become a reality. Essentially the Decree stipulated that all individuals who could be suspected of disloyalty to the constitution on account of real or alleged extremist activities were to be debarred from employment in the civil service. The novelist Peter O. Chotjewitz spoke for many when he described the Decree as nothing less than a 'war on culture from above'; in the same vein the political scientist Oskar Negt termed it a 'preventive counter-revolution'. Certainly, the Decree engendered a system of political vetting and ideological screening which, both in scale and in method, was bound to stir memories of the apparatus fashioned by National Socialism for weeding out undesirables from the state service. Precisely this comparison was drawn by Alfred Andersch in January 1976 in his poem on Article 3(3) of the Basic Law: 'A nation of | ex-Nazis | and its fellow travellers | is once again | engaged in its favourite sport | the witch-hunt for | Communists | Socialists | humanists | dissidents | leftists . . . a smell is spreading | the smell of a machine | which produces gas.'[14] This provocative assessment of the Federal Republic as, at least in some respects, a modern, more efficient version of a fascist state was, of course, not dissimilar to the terrorists' own analysis. Other writers tried to address the issue in more measured fashion by focusing on the fate of individuals who had fallen victim to the procedures sanctioned by the Decree. Among the many works on this theme were Franz Xaver Kroetz's one-act play *Verfassungsfeinde* (1973), Peter Schneider's story . . . *schon bist du ein Verfassungsfeind* (1975), Heinrich Böll's short story 'Du fährst zu oft nach Heidelberg' (1977), Hans-Peter de Lorent's novel *Die Hexenjagd* (1980), and Jürgen Albertz's novel *Die zwei Leben der Maria Behrens* (1981).

The atmosphere of suspicion and hysteria reached fever pitch in the autumn of 1977 with the terrorist assassinations of the Chief Prosecutor (Siegfried Buback), a high-ranking banker (Jürgen Ponto), and the head of the Federation of German Industry (Hanns Martin Schleyer). The powers of the police now seemed to be so great, if not to say arbitrary, that critical intellectuals and liberal-minded politicians felt called upon to defend the democratic state with renewed vigour. A paperback entitled *Briefe zur Verteidigung der Republik*, containing contributions by some thirty authors, appeared in the autumn of 1977 and quickly sold in excess of 100,000 copies.

14 One of the earliest publications of Andersch's poem was in *Der lange Marsch. Zeitung für eine Neue Linke* (West Berlin, Feb. 1976), 16; it was subsequently published in Klaus Wagenbach *et al.* (eds.), *Vaterland, Muttersprache: Deutsche Schriftsteller und ihr Staat seit 1945* (Berlin, 1994), 297–8.

Rob Burns and Wilfried van der Will

Another such volume, *Briefe zur Verteidigung der bürgerlichen Freiheit*, followed a year later. Here the contributors argued that police, administrative, and judicial practices were falling short of true democratic standards and that the computer perfectionism of criminal and ideological investigation posed a far greater threat to civil liberty than the atrocities of the terrorists. In short, many people now feared that the Federal Republic had, to quote an analysis in *Der Spiegel*, embarked on the fatal descent into the surveillance state. It was an index of the extent to which Germany was gripped by this mood that it produced responses in a variety of creative media.

In confronting the twin challenge posed by terrorism and state security the New German Cinema frequently courted controversy. Margarethe von Trotta's *Die bleierne Zeit* (1981), inspired by the relationship between the terrorist Gudrun Ensslin and her sister, and Reinhard Hauff's award-winning film *Stammheim* (1986), a documentary reconstruction of the Baader–Meinhof trial, were both condemned by some critics for appearing to side with the Red Army Faction. In Fassbinder's *Die dritte Generation* (1979) the modern urban guerrillas are portrayed as mere adventurers, lacking ideals and political commitment and motivated purely by the need to escape their vacuous existence in an affluent society. In their naïvety they are manipulated by American capital in the form of a multinational electronics firm which finances their exploits in the hope of boosting its sales, since its computers are used in tracking down terrorists. This theme also occurs in Alexander Kluge's *Der starke Ferdinand* (1976), whose central character describes himself as a 'radical activist in security matters'. Employed by the German branch of a multinational corporation, he transforms the firm's security forces into a ruthless commando unit whose course of instruction is completed by joint manœuvres with a neo-Nazi paramilitary gang. The suggestion of collusion between industry and the state security forces is also a feature of Böll's *Die verlorene Ehre der Katharina Blum* and this aspect of the story is given extra prominence in Volker Schlöndorff and von Trotta's cinema adaptation. More than the book the movie foregrounds the role of the state surveillance apparatus, both by highlighting its many eavesdropping practices and by the dramatic representation of the high-powered military operations which are mounted to storm Katharina's apartment and, later, to effect the capture of her lover. The film's basic plot-line, an innocent caught up in the ugly climate of a terrorist witch-hunt, resurfaces in Hauff's *Messer im Kopf* (1978), based on a script by Peter Schneider. Other authors, notably Heinrich Böll, Wolf Biermann, and Peter Steinbach, contributed to the film which most successfully captured the oppressive atmosphere permeating German society in the autumn of 1977. In a remarkably swift response to the traumatic events of that time, which culminated in the hijacking of a Lufthansa jet, several terrorist assassinations, and the suicides of the leading RAF members in their high-security cells, a number of prominent directors, including Schlöndorff, Kluge, Fassbinder, and Edgar Reitz, collaborated in the making of the film *Deutschland im Herbst* (1978). In a *mélange* of documentary footage and fictional episodes they laid bare their fears about the fatal threats to civil society posed by the forces of law and order. Their own mood is best summed up by one of the intertitles: 'Once atrocity has reached a certain point, it no longer matters who started it. It should just stop.'

In one episode in *Deutschland im Herbst* the poet and singer Wolf Biermann gives a moving performance of his text 'Das Mädchen aus Stuttgart', a clear reference to Gudrun Ensslin. Not surprisingly, the political events of the 'German Autumn' also found their way into the repertoire of other *politische Liedermacher* such as Franz-Josef Degenhardt, Dieter Süverkrüp, and Wolfgang Neuss; but more strikingly, perhaps, the overbearing mood of the time left its mark on the *Polit-Rock* of the German New Wave which developed in the late 1970s and early 1980s. In particular, punk bands like Katapult gave raucous expression to their view of Germany as a 'Big Brother' society: while Extrabreit intoned 'Day and night they'll be with you | the police', Abwärts portrayed the Federal Republic as a 'state of catastrophe', chorusing 'We are living in a computer state'. Such ideas were also taken up by more mainstream rock artists like Udo Lindenberg and the band Ideal, which, in the title of one of their most popular songs, visualized Germany in the grip of a new 'Ice Age'. The state's eagerness to deploy the most advanced technology in its defence and to subject its citizens to comprehensive computer screening was captured to brilliant comic effect by Udo Lindenberg in his song 'Datenbank':

> I have a nice new identity card
> with a long number on it in case I forget who I am . . .
> I travel about a lot, hither and thither, on long trips
> at the airport I get out my ID card
> a little dogsbody shoves the thing in the computer, what does it do
> it goes ratter, ratter, ratter
> and then I'm in a flutter . . .
> I say, take it easy, man, you know what it says
> that the Republic will anyway soon go down the drain because of
> oddballs like me

The extensive cultural legacy of the 'German Autumn', and of the social syndrome it epitomized, also encompassed prose fiction, notable examples of which included Max von der Grün's *Stellenweise Glatteis* (1973) and *Flächenbrand* (1978), Otto F. Walter's *Die Verwilderung* (1977), Franz-Josef Degenhardt's *Brandstellen* (1975) and *Die Mißhandlung* (1979), Peter O. Chotjewitz's *Die Herren des Morgengrauens* (1978), and F. C. Delius's *Ein Held der inneren Sicherheit* (1981). The most comprehensive attempt at reflecting the absurdities of the surveillance state was Böll's *Fürsorgliche Belagerung* (1979). In this panoramic novel he showed how the sophisticated police apparatus deployed to guard an influential newspaper proprietor, Fritz Tolm, paradoxically causes insecurity, ultimately fails to provide an effective shield against terrorists determined to defeat the police, and, in the final analysis, only succeeds in producing what Böll termed 'casualties of security'. Not only are the lives ruined of entirely innocent people who happen to become enmeshed within the extensive security network, but both the police themselves and their charges fall prey to paranoia. The coldly calculating attitude of the terrorists proves to be but the mirror-image of that of the capitalist entrepreneurs. Through sinister channels some of the latter's profits reach the terrorists and help to finance their operations, a connection which reveals them to be the perverted offshoots of capitalism rather than an alternative to it. Police surveillance, apart from being an index of the state's own insecurity, is portrayed as only one of the cancers eating away at the safety of its citizens. Another is the invasion of privacy by the hacks of the gutter press working in collusion with the secret police, thus in effect doubling the apparatus of surveillance. A further cancer is the voracious appetite of the modern economy, best illustrated in the novel by huge excavators that raze villages and whole landscapes in order to exploit the deposits of lignite as fuel for electricity-generating stations. Tolm, himself displaying the typical features of the capitalist shark, gradually comes to the realization that the whole 'system' is corrupt and must eventually be supplanted by a new kind of socialism. He draws ever closer to his sons who, imbued with the values of the anti-authoritarian student movement, have broken with social conformity. The one has withdrawn into a rural idyll and the other into a Green commune; but even these milieux are not immune from the attentions of the surveillance state. What the retreat into such environments indicates, however, is the need for a social utopia predicated on an acute postmodern awareness about the lethal contradictions of the existing social system.

In accordance with his principle 'art must go too far', Böll used fictional prose to transpose actuality into its most negative form in order to posit the hope that it could be transcended. *Fürsorgliche Belagerung* must therefore be seen as part of a political discourse about the necessity to preserve the freedom of democratic society from the encroachments of the surveillance state. In other words, Böll was not advancing the thesis, in fictional form, that the Federal Republic had fallen into the hands of Big Brother. It was 'neither an ideal democracy nor a police state', he declared, and remained firm in his belief that no such totalitarian state would be established. Like Böll's novel, the culture of the 'German Autumn' gave vent to deep concern about the course on which German society was apparently set. By its very existence, however, that culture attested to the pluralism of opinion and creative expression which, despite some uncomfortable authoritarian challenges, continued to develop throughout the whole period. It was similarly paradoxical that the anti-authoritarian student movement, while in its most extreme form giving rise to urban terrorism and sectarian intolerance together with the inevitable law-and-order backlash, nevertheless made social protest an accepted part of civil society and thus helped transform the political culture in Germany. Crucially, the critical intellectuals now acquired thousands of like-minded allies in a younger generation whose zest for political and cultural change was equally great. This alliance became most visible in the peace protests of the early 1980s, when writers like Böll and Grass found themselves part of a mass movement and were clearly content to be used as celebrities so that demonstrations, such as that at the nuclear missile base in Mutlangen in late 1983, would receive maximum media exposure.

The Postmodern Turn

The association of many critical intellectuals with a broader movement of protest—and, equally, the love–hate relationship with that movement on the part of others—was symptomatic of fundamental changes in awareness and cultural creativity which were taking place in the late 1970s and 1980s. These went far beyond the isolated, though related, criticism of modernism which could be found within the literature and thought of the nineteenth century (Goethe, German Romanticism and Post-Romanticism, Nietzsche, etc.) or in the 'Critical Theory' of the Frankfurt School. Doubts about the trajectory of modernism were voiced in many fields simultaneously, inspiring a number of new trends in politics, philosophy, the social

Rob Burns and Wilfried van der Will

16. Celebrity blockade at Mutlangen, September 1983.
The NATO 'dual-track' decision (12 December 1979), which provided for the deployment of American medium-range nuclear missiles in Western Europe (over half of them in the Federal Republic), triggered the spectacular revival of the *Friedensbewegung*, beginning with the Krefeld Appeal (launched in November 1980) and climaxing, in late October 1983, in the largest protest demonstrations in German history. In that so-called 'hot autumn' the peace movement embarked on a programme of direct non-violent action, the prelude to which was a three-day blockade of the US military base at Mutlangen. Over 150 public figures took part, including the Nobel laureate Heinrich Böll (left of picture), the SPD candidate for Chancellor in the 1990 elections, Oskar Lafontaine (centre), and the Green Party members of the Bundestag and co-initiators of the Krefeld Appeal, ex-NATO General Gert Bastian and Petra Kelly (foreground, centre and right, respectively). Four years later the INF Agreement signed by Reagan and Gorbachev led to the removal of the missiles.

sciences, literature, film, and the visual arts, which collectively amounted to a postmodern turn in the development of culture. This epochal change had its roots in the secular social shifts outlined earlier. For it was from within the diffuse, sophisticated service class, and in particular from within the intelligentsia working in the 'knowledge industries', that demands issued for a rethink of the old verities of technological progress and for a new agenda to be set for both politics and the arts.

The most visible expression of postmodernism, and hence the area where the term initially seemed most easily applicable, was in architecture. Against the puritanical functionalism of the Bauhaus with its unadorned boxes of steel, concrete, and glass that might arbitrarily house offices, flats, department stores, or universities, against this grey geometry of pure economic efficiency, a desire for colour, non-rectangular lines, decoration, and playful elegance began to assert itself. The towns as patrons or supervisors of this new architecture, seeking to create a friendlier environment for the life of the urban community in place of the repellent, flat façades of modernist design, now turned to architects like James Stirling who, drawing on a rich repertoire of historical styles, was responsible for the main architectural event of the 1980s, the Neue Staatsgalerie in Stuttgart (completed in 1984). Features reminiscent of ancient Egypt, traditional European structures, modernism, and the colours of pop art are all present in an architectural ensemble that, eschewing repetitiveness, opens up new geometrical perspectives at every turn. Despite its eclecticism this building attains a kind of harmony in which oppositional elements happily coexist: Romanesque arches and windows alongside Egyptian cornices or the combination, within the same wall, of concrete, sandstone, and travertine. This architecturally hybrid edifice thus epitomizes many of the ideas commonly associated with postmodernism: the pluralism of styles and the relativity of value systems; the carefree syncretism of forms and philosophies merrily suggesting that 'anything goes' (Paul Feyerabend); the notion of contemporary culture as a nostalgic re-enactment of, or ironic quotation from, previous cultures; the dissolution of the boundary between high and popular culture; the delight in retrieving urban areas in which an informal culture of civic interaction may thrive; and the irreverence towards dogma and monolithic authority.

Similar tendencies were present in the sculpture and painting of the 1970s and 1980s. Joseph Beuys sought to show in his work how individual life manifested itself as an energy which could shape material. All that remained of the notion of art was the public

17. James Stirling's Neue Staatsgalerie, Stuttgart (1984).
The postmodern fusion of styles that characterizes this building is illustrated by the outdoor
sculpture court in the centre of the museum (top) in which a number of architectural quotations
are brought together: the court and its sculptures are redolent of the Renaissance
piazza; the high walls which surround it, complete with the flora on top, recall the ruins of
Hadrian's Villa and have the effect of suggesting a dome where there is only sky; the sunken Doric
portico on one side contrasts with the modern staircase on the other; the centre of this rotunda,
which appears to demand an altar or some such symbolic icon, is marked only by the grill of a
drain. Through the openings left in the high wall and the doorway to the pedestrian ramp curving
up the rotunda can be seen the pop-art colours of the cylindrical pedestrian railings beading the
building (bottom).

demonstration of such shaped material as isolated object. The extreme anti-élitism of Beuys is evident in his exhibition pieces which appear to be saying that art is an unfinished document of life to stimulate the senses, not a finished masterpiece in its own right. In painting, Georg Baselitz, Markus Lüpertz, Karl Horst Hödicke, and others followed international trends towards the abandonment of modernist, avant-garde positions in favour of the reinstatement of representational art. Their work shows an antipathy towards any unified style, favouring instead the calculated experiment with a multiplicity of mannerisms. These tendencies are commonly seen as dating from 1977, the year in which the Galerie am Moritzplatz was founded in Berlin and the exhibition *Forum junger Kunst* was staged in Recklinghausen. Modernist painting, particularly abstract art, increasingly lost its attractions as it came to be regarded as too remote from ordinary social life.

In musical composition, too, a marked reaction against modernism became evident. Hans Werner Henze had already rejected serialism as doctrinaire in the 1950s and turned instead to more melodic, harmonically more traditionalist music of a lush, distinctly Italianate flavour, a style which reached a climax in his opera *Die Bassariden* (1965). In the 1970s, when he put himself at the service of the (West) German Communist Party (DKP), he composed politically committed music in an atonal, yet anti-élitist vein. For example, he wrote the score for the film version of Böll's narrative *Die verlorene Ehre der Katharina Blum* (1975) and in his atonal opera *Wir erreichen den Fluß* (1974–6), based on a text by Edward Bond, he gave vent to his pacifist passion. It was in this latter work, as well as in his opera *Die englische Katze* (1983) and in his Seventh Symphony (1984), that, in accordance with the precepts set out in his *Exkurs über den Populismus* (1979), he quit 'the ghetto of modernism' in order to reach a wider public. Thus, in Henze's work atonality is mixed with neo-Romantic and neo-Classicist borrowings. Historical reminiscences together with vulgar, popular, and esoteric tones are used to achieve a theatricality full of realism and a lucidity replete with illusions. Such dialectical tension is abandoned in another representative of postmodern music, the Polish composer Krzysztof Penderecki, who, at least for a while in the 1980s, dominated the innovative musical scene in Germany and became the most outspoken opponent of avant-garde modernism:

It is not only the public that yearns for music in a pure major key, I do too. I had no intention of composing atonal clusters forever or dense, opaque harmonies. . . . Schönberg was certainly important but you can forget about

Rob Burns and Wilfried van der Will

... all those Darmstadt disciples of the so-called Schönberg School. . . . I find it basically wrong that in the New Music harmonic tensions are not resolved. . . . A richly orchestrated unison following an atonal chord is surely wonderful, you can simply relax and breathe a sigh of relief.[15]

The predilection for evoking, quoting, and distorting old masters is particularly evident in Wolfgang von Schweinitz's String Sextet (1978) and Volker David Kirchner's *Idyll für Orchester* (1982), which both bear the nostalgic subtitle 'Hommage à Franz Schubert'. However, the danger of the postmodern tendency here is that it may lead to a self-indulgent, pompous, and repetitive amalgam of well-known musical sound bites which, as in the case of Klaus Schulze's synthesizer composition *Phantasien* (1978), hovers uncomfortably between Electronic Rock and Mahler. While the extreme subjectivism and anti-rationalism of this music may thus end in an epigonal 'sparrows' chorus of the postmodernists' (Peter Sloterdijk), its basic creative impetus nevertheless stemmed from a powerful epochal experience, one which von Schweinitz formulated as follows:

The optimistic belief in progress, for centuries the driving force behind cultural development, has been shattered. Rationalism has proved incapable of establishing order and reason in the world, a hypertrophied materialism has been unmasked as a vicious circle of frustration. It dawns on us today to what extent we are estranged, socially and psychologically, within this rationalist and materialist world. This realization creates the need for rehumanization, a yearning which unleashes productive energy.[16]

In the 1970s the young intelligentsia, flanked by older freelance writers like Böll, Enzensberger, and Grass, began to display a deep-seated scepticism towards the typically modernist belief that an egalitarian, affluent society could be fashioned in the wake of technological advance. For these intellectuals modernism meant the subjection of nature to science and its exploitation by machine technology, with society itself being made into an object of social engineering on the basis of loudly propagated ideological designs. In his cycle of cantos *Der Untergang der Titanic* (1978) Enzensberger chose one of the most potent symbols of the modernist credo and subjected it to postmodern scepticism. In political terms, the unbounded optimism about the nature of social progress could be found in the East as well as the West, promoted on the one hand by totalitarian dogmatism and on the other by democratic reformism. It was this faith in the wisdom of ideological edifices in East and West which was undermined in the most distinguished and extensive

15 ' "Ein Verlangen nach reinem Dur". SPIEGEL-Gespräch mit Krzysztof Penderecki', *Der Spiegel*, 41 (5 Jan. 1987), 145.
16 Wolfgang von Schweinitz, 'Standort', *Neue Zeitschrift für Musik*, 1 (1979), 19.

prose epic of the time, Uwe Johnson's four-volume *Jahrestage: Aus dem Leben von Gesine Cresspahl* (published 1970–83). Set in New York, Mecklenburg, and a number of subsidiary sites like London, Copenhagen, and Prague, this novel presents in a series of diary entries from 21 August 1967 to 20 August 1968 the thoughts of an ordinary white-collar worker, Gesine Cresspahl, who is disgusted equally by American imperialism and Stalinist socialism. Despite her general pessimism Gesine upholds the fragile vision of a 'third way' in which the historical advances of bourgeois society might be married to the ideals of social justice and equality. The novel ends when the Prague Spring, in which just such an experiment was begun historically, is brought to an end by Warsaw Pact troops occupying Czechoslovakia, an action that signalled the demise of all possibilities for reform in the countries of so-called real socialism and thus effectively destroyed the dream of the 'third way'.

In the light of the defeat or disintegration of totalitarian ideologies and the incremental destruction of the environment, the tenets of modernism had to be rethought, entailing significant changes in the cultural and political agenda which were especially pronounced in Germany. At a minimalist level this postmodern condition manifested itself in a 'new inwardness'. Equally dejected by the innate totalitarianism of both right- and left-wing ideologies and by the anti-authoritarian movement's critique of them, writers like Rolf Dieter Brinkmann (*Rom, Blicke*, written 1972, published 1979), Peter Handke (*Als das Wünschen noch geholfen hat*, 1974), and Botho Strauß (*Die Widmung*, 1977) despaired of the possibility of collective action. In their works they sought to capture the fate of the disconsolate individual within the alienating structures of the big cities (Rome, London, Paris, Berlin) which, though blighted by modernism, yet offered the excitement of unexpected perceptions and the seductions of multicultural consumption. The disjunctures, diffuseness, and second-hand quality of everyday experience, epitomized by the mêlée of the TV programme schedule, bred a new multi-layered awareness which called for a neo-Romantic reconciliation of reason and fantasy, past and present, adherence to locality and exposure to global life; or, as Botho Strauß put it in *Der junge Mann* (1984):

Where others only perceive glittering decay he sees transitions and transformations, he sees the abundant market of difference which arises out of the essential uncertainty and openness of this society. . . . As far as the element of time is concerned, here too an extended awareness, a multiple consciousness must protect us from the uniform and coercive regimes of progress, from utopia, and every so-called 'future'. . . . We need circuits

Rob Burns and Wilfried van der Will

which connect the Then and the Now and finally, we need the living unison of everyday awareness and dream.[17]

There was talk at the time of a *Tendenzwende*, meaning a reorientation of the literary and student intelligentsia towards subjective experience and hedonistic contentment. The ready involvement in the collectivism of the far left was now abandoned, as were all attempts at mobilizing the masses in pursuit of ideological objectives. A 'Me'-generation began to reject politics as the self-estranging struggle for an ultimate goal which demanded the subjugation of the individual to the dictates of leaders and collectives. New journals founded towards the end of the 1970s, like *Freibeuter* and *Konkursbuch*, mirrored this mood. They developed the argument, first advanced by Horkheimer and Adorno in *Dialektik der Aufklärung*, that technological rationality was tyrannical, reduced individuals to numbers, and had as its most powerful executors the legal and political bureaucracies of modern states which, by curtailing individual liberty, were a perversion of enlightened reason. This pessimistic impetus was sustained in Peter Sloterdijk's philosophical essays, notably *Kritik der zynischen Vernunft* (1983), in which the reflecting individual, comfortably embedded in affluence, compromises the demands of his critical reason and withdraws into the position of a cynical voyeur.

In contrast to such cynicism and passivity an openly combative response came from the new social movements whose members, retreating from the 'grand narratives' of existing ideologies, took up critical positions closely reflecting their personal experience as women, as citizens, as consumers, etc. Nevertheless, the critique of the old nostrums of ideology, which soon occasioned debates, even within the established political parties, about the necessity for a *Wertwandel*, frequently required the commitment to new 'grand narratives', such as the development of an ecological reconciliation of nature and technology. Within the fictional confines of a literary tale such a reversal of a 'grand narrative', namely the change-over from an age-old patriarchy to a new, female-dominated history, is shown in *Der Butt* (1977) by Günter Grass. This master of German prose was in a sense articulating an idea whose time had come. While this vision of a society free from masculine domination was shared by the women's movement, many of its protagonists nevertheless opposed a simple turning of the tables on the grounds that merely replacing a patriarchal system with one based on matriarchal privilege would repeat the history of repression by inverting the stereotypes of gender. A much more complex set of problems confronted women demanding an equally complex range of answers.

17 Botho Strauß, *Der junge Mann*, (Munich, 1987), 11.

The Cultural Projections of Feminism

Like other protest movements, the new feminism of the 1970s and 1980s reflected the development of culture in an era characterized not just by greater creative diversity but also by the tensions between modernism and postmodernism. In line with the view, expressed at the beginning of the nineteenth century by the utopian socialist Charles Fourier, that 'the furtherance of the rights of women is a general precondition of all social progress', the West German feminist movement insisted that the constitutional guarantee of full equality between men and women (Article 3(2)) had remained a mere promise. Apart from being underrepresented in politics, the state administration, the judiciary, the universities, the media, and industry, women suffered discrimination at the most basic and personal level, namely in terms of legal limitations on the control over their own bodies. The campaign in the early 1970s to abolish the abortion laws marked the emergence of the women's movement as a coherent political force. The struggle for the right to a 'dignified abortion'—in Alice Schwarzer's words, 'the precondition of emancipation'—not only united women of quite different ideological persuasions, it also articulated an interest with which the vast majority of ordinary women could identify, thereby taking feminism beyond the student movement, where it had originated, into the arena of mass politics.

This struggle for women's rights obviously continued a central concern of modernism, the drive for greater equality and emancipation. At the same time, however, the movement developed key elements of the postmodern critique of society, targeting the aggressive psychology of the male, the subordination of nature to modern science and technology, and the dominance of the military–industrial complex within the economy. In short, the new feminism demanded a 'comprehensive cultural revolution' predicated on the premiss that 'the personal is political': 'Everything needs to be changed: the way we think—the discourse of power; the way we live—the family; the way we work—the technological-industrial complex; indeed, the way we laugh, love, cry, and dream.'[18] Confronted by a culture industry in which women were marginalized, feminists in the mid-1970s realized that they needed to create their own public sphere in which women would be central. The result was the transformation of feminism from a political programme into a multifaceted counter-culture with its own networks of communication.

Given the loose structure of the women's movement, its most

18 Gabriele Dietze (ed.), *Die Überwindung der Sprachlosigkeit* (Darmstadt and Neuwied, 1981), 8.

Rob Burns and Wilfried van der Will

pressing requirement was a regular publication which would facilitate communication between the many autonomous women's groups that had sprung up in the Federal Republic in the first half of the 1970s. This need was partially met by the magazine *Courage*. Founded in September 1976 and appearing monthly until 1984, it addressed a broad range of topics: work, culture, psychology, lesbianism, prostitution, ecology, and women's history. In January 1977 Alice Schwarzer founded *Emma*, which, unlike *Courage*, was written and produced by professional (women) journalists and aimed at an audience much broader than that constituted by the organized women's movement. The magazine, readily available at kiosks and newsagents, quickly built up its circulation to 120,000 (compared with 60,000 for *Courage*). Such figures supported the calculation that by the end of the 1970s about half a million women in the Federal Republic would come into regular contact with feminist ideas via the medium of the printed word. Moreover, a multitude of women's newspapers, magazines, and journals followed in the wake of *Courage* and *Emma*, including a host of regional organs and an array of specialist publications devoted to particular fields of activity, such as the music paper *Troubadora*, the magazine on the visual arts *Kassandra*, and the feminist film journal *Frauen und Film*.

Founded in 1974 by Helke Sander, *Frauen und Film* was one of several pioneering developments that helped forge an environment capable of sustaining a feminist film culture. In the previous year Sander, together with Claudia Alemann, had organized the first German women's film festival and workshop in Berlin. In 1977 that city also became the site for the first *Frauenkino*, thus providing a model for autonomous women's cinemas (showing films by women to women) that was quickly emulated elsewhere in Germany. Following the 1979 Hamburg Film Festival, where women found their interests still woefully underrepresented, an Association of Women Film-Workers was established. Its first act was to issue a manifesto with over eighty signatories demanding that 50 per cent of all film subsidies should be allocated to female directors and that special support should be provided for the distribution and exhibition of films made by women. Although these objectives were never attained, untypically generous funding for films by and about women was in fact granted throughout the 1970s by the public broadcasting corporations. Through its current affairs programmes, documentaries, shorts, and feature films West German television provided ample coverage of the many issues raised by the new women's movement and in the process gave many feminist directors their entrée into film production. It is this combination of factors which explains why the number of women directors, scriptwriters, editors, producers, and technicians continued to grow throughout the 1970s and why the Federal Republic came to possess 'proportionately more women film-makers than any other film-producing country'.[19]

The *Frauenfilm*, 'a film-making practice defining itself outside the masculine mirror',[20] embraced a great variety of themes and styles as the paradigmatic cases of Margarethe von Trotta and Helke Sander show. Born in 1942, von Trotta worked initially as an actress before embarking on a collaboration as both writer and director with her husband, Volker Schlöndorff. However, she quickly came to resent the fact that 'the public by and large only acknowledged Volker . . . and regarded me as an appendage'.[21] After opting to direct in her own right von Trotta became the first West German woman film-maker to achieve popular success outside the Federal Republic (only two others, Helma Sanders-Brahms and Doris Dörrie, were able to attain such recognition). Frequently employing star actresses like Hanna Schygulla, Barbara Sukowa, and Jutta Lampe, von Trotta's films rarely depart from the style of classical narrative cinema. Addressing the question of whether it was possible to identify a specifically female form of aesthetics in film, she reflected that for her it lay primarily 'in the choice of themes and in the respect, sensitivity, and care with which we approach the people we are presenting'.[22] In accordance with this view von Trotta's films could be said to cohere as an *œuvre* in so far as they all show female characters 'actively engaged in a struggle to define their lives, their identities, and their feminist politics in a situation where the dominant discourse constantly undermines their efforts or forces them into destructive positions through controlling what choices are available'.[23] This was certainly true of von Trotta's best-known film, *Die bleierne Zeit* (1981), which took up two themes repeatedly addressed by German feminist cinema, namely the interpersonal relationships between women and the confrontation with a specifically German historical past. Loosely based on the story of Christiane and Gudrun Ensslin, the film is, however, less an examination of urban terrorism than a reflection on a particular generation formed in the 'leaden times' of the 1950s and on sisterhood in both the personal and the political sense.

In contrast to the career of von Trotta, who moved to Italy in the late 1980s and managed to secure relatively large budgets for her later films like *Rosa Luxemburg* (1986) and *Paura e amore* (1988), that of Helke Sander took shape within a cultural environment bounded by alternative politics and low-budget film-making. Between 1966 and 1969 she studied at the Berlin Academy of Film and

19 Thomas Elsaesser, *New German Cinema* (Basingstoke, 1989), 185.
20 Marc Silberman, 'Film and Feminism in Germany Today', *Jumpcut*, 27 (1982), 41.
21 'Gespräch zwischen Margarethe von Trotta und Christel Buschmann', *Frauen und Film*, 8 (1976), 31.
22 Hans-Jürgen Weber (ed.), *Heller Wahn: Ein Film von Margarethe von Trotta* (Frankfurt am Main, 1983), 103.
23 E. Ann Kaplan, *Women and Film* (New York and London, 1983), 104–5.

Rob Burns and Wilfried van der Will

Television and then went on to make a number of documentaries and didactic films dealing with, amongst other things, the social pressures facing working-class women (*Eine Prämie für Irene*, 1971) and the problem of contraception (*Macht die Pille frei?*, 1972). Despite the opportunities offered by German television Sander complained that feminist film-makers were patently disadvantaged. Indeed, it was her own experience of such discrimination (amounting in her view to a kind of *Berufsverbot*) that prompted her considerable efforts to create autonomous institutions for the furtherance of women's film-making. As Thomas Elsaesser has observed, Sander's career can thus 'be read symptomatically in the way that it quite deliberately marks and documents the women's movement and its impact on the private as well as public lives of her characters, at once autobiographical and representative'.[24]

That project was successfully realized in three essentially autobiographical fiction films, *Die allseitig reduzierte Persönlichkeit* (1977), *Der subjektive Faktor* (1981), and *Der Beginn aller Schrecken ist Liebe* (1984). In the second film in this quasi-trilogy (the only one where Sander does not play the lead role) the narrative focuses on the years 1967 to 1970 as seen from the vantage-point of 1980 and traces the growth of the new feminism out of the West German student movement. Centring on Anni, a young mother who moves into a *Wohngemeinschaft* with her little son Andres, the film presents this collective household as a microcosm of the student movement in order to illustrate both its internal contradictions and subsequent fragmentation. Chief among the former was the flagrant disparity women perceived between the anti-authoritarian rhetoric deployed in the public sphere by their male comrades and the latter's wholly authoritarian and patriarchal behaviour in their private life. While the men attended demonstrations and engaged in political debate, the women were still expected to look after the children or perform the purely menial tasks and were thus effectively marginalized in the political discourse. In the film this attitude is typified by Matthias, a socialist intellectual quite unable to translate his theoretical belief in female equality into the practice of everyday life. Such indifference to women's interests leads Anni—as in reality it did Sander—to form the Action Committee for the Liberation of Women, the nucleus of the new women's movement. Eventually the commune disintegrates and the directions in which its members disperse symbolize the strategies pursued by various factions within the broader student movement after its dissolution: Anni's ultra-dogmatic lover, Uwe, falls prey to the rigid sectarianism of Maoist cadre parties, while Till, the only male to reflect his anti-

24 Elsaesser, *New German Cinema*, 189.

authoritarian principles in his personal relationships, paradoxically ends up in the political cul-de-sac of urban terrorism. The positive legacy of the student movement is clearly represented by Anni herself, for the feminism she champions is no separatist one but rather a model of activism which seeks to integrate women's struggles within those of the broader community. As such it prefigures the politics of the locality which in the 1970s paved the way for the Green movement and the mass peace protests of the 1980s, a reading the film underscores by associating the adolescent Andres with the issues of nuclear power and atomic weapons.

The 'subjective factor' of the title extends beyond an allusion to the feminist axiom 'the personal is political', and comments in self-reflexive fashion on the film's means of representation. Eschewing the illusionistic realism of classical narrative cinema, Sander employs a variety of filmic practices, in particular those pertaining to the documentary code. Yet despite the use of newsreel, press photographs, hand-held camera, and narratorial voice-over (provided by Sander herself) the film should not be seen as some simple affirmation of the documentary as a vehicle of objective truth. Rather, by continually foregrounding the split between the fictional and the documentary discourse and by highlighting her own role in structuring the film, Sander juxtaposes elements 'that remain distinct and comment upon each other, that invite the spectator to make some kind of critical connection between them . . . and thus provoke interpretation of depicted events from a variety of perspectives'.[25] When asked about the notion of a 'feminine aesthetic', Sander remained sceptical, observing, for example, that women filmmakers were often drawn to video and documentary production for financial rather than aesthetic reasons. Writing in 1978 she likened the situation of women to that of Kaspar Hauser: 'We must first learn to see with our own eyes and not through the mediation of others.'[26] In short, the process of emancipation as conceived by Sander required women to transform their entire perception of the world *qua* women, regardless of the artistic medium within which they had chosen to work.

Feminist writers of the 1970s and 1980s were acutely aware of this challenge and determined to show that woman could truly become 'the subject through which the world is presented instead of reiterating male-defined perspectives that permit only inauthentic visions of women's lives'.[27] Initially, as in the cinema, women revealed a distrust of conventional fiction and a preference for ostensibly more authentic forms of narrative that were either documentary in character—such as the volume edited by Erika Runge,

25 Richard W. McCormick, *Politics of the Self: Feminism and the Postmodern in West German Literature and Film* (Princeton, 1991), 225.
26 *Frauen und Film*, 15 (1978), 7.
27 Juliet Wigmore, 'Feminist Writing in West Germany', in Keith Bullivant (ed.), *After the 'Death' of Literature* (Oxford, New York, and Munich, 1989), 89.

Rob Burns and Wilfried van der Will

Frauen: Versuche einer Emanzipation (1969)—or based on personal experience, like Karin Struck's novel in diary form, *Klassenliebe* (1973). The use of autobiographical narrative in order to address problems confronting women generally is best exemplified by Verena Stefan's *Häutungen* (1975), which became a seminal text for the new women's movement in Germany. The title image of a snake shedding its skin reflects the way in which Stefan's first-person narrator detaches herself from a world experienced as stiflingly male and gradually evolves a new self. She comes to see her own body as the primary site of her exploitation, a realization which collapses the notion that the personal and the political are discrete spheres of experience. The untenability of this view is illustrated by the two men with whom the protagonist becomes emotionally and sexually involved. Although both in their different ways—one as a member of the Black Panthers, the other as an activist in the student movement—are committed to the struggle against inequality, like the men in Sander's *Der subjektive Faktor* they are incapable of recognizing the mechanisms of oppression operating in their own relations with women. As Stefan ruefully remarks of Dave, the Black Panther, 'he fought the domination of the whites over the blacks and yet reasserted daily the domination of men over women'.[28] Such experiences induce a radical change of consciousness in Stefan's narrator, with the final destination on her voyage of self-discovery turning out to be lesbianism and radical feminism. Although published by Frauenoffensive, a small independent publishing venture run by a feminist collective, *Häutungen* had sold 140,000 copies by 1979. It became an indispensable book for consciousness-raising groups, for the particular problems it confronted, the learning processes it embodied, and the style of narrative, which both invited identification and explored new forms of mediating female experience, all made it ideally suited to the needs of women intent on laying bare their own past but possibly lacking the confidence and means of expression to do so.

The sense of personal liberation that ensues when a woman extricates herself from a relationship with a man is a theme addressed by a number of writers such as Birgit Pausch in *Die Verweigerungen der Johanna Gauflügel* (1977) and Karin Petersen in her novel *Das fette Jahr* (1978). Equally, autobiographical and biographical writing focused on the author's relations with her parents. Typically the father is characterized by his remoteness and emotional detachment, as in Elisabeth Plessen's *Mitteilung an den Adel* (1976) and Barbara Bronnen's *Die Tochter* (1980), or alternatively as a figure who, through his general patriarchal attitudes or

28 Verena Stefan, *Häutungen* (Munich, 1975), 35.

particular political beliefs, exerts a shaping influence on his daughter. Texts like Ruth Rehmann's *Der Mann auf der Kanzel* (1979) or Brigitte Schwaiger's *Lange Abwesenheit* (1980) explore the process by which the authors, in seeking to come to terms with that paternal influence, cast light on their own personality. Although often tinged with greater authorial sympathy, representations of the mother–daughter relationship, like Karin Struck's *Die Mutter* (1975) or Katja Behrens's *Die dreizehnte Fee* (1983), are seldom any less problematical. In her autobiographical novel *Gestern war heute* (1978) Ingeborg Drewitz provides a family portrait spanning five generations in which history is presented from a predominantly female perspective, with the various fathers and husbands mostly appearing as marginal or indeed silent figures.

Feminist writing also concerned itself with history's 'silent' women, namely those who, like Clara Schumann in Elfriede Jelinek's play *Clara S.* (1981), sacrificed their own creative potential on the altar of the male artistic genius or others who were quite simply consigned to marginality by male-centred historiography. Examples of the latter include Ria Endres's *Milena antwortet* (1982), written from the perspective of Kafka's epistolary correspondent, Milena Jesenská, and Karin Reschke's *Verfolgte des Glücks. Findebuch der Henriette Vogel* (1982), which constructs the life-story of the woman otherwise known only for her suicide pact with Heinrich von Kleist. Another way in which women writers vacated the terrain of the male perspective in order to write 'herstory' was by establishing a narrative framework that fused the contemporary and the mythological. Most notably deployed by Christa Wolf in *Kassandra* (1983), this technique is also apparent in a trilogy of novels by Barbara Frischmuth. In *Die Mystifikation der Sophie Silber* (1976) the central character's encounter with the world of spirits in the form of the fairy Amaryllis Sternwiese is not in fact a mystifying experience, for by removing herself from contemporary reality Sophie sets in motion a process of enlightenment through which she is enabled to liberate herself and embark on a new life. Cast as a modern Orpheus the heroine in Ulla Berkéwicz's *Michel, sag ich* (1984) ventures forth from her rural idyll and descends into the underworld of Frankfurt in search of her lost lover. Similarly, in her play *Krankheit oder Moderne Frauen* (1987) Elfriede Jelinek presents her protagonist Camilla as a latter-day Medea who at one point remarks, 'I am ill, therefore I am.' As Sigrid Weigel has observed,[29] Jelinek here echoes (and satirizes) a common image of women in feminist writing which employs illness as a metaphor for femininity. In some cases this is rendered by fairly conventional albeit harrowing realism,

29 Regula Venske and Sigrid Weigel, ' "Frauenliteratur"— Literatur von Frauen', in Klaus Briegleb and Sigrid Weigel (eds.), *Gegenwartsliteratur seit 1968* (Munich, 1992), 262.

as with Maria Erlenberger's 'report' of being treated for anorexia nervosa and schizophrenia in *Der Hunger nach Wahnsinn* (1977) or Gisela Elsner's novel *Abseits* (1982), in which a middle-class Munich housewife is propelled by her remorselessly oppressive family life into mental depression, drug addiction, and ultimately suicide. More strikingly, however, the focus on the body as a unique site of experience prompted women writers to rethink basic literary categories in the search for a language that would 'speak the body' anew (Luce Irigaray).

This was a difficulty Verena Stefan had also confronted, for in the introduction to *Häutungen* she remarks on the problem of writing about women's bodies and female sexuality in view of the intrinsic sexism of the German language: 'Each word must be twisted and turned before it can be used. . . . In writing I ran straight up against language.'[30] One of the ways she chose to escape from this impasse, however, provoked criticism from some feminists who detected a biological determinism at work in Stefan's use of nature imagery when discussing the female body. It was not least the desire to avoid cliché and open up new perspectives which motivated other women writers to experiment in more radical fashion with language and narrative form. In the title text of Anne Duden's prose volume *Übergang* (1982) a brutal attack on the first-person narrator is the catalyst for a mode of perception in which her violated body becomes the sole locus of experience and the boundaries between the physical and the mental, between inner and outer self, are dissolved. While this gives rise to a form of articulation which renders the narrator's past as well as her present state through metaphors of physical sensation, Duden nevertheless leaves the syntactical structure of language intact. By contrast, Pola Veseken pushes language almost to breaking-point and in the direction of an asocial discourse that resists instrumentalization as conventional communication. In her voluminous, episodic novel *Altweibersommer?* (1982) writing is the means to undo the first-person reference, 'to discover what under certain circumstances one might term the "ego" and how it might be unpacked', as the narrator puts it. She has acquired the tools of psychoanalysis and by working with association, dreams, and slips of the tongue she accesses her unconscious and expands memory to encompass elements registered in her body as painful symptoms. Veseken's attack on the discursiveness of language is thus the process whereby the feminine libido, the existence of which is denied by Freudian psychoanalysis, gains release. In short, she uses the means of psychoanalysis in order to deconstruct its very assumptions.[31]

A similar act of deconstruction is effected by Elfriede Jelinek in

30 Stefan, *Häutungen*, 4.
31 Pola Veseken, *Altweibersommer?* (Frankfurt am Main and Basle, 1982), 18. See Renate Becker, *Inszenierungen des Weiblichen* (Frankfurt am Main, Berne, New York, and Paris, 1992), 237.

her controversial, bestselling novel *Lust* (1989). Through her mimetic reproduction of pornography Jelinek succeeds in bringing to the fore what above all characterizes this form of discourse, namely the absence of the female subject. This is reflected, firstly, in the denial of a voice to Gerti, the book's protagonist, and, secondly, in the prevalence of passive verbs, which serves to underscore Gerti's status as (sexual) object. Jelinek transcends the mimetic level, however, in the multiplicity of voices in which her narrator speaks.[32] *Lust* may describe a seemingly endless succession of sexual acts but in the process Jelinek draws on a formidable arsenal of rhetorical devices— assonance, alliteration, metaphor, metathesis, and paronomasia— in order to ridicule the language of pornography. With the sentence 'you are invited to look on' the narrator not only identifies her own role as the creator of the images, but she also defines the position of the (male) reader as viewer and voyeur. Moreover, the frequency and acerbity of the direct address renders this position highly uncomfortable. Elsewhere the narrator intervenes to establish her own sense of involvement with the narrative, either in the form of an ironic interjection or in an open display of identification with Gerti and her suffering. Ultimately, then, *Lust* is not, as some reviewers saw it, the attempt to emulate pornography but rather the unmasking of sex as a gross display of masculine power and violence.

The whole question of violence against women was, in fact, brought to public attention in Germany primarily by the efforts of the feminist movement which, after years of campaigning, persuaded the established politicians that here was a problem demanding official recognition and financial measures. By the end of 1983 there were, according to government figures, some 150 women's shelters in the Federal Republic and it was estimated that at that time about 40 per cent of all feminist projects were related in some way to this issue. These were, of course, essentially a defensive response to male violence. In fiction, however, women were increasingly portrayed as breaking out of their powerlessness and going on the offensive. In Libusa Moníková's *Eine Schädigung* (1981) the protagonist beats a policeman to death after he has raped her, a theraputic act of retribution which 'brought her from a state of silence to one of articulacy in which she could find a name for herself again'. In particular, women writers turned to the popular genre of the crime story and the detective novel as the narrative form where this role reversal could most easily be effected, and the late 1980s witnessed a spate of such books with titles like Sabine Deitmer's *Bye-bye Bruno. Wir Frauen morden* (1988) and *Auch brave Mädchen tun's: Mordgeschichten* (1990), Doris Gercke's *Weinschröte, du mußt hängen* (1988), and Katrin

32 Renate Becker, 'Schreiben als Diskurskritik' (unpublished paper, 1990), 18–19.

Rob Burns and Wilfried van der Will

Skafte's *Lauter ganz normale Männer: Ein Krimi—nur für Frauen* (1990). As is the case with Pieke Biermann's *Violetta* (1990), a detective story featuring a women's commando unit that beats up sexist men, what distinguishes such feminist crime fiction from the traditional type is not (just) that the figures of 'law and order' are women. Rather, as Isabel Morf has pointed out, there is a distinct shift in the scale of moral values: 'the actual crime is the behaviour of the victim and the murder helps establish a new code in accordance with which atonement is unnecessary and the murderers mostly go unpunished.'[33] On the other hand, it might be argued, by giving woman the essentially male role of avenger—a trend which, coincidentally, became fashionable in the Hollywood cinema of the early 1980s as epitomized by films like *Lipstick* and *Handgun*—such literature merely succeeded in idealizing once more stereotypical patterns of masculinity paradoxically projected in female guise.

The appropriation of established literary models by feminist writers clearly brought with it the danger that the new might actually be absorbed by the old, in other words, that the dominant culture would reassert itself by imposing the inherent inertia of traditional form on new content. Conversely, the dominant culture had its assimilative powers tested by the need to incorporate new themes and perspectives. This was just as true in the other arts as in the field of literature. In this respect, literary developments were only the reflection of a more extensive process whereby the dominant culture became significantly broadened and, while working to defuse the threat of oppositional forms by assimilating them into its culture industry, actually had to integrate and, indeed, co-opt new cultural demands. To some extent, this dialectic of integration and dissemination also operated in relation to the culture of ethnic minorities.

Problems of the Multicultural Society

While cultural output in the Federal Republic steadily diversified in the course of the 1970s, it nevertheless remained bounded by ethnocentricity and Eurocentricity. Yet the federal government's policy of encouraging worker migration had by then brought about significant demographic changes. By 1972 there were 3.5 million resident foreigners in West Germany, rising to 4.67 million, or 7.6 per cent of the total population, ten years later. These were faced with a range of problems relating to their living and working conditions, legal status, and civic rights, for Germany had effectively become a

33 Isabel Morf, 'Es war Mord am Mann', *Freitag*, 22 (24 May 1991), 8.

country of immigration while making it difficult for its economic migrants to attain full citizenship. It was essentially the latter's alterity, their felt sense of 'otherness', which was given expression in a variety of cultural forms. From the outset 'guest workers', so called, had been motivated to write about their experience, not least because this was one way of coming to terms with the problems they encountered. However, it was not until the beginning of the 1980s that concerted efforts were made to recuperate and promote 'this dispersed, neglected, and suppressed literature'. This formulation was used in a programmatic essay entitled 'Literatur der Betroffenen' (1981), which was co-authored by the Italian Franco Biondi and the Syrian Rafik Schami. They organized a special series for the publication of literary works in German by immigrant writers called *Südwind. Gastarbeiterdeutsch*, itself a direct result of the newly founded Multinational Association for Literature and Art. The latter was conceived not as a means of facilitating access to German culture, which was summarily dismissed as 'a culture of the educated middle class for the educated middle class',[34] but as an instrument of 'cultural resistance' that might help a multinational culture 'attain liberation'.[35] These terms suggested affinities with the older tradition of working-class culture, on the one hand, and with the political goals pursued by the liberation movements of the Third World, on the other. Consequently, this 'literature of the affected', which gave priority to the authenticity of experience over the attainment of formal perfection, was intended to foster solidarity among immigrant workers and between them and the indigenous working population.

An influential forerunner of this type of writing was Vera Kamenko's *Unter uns war Krieg* (1978), an autobiographical account of emigration which covers the period from Vera's birth in Yugoslavia in 1947 to her imprisonment in Germany for the accidental killing of her young son in Berlin in 1972. One of the most interesting features of this painful narrative, which was further popularized in a song by Bettina Wegner, concerns Kamenko's struggle with language. For much of the time in Germany she exists in a sort of linguistic twilight zone, for her exclusive medium of communication is the rudimentary German spoken amongst foreigners of different nationality. One consequence of this is a partial alienation from her native Serbian. As Jeanette Claussen has suggested, this might also explain why Kamenko chose to write her story in German, for this is how she experienced events leading up to her imprisonment. Hence her grappling with the language while writing is but 'an extension of her daily struggles to communicate and

34 Franco Biondi and Rafik Schami, 'Literatur der Betroffenen: Bemerkungen zur Gastarbeiterliteratur', in Christian Schaffernicht (ed.), *Zu hause in der Fremde: Ein bundesdeutsches Ausländer-Lesebuch* (Fischerhude, 1981), 124.
35 Ibid. 146.

Rob Burns and Wilfried van der Will

survive in Germany'. Vera's language is broken German in a double sense, for she 'breaks the language out of necessity, to break the silence'.[36] The value of *Unter uns war Krieg* is thus twofold: first, it demonstrates the ways in which cultural, ethnic, and gender differences are structured by language itself; and, secondly, 'Vera's story can help women come closer to knowing the meaning of their own oppression through the recognition of what they have in common with her'.[37] Moreover, Kamenko's hope that by her example she might inspire others to write about their experiences was amply realized in a considerable body of literature by foreign women writers such as Saliha Scheinhardt, Alev Tekinay, and Aysel Özakin.

The first half of the 1980s witnessed a significant growth of interest in German literature written by immigrants. The cultural sections of party-affiliated foundations, church organizations, the German Writers' Union, a number of prestige theatres, the German broadcasting corporations, and several major publishing houses all sought to draw the attention of a wider public to such writers. A key role in this process was played by the Munich Institute for German as a Foreign Language. Not only did its work help confer academic respectability on a hitherto neglected field of study, but it also opened up further opportunities for publication, first through the literary contests it organized from 1979 onwards and secondly through the establishment of the Adelbert von Chamisso Prize, an award (currently DM15,000) devoted to literature written in German by foreign authors.

A further contribution towards establishing a multicultural awareness in Germany was made by the New German Cinema through such studies in prejudice as Fassbinder's *Katzelmacher* (1969) and *Angst essen Seele auf* (1974) and Helma Sanders-Brahms's *Shirins Hochzeit* (1976). In the 1980s immigrant film directors added to this repertoire, most notably Tevfik Baser, whose central concern was with the special difficulties Turks encountered in adapting to life in the Federal Republic on account of a predominantly patriarchal Muslim culture. The eponymous location of Baser's first feature, *40 m² Deutschland* (1986), is the flat in a Hamburg tenement building in which Turna, newly arrived from Turkey, is literally incarcerated by her husband in his fanatical desire to protect her from what he regards as the moral depravity of German society. What makes the film such a particularly harrowing experience is that it is shot almost entirely from Turna's point of view. As in Chantal Akerman's *Jeanne Dielman, 23 Quai du Commerce, 1080 Bruxelles* (1975) —and the Belgian director's technique of positioning the camera at a woman's eye-level is also employed by Baser—the viewer must undergo

36 Jeanette Claussen, 'Broken but not Silent: Language as Experience in Vera Kamenko's *Unter uns war Krieg*', *Women in German Yearbook*, 1 (1986), 123.
37 Ibid. 120.

directly the claustrophobic tedium which now constitutes Turna's experiential world and which is only punctuated by the drama of having to tend her husband during his epileptic fits. Otherwise Turna's sole contact with the outside world comes in the form of brief exchanges in sign language with a child in a neighbouring apartment and in her observation of a prostitute conducting business on the street corner below. That the latter is occasionally shown rejecting the custom of certain men seems to imply a freedom of will denied to Turna herself, who is sexually at the beck and call of a husband intent on siring a male offspring. Significantly, on only one occasion—when Dusun learns of his wife's pregnancy—does the camera retreat from Turna's prison, thus sparing the viewer the prolonged, self-centred jubilation this news elicits. Dusun, however, does not live to see the birth of his child, for he suffers a fatal epileptic attack, leaving Turna to secure a release of sorts as she finally plucks up the courage to step over the corpse of her husband, who even in death maintains the role of his wife's jailor by blocking the doorway. That the camera declines to follow her as she staggers into the bright sunlight of the street would seem to suggest that Turna's liberation is relative and that a whole set of new problems await her in the foreign environment to which she has only now gained access.

This conclusion acquires further credence in the light of Baser's second feature, *Abschied vom falschen Paradies* (1989). Loosely adapted from Saliha Scheinhardt's *Frauen, die sterben, ohne daß sie gelebt hätten* (1983), a story based on real events, the film portrays the experience of Elif, a young Turkish mother convicted of the murder of her brutal husband. The narrative is constructed on the paradoxical premiss that incarceration is at the same time a form of emancipation. As with Vera Kamenko—but unlike the heroine of *Shirins Hochzeit*, for whom Westernization merely entails exchanging one form of bondage for another—imprisonment brings to an end the cultural and linguistic isolation to which an immigrant has been subjected in open society, for it is only in gaol that Elif has any sustained contact with Germans, the German language, and Western culture. The film's grimly pessimistic conclusion merely inverts the initial paradox: with her sentence cut for good behaviour and her familial and cultural ties to her homeland now severed, Elif is to be sent back by the authorities to Turkey where she faces either another trial and (longer) period of imprisonment for the same crime or certain death at the hands of an avenging brother-in-law.

While garnering considerable critical acclaim, Baser's films were roundly denounced by the Turkish community in the Federal Republic. Such controversy paled into insignificance, however, in comparison with that triggered by Günter Wallraff's *Ganz unten* (1985), which, like no other cultural intervention, succeeded in placing the situation of Germany's immigrant workers on the political agenda. Deploying once again his Scarlet Pimpernel approach to investigative journalism, Wallraff disguised himself as a Turkish worker and assumed the identity of a real immigrant, Ali Levent Sinirlioglu, in order to penetrate West Germany's illegal labour market. Equipped with a hidden video camera and microphone, he then for some two years recorded his experiences in a variety of dangerous, insanitary, and badly paid jobs, working at McDonald's, in the Thyssen steelworks, as a chauffeur for the subcontractor Vogel, and as a human guinea-pig in the pharmaceutical industry. He also reported on how he was treated in pubs, at the soccer match between Turkey and West Germany, and at a political rally in honour of Franz Josef Strauß. In a dramatic climax Ali/Wallraff cons Vogel into participating in a (staged) transaction in which the subcontractor believes he will receive tax-free remuneration in exchange for providing Turkish workers to repair a nuclear reactor emitting lethal doses of radiation.

In many respects *Ganz unten* is a paradigmatic text for cultural studies: first, it was a multimedia event, for as well as appearing in a paperback edition it was serialized in *Der Spiegel*, and using mainly the video footage the director Jörg Gfrörer released a cinema version which was subsequently screened on television; secondly, it was interdisciplinary in method, combining the discourses of fiction, the documentary, and participant observation as applied in modern sociology; and, finally, it transgressed the division between high and popular culture. Its special status within the latter derived not least from the fact that *Ganz unten* made publishing history, being translated into twenty languages (including Turkish) and selling more copies in a shorter period of time than any other postwar European book, including well over 3 million in the Federal Republic alone. Moreover, by prompting the German trade unions finally to confront the exploitation of immigrant workers and compelling the government actually to enforce laws regulating the employment of foreign labour, Wallraff provided powerful ammunition against those who would argue that the written word has long since ceded its political potency to the popular media of film and television. The film version of *Ganz unten*, in fact, was beset with problems in Germany, principally because the major distributors and television channels took fright at the potential legal repercussions,

18. Günter Wallraff, *Ganz unten* (1985).

Born in 1942, Günter Wallraff has been a constant thorn in the flesh of the establishment from the moment he refused to do military service in the early 1960s. His experiences as a worker with various industrial firms provided the material for *Wir brauchen Dich* (1966), after which he wrote for the political magazines *Pardon* and *konkret*. A member of Gruppe 61, Wallraff helped found the breakaway organization Werkkreis Literatur der Arbeitswelt. Further undercover exploits gave rise to *13 unerwünschte Reportagen* (1969), *Neue Reportagen* (1972), *Ihr da oben, wir da unten* (1973), the *Bild-Zeitung* exposé *Der Aufmacher* (1976), and, most notoriously, *Ganz unten*, which cemented Wallraff's reputation as a 'postmodern Robin Hood' (Heiner Müller): a master of disguise capable of fooling even his arch-enemy, Franz Josef Strauß (see top right), Wallraff donated some of the proceeds from his 3 million bestseller towards a centre for *Gastarbeiter*, but was driven into exile in Holland by the hounding he received from the lawyers, the media, and the state surveillance forces.

especially since German law forbids recording people without their permission. In truth, however, the film is a somewhat pallid affair, not least because it can never quite decide what generic codes to follow and thus falls rather uneasily between the two stools of direct cinema (where the director is conceived merely as an intermediary between the subject-matter and the viewer) and the social documentary (which deploys a variety of techniques in the service of some preconceived statement or narrative). Paradoxically, the film's one great strength is at the same time its major weakness: while those who would charge Wallraff with fabricating his material could scarcely contest the recorded evidence of Vogel repeatedly condemning himself by his own testimony, through its excessive focus on Vogel the film risks demonizing him as a manifestly nefarious, but not necessarily typical, small-time entrepreneur.

With his book Wallraff achieved the not inconsiderable feat of attracting criticism from both the right and the left. While German industry resorted once again to its tried and trusted counter-offensive against Wallraff, involving high-profile media denunciations and court cases (most of which they lost), the author found himself the butt of attacks by both German and Turkish left intellectuals. One charge levelled against Wallraff was that of tendentiousness, namely that the author merely set out to prove what he knew to be the case all along, and that the text amounted to little more than preaching to the converted. Certainly, the book's exposé of the unacceptable face of German industry reinforced the picture that had emerged from Wallraff's documentary prose of the 1960s and 1970s. But to focus attention exclusively on the inhuman and illegal conditions to which many immigrant labourers were subjected in Germany was to ignore the most disturbing element of the book. For as Anna Kuhn has passionately argued, Wallraff's most damning indictment of German society concerned 'the prevalent xenophobia' he uncovered and 'the parallels that were evoked between contemporary hostility to Turks and National Socialist anti-Semitism'.[38] In the light of the recrudescence of racist violence which greeted the influx of political asylum seekers in Germany post-unification, Ganz unten now seems gruesomely prophetic.

On the other hand, Wallraff faced the charge of inverted racism, with his book seen as presenting a patronizing and stereotyped portrait of the Turks as ignorant, unskilled, credulous, and pitiful. While it is true that Ganz unten tends towards a rather one-dimensional image of the Turk, it is necessary to bear in mind two other aspects of the text. The first concerns the persona of Wallraff's Ali. For if Wallraff plays him as a cliché of the dumb and gullible immigrant

38 Anna K. Kuhn, 'Bourgeois Ideology and the (Mis) Reading of Günter Wallraff's Ganz unten', New German Critique, 46 (1989), 193.

Rob Burns and Wilfried van der Will

worker, then this performance is primarily for the consumption of his adversaries and it is not in this exclusive guise that the reader perceives him. On the contrary, the ostensibly naïve Ali is shown to outwit that most astute of politicians, Franz Josef Strauß, just as he is able to dupe the unscrupulous Vogel by casting him as the unwitting protagonist in the book's climactic drama, the nuclear reactor hoax. Secondly, it is part of the political 'subtext' of *Ganz unten*—repeatedly underscored by the nature of Wallraff's authorial reflections—that he is presenting the particular oppression of Turks as 'paradigmatic for the experience of oppression in general'.[39]

From the late 1970s onwards animosity towards foreigners in Germany was to all intents and purposes synonymous with hostility to Turks, who constituted roughly one-third of the total number of immigrants in the Federal Republic. By both addressing and universalizing that oppression *Ganz unten* represented a model text for the 'literature of the affected' advocated by Biondi and Schami. Yet by then that particular trend had been superseded by a conception of literature as cultural mediator that eschewed adversarial politics and sought to foster reconciliation between foreigners and Germans. This was above all the project of the Ararat Publishing House, founded in 1977 by Ahmet Dogan with the aim of 'familiarizing the German public with Turkish culture . . . and the Turks in emigration with German culture'.[40] In accordance with this commitment to biculturality many texts were produced in bilingual editions and the Ararat catalogue included works of Turkish folklore and classic authors such as Nazim Hikmet as well as the writings of lay and professional writers resident in the Federal Republic. The spirit of this venture was epitomized by two authors in particular: Yüksel Pazarkaya, who consistently argued for a creative synthesis of Turkish and German culture to the mutual benefit of both, and Aras Ören, who moved to Berlin in 1969 and was the first winner of the Chamisso Prize. Although Ören continued to write in Turkish (and had his work appear in translation with established German publishers), his audience was a cosmopolitan one. Precisely because the culture shock for Turks was greater than for immigrants from distinctively European nations, the Turkish community in Germany gradually built up a cultural infrastructure (encompassing shops, newspapers, schools, libraries, religious centres, sports associations, theatre groups, and cinemas) which provided the broader context for the binational mediation of culture and literature.

The ranks of those championing the cause of multiculturalism in Germany were swelled in the 1980s by prominent politicians from all the major parties, ranging from the Greens' Daniel Cohn-Bendit,

39 Arlene Akiko Teroaka, 'Talking "Turk": On Narrative Strategies and Cultural Stereotypes', *New German Critique*, 46 (1989), 119.
40 Ahmet Dogan, 'Kulturvermittlung und Folklore: Gespräch Helmut Hartwig–Ahmet Dogan', *Ästhetik und Kommunikation*, 44 (1981), 38.

Director of Multicultural Affairs on the Frankfurt City Council, to Heiner Geißler, formerly General Secretary of the CDU. These understood multiculturalism not merely as an uneasy coexistence of cultures imported from various corners of the globe, but, to a greater or lesser extent, as an interactive practice predicated on mutual tolerance. In Geißler's view the concept of the multicultural society will prove to be as central to the new Germany as that of the social market economy was to the development of the old Federal Republic.[41] Cohn-Bendit, for his part, defined multiculturalism quite simply: 'The immigrants try to create for themselves a feeling of being at home in a foreign country. In so doing they are shaped by that foreign society, which they shape in their turn. In this way new, interrelated home environments can develop';[42] or, as Aras Ören expressed it in the title of one of his books, 'abroad is also home'. Lest one impute a hopelessly naïve anthropological optimism to their authors, these quotations must be read as programmatic statements about the political and cultural future of German society rather than as assessments of an already established practice of multicultural interaction in which different cultural identities would be both preserved and enhanced.

Americanization and National Identity

The fear of being assimilated by a foreign culture was not unique to West Germany's immigrant population, for national identity was a significant problem for the Germans themselves. Moreover, wherever that debate surfaced—on the left or on the right, within the post-1945 or the post-1968 generation—it invariably meant engaging with the considerable influence exerted on Germany by the United States, which went far beyond the military and economic spheres. During the Cold War, of course, the Federal Republic served as the West's most important buffer-state that was to halt the westward expansion of the Soviet empire. West Germans, on the whole, willingly accepted that role and quickly learnt to take their political and ideological cues from America, just as they were more than happy to emulate its consumerism. However, the special relationship between the Federal Republic and the United States by no means pre-empted criticism from within West Germany of its most valuable ally. Emanating from sections of the German left this criticism focused on the United States's role as an imperial power with hegemonic aspirations, as evidenced by its interventions in Vietnam, Chile, El Salvador, and elsewhere in the Third World. It

41 Heiner Geißler, 'Wir sind ein Einwanderungsland', *Die Zeit* (15 Nov. 1991), 7.
42 Daniel Cohn-Bendit and Thomas Schmid, 'Wenn der Westen unwiderstehlich wird', *Die Zeit* (22 Nov. 1991), 5.

Rob Burns and Wilfried van der Will

was not, however, until the NATO 'dual track' decision of 1979 and the mass peace protests of the early 1980s that this perception of the United States began to gain widespread support. For despite the success of Brandt's *Ostpolitik* the West German public could by then no longer be deflected from the disillusioning realization that the period of détente in the 1970s had in fact amounted to an intense arms race between the Soviet Union and the United States, with the respective territories of the two Germanies being treated as the forward strategic bases of the two superpowers. Hence the Protestant pastor and former Mayor of West Berlin, Heinrich Albertz, could announce that 'we are an occupied country',[43] while in the same vein the distinguished theologian Helmut Gollwitzer proclaimed in 1981: 'No West German can tolerate this unconditional subordination of the interests of our people to foreign interests, this delivery of the existence of our people into the hands of a foreign government.'[44]

Albertz and Gollwitzer were of a generation which had experienced directly the horrendous consequences of a national pride poisoned by racism and rampant chauvinism, and their views betrayed neither a new German nationalism nor an inherent anti-Americanism. Yet prominent voices could also be heard at this time whose antipathy towards the United States was as much cultural as political. In an interview in 1981 the writer Gerd Fuchs accused the Americans with unmistakable bitterness: 'These people have taken away our honour. A whole nation has been turned into an accomplice. This amounts to both cultural and political poisoning'; while his fellow author Hermann Peter Piwitt bemoaned the occupation of his country by a 'Yankee culture' and posed the question, 'How can I defend myself against everyday colonialism?'[45] In the course of the 1980s the growth of post-materialist values in Germany provided a further inflection of this criticism. America was now seen as the leading exponent of modernism and cultural imperialism, symbolized by the twin icons of global consumerism, Coca-Cola and McDonald's. In contrast, critical attitudes in the late 1960s and 1970s tended to focus on a condemnation of US politics and not, that is to say, on a wholesale rejection of the American way of life. After all, even the German student movement, while vociferously denouncing the policy on Vietnam, nevertheless looked to the United States for its initial inspiration and drew its role models from the 'Beat' movement and other elements of American subculture. The same ambivalence was also apparent with regard to the two areas of popular culture that arguably represented America's most successful export articles, rock music and Hollywood cinema.

43 Heinrich Albertz, 'Wir sind doch ein besetztes Land', in Dieter Hoffmann-Axthelm and Eberhard Knödler-Bunte (eds.), *Wie souverän ist die Bundesrepublik?* (Berlin, 1982), 115–19.
44 Quoted in *Die Zeit* (30 Oct. 1981).
45 Ibid., both quotations.

At the consumer level, at least, the supremacy of the American (and British) music industry remained virtually unchallenged in Germany: the record sales of American rock and pop artists far outstripped those of their German counterparts; the Federal Republic was very quickly targeted as the country in Europe (apart from Britain) where not only the megastars but also the cult figures of the American rock scene would be guaranteed sell-out tours; German discotheques pumped out music for the latest dance trends from the United States; and rock clubs in the late 1960s and 1970s regularly featured German groups whose repertoire consisted of endless cover versions of American and British hit songs. Even those few German bands which succeeded in attracting an international following did so largely on the basis of instrumentals, like the psychedelia albums of Tangerine Dream or the synthesizer rock of Kraftwerk. For all the diversity of musical trends in Germany—from rock 'n' roll to heavy metal, from soul music to Electronic Rock, from psychedelia to jazz rock—the common denominator remained the absence of German lyrics. The sole exception to this in the 1970s were politically oriented bands like Ton Steine Scherben, BAP, Floh de Cologne, Udo Lindenberg und sein Panikorchester, and feminist bands such as Bonner Blaustrümpfe, Insisters, and Lysistrata. Undoubtedly, the attraction of Anglo-American rock can be explained primarily in musicological terms, for it stood in marked contrast to the one form of pop music which was traditionally sung in German, the *Schlager*. These predominantly lightweight orchestral confections, served up by the likes of Roy Black, Cindy und Bert, Heino, and Mary Roos, were regarded with disdain by young people drawn to the ostensibly rebellious nature of rock with all its associations of sex, drugs, long hair, and flamboyantly nonconformist lifestyles. The linguistic divide was illustrated perfectly by the two television programmes which, in the 1970s and for most of the 1980s, represented the flagship of these respective forms of music: whereas Dieter Thomas Heck's show 'Hitparade' refused to countenance any song not performed in German, 'Formel Eins' featured mainly American and British artists and its weekly run-down of the pop charts always included those from the United States and Britain as well as the German ones.

The late 1970s, however, witnessed the emergence of a new musical trend in West Germany, dubbed *Neue Deutsche Welle*, the essential feature of which was its combination of rock music with German lyrics. Explaining this phenomenon partly in sociological terms, Sabine von Dirke situates the origins of the German New

Rob Burns and Wilfried van der Will

Wave in the counter-cultural groups within the Federal Republic, noting that the main difference between the 1960s and the late 1970s was the lack of a protest movement or counter-culture in the United States equivalent to the West German one. Thus not only did America no longer function as a role model but also there developed within the West German protest culture of the late 1970s and early 1980s 'a distinct sense of withdrawal from the hegemony of the United States, its politics, and popular culture'.[46] In its original form the *Neue Deutsche Welle* was inspired by punk rock and, as with British punk, attracted a politically heterogeneous audience, ranging from neo-Nazi skinheads, on the one hand, to *Spontis* from the alternative scene, on the other. What these diverse constituencies had in common, however, was a sense that politically as well as musically punk was 'against the system'. With its preference for crude amplification and for the basic instrument constellation of bass, guitar, and drums punk cocked a snook at mainstream rock and its constant striving for technical sophistication; while the raucous vocals and militant posturing adopted by bands like Ätzttussis, Tote Hosen, S.Y.P.H., and the Nina Hagen Band were clearly designed to be as provocative as possible. If the basic gesture of punk was oppositional, then it was only logical that its scream of defiance should be uttered in German. Although the original *Neue Deutsche Welle* was relatively short-lived—and soon, in fact, gave way to parodistic and altogether blander forms, like the *Neue Deutsche Fröhlichkeit* of bands such as Trio, which belied the music's countercultural origins—it nevertheless left its imprint on rock music generally in the Federal Republic and prepared the way for the success of more mainstream rock performers like Spliff, Marius Müller-Westernhagen, Wolf Maahn, Klaus Lage, Herbert Grönemeyer, and Rio Reiser, who either were directly associated with anti-establishment attitudes or at least made use of German lyrics as a medium for voicing critical sentiments. This in turn led to the launch in December 1993 of Viva-TV, a music video channel aiming to rival the Anglo-American-dominated MTV Europe by devoting 40 per cent of its programming to German artists. Another type of music, traditional Bavarian oompahpah folk—typified by the Naabtal Duo's million-seller hit single of 1989, 'Patrona Bavariae'—continued to draw large audiences, testifying to the fact that a certain style of *Gemütlichkeit* will not go away, much as it may be disliked by intellectuals for its 'blood-and-soil' connotations.

The 'new wave' in German cinema proved to be of considerably longer duration and, much more so than rock music, was involved

46 Sabine von Dirke, 'New German Wave: An Analysis of the Development of German Rock Music', *German Politics and Society*, 18 (1989), 68–9.

in a love–hate relationship with its American counterpart. Negative attitudes towards American cinema—epitomized by Hans Jürgen Syberberg's caustic description of Hollywood as 'the great whore of show-business'[47]—were largely founded on the contempt for commercialism that was harboured by so many of the directors associated with the New German Cinema. Certainly, at the commercial level the West German film industry never managed to escape from the iron grip of American capital. Film distribution in particular continued to be dominated by companies under American control, which by the end of the 1970s had been extended over four out of the six largest distributors in the Federal Republic. Between 1955 and 1978 the West Germans' share of their domestic market plummeted from 47.3 to 8 per cent. A decade and a half later the figure had risen only slightly to 10 per cent, with most of the other 90 per cent of distributors' fees being paid for the hire of American films. Similarly, film production in Germany declined steadily from the mid-1950s onwards. In 1977, the *annus mirabilis* of the New German Cinema, there were fifty-one films produced in the Federal Republic, less than half of the equivalent figure for 1955, although admittedly at that time the domestic film industry was content to churn out an endless stream of kitsch and shallow entertainment. It was, of course, the unmitigated commercialism of the *Opas Kino* which had inspired the disdain of younger German directors in the early 1960s. The older generation of film-makers were castigated for merely aping the worst excesses of the American film industry and for their unwillingness to challenge the dominance of Hollywood by creating an indigenous cinema of artistic distinction. And yet, the antipathy the young generation felt towards Hollywood as an industry did not necessarily extend to that tradition of film-making or, indeed, to the films themselves (nor, as the careers of Wim Wenders, Volker Schlöndorff, Percy Adlon, Wolfgang Petersen, and Doris Dörrie attest, were West German directors deterred from working in America). Even in 1966 Schlöndorff, for example, could happily state that he had made his second feature, *Mord und Totschlag* (1967), with the American action films of the 1930s very much in mind, since, for him, they mirrored those times more vividly than many a documentary. More strikingly, Rainer Werner Fassbinder never sought to conceal the formative influence that the classic Hollywood models of the gangster movie and the melodrama had exerted on his own work. Ironically, two of Hollywood's greatest exponents of those genres were prototypes of the Americanized German, Fritz Lang and Douglas Sirk (Detlev Sierck). While the latter was a particular source of inspiration for Fassbinder, Lang

47 Hans Jürgen Syberberg, *Hitler, Ein Film aus Deutschland* (Reinbek, 1978), 47.

Rob Burns and Wilfried van der Will

could be regarded as the 'lost film father'[48] of Wim Wenders, who, perhaps more than any other recent German film-maker, revealed an uneasy love for America.

The impact of American popular culture on Wenders's biography has been well documented, not least in his own admission that it was the attractions of pinball machines and rock 'n' roll which deflected him from his adolescent ambitions of joining the priesthood. Born in August 1945, Wenders belonged to the generation of German cinema-goers reared on the dubbed old Hollywood movies that in the late 1940s and throughout the 1950s were dumped on the German market by American distributors. Indeed, at one level his work is a homage to American cinema: it draws on Hollywood genres (the road movie, the thriller, the 'buddy' movie), is replete with allusions to Hollywood giants like John Ford, Howard Hawks, and Alfred Hitchcock, and even features acting appearances by American directors (Samuel Fuller, Nicholas Ray, Dennis Hopper, and Roger Corman). And yet, Wenders neither slavishly copies nor parodies Hollywood cinema; rather, he makes thrillers without thrills (*Die Angst des Tormanns vor dem Elfmeter*, 1971, *Der amerikanische Freund*, 1977), emotional narratives without emotions (*Alice in den Städten*, 1973, *Paris, Texas*, 1984), and road movies fused improbably with the quintessentially German form of the *Bildungsroman* (*Falsche Bewegung*, 1975, *Im Lauf der Zeit*, 1976). Wenders's ambiguous fascination with things American ultimately transcends the cinema, however, for in all his work prior to *Hammett* (1982) he was preoccupied, as he himself noted in 1978, with one particular theme, the Americanization of Germany.[49]

In a celebrated remark in *Im Lauf der Zeit* one of Wenders's characters, unable to get a pop song out of his head, observes: 'The Yanks have colonized our subconscious.' While this film both celebrated and criticized the influence of American culture in Germany, the mood of Wenders's next film was less ambiguously an expression of regret about cultural colonization. *Der amerikanische Freund* tells the story of Jonathan Zimmermann, a Hamburg picture-framer suffering from a rare blood disease, who, through his association with an American exile, Tom Ripley, becomes involved first in the sale of forged paintings and then in the murder of two American gangsters operating in the international pornography business. Based on a Patricia Highsmith novel, *Ripley's Game*, the film alludes through its very title to the special relationship between Germany and the United States and explores the various personal, economic, and cultural repercussions of American friendship. In making him his 'buddy' Ripley undermines Jonathan's relationship with his wife,

48 Kathe Geist, *The Cinema of Wim Wenders: From Paris, France to Paris, Texas* (Mich., 1988), 65.
49 *Time* (20 Mar. 1978), 58.

Marianne, and seduces him with the thrill of violence such that this placid and gentle man can celebrate the successful performance of his second contract murder with an exultant, almost orgasmic scream. Money is a further factor in Jonathan's corruption, for although he supposedly agrees to the murders as a means of safeguarding the financial future of his wife and child, he becomes increasingly fascinated by Ripley's wheeler-dealings. In allegorical terms, then, Jonathan's seduction by the lure of the underworld represents the Federal Republic's collusion in the manœuvrings of American capital. That the exploitation of Europe is cultural as well as economic is evident from the stark contrast between the two men: on the one hand, the sensitive European artisan with a lovingly aesthetic relationship to his craft and, on the other, the philistine cowboy, whose Hamburg villa is decked out with all the trappings of Americana, such as a Rockola jukebox and a Coca-Cola machine. When Ripley describes his aim in life with the words 'I make money', his unwitting association of himself with the process of counterfeiting is but one of many verbal and visual allusions to America as the source of fakery. For example, the hospital in Paris where Ripley's crony procures the bogus diagnosis of Jonathan's illness as terminal is an American institution. Moreover, as Jonathan holds the forged medical document in his hands a rack focus links this to a further image of a fake duplicate, namely the miniature replica of the Statue of Liberty on the Seine below him.

It is no coincidence that Wenders chose to shoot this sequence in a part of Paris called 'little Manhattan', for although the film uses four metropolitan locations—New York, Hamburg, Paris, and Munich—the editing is clearly designed to render these cities mutually indistinguishable. These homogeneous cityscapes are just one facet of Wenders's Americanized filmic world that James Franklyn has aptly characterized as 'a pop culture universe . . . sterilized by American technology and the impersonal values of the consumer society'.[50] In *Der amerikanische Freund* Wenders extends the critique of Americanization to encompass the cinema itself, for Jonathan surrounds himself with the paraphernalia of early cinema such as a zoetrope, a stereopticon, and a moving light picture. If this is the cinema in the age of innocence, then Ripley and the gangsters represent its ultimate commercial corruption, pornography. Significantly, the present Ripley gives to Jonathan as a symbol of his friendship is an optical device showing naked women and, equally significantly, the 'innocent' Jonathan takes as much delight in this toy as his 'corrupt' buddy does. Unlike the old woman in *Im Lauf der Zeit*, who laments the cinema's loss of idealism and prefers to

50 James Franklyn, *New German Cinema: From Oberhausen to Hamburg* (London, 1983), 152.

Rob Burns and Wilfried van der Will

close her provincial picture house rather than show the dross foisted on her by the American distributors, Jonathan gradually succumbs to the forces of depravity.

In the novel the Mafiosi are connected with the gambling business rather than pornography and the film's other numerous infidelities to the original include the ending. With Highsmith the bond between the two men is sealed in the ultimate fashion as Jonathan becomes the victim of a bullet intended for Ripley. Wenders, however, reinstates the notion of resistance to American corruption, for although Jonathan dies (from his illness), he does so with Marianne at his side and not before he has divorced himself from his American friend by driving off and abandoning Ripley. Moreover, as if in an attempt to reclaim his lost innocence, Jonathan utters his dying words in the Swiss dialect of his childhood. *Der amerikanische Freund*, in fact, prefigured a modest act of resistance on the director's own part. Impressed by Wenders's adaptation of the Highsmith novel, Francis Ford Coppola invited him to Hollywood to direct another 'thriller', *Hammett*, a project that was to be dogged not least by the German film-maker's reluctance to fall in with the demands of the American studio system.

In Wenders's view the main reason why the Federal Republic proved so susceptible to American 'colonization' was that the postwar generation of which he was a part had willingly embraced American culture as a means of breaking with the Nazi past: 'The need to forget twenty years created a hole and people tried to cover this . . . by assimilating American culture. One way of forgetting the past, and one way of regression, was to accept the American imperialism.'[51] It was not the least of the New German Cinema's achievements that in the late 1970s it sought to confront that collective amnesia by critically opening up the German past and relating it to the present. Dissimilar though they were in terms of both their filmic strategies and political perspectives, Syberberg's *Hitler— Ein Film aus Deutschland* (1977), Fassbinder's *Die Ehe der Maria Braun* (1978), Kluge's *Die Patriotin* (1979), and Sanders-Brahms's *Deutschland, bleiche Mutter* (1979) all made a significant contribution to the interrogation of German history. Ironically, however, it was yet another American cultural export, the eight-hour television series *Holocaust*, which greatly stimulated this process of confronting the Nazi past in Germany. An admixture of soap opera and documentary drama, *Holocaust* was the first commercial film to represent the 'reality' of the Final Solution in fictional form, attracting an audience of over 20 million West Germans when it was broadcast in January 1979. Moreover, the film's impact transcended these brute statistics, for

51 Jan Dawson, *Wim Wenders* (Toronto, 1976), 7.

it ignited a public debate that made *Holocaust* a media event without parallel in the history of the Federal Republic. Among the many contributors to this discussion was the director Edgar Reitz, whose vehement critique of *Holocaust* culminated in the following accusation: 'The most serious act of expropriation there is occurs when people are deprived of their history. With *Holocaust* the Americans have taken away our history.'[52] As a conscious riposte to this act of cultural larceny Reitz set to work on a television series of his own, which was originally to be called 'Made in Germany' but which, when broadcast in 1984, bore the even more provocative title of *Heimat*. In the same article in which he denounced *Holocaust* Reitz elaborated the principle that would inform his own project: 'There are thousands of stories among our people worth filming, which are based on the irritating minutiae of experience. These stories individually would not appear to contribute to the assessment or explanation of history, but, taken together, they would actually fill this gap.'[53] What followed was a sixteen-hour film telling the story of the Simon family over four generations and centring on the figure of Maria, who spends her entire life in the Hunsrück village of Schabbach. In a manner analogous to Thomas Mann's approach in *Buddenbrooks* Reitz shows life on the margins of history where the grander political events and social developments only impinge on the narrative in so far as they are of direct significance for the lives of his provincial characters. '*Heimat* and nation', he stated, 'are contradictory terms'[54] and it is the former which, for Reitz, is the source of an authentic German identity.

Reitz was, of course, fully aware of the ideological baggage attached to the concept of *Heimat* and of the perversion it had undergone not just in the films of the Third Reich but also in the post-war German cinema. While his film was clearly not designed to extend that particular tradition, neither did it correspond to the critical *Heimatfilm* of the early 1970s, movies like Schlöndorff's *Der plötzliche Reichtum der armen Leute von Kombach* (1970), Hauff's *Mathias Kneißl* (1971), or Fassbinder's *Wildwechsel* (1972), which sought to deconstruct the genre by inverting its conventions. Rather, Reitz's aim was 'to present a practical confrontation with everything that [the concept of *Heimat*] triggers in people's feelings, positive and negative, in this peculiar morass of experiences and passions and fears'.[55] The public's response to *Heimat* seemed to indicate that he had only succeeded on the first of these counts, for the film struck an amazingly popular chord with the West German television audience (each episode being seen by 9 million viewers on average and with a total of 20 million West Germans watching at least one of

52 Edgar Reitz, 'Unabhängiger Film nach Holocaust?', in Edgar Reitz, *Liebe zum Kino: Utopien und Gedanken zum Autorenfilm 1962–1983* (Cologne, 1984), 102.
53 Ibid.
54 Anna Mikula, 'Edgar Reitz, ein Deutscher', *Zeit-Magazin*, 44 (26 Oct. 1984).
55 Quoted in Anton Kaes, *From Hitler to Heimat* (Cambridge and London, 1989), 167.

Rob Burns and Wilfried van der Will

the eleven instalments). Moreover, the film became a media event in Germany, second only to the American series that had provided the catalyst for its production. In the ensuing debate Reitz had to face two particular charges. The first—formulated starkly in Timothy Garton Ash's question 'What about Auschwitz?'[56] and sardonically in Gertrud Koch's observation that fascism seems to be imported into Schabbach from a Berlin brothel (by Lucie, Edward Simon's wife)[57]—centred on the accusation that in its portrayal of a community seemingly exonerated from complicity in the crimes of National Socialism the film presented a sanitized version of recent German history. Secondly, despite the convincing narrative breadth of this series and its realism in depicting the life of a provincial community where the atrocities of National Socialism remained marginal, it was difficult to avoid the gloomy conclusion that Reitz's project of 'repossessing our history' had merely inspired a national sense of loss. The collective amnesia afflicting German society 'seemed to have been lifted only at the price of nostalgia'.[58] This judgement would appear to be borne out by the sequel to *Heimat*, which, although harvesting critical acclaim both at home and abroad, proved a flop with German television audiences. Doubtless this was not unrelated to the fact that in *Die zweite Heimat* (1993) Reitz foresook both the Hunsrück and the historical sweep of the original film in order to pursue the musical career of Maria's youngest son, Hermann, and his experiences in a bohemian community in the Munich of the 1960s. Ironically, too, what undoubtedly helped stoke the nostalgia surrounding the first series was precisely that element which distinguished it from the classic *Heimatfilm*, namely the way in which by its ending the film undermines the spurious idyll of regional life. For, as Anton Kaes has argued, the later episodes in the series mercilessly document the rapid decline of *Heimat* after 1945 and the full weight of criticism thus 'falls on the Federal Republic which, the film implies, has lost all traces of identity in the course of its Americanization'.[59]

The critical discussion of *Heimat* centred on Reitz's endeavour to reinterpret recent German history by bringing to bear a perspective from below, retracing the lived experience of the common people in a rural environment. At the same time there were attempts by professional historians to reassess the Nazi past which, in a much more problematical way than was the case in *Heimat*, downplayed the fact that Germany had become involved in a deliberate policy of genocide and mass murder under the Hitler regime. When Jürgen Habermas, not himself a historian but a philosopher and astute observer of the cultural scene, accused these revisionist scholars of

56 Timothy Garton Ash, 'The Life of Death', *New York Review of Books* (19 Dec. 1985).
57 'Diskussion mit Friedrich P. Kahlenberg, Gertrud Koch, Klaus Kreimeier und Heide Schlüpmann', *Frauen und Film*, 38 (May 1985).
58 Elsaesser, *New German Cinema*, 278.
59 Kaes, *From Hitler to Heimat*, 191.

whitewashing German history, he unleashed what became known as the *Historikerstreit*. Ernst Nolte, Andreas Hillgruber, Klaus Hildebrand, and Michael Stürmer, all of them academically respected representatives of their subject, were taken to task by Habermas in an essay in *Die Zeit* (11 July 1986) substantially because they sought to relativize the crimes of National Socialism (which they did not deny as such) and to stress those of Stalinism, while at the same time insisting on the degree of suffering endured by the German people. Habermas's main concern was that the procedures of this neo-historicism relied exclusively on the reconstruction of the good or bad faith of the participants in these particular historical events. The historian, Habermas suggested, thus became chained to a myopic perspective and lost sight of the enormity of the crime. This could happen all the more easily because the legislative preparation, planning, and bureaucratic management of mass annihilation in the Third Reich had the appearance of normality and its efficient implementation presupposed the basic structures of an orderly conduct of social affairs.

Habermas, rightly, suspected an ulterior motive in the writing of the neo-historicists, namely their desire to reinstate historiography as a means with which to prop up the Germans' sense of national identity. Hillgruber, for one, had clearly stated this intention when he demanded that contemporary historians should describe the present as a period which would culminate in the unification of Germany on the basis of self-determination. While one might quarrel with a methodology predicated on political prognostication, the explicit desire for all Germans to be allowed to express their opinions freely was, of course, in itself quite unexceptionable. However, the concept of the nation-state had never been more profoundly undermined than in Germany, where nationalism had been perverted into the political and moral disaster of National Socialism. Nolte's insistence that Hitler had to a large extent been aping the atrocities of Stalin could not explain away the singularity and scale of the fascist crimes, let alone legitimate them. If the revisionist historians' attempt to uphold the continuity of a civilized German identity had to be abandoned, and if, as Habermas and his supporters presupposed, the ruptures of German history had to be accepted, then how could German identity be positively conceived in the present? In contrast to renewed attempts at reconstituting Germany as a 'community shaped by destiny' (*Schicksalsgemeinschaft*) or as an ethnically or culturally unique nation, Habermas proposed a patriotism based on allegiance to the constitution (*Verfassungspatriotismus*). Despite the cold rationalism of this common bond forged by

Rob Burns and Wilfried van der Will

allegiance to the Basic Law, it offered the possibility of a viable consensus within a society suffused by ideological, political, and cultural pluralism. The envisaged concept of patriotism was underpinned by the pledge to preserve the existing social diversity by giving it a legal framework of reference whose high-minded humanitarianism it was in the interests of the vast majority to defend. Certainly, it remained a fundamental prerequisite for establishing any rational concept of national identity in Germany (and elsewhere) that society be not subject to a culture industry which merely functioned as an instrument of one-dimensional mass manipulation.

At the conclusion of the period discussed in this chapter—which at the same time marked the end of the old Federal Republic—there was no sign that the democratic foundations of West Germany had become insecure. Moreover, just as the democratic ethos had taken root, so the culture of that society had diversified. That is to say, a culture industry which operated merely as the manipulative tool of big business and the ruling class, as Horkheimer and Adorno had originally suggested, was not in evidence. Rather, as we have demonstrated, the culture industry itself underwent diversification and increasingly opened up media spaces in which a continuing public discourse on society's changing needs and values could establish itself, thus reviving traditions of rational enlightenment and political emancipation. Culture found itself drawn into a new proximity to politics; or, as Habermas observed in the late 1980s, a 'new intimacy' between the two spheres could be discerned. While Habermas believed that the rediscovered interest of politicians in culture was motivated in the main by their desire to find fresh legitimatory instruments to compensate for their failure of leadership in the economic sphere, he also had to concede, somewhat grudgingly, that the real impetus for cultural reorientation originated in society itself. He recognized 'that through the debates conducted by a politically alert public and driven on by the new social movements, the cultural orientations of the population at large are being fundamentally reshaped'.[60] Far from repeating the thesis on the culture industry advanced by his Frankfurt School mentors, Habermas expressed the hope that 'the incorporation of culture within the political debate might even foster possibilities of enlightenment'.[61] Precisely this sentiment had been foreshadowed in the writings of Hilmar Hoffmann, who envisaged a society where the 'pleasure of public controversy' was central to the notion that culture should provide 'spaces of self-realization for all'.[62]

We would therefore conclude that the vision of the 'culture

60 Jürgen Habermas, 'Die neue Intimität zwischen Kultur und Politik' (Dec. 1987), in Jürgen Habermas, *Die nachholende Revolution* (Frankfurt am Main, 1990), 17.
61 Ibid. 10.
62 Hilmar Hoffmann, *Kultur für morgen: Ein Beitrag zur Lösung der Zukunftsprobleme* (Frankfurt am Main, 1985), 211.

society' must be regarded both as a goal in whose name political actions can be legitimated and as a necessary discursive process in which the whole of German society is involved in the pursuit of a consensus on values and national identity within a situation of accelerating social change (modernization). This vision found itself relegated to the sidelines, first by the unification of Germany and then by the economic recession of the early 1990s. The energies that had brought about a sea change in the political culture of West Germany, together with those that had toppled the regime in East Germany, were now absorbed by other pressing issues. However, while the 'new intimacy' between culture and politics began to evaporate in the face of drastic reductions in the local, regional, and federal budgets for culture, the pluralism of the democratic structures, the richness in the forms of cultural expression, and the intensity of the debate on the basic orientations of the individual and society survived.

Suggested Further Reading

The following studies trace developments in the political culture of the Federal Republic since the late 1960s:

Brand, Karl-Werner, Büsser, Detlef, Rucht, Dieter, *Aufbruch in eine andere Gesellschaft: Neue soziale Bewegungen in der Bundesrepublik*[2] (Frankfurt am Main and New York, 1986).

Burns, Rob, and **van der Will, Wilfried**, *Protest and Democracy in West Germany: Extra-Parliamentary Opposition and the Political Agenda* (London, 1988).

Fohrbeck, Karla, and **Wiesand, Andreas,** *Von der Industriegesellschaft zur Kulturgesellschaft* (Munich, 1989).

Greiffenhagen, Martin, and **Greiffenhagen, Sylvia**, *Ein schwieriges Vaterland: Zur politischen Kultur im vereinigten Deutschland* (Munich and Leipzig, 1993).

Markovits, Andrei S., and **Gorski, Philip S.**, *The German Left: Red, Green and Beyond* (Cambridge, 1993).

The general surveys of culture in the Federal Republic listed below, while written from different analytical perspectives, concur in identifying cultural pluralism as a significant feature of the period:

Benz, Wolfgang (ed.), *Die Geschichte der Bundesrepublik Deutschland*, iv. *Kultur* (Frankfurt am Main, 1989).

Glaser, Hermann, *Die Kulturgeschichte der Bundesrepublik Deutschland*, iii. *Zwischen Protest und Anpassung 1968–1989* (Frankfurt am Main, 1990).

Hermand, Jost, *Die Kultur der Bundesrepublik Deutschland 1965–1985* (Munich, 1988).

The following may be consulted for a more detailed analysis of special aspects of cultural development:

Rob Burns and Wilfried van der Will

Education and Media:

Baumert, Jürgen, *et al.*, *Das Bildungswesen in der Bundesrepublik Deutschland* (Reinbek, 1990).

Bausch, Hans, *Rundfunkpolitik nach 1945* (Munich, 1980).

Hilgemann, Susanne, *Kabel- und Satellitenfernsehen: Die Entwicklung in der Bundesrepublik Deutschland unter ökonomischen, politischen und inhaltlichen Aspekten* (Bonn, 1988).

Holzer, Horst, *Medien in der BRD: Entwicklungen 1970–1980* (Cologne, 1980).

Meyn, Hermann, *Massenmedien in der Bundesrepublik Deutschland* (Berlin, 1985).

Literature, Writers, and Politics:

Ackermann, Irmgard, and **Weinrich, Harald** (eds.), *Eine nicht nur deutsche Literatur: Zur Standortbestimmung der 'Ausländerliteratur'* (Munich, 1986).

Briegleb, Klaus, and **Weigel, Sigrid** (eds.), *Gegenwartsliteratur seit 1968* (Munich, 1992).

Bullivant, Keith (ed.), *After the 'Death' of Literature: West German Writing of the 1970s* (Oxford, New York, and Munich, 1989).

Parkes, Stuart, *Writers and Politics in West Germany* (London and Sydney, 1986).

Reeg, Ulrike, *Schreiben in der Fremde* (Essen, 1988).

Schnell, Ralf, *Die Literatur der Bundesrepublik* (Stuttgart, 1986).

Suhr, Heidrun, 'Ausländerliteratur: Minority Literature in the Federal Republic of Germany', *New German Critique*, 46 (1989), 71–103.

Wagenbach, Klaus, *et al.* (eds.), *Vaterland, Muttersprache: Deutsche Schriftsteller und ihr Staat seit 1945* (Berlin, 1994).

Cinema:

Elsaesser, Thomas, *New German Cinema* (Basingstoke, 1989).

Franklyn, James, *New German Cinema: From Oberhausen to Hamburg* (London, 1983).

Kaes, Anton, *From Hitler to Heimat* (Cambridge and London, 1989).

Knight, Julia, *Women and the New German Cinema* (London, 1992).

McCormick, Richard, *Politics of the Self: Feminism and the Postmodern in West German Literature and Film* (Princeton, 1991).

Sandford, John, *The New German Cinema* (London, 1980).

Classical and Popular Music:

Dibelius, Ulrich, *Moderne Musik*, ii. *1965–1985* (Munich, 1988).

Koch, Albrecht, *Angriff auf's Schlaraffenland: 20 Jahre deutschsprachige Popmusik* (Frankfurt am Main and Berlin, 1987).

7

Unification and its Aftermath: The Challenge of History

GODFREY CARR

GEORGINA PAUL

We are somebody again. But who?
(Headline, *Wochenpost*, 15 July 1993)

THROUGHOUT the summer and autumn of 1989 the world looked on in astonishment as the communist regimes of Eastern Europe collapsed before the eye of the television and photojournalists' cameras. But of all the extraordinary images of that period, none were more extraordinary or more emotive than those relayed from Berlin on the evening of 9 November and during the days that followed of crowds mingling at the now open checkpoints of the Berlin Wall and revellers with sledgehammers celebrating the end of enforced separation. In the twenty-eight years since its construction in August 1961, the Berlin Wall had come to serve as a powerful cultural symbol of the post-1945 division between East and West, communism and capitalism. The public spectacle of its fall, its transformation from divisive border to festive meeting-point and site of symbolic reunion of a divided nation seemed to herald a new historical era, a New World Order based on co-operative community instead of ideological confrontation.

Of course, the media spectacle concealed a more complex reality. By 3 October 1990, the day of German unification when the five new *Länder* of eastern Germany, together with a reunited Berlin, formally acceded to the Federal Republic under Article 23 of the Basic Law, the euphoria of 1989 had given way to a more sober mood. The new Germany was faced with daunting responsibilities. The most pressing of these was the rebuilding of the economically and ecologically ruined eastern *Länder* and the construction of a united nation from the legacy of two ideologically opposed systems. The task was compounded by the challenge of coping with a vastly increased influx of immigrants, both legal and illegal, many of them claiming the protection of the Federal Republic's liberal asylum law. This put pressure on a social support system already under strain from the commitments of unification and rapidly became the target of popular resentment, especially in the socially destabilized eastern *Länder*. Calls for tolerance and generosity as the proper values of liberal democracy were countered by the rise of vociferous and violent extremist right-wing groups harking back to the ultra-nationalist and racist ideology of the Nazi period. The Federal Republic's democratic credentials, painstakingly established over forty years, seemed suddenly under threat from the ghosts of the past.

At the same time, Germany had to come to terms with a new international status. The Two-Plus-Four talks between the two governments of the Federal Republic and the GDR and the four Allied Powers, initiated in May 1990 and concluded with the agreement of 12 September 1990, effectively put an end to the residual rights of the victors of the Second World War and thus to what one commentator called the 'grace of dependency'. Now a fully fledged member of the international community, the expanded Federal Republic was faced with the complex task of reconciling conflicting demands: on the one hand, the need to allay the historically based fears on the part of its neighbours of a larger Germany with the economic and military strength that this entailed; on the other, the expectations of its NATO allies and the United Nations of German participation in their international undertakings. The delicacy of the German position became immediately evident during the Gulf conflict of early 1991. Only months earlier the federal government had been at pains to reassure the international community of Germany's commitment to peace; now it found itself under pressure on two fronts: from the NATO allies to contribute troops as well as funds to the war effort, and from street demonstrations within Germany itself to uphold an anti-militarist stance. In the event, German military participation in the Gulf War was limited to the stationing of troops in Turkey, thus complying with the clause in the constitution which permitted German military activity outside Germany only for the purpose of defence of a NATO ally.

The united Germany's location at the geographical heart of a restored, undivided Europe posed further problems. Here, too, it was a matter of reconciling conflicting commitments: on the one hand, a revived historical interest in Eastern Europe and the newly recreated Baltic states, and a sense of duty, reinscribed not least by the Two-Plus-Four Agreement, towards the economically and politically disintegrating Soviet Union; on the other, Germany's continuing centrality to the European Community.

The rhetoric of the unification speeches stressed unity and freedom, values enshrined in the now all-German constitution. 'The Germans', proclaimed President Richard von Weizsäcker on 3 October, 'have become calculable, reliable, and respected partners.' But there was also an acknowledgement of difficulties ahead: 'Both internally and externally there are pressing problems. . . . We are also aware how difficult it will be to do justice to the expectations which reach us from all points of the compass.'[1]

Cultural Unification: A Western Takeover?

With the unification of Germany in 1990, two cultures came together which for forty years had undergone quite different ideological developments. The accession of the territory of the GDR to the Federal Republic meant the integration of the GDR into the existing social, political, and economic structure of its former ideological opponent. Many Western commentators in 1989 and 1990 spoke of the 'victory of capitalism', and while for the people of East Germany unification brought liberation from the totalitarian state, it also meant that, like a nation in defeat, they had to reorient entirely towards the values of the 'victor'.

In the GDR, cultural activity had been intimately bound up with the ideological interests of the socialist regime; typically for the totalitarian state, cultural production had been subject to strict ideological control, but it had also served as an essential instrument through which the regime could win international prestige. In essence, state subsidization of the arts in the West had had a similar motivation: the political promotion of the Federal Republic as a *Kulturstaat* (cultural state) was bound up both with internal interests—the promotion of national identity on the basis of cultural tradition—and with the prestige of the state in a larger international community. It is not surprising, given the significance attached to the cultural sphere throughout the history of the Federal Republic, that it should have gained explicit mention in the Unification Agreement of 1990; but nor is it surprising that the clause in the Agreement pertaining to culture set certain ideological emphases which were to determine the adaptation of cultural activity in the former GDR to the cultural values of the West. 'In the

1 'Ansprache des Bundespräsidenten Dr. Richard von Weizsäcker' (3 October 1990), in *Die Vereinigung Deutschlands im Jahr 1990. Verträge und Erklärungen*, issued by the Presse- und Informationsamt der Bundesregierung (Bonn, 1991), 248, 243.

years of separation,' the opening paragraph of Clause 35 of the Unification Agreement states,

art and culture were—despite the different development of the two states in Germany—a basis of the continuing unity of the German nation. In the process of the state unification of the Germans on the path to European unity, art and culture have an independent and essential contribution to make. The status and prestige of a united Germany in the eyes of the world are dependent not only on its political weight and economic achievement, but equally on its importance as a cultural state [Kulturstaat].[2]

The terms of the Agreement involved value judgements with regard to the culture of the former GDR, implying the recognition of cultural activity in the socialist state only to the extent that this was seen as being part of the heritage of the German nation as a whole. Clause 35 included a commitment to the preservation of 'cultural substance' in the new Länder, but at the same time the commentary on the Agreement stated explicitly: 'The cultural development in the German Democratic Republic took in part a different course from that in the Federal Republic of Germany. Not all artistic activities in the acceding territory can be continued in the same form as hitherto.'[3]

In keeping with the principle of the adaptation of the former GDR to the federal system of West Germany, the administrative and financial responsibility for cultural institutions passed at unification from central government to government at Länder and local community level. In view of the potential lack of funds available for the cultural sphere, particularly in major cultural centres such as Berlin and Dresden, the financial resources of the Länder and local communities were to be supported by two transitional measures: the possibility of financial aid from federal funds, and the temporary continuation (until 31 December 1994) of the cultural fund (Kulturfonds) of the GDR for the promotion of culture, art, and artists.

For 1991, the first year of unification, a total of DM900 million of federal funds was set aside for the preservation and promotion of culture in the new Länder. Of this sum, DM600 million were allotted to the 'Programme for the Preservation of Cultural Substance', which took as its focus the support of cultural institutions and events of supraregional significance. In early 1991 a list of major institutions considered as priorities for financial support was drawn up, encompassing all the regions of the new Länder. The list included theatres, opera houses, orchestras, film studios, art galleries, museums, libraries and archives, and major historical monuments,

2 Die Vereinigung Deutschlands im Jahr 1990, 125.
3 Manfred Ackermann, Der kulturelle Einigungsprozeß. Schwerpunkt: Substanzerhaltung (Forum Deutsche Einheit: Perspektiven und Argumente 7; Bonn-Bad Godesberg, 1991), 55–6.

as well as places of memorial (the sites of concentration camps in the area of the former GDR, for example). A further DM300 million were allotted to the 'Infrastructure Programme', which focused on the promotion of cultural activity at local community level: artistic activities (art exhibitions, music, literature, film), libraries and local archives, and also youth education and socio-culture (clubs, community centres, and so on) held to be essential to the cultural life of the community. Berlin, as the capital of the united Germany, received exceptional status and additional funding of DM80 million for specific institutions of European significance.

Of course, the reorganization process involved changes and sacrifices. Unlike the GDR, which, in return for ideological concessions, had offered generous financial and organizational support to individual artists and writers in order to ensure cultural production in its own interests, the now expanded Federal Republic had no specific interest in a particular kind of ideologically conformist cultural production. As a result, and despite the temporary continuation of the cultural fund with the aim of supporting individuals (in contrast to the institutional focus of federal and regional funding), individual artists and writers for the most part now had to adapt to Western-style competition in the cultural market-place. Local community culture also suffered. In the GDR, socialist ideology had meant that the majority of local cultural institutions were centred on the work-place. As former GDR companies were closed down or sold off to (mainly west German) buyers under the auspices of the *Treuhandanstalt*, these cultural facilities fell away. The resources of the 'Infrastructure Programme' were only adequate for a partial restructuring of local community cultural life under these circumstances. Problems associated with the general reorganization of cultural activity after unification were compounded by the widespread dominance of westerners in the new local and regional cultural administrations (as in all social and political administrative areas), outsiders, then, who had a necessarily scanty acquaintance with the communities in which they were now working and little respect for the socialist cultural legacy.

In cultural areas beyond the sphere of public administration and funding, restructuring took place according to the law of the market. Western publishing houses were quick in taking over former state- and Party-owned newspapers and magazines, seeking to exploit the east German thirst for information after decades of ideologically controlled media. Between early 1990 and mid-1992, some thirty newspaper publishers were set up in eastern Germany (only one a purely east German concern) with a total of eighty-four titles;

only seventeen, with a total of thirty-seven titles, survived. There were some spectacular misjudgements. The west German Burda Verlag, for example, was rumoured to have lost DM140 million in the failed project of setting up an east German equivalent to the Springer Verlag's *Bild-Zeitung* under the title *super*. On the whole, east German newspaper readers proved resistant to change. West German national dailies made only limited inroads into the east German market, with most readers remaining faithful to the former SED-owned, now western-owned, regional newspapers (fifteen titles, total circulation in 1993 of 7 million). Only one former GDR national weekly, the *Wochenpost*, owned by the Hamburg-based company Gruner + Jahr, but employing mostly east German journalists, succeeded in gaining significant circulation in west Germany.

The main beneficiary of the absence of a free press in the GDR had been the book trade: as Chapter 4 demonstrated, the GDR had enjoyed renown as a highly developed reading culture (*Leseland DDR*), with literature replacing the press as the main forum for critical public debate. The initial effect of the opening of the borders was a turn away from extant GDR literature, whose critical role had now become obsolete. Some publishers were able to profit from publishing documentation and commentary on the events of 1989 and revelations concerning the functioning of the socialist regime (Forum Verlag, set up in Leipzig in 1989 by a group of young GDR intellectuals, ran its business entirely on this basis in the initial phase). On the whole, however, it was a matter of adapting to new consumer demands. In the period following the opening of the Berlin Wall travel literature, self-help books, and erotica dominated the bookshops in eastern Germany. With the stabilization of the market, publishers' lists found a profitable recipe in popular literature (notably detective novels and thrillers) and local history, catering for the revival in regional identity. Major GDR literary publishers, such as Aufbau Verlag, who tried to retain their profile without western support, were soon facing heavy losses, despite draconian staff cuts. (Interestingly, however, by early 1993 the first comparisons of separate bestseller lists for the old and new federal *Länder* showed that east German readers were returning to their 'own' authors: three new publications by former GDR writers—novels by Erwin Strittmatter and Christoph Hein, and the correspondence between Christa Wolf and Brigitte Reimann, all appearing in Aufbau—featured among the eastern top ten for June while remaining absent from the western list.)

If the publishing landscape showed signs of only partial adaptation to Western tastes, the picture in the electronic media and entertainment industries revealed a more clear-cut Westernization of the east. In general, the 'backlog demand' (*Nachholbedarf*) in the east for Western cars, electrical goods, and all the accoutrements of the modern Western lifestyle was the most significant factor in the German economic boom of 1990–1. In terms of mass popular culture, unification seemed relatively unproblematical.

Figures for the video industry may serve as an illustration of general trends. Between the opening of the Berlin Wall in November 1989 and early 1991, some 3,000 video shops set up business in the east, many in the hastily converted sheds and garages of would-be east German entrepreneurs, and most in co-operation with western partners. Whereas in January 1990 only 2 per cent of eastern German households had a video recorder, by April 1991 the figure had risen to 25 per cent (compared with 48 per cent in the west) and by April 1992 to 30 per cent (52 per cent). Of 4.8 million videos delivered to video loan businesses in Germany in 1990, 2 million went to eastern businesses. Initially the backlog demand focused on older films rather than the latest video hits (probably because the former were cheaper to hire), but also on violent action films and pornography which had been taboo under the socialist regime. By April 1992 video trade reports noted a normalization of business in the east. By then some 800 of the 3,000 new video shops in the east had folded, but overall profits were up. The focus of demand had shifted to recent video releases, hobby and children's videos, the same pattern as business in the west.

A similar picture emerges from the figures of the music industry. Sales of LPs and cassettes, weakened by the rise of the CD in the west, increased considerably under the influence of the eastern market in 1990–1. Again, demand concentrated initially not on recent music, but on US and British 'oldies', only to fall broadly in line with western trends by mid-1992, although a renaissance of interest in former GDR bands like Die Puhdys signalled the same revival of old GDR loyalties as that observed in the publishing trade. By then, though, sales of CDs—and CD players—were also significantly increasing in the east.

Commercial television was another area to profit from unification, although here the patterns in the east and west were rather different. Problems with the reception of state television channels in some areas of the former GDR and lack of cable facilities (by January 1993, only 12 per cent of the 6.4 million TV households in eastern Germany had cable TV, as opposed to 70 per cent of the 27 million TV households in the west) resulted in a rapid spread of satellite television. Between November 1989 and the end of 1991, some half a million satellite dishes had been sold in the east; by January 1993 the figure had risen to 1.3 million (just under 20 per cent of all TV households) as opposed to 2.3 million in the west (less than 10 per cent). By May 1993 the two main state channels, ZDF and ARD, were considering going on satellite frequency.

However, perhaps the most spectacular example of eastern German consumption, since it affected the street scene, was the rush to buy that most German of vanity symbols, the car. The Trabant, with its plastic bodywork and noisy two-stroke engine, became the epitome of east German inferiority. Some chose to express their resistance to the west German takeover by retaining and driving their Trabant with pride. But many were eager to be rid of this embodiment of their perception of themselves as second-class citizens. Car sales boomed. In 1990, over a million cars were sold in eastern Germany, 285,000 of which were new registrations, mainly from Western European production. This was followed by 730,000 new car sales in 1991, bought from savings or under credit agreements. In 1989 there were only 235 cars per thousand of the population in east Germany (as compared with 479 per thousand in the west); by the end of 1991, the figure had risen to 353 per thousand (489) and by 1993, prognoses suggested that the figure would rise to 433 (502) by the end of the year.

Notwithstanding the relatively speedy adaptation of consumer behaviour in the new *Länder* to patterns familiar in the west, the cultural divide between eastern and western Germany remained, at least in terms of popular attitudes. In the east, resentment grew at the manner of unification as factories closed, institutions were 'wound down' (*abgewickelt*), unemployment rose, and the large-scale investors stayed away. Living costs rose dramatically while wages, for those in work, remained below levels in the west. Professional qualifications gained in the GDR were often no longer recognized, making retraining necessary for many who had exercised their profession for years. In some professions—teaching, for example—pensionable service was recognized only from the date of unification.

Women, in particular, seemed the losers in the unification process. In the GDR, over 90 per cent of women of working age had been in employment, supported by an efficient childcare and kindergarten system. Of course, it had been in the economic interests of the state to support the female work-force, and perhaps in its ideological interest to integrate children at an early age into the socialist education system. But for women it had meant a large degree of economic independence and the welcome possibility of

Godfrey Carr and Georgina Paul

combining career and family. As ever in times of high unemployment, women were hard hit by the collapse of the east German economy after 1989, and further burdened by kindergarten closures due to lack of public funds. By May 1993, 60 per cent of the million-plus unemployed in eastern Germany were women. A reflection of the problems faced by women, as well as general social instability, was the dramatic fall in the birth-rate in the new *Länder* in the period following unification. In 1990, the birth-rate fell by 12.2 per cent compared with the previous year, and in 1991 by a further 38.8 per cent, while the number of births in west Germany rose by 6.2 per cent in 1990 and remained at almost the same level in 1991.

A further bone of contention was the abortion law. Following a legal compromise after unification, the abortion law of the GDR—abortion on demand within the first twelve weeks of pregnancy—continued to pertain in the eastern *Länder* for a transitional period of two years, during which time the federal parliament was committed to reach agreement on an amendment of the ever controversial Paragraph 218 of the Criminal Code which in the old *Länder* permitted abortion only on medical, eugenic, criminological (i.e. in cases of rape), or social grounds. In June 1992 an amendment was passed adopting former GDR law for the whole of Germany, only to be confronted with a repeat of the political manœuvring of the 1970s as the CDU/CSU appealed to the Constitutional Court. In May 1993 the Court ruled that abortion was against the constitution and therefore illegal, though not a punishable offence. In effect, this meant that abortion was no longer covered by medical insurance, making the operation a matter of personal finance in the event of women finding a doctor willing to be party to what had been declared an illegal undertaking. In addition, the Court ruled that all women wishing to have an abortion were required to be interviewed by health service workers with the specific aim of dissuading them from the operation. To women in both east and west this seemed an unwarranted affirmation of the principle of state intervention in women's self-determination; but for women in the east, accustomed to greater freedom of decision, it was a particularly backward step. Following the ruling, the matter was returned to parliament. During 1993–4, all parties drew up draft proposals for a fresh amendment, with those in favour of minimal state intervention attempting to find a wording compatible with the judgement of the Constitutional Court, and those against abortion attempting to consolidate their position. No proposal proved capable of attaining a parliamentary majority, and by the autumn of 1994 it seemed unlikely that any amendment would be passed before the general elections in October. The Constitutional Court ruling continues to pertain until such time as a new law is passed.[4]

In western Germany, meanwhile, unification was posing an increasing threat to accustomed economic prosperity. The burden of financial transfers from west to east, funded amongst other measures by a 'solidarity tax' levied on west German incomes, was compounded by the effects of world recession which hit Germany all the harder after the unification boom of 1990–1. Here, too, unemployment rose, topping 3 million in early 1993, the highest level since the oil crisis in the mid-1970s. Predictably this caused resentment towards the east. Moreover, it was all too easy for easterners and non-Germans to ignore the real sense of loss experienced by many in the west when the new Germany was proclaimed. Brought up to consider themselves Federal German citizens and proud of their state's achievements, many found it psychologically almost impossible to include the regions east of the former border in their concept of Germany. A physical expression of this attitude in the early days was the marked reluctance of so many in the west to drive into the east.

The new Germany was in a state of transition. In this climate of uncertainty and change, many found refuge in a cultural identity which in reality was itself in a process of flux, underpinning this identity with prejudice. The westerners felt that their cousins from the east wanted all the benefits of the hard work of the post-war years without making any effort, and the easterners felt that they had borne an unfair burden of deprivation after the war only to find that the society and culture which they had nevertheless built up were threatened with destruction by an arrogant and exploitative west. In short, the Berlin Wall had fallen, but 'the wall in people's heads' remained.

The Problem of Cultural Identity

'In the years of separation art and culture were—despite the different development of the two states in Germany—a basis of the continuing unity of the German nation.' As already shown, this apparently objective statement in the Unification Agreement about the role art and culture had played in preserving a unified identity of Germany in the period of division concealed a political agenda. The idea that culture had held together and preserved a German identity was in fact illusory, and the extent of the different development between the two German states became ever more evident

4 For a more detailed account of the abortion debate, see Elizabeth Clements, 'The Abortion Debate in Unified Germany', in Elizabeth Boa and Janet Wharton (eds.), *Women and the Wende: Social Effects and Cultural Reflections of the German Unification Process* (=German Monitor, 31 (1994)), 38–52. A full analysis of the effects of the collapse of socialism in Eastern Europe on women can be found in Barbara Einhorn, *Cinderella Goes to Market: Citizenship, Gender and the Women's Movement in Eastern Europe* (London, 1993).

Godfrey Carr and Georgina Paul

after unification. In the sentence quoted there are echoes of a German view of culture dating back to the eighteenth century in which cultural unity was elevated as a goal to be pursued as a substitute for a political unity that was clearly impossible. In reality, just as Germany has enjoyed little economic and political unity, so too there has been little cultural unity.

The very existence of the term *Kulturstaat* in German is itself significant. In other Western countries the word 'state' on its own usually presupposes a national culture which takes in economic, political, scientific, and cultural activity. The German words *Kulturstaat* and *Kulturnation*, however, indicate something over and above a particular political entity. This wider meaning was deliberately exploited by Günter Grass when in 1990 he proposed a confederation of the two Germanies rather than one unified state. The longing for unity, he argued, could be satisfied by the fact that both states were members of the one German *Kulturnation*. By using the term *Kulturstaat* in an official document ('The status and prestige of a united Germany in the eyes of the world are dependent not only on its political weight and economic achievement, but equally on its importance as a *Kulturstaat*'), the government minimized the marked differences between culture in the GDR and the Federal Republic, and posited a high degree of continuity with the past.

To those charged with directing cultural affairs in the united Germany the notion that a particular German cultural unity had been preserved intact over the forty years of division must have seemed bizarre. Ulrich Roloff-Momin, the Senator in charge of cultural matters in Berlin, described the situation in his own city as follows: 'We are living in a city in which two social systems are impinging on each other, that is two worlds which since 1945 have grown apart in their own extremely different ways, not only materially but also culturally.'[5] He went on to explain that the gap was not so much in the way that plays or music were put on and performed, as in the basic attitudes to cultural activity of those concerned. In West Germany the emphasis had been on individual effort, achievement, and responsibility whilst in East Germany the emphasis was on teamwork and the general good of the community. These are fundamentally different approaches both to the production of culture and to its role in society.

Through a combination of parochialism and cosmopolitanism German culture since the Second World War had managed by and large to steer clear of the difficult issue of what it meant to be German. Precisely this issue was now, however, thrust into prominence by unification, which brought with it first a cultural maelstrom and

5 Ulrich Roloff-Momin, quoted in Dieter E. Zimmer, 'Berliner Aufstände und Abgründe', *Die Zeit* (10 Sept. 1993), 60.

then a profound trauma. The depth of this cultural trauma in Germany is seen most obviously in the realm of architecture and especially in Berlin. The many ugly gaps in the very heart of the city which were the legacy of the Cold War now had to be filled, but how and to what end?

The difficulties arising from the symbolic value attaching to civic architecture were already evident in the restoration of the Quadriga on the Brandenburg Gate. Damaged by revellers during the New Year celebrations of 1990, the famous sculpture was taken down for restoration and was not in place during the festivities of 3 October—perhaps an example of negative and involuntary symbolism. It was rebuilt according to Schinkel's original drawings of 1813 featuring the Iron Cross and Prussian eagle in the victory wreath held aloft by the central figure of the goddess Eirene. Significantly, these had been removed in the GDR restoration of 1958 because of their association with German imperial aspirations and militarism. While the restoration of the Quadriga to its earlier state was in keeping with a trend, noticeable from the mid-1980s, towards the reinstitution of cultural symbols previously considered ideologically unacceptable (the rehabilitation of the statue of Frederick the Great on Unter den Linden in 1986 was an earlier manifestation of this trend in the GDR), the reappearance after unification of the Iron Cross and eagle for a time added fuel to the fears among Germany's neighbours of a revival of German nationalism and aggression.

Unification and the decision to make Berlin the capital of the new Germany produced powerful commercial and political pressures to give expression to the changed situation in appropriately impressive buildings so as to overcome once and for all the legacy of the Second World War and the ensuing long years of division. At first planning began with great confidence. An international competition was held to produce ideas for redeveloping the area round the Brandenburg Gate, and one architect even proposed an ambitious scheme to cover the whole area with a gigantic roof. As the economic depression deepened and plans were looked at again, fundamental questions began to be asked, about what should be demolished, what restored, and what built anew, and by whom. A reflection of the indecision and sudden lack of confidence was the mock life-size façade in wood and plastic of a restored Berlin Schloss which was donated by an industrialist and founder of a society devoted to recreating the building. A great success with Berliners, it nevertheless highlighted the major problem faced by the city in finding architects equal to the task of producing buildings to stand comparison with Schinkel's Altes Museum and Neue Wache and

Raschdorf's Berlin Cathedral. The façade served as an amusing temporary solution, but the unfilled area behind it was a disturbing reminder of how difficult it would be to find a culturally acceptable answer to the unresolved problems of the past.

A particularly revealing example of cultural confusion in relation to the past was the restoration at great expense of the Prussian Landtag to house the Berlin regional parliament. The actual decision to restore it and the choice of architects were both arrived at undemocratically by the then President of the parliament, Jürgen Wohlrabe, and proved contentious issues. The building is a microcosm of German history. Built in 1899, it was here that the workers and soldiers councils met at the end of the First World War and decided against a republic of soviets. The founding conference of the Communist Party took place in it, and in 1933 it became a People's Court; later it was turned by Göring from a 'house of hot air' into a 'house for airmen', and in 1949 Wilhelm Pieck proclaimed the foundation of the GDR from it. After its splendid restoration it is now too big for the reduced Berlin administration which is due to move into it. The building has three possible addresses. The President of the House of Deputies found the original address Niederkirchnerstrasse unsuitable because the name commemorated a communist resistance fighter, and opted instead for Berlin Central, whilst the CDU group refer to it as the Prussian Parliament.

Plans to redevelop the Alexanderplatz with massive skyscrapers had to be abandoned because the east Berliners rebelled against the idea, pointing out in discussions that it was the 'last central square left to the "Ossis"'. There was also a furious debate as to whether to restore or demolish buildings from the Nazi era such as the Reichsbank and the Air Transport Ministry. In the end the decision was taken to restore and convert them to other uses, but there will be many more such dilemmas as Berlin tries to make itself once more a metropolis like London or Paris. Other parts of Berlin such as the Potsdamer Platz are being rebuilt by large concerns such as, in this case, Daimler Benz. A leading figure in the firm, Manfred Gentz, stressed the crucial importance of developing a united vision of what Berlin should look like in twenty years' time with ideas drawn from the worlds of politics, economics, science, and culture. One way of focusing this vision was the (unsuccessful) bid for the Olympic Games in the year 2000, but, in discussing the plans associated with the bid, Gentz identified as one of the major problems the difference between the view the Berliners themselves have of their city and the perceptions of those from outside coming into the federal capital.[6]

6 Interview with Manfred Gentz in *Der Spiegel*, 16 (19 Apr. 1993), 146–53.

The architectural and developmental problems of Berlin were mirrored elsewhere in the country. In Dresden, for instance, the Schloss was rebuilt, and a group was formed which was dedicated to restoring the cathedral using as far as possible the stones from the existing rubble and by means of computer modelling replacing them in their original positions. For many citizens short of decent homes this was pure madness. In Leipzig the Passagen were desperately in need of restoration, but there were fears that much of their original character might be destroyed in the process.

Perhaps the most striking example of these architectural dilemmas is again in Berlin, where there has been a fierce dispute over the future of the Palast der Republik. A relic of the communist regime in a very prominent site, it was quickly condemned to demolition by the new city government, ostensibly because of the health hazard posed by the asbestos built into it. Most easterners, however, felt that this decision was just one more example of cultural dictatorship by the west motivated by an obsessive desire to eradicate all reminders of the former regime from the new capital. What the western politicians had failed to appreciate was that despite its garish exterior the building epitomized that eastern communal culture identified by the Berlin Senator for Cultural Affairs. It was here that citizens of East Berlin were married, celebrated birthdays, and took part in a range of leisure pursuits, all at very little cost. It was open to all and affordable by all. As such, it represented a much appreciated facility for urban cultural and social life unparalleled in the west of the country. Soon there was a powerful movement devoted to its preservation and the demolition order was suspended pending further talks. Common to all these affairs is a hesitation between the desire, on the one hand, to link up with the past and, on the other, to affirm the foundation of a new state with emphatically modern, indeed daring architecture. But what the debates reveal above all else is the dilemma of attempting to express a unified cultural identity in public buildings which are manifestations of a history of political discontinuity and ideological antagonism. The deserted and boarded-up Palast der Republik, its fate still undecided after four years of argument, epitomized the continuing lack of a spirit of common identity among the Germans following unification.

A wave of historical revisionism unleashed by the political watershed of 1989–90 and the sense of a need for a redefinition of cultural values, coupled with indecision about the way forward, also had repercussions for the literary scene. The dissolution of the GDR and the rapid move towards unification in 1990 was accompanied

Godfrey Carr and Georgina Paul

by a fiercely raging debate in the literary review sections of the press which, as it progressed, put a question mark over many of the assumptions of the post-1945 era about the role of the intellectual in German society. The catalyst for the 'literature debate', as it came to be known, was the publication in June 1990 of a short text by the prominent GDR writer Christa Wolf, entitled *Was bleibt*, a literary treatment of the surveillance of an individual identifiable with Wolf herself by the GDR state security police (*Stasi*). Intended no doubt as a contribution to public debate on the nature of the GDR as a surveillance state, it was taken by a number of western reviewers as an opportunistic attempt by Wolf to number herself after the event among the victims of the GDR regime. Wolf, hailed in the West throughout the 1970s and 1980s as one of the GDR's leading oppositional writers, found herself now described as a 'state poet' and the subject of vitriolic personal attacks. Prominent left-wing intellectuals in the Federal Republic, foremost amongst them the doyen of the Gruppe 47, Walter Jens, sprang to Wolf's defence, seeing in these attacks a concerted campaign to discredit the whole of the GDR's oppositional culture. It was pointed out that it was precisely those writers and intellectuals previously seen as dissident who were now the target of public revilement, not those who had been fully co-operative with the GDR regime such as the Writers' Union president, Hermann Kant. Matters were complicated by subsequent revelations that many writers associated with opposition to the regime, including Wolf and the dramatist Heiner Müller, had been at some time involved in collaboration with the *Stasi*.[7]

The existence of the *Stasi* records proved a major problem in all spheres of public life. A new concept entered the vocabulary of the former West Germans, that of the 'unofficial collaborator' (*Inoffizielle Mitarbeiter* or *IM*). As Marion Gräfin Dönhoff indicated, there may have been as many as 100,000 of these in addition to the 100,000 official members of the state security apparatus.[8] Together they were responsible for producing some 180,000 kilometres of personal files, from which at any time material could emerge which was controversial and likely to undermine the position of an individual from the east—a number of political reputations were irretrievably damaged by such information being made public, for example. But revelations of *Stasi* involvement also proved a significant factor in the reassessment of GDR literature. A cloud of disrepute came to hang over many writers previously regarded as moral authorities as their earlier political allegiances were debated and the privileges they had enjoyed under the socialist regime were held up for public scrutiny. For a time, it was suggested that the only

7 Full documentation of the literature debate and a volume of commentary on the issues involved can be found respectively in Thomas Anz (ed.), *Es geht nicht um Christa Wolf. Der Literaturstreit im vereinten Deutschland* (Munich, 1991), and Karl Deiritz and Hannes Kraus (eds.), *Der deutsch–deutsche Literaturstreit oder 'Freunde, es spricht sich schlecht mit gebundener Zunge'* (Hamburg and Zurich, 1991).
8 Marion Gräfin Dönhoff, 'Niemand kann ein ganzes Volk durchleuchten', *Die Zeit* (10 Sept. 1993), 4.

9 See e.g. Heinz
Ludwig Arnold with
Gerhard Wolf (eds.),
*Die andere Sprache. Neue
DDR-Literatur der 80er
Jahre (text + kritik*;
Munich, 1990); and
Peter Geist (ed.), *Ein
Molotow-Cocktail auf
fremder Bettkante. Lyrik
der siebziger und
achtziger Jahre von
Dichtern aus der DDR*
(Leipzig, 1991).
10 See Wolf
Biermann, *Über das
Geld und andere
Herzensdinge. Prosaische
Versuche über
Deutschland* (Cologne,
1991), and *Der Sturz des
Dädalus oder Eizes für
die Eingeborenen der
Fidschi-Inseln über den
IM Judas Ischariot und
den Kuddelmuddel in
Deutschland seit dem
Golfkrieg* (Cologne,
1992), two collections
of essays, articles, and
speeches by Biermann
from the period
1990–2.
11 Karen Leeder offers
some very useful
insights into the
ideological motives—
and blind spots—
within the debate on
GDR literature in her
article ' "Eine
Abstellhalle des
Authentischen":
Postmodernism and
Poetry in the New
Germany', in Arthur
Williams and Stuart
Parkes (eds.), *The
Individual, Identity and
Innovation. Signals from
Contemporary Literature
and the New Germany*
(Berne, 1994), 201–20.
12 Frank
Schirrmacher,
'Abschied von der
Literatur der
Bundesrepublik', *
Frankfurter Allgemeine
Zeitung* (2 Oct. 1990),
Book Fair Suppl., 1.

identifiable group of writers and artists to have preserved their integrity within the GDR was that working within the predominantly young alternative scene generally associated with the Prenzlauer Berg area of Berlin, many of whose texts were presented to the wider public for the first time following the *Wende* of 1989.[9] It was perhaps also a factor in the sudden approval and recognition meted out to this alternative, anarchic culture by western critics that the linguistic experimentation which particularly characterized the texts of the Prenzlauer Berg poets lent itself to critical analysis in postmodernist terms, so that the aesthetic divide between western and eastern literature seemed at its narrowest here. However, with revelations in late 1991 that a number of writers associated with the Prenzlauer Berg scene had themselves collaborated with the *Stasi*, including Sascha Anderson, one of the scene's most prominent figures, the cloud of disrepute threatened to engulf the literary production of the younger, 'drop-out' generation too. The claim to moral integrity became the preserve of those writers who had left or been forced to leave for the West, and some, notably Wolf Biermann, used this as a platform from which vociferously to criticize former colleagues.[10] It is of course worth noting that all kinds of interests, political, personal, and aesthetic, were at work—and still are—in the battle to establish a new historical view of GDR literature and culture, and that the often emotive, not to say aggressive, tone of the debate in its early stages was an indication of the ideological stakes involved.[11]

The controversy did not stop at the reassessment of GDR literature, however. In an article published on the eve of unification, Frank Schirrmacher, *Feuilleton* editor of the *Frankfurter Allgemeine Zeitung* and, with Ulrich Greiner of *Die Zeit*, one of Christa Wolf's most vociferous detractors, called for a 'farewell to the literature of the Federal Republic'. He identified such dominant figures of the Federal Republic's literary scene as Günter Grass, Heinrich Böll, and Siegfried Lenz as participants in a 'conscience industry' who, far from standing in opposition to the social order of which they wrote so critically, had, like their counterparts in the GDR, been implicated in the legitimization of the state through their didactic approach to the theme of German guilt and their projection of democratic consciousness.[12] Schirrmacher's article concluded with an appeal for a literature uninvolved in politics, a theme taken up by Ulrich Greiner in *Die Zeit* a month later in an article condemning the German 'aesthetic of political conviction' (*Gesinnungsästhetik*) which, he argued, had dominated both the production and the public reception of literature in the two German states throughout the post-war era.[13] Hailing the end of the literature of the GDR and the Federal Republic, Greiner looked forward to a new literary era in which aesthetics and (social) morality would no longer be forced into what he termed a 'marriage of convenience'—a projection which flew in the face of much of the German cultural tradition, not only since 1945, and so implied as summary a disregard for the past as some of the more futuristic suggestions for the rebuilding of central Berlin.

Intellectual Debate and Political Culture

In essence, the arguments of Schirrmacher and Greiner in the literature debate were symptomatic of a more general questioning of many of the moral and political certainties which had come to characterize both Germanies in the post-war period. This opened up a space for public exchange and dialogue which was only appropriate to the inception of a new historical era, and, contrary to the suggestion that writers should now begin to withdraw from intervention in the political arena, many established intellectual figures from both east and west were active in putting forward their views on issues of topical debate in press articles, essays, and television interviews. But the fact they were themselves clearly having problems in keeping up with the breakneck pace of historical developments, together with the sheer mass of conflicting suggestions and viewpoints, combined with a more general creeping popular disillusionment with politics following the euphoria of 1989 to create a curious sense of vacuum and lack of moral leadership.

One expression of the difficulty intellectuals faced in critically assessing the present was the debate which flared up briefly in 1990 about a possible German 'third way' between capitalism and communism embodied in a reformed GDR. Günter Grass argued passionately that political unity for the German people was very risky, and that it would be much better for them and their neighbours if they continued to live in two states linked possibly in a confederation and expressing their unity as Germans through their culture. Grass was clearly horrified at the sudden merger of the two states and the apparent total victory of capitalism. His thinking was dominated by his own memories of the Nazi era and of the Holocaust. After Auschwitz he fundamentally distrusted his fellow Germans and felt that the only safe form of German unity was cultural unity. He used terms like 'new colonial masters', 'robber-baron mentality', 'first- and second-class Germans', and a 'process of cultural

13 Ulrich Greiner, 'Die deutsche Gesinnungsästhetik', Die Zeit (2 Nov. 1990), 59–60.

colonization' in order to describe what was going on in the former GDR.[14] His hope that a new GDR might offer a 'third way' was shared by Heiner Müller, who started to develop a theory of 'retardation', seeing in this a quality which the east had to offer to counter the 'total acceleration' embodied by the west.[15] The notion of a 'third way' has many antecedents in German cultural and political history and has usually been an indication of an attempt to avoid the political constraints of the present. The lack of realism in Grass's emotional appeal was made very evident by the response of Monika Maron, a former GDR writer who had moved to West Germany in 1988. She promptly took him to task for idealizing existence within the former communist state in order to support his argument against unification. She dismissed his suggestion that life there had been slower and less pressurized and had afforded more opportunities for real discourse, arguing instead that in a corrupt, repressive, conspiratorial society any apparent closeness and solidarity among citizens was a defensive response to the ever present spies of the state. In a series of articles Maron dealt scathingly with those left-wing German intellectuals who continued to bemoan the loss of a socialist utopia that they themselves had not been willing to live in; but she was equally severe in her attacks on established GDR writers such as Stefan Heym for condemning east German consumerism, since they had previously enjoyed the material goods and the freedom to travel which the general populace had so much desired. Maron's hard-headed, somewhat cynical, and yet generally optimistic reaction to unification was very different in tone from the alarm and outrage of older writers such as Grass and Heym. She saw the difficulties and the dangers but in her case memories of Nazism did not undermine her confidence in the ability of the Germans to cope with unification.[16]

In marked contrast to Grass, one prominent writer of the older generation in the Federal Republic openly rejoiced at the turn of political events. Martin Walser had long campaigned for unification at a time when most thought the idea was a lost cause. He had repeatedly affirmed the right of the Germans to unity and true nationhood, despite the crimes committed by the Nazis. In newspaper articles after unification he rejected Grass's advocacy of the *Kulturnation* as a feeble substitute for national pride, and argued that without the restoration of a normal concept of nationhood to the Germans there could be no hope of taking the initiative from the newly emergent extreme right, either in its intellectual or in its hooligan manifestations. Walser refused to allow himself to be terrified by such people, viewing them simply as a passing phenomenon,

14 See Günter Grass, *Gegen die verstreichende Zeit. Reden, Aufsätze und Gespräche 1989–1991* (Hamburg and Zurich, 1991).

15 See Heiner Müller, 'Zur Lage der Nation'— *Heiner Müller im Interview mit Frank M. Raddatz* (Berlin, 1990), esp. the section 'Stirb schneller, Europa', pp. 25–42.

16 A selection of Maron's articles commenting on unification and the role of intellectuals in the debate surrounding it is included in Monika Maron, *Nach Maßgabe meiner Begreifungskraft. Artikel und Essays* (Frankfurt am Main, 1993); see esp. 'Das neue Elend der Intellektuellen', pp. 80–90, 'Fettaugen auf der Brühe', pp. 99–102, and 'Zonophobie', pp. 112–20. Stefan Heym's views, attacked by Maron in 'Das neue Elend', were set out in articles repr. in Stefan Heym, *Filz. Gedanken über das neueste Deutschland* (Munich, 1992).

a reflection of a general disorientation and temporary inability to identify with the new Germany.

If, on the general issue of unification, Walser's optimism seemed more justified than Grass's pessimism, on the specific issues of racism and right-wing aggression Grass was certainly more aware of the potential for tragedy. In the first three years after unification the instances of violence against asylum seekers and other foreigners in Germany escalated frighteningly. Two major arson attacks in the former GDR, at Hoyerswerda in September 1991 and Rostock in August 1992, caught the headlines especially, and then just as the west Germans were feeling that this was a problem confined to the east there came Mölln in November 1992 and Solingen in May 1993. In the wake of these atrocities there was a general sense of outrage coupled with a deep uncertainty among both politicians and the general public as to how best to react. At the same time there was a painful awareness that the Germans, because of their recent history, should respond both vigorously and effectively. After the first incidents there were impressive torchlight processions in many major cities expressing solidarity with the victims. These mass popular demonstrations revived the methods of the extra-parliamentary citizens' initiatives of the 1970s and 1980s, but were in turn criticized in some sections of the media as being mere empty gestures, a placebo to the conscience. One could perhaps see in such criticisms some correspondence with Schirrmacher's notion of a 'conscience industry' in the old Federal Republic. The effect was debilitating. The energy of protest became diffused, and the demonstrations were not repeated after later attacks. Moreover, the subsequent tightening of the asylum law, while politically pragmatic in the face of large-scale immigration, could all too easily be read as a move to appease nationalist and racist sentiment.

For all the articles, essays, media interviews, and television appearances, there was a remarkable absence of authoritative and considered theorizing about the process of unification and its consequences. Rüdiger Bubner spoke of a 'resounding silence' on the part of the intellectuals and Ivo Frenzel remarked on a 'deficiency of theory relating to the change'. It may be wrong, of course, to expect writers to theorize about these matters, but the expectations related to the previous role played by writers in both parts of Germany. In the polarized situation of the Cold War they had indeed acted as moral consciences to the nation, providing a focal point for opposition to the government when this was not forthcoming through the political system. In the new situation of unity either this role will have changed fundamentally or it will have to adapt to new parameters. Some intellectuals themselves take a pessimistic view of the effectiveness of their resistance. Günter Kunert, for instance, in an interview with the psychiatrist Hans-Joachim Maaz, observed sardonically that without the efforts of writers and intellectuals in the GDR the collapse of that state might have occurred twenty years earlier.[17] He went on to accuse his fellow writers of having so effectively shored up the system that they now have an ever declining influence on public opinion. He noted, on the one hand, a growing unwillingness on the part of the public to inform themselves by reading and, on the other, a fatal readiness among intellectuals in the past to discredit themselves by falling into what he calls the 'sense trap'. By this he means their incorrigible desire to rush in and interpret a situation when it is in its most critical and complex phase.

The potential role of culture in promoting political and social reconciliation in this remarkable phase of German history is a complex one, but must lie in trying to get Germans to rethink their past, and not just the period of Nazi Germany but also the consequences since the end of the Second World War. Heiner Müller, who was less damaged than some by the accusation of having had contacts with the *Stasi*, nevertheless acknowledged that it might now be time for prominent literary figures like himself to stop pronouncing on contemporary politics. He greeted the liberation of literature from its function as an 'articulator of political issues', but suggested that it had a role to play in a new constructive examination of the recent past. It would no longer have to perform in a documentary capacity but could function autonomously. One major problem for writers, however, was how to find the appropriate language and images in which to describe the new Germany. Plays by Herbert Achternbusch (*Auf verlorenen Posten*, 1990), Botho Strauß (*Schlußchor*, 1991), and Klaus Pohl (*Die schöne Fremde*, 1991) resorted to allegory in order to convey the complex relationship of the new Germany to the former GDR and to its Nazi past. Common to all of them was an awareness that a critical view of the past is a key to defining the new state and overcoming the formidable tensions and resentments within it.

A similar view of the past pervaded the writings of Jürgen Habermas on unification. He warned against facile comparisons between the post-unification situation and the period immediately after the Second World War. What he found particularly suspect was the notion that both Germanies had alien cultures imposed on them by the occupying powers and must now find their way back to a common tradition. For Habermas, what happened in the Federal

17 Günter Kunert, 'Neues Spiel, neues Unglück' (dialogue with Hans-Joachim Maaz), *Die Zeit* (29 Nov. 1991), 60.

Godfrey Carr and Georgina Paul

Republic was a happy break with a fateful continuity in German history and the chance for Germans at last to walk 'with an upright gait'. Habermas believed that it was precisely the critical oppositional role played by writers and intellectuals in West Germany in the post-war period which now made possible a new and much more productive assessment of the past not only in the former GDR, but in the whole of the new Federal Republic.

As these and other writers and intellectuals realized, unification had started to melt the ice which, since the Second World War, had surrounded so many fundamental questions about the role and future of German society. And yet, it may seem ironic that the renewed debate about the nature of German culture, identity, and nationhood should come at a time when the validity of the nation-state was itself being called into question by historical and economic developments. The ratification of the Treaty of Maastricht and the establishment of the European Union in 1993 were just one manifestation of a universal trend towards the greater political and economic interdependence of nations which has characterized the late twentieth century. Interdependence, itself not a new concept, has nevertheless been strengthened by the growth in sophistication of global media and communications networks which have in turn had significant repercussions for cultures hitherto shaped largely by the relation to individual historical traditions. While national differences clearly remain, the increasing influence of vast multinational corporations and technological exchange on the cultural sphere of the rich industrial countries of the world is reflected in a noticeable homogenization in some forms of cultural expression and production, particularly in the area of mass popular culture. The levelling effect of such widespread commercialization can perhaps be seen most clearly among the young. Surrounded by the products of this commercially driven international culture—popular music, television, film, video, and also computer technology—young people in Germany have less to differentiate them from their peers in other industrialized countries than their counterparts of a generation ago. In more general terms, culture is becoming ever more a matter of lifestyle in a manner which transcends national boundaries.

A further issue in the forefront of public debate which is also related to the decline of old notions of national identity is multiculturalism. The after-effect of labour policies of the 1950s and 1960s has meant that Germany, like a number of other Western European countries, has to all intents and purposes become a multicultural society. The traditions of ethnic groups now well-established in Germany are increasingly contributing to the cultural life of the nation—witness, for example, the growing body of literature in German written by those of non-German descent. In this respect, the idea of a specifically German cultural identity is revealed as a fallacy. Moreover, as a result of racist attacks which have afflicted not only recent immigrants, but families who have lived in Germany for generations, politicians are being forced to rethink the Federal Republic's rigid citizenship laws in order to allow ethnic groups to be better represented in political and local community life.

These processes make it difficult for Germany to define itself in terms of its cultural heritage as it was wont to do. There are those, however, who refuse to accept this radically changed situation and who are still determined to escape from an uncomfortable reality into cultural nationalism as a well-tried substitute for politics. As a pendant to the activities of fascist thugs on the streets trying to replace political debate with violence there has been a re-emergence of salon nationalists trying to revive interest in the anti-capitalist, cultural conservatives of the past such as Lagarde, Langbehn, Moeller van den Bruck, Spengler, Klages, and Jünger. Here again an attempt is being made to establish a continuity with the past which is untenable in the present situation. Curiously, in France the same thinkers are being celebrated among extreme right-wing intellectuals as potential prophets of a new European nationalism, evoked to counter the imagined threat of the total Americanization of society. The attempt seems curiously dated. All these figures from Germany's past wrote from an overwhelming sense of resentment which fuelled their cultural nationalism. The gap between the Germany which they dreamed of and the one in which they actually lived does not exist today.

The answer must surely lie elsewhere. It is the friction between objective economic and social developments and the intellectual striving to find forms in which to respond productively to these developments, not to deny them, that has always ensured cultural vitality. There is no reason to suppose that this productive friction will not be forthcoming as Germany moves into the twenty-first century, nor that creative responses will not be found that are both appropriate to and, indeed, formative of its changing culture. Despite the concerns of some at the apparent domination of the forces of capitalism and commercialization in the era after the Cold War, the total industrialization of culture as envisaged by Horkheimer and Adorno in the 1940s is not really in prospect. There remains, and no doubt will always remain, the possibility of intellectual and artistic intervention; and, not least, the spread of the discipline of cultural studies in German universities would seem a healthy sign of the continued impetus towards the kind of critical awareness that militates against passivity.

Though the huge economic and social problems posed by unification cannot be underestimated, Germany is at last a united, free, and democratic state. It will now be able to develop a pragmatic sense of itself as a nation which embraces a variety of traditions and identities. As it does so, the opportunity should be there for cultural developments of increasing richness and diversity.

Suggested Further Reading

The following works give a general picture of the events and immediate aftermath of unification:

Ardagh, John, *Germany and the Germans* (London, 1991).

Friedrich, Wolfgang-Uwe (ed.), *Totalitäre Herrschaft—Totalitäres Erbe, German Studies Review*, Special Issue (Fall 1994).

Fritsch-Bournazel, Renata, *Europe and German Unification* (New York and Oxford, 1992).

James, Harold, and **Stone, Marla** (eds.), *When the Wall Came Down: Reactions to German Unification* (New York and London, 1992).

Books and articles listed below deal with the question of German identity and the renewed confrontation with the past:

Augstein, Rudolf, *Deutschland, einig Vaterland* (Göttingen, 1990).

Grass, Günter, *Two States—One Nation: The Case Against German Reunification* (London, 1990).

Habermas, Jürgen, *Staatsbürgerschaft und nationale Identität: Überlegungen zur europäischen Zukunft* (St Gallen, 1991).

Knoblich, Axel, Peter, Antonio, and **Hatter, Erik** (eds.), *Auf dem Weg zu einer gesamtdeutschen Identität* (Cologne, 1993).

Mayer-Iswandy, Claudia (ed.), *Die Nation zwischen Traum und Trauma: Transatlantische Perspektiven zur Geschichte eines Problems* (Tübingen, 1994).

Meier, Charles S., *Die Gegenwart der Vergangenheit: Geschichte und die nationale Identität der Deutschen* (Frankfurt am Main and New York, 1992).

Schneider, Peter, *Extreme Mittellage: Eine Reise durch das deutsche Nationalgefühl* (Reinbek, 1990).

The implications of unification for women are addressed in the following work:

Boa, Elizabeth, and **Wharton, Janet** (eds.), *Women and the Wende: Social Effects and Cultural Reflections of the German Unification Process*, (= *German Monitor*, 31 (1994)).

For more background to developments in the media and the general cultural debate since unification the following would be useful:

Anz, Thomas (ed.), *'Es geht nicht um Christa Wolf': Der Literaturstreit im vereinten Deutschland* (Munich, 1991).

Brockmann, Stephen, 'The Reunification Debate', *New German Critique*, 52 (Winter 1991), 3–30.

Deiritz, Karl, and **Kraus, Hannes** (eds.), *Der deutsche Literaturstreit oder 'Freunde es spricht sich schlecht mit gebundener Zunge'* (Hamburg, 1991).

Heinrich, Arthur, and **Naumann, Klaus** (eds.), *Alles Banane: Ausblicke auf das endgültige Deutschland* (Cologne, 1990).

Meyer, Hermann, *Massenmedien in der Bundesrepublik Deutschland: Alte und Neue Bundesländer* (Berlin, 1992).

Stolte, Dieter, *Fernsehen am Wendepunkt* (Munich, 1992).

Williams, Arthur, Parkes, Stuart, and **Smith, Roland** (eds.), *German Literature at a Time of Change 1989–1990: German Unity and German Identity in Literary Perspective* (Berne, 1991).

Williams, Arthur, and **Parkes, Stuart** (eds.), *The Individual, Identity and Innovation: Signals from Contemporary Literature and the New Germany* (Berne, 1994).

Chronology of Events

1870–1	Franco-Prussian War
1871	Proclamation of the German Empire
	Charles Darwin, *The Descent of Man*
1873	*Kulturkampf* legislation introduced in Prussia
1875	Gotha Programme of the Social Democratic Party (SPD)
	Thomas Mann born
1876	Opening of the Bayreuth Festival and the first complete performance of *The Ring*
	Invention of the telephone (Bell)
1878	Anti-socialist legislation passed (and remains in effect until 1890)
1879	Albert Einstein born
	Henrik Ibsen, *A Doll's House*
1881	Invention of prototype reproduction process (Georg Meisenbach)
1883	Death of Karl Marx and Richard Wagner
	August Bebel, *Die Frau und der Sozialismus*
1888	Year of the three Kaisers: Wilhelm I, Friedrich III, and Wilhelm II
1889	Founding of the Second International
	Founding of the Freie Bühne in Berlin
	Social security legislation introduced in the German Reich
1890	Following Reichstag elections the SPD is for the first time the largest party in terms of votes (1.5 million, 20%)
	Dismissal of Bismarck as *Reichskanzler*
1891	SPD adopts a Marxist platform with its Erfurt Programme
1892	First Munich Secession
1893	Invention of the diesel engine
1894	Founding of the Alldeutscher Verband
	Otto Brahm becomes director of the Deutsches Theater
	Founding of the Worpswede Artists' Colony
1895	First public motion picture performances in Paris and Berlin
	Discovery of X-rays (Röntgen)
1896	Appearance of *Jugend* and *Simplicissimus*
	Bürgerliches Gesetzbuch (Civil Code) passed (and takes effect 1 January 1900)

Imperial Germany

1898	Death of Otto von Bismarck
	Bertolt Brecht born
	Beginning of the construction of the German fleet
	Discovery of radium (Marie Curie)
1899	Boer War (until 1902)
1900	Sigmund Freud, *Die Traumdeutung*
	Death of Friedrich Nietzsche
	Beginnings of the *Wandervogel* movement
	Development of quantum theory (Max Planck) and the Zeppelin airship
1901	Thomas Mann, *Buddenbrooks*
1903	Founding of the Ford motor factory
	First motorized flight
1905	Max Reinhardt becomes director of the Deutsches Theater
	Artists' colony *Die Brücke* founded in Dresden by Ernst Ludwig Kirchner
	Theory of relativity developed by Einstein
1910	Appearance of Herwarth Walden's *Der Sturm*
1911	Artists' colony *Der blaue Reiter* founded in Munich by Wassily Kandinsky
1912	SPD becomes the largest party in the Reichstag (110 deputies out of 397)
	Sinking of the *Titanic*
1913	Death of August Bebel, co-founder and Chairman of the SPD
	Walden's 'First German Autumn Salon' in Berlin
	Stellan Rye, *Der Student von Prag*
1914	Outbreak of the First World War; war credits approved by all the parties in the Reichstag including the SPD (4 August)

The Weimar Republic

1918	The 'November Revolution': the abdication of Wilhelm II, the proclamation of the Republic by Scheidemann (9 November), and the signing of the armistice between Germany and the Allies (11 November)
	Founding of the German Communist Party (KPD)
1919	Assassination of Karl Liebknecht and Rosa Luxemburg
	Elections to the National Assembly and Friedrich Ebert elected President
	Soviet Republic proclaimed in Munich, headed by Toller and Niekisch
	Adoption of the constitution by the National Assembly (11 August)
	Robert Wiene, *Das Cabinet des Dr Caligari*
1920	Versailles Treaty comes into force (10 January)
	Foundation of the Nazi Party (NSDAP)
	Kapp *putsch* defeated by a general strike
1921	Widespread strikes leading to conflict with the army and the police

1922	Assassination of Walther Rathenau, Minister for Foreign Affairs
	Thomas Mann's 'Von deutscher Republik' given as a speech in Berlin
1923	Occupation of the Ruhr by French troops
	Formation of a new government under Gustav Stresemann
	Hitler/Ludendorff *putsch* in Munich fails (9 November)
	Raging inflation: $1 = 4.2 billion marks by the end of December
1924	Dawes Plan regulating reparations payments
1925	Following Ebert's death Hindenberg is elected President
1926	Plebiscite on the expropriation of the aristocracy (rejected)
1927	KPD sets up a central organization for agitprop and demands a 'red front' for cultural struggle
	Collapse of the Berlin stock exchange
1928	Following elections a grand coalition is formed under Hermann Müller (SPD)
	League of Proletarian Revolutionary Writers (BPRS) established
	Bertolt Brecht, *Die Dreigroschenoper*
1929	Signing of the Young Plan on reparations, repeatedly attacked by the right
	Death of Gustav Stresemann
	Wall Street Crash, causing the withdrawal of foreign capital (25 October)
1930	Brüning forms a cabinet without parliamentary support, thus marking the end of parliamentary rule and the beginning of government by Presidential decree
	Unemployment reaches 3 million
	In elections the NSDAP wins 107 seats to become the second largest party in the Reichstag (14 September)
	Josef von Sternberg, *Der blaue Engel*
1932	Hindenburg re-elected President
	In the national elections the Nazis become the largest party with 38% (31 July)
	Slatan Dudow/Bertolt Brecht, *Kuhle Wampe*
1933	Hitler becomes Chancellor (30 January)
	Reichstag fire (27 February)
	Passage of the 'Enabling Law' (23 March) and *de facto* cancellation of the Weimar constitution
	In the March elections, with unemployment at 6 million, the NSDAP wins 17.3 million votes (43.9%)

1933	Burning of the books (10 May)
	One-party state proclaimed (14 July)
	Creation of the Reich Chamber of Culture (Reichskulturkammer)
1934	'Night of the Long Knives', the purge of the SA (30 June)
	With the death of Hindenburg Hitler becomes *Führer und Reichskanzler* (2 August)

The Third Reich

6th Party Congress at Nuremburg, filmed by Leni Riefenstahl in *Triumph des Willens*

1935 Reintroduction of conscription and the proclamation of the Nazi race laws

German occupation of the Rhineland in defiance of the Versailles Treaty

Carl von Ossietzky, held in a concentration camp since 1933 (and dying there in 1938), is awarded the Nobel Peace Prize

1936 Unemployment nil

1937 Exhibition of Degenerate Art (*Entartete Kunst*) in Munich

1938 *Anschluß* of Austria (13 March)

As a result of the 'Appeasement' policy the Sudetenland is ceded to Germany

Reichskristallnacht (9 November) when the SA vandalizes Jewish shops and synagogues

Leni Riefenstahl, *Olympiade*

1939 German troops march into Prague (15 March)

Hitler–Stalin Pact (23 August)

Wehrmacht invades Poland (1 September); Britain and France declare war on Germany (3 September)

1940 Veit Harlan, *Jud Süß*

1942 At the Wannsee Conference Heydrich announces the 'Final Solution of the Jewish Question' (20 January), which is implemented principally at the extermination camps at Auschwitz-Birkenau, Majdanek, Treblinka, Sobibor, and Chelmno

1943 Brutal clearance of the 'Warsaw Ghetto' (19 April–16 May)

1944 Von Stauffenberg plot to kill Hitler (20 July) fails

1945 Yalta Conference where Roosevelt, Stalin, and Churchill agree the division of Germany into four zones of occupation (4–11 February)

Hitler commits suicide (30 April)

Capitulation of the Wehrmacht (7–9 May)

The German Democratic Republic (GDR)

1945 Soviet military administration approves the formation of 'anti-fascist' parties

At the Potsdam Conference (17 July–2 August) the Allies agree on the denazification, demilitarization, and decentralization of Germany

Creation of the Kulturbund

1946 Establishing of DEFA film company in East Berlin

Founding of SED (Socialist Unity Party) through the merger of the KPD and SPD

First edition of *Neues Deutschland*, the daily paper of the SED Central Committee

1947 All-German Writers' Congress

1948 Currency reform (23 June)

Brecht founds the Berliner Ensemble

1949	Founding of the German Democratic Republic (7 October)
	Launching of *Sinn und Form*
1950	3rd Party Conference of the SED where the Party Executive is changed to the Central Committee; Chairmen of the Party are Wilhelm Pieck and Otto Grotewohl
	GDR joins COMECON
1951	SED campaign against 'formalism' and 'decadence' in favour of 'socialist realism'
	Censorship apparatus established
	165,648 East Germans flee the GDR
1953	Workers' uprising (17 June) in East Berlin and other towns is suppressed by Soviet troops
	391,390 East Germans move to West Germany and West Berlin
	Walter Ulbricht elected First Secretary of the SED Central Committee
1954	USSR proclaims the sovereignty of the GDR
	Creation of the Ministry of Culture
1955	'Thaw' in Eastern Europe (until 1957)
1956	Creation of the Nationale Volksarmee (18 January)
	Failure of the Hungarian uprising leads to renewed cultural repression
	Death of Bertolt Brecht
	All-German team takes part in the Melbourne Olympic Games
1957	Show trial of the so-called *Harich-Gruppe*: Wolfgang Harich, editor of the *Deutsche Zeitschrift für Philosophie*, is sentenced to ten years
	Ulbricht proposes a German Confederation as an interim move towards German reunification
	Heiner Müller, *Der Lohndrücker*
1958	Abolition of rationing
	Bruno Apitz, *Nackt unter Wölfen* (the film version directed by Frank Beyer is released in 1963)
1959	SED initiates the *Bitterfelder Weg* (24 April)
	Uwe Johnson, *Mutmaßungen über Jakob*
1960	Trading Agreement between GDR and West Germany
1961	Building of the Berlin Wall (13 August)
1962	Conscription introduced (24 January)
	Peter Huchel removed as editor of *Sinn und Form*
1963	SED introduces the 'New Economic System' and allows the debate of past errors in cultural works
1964	Robert Havemann is dismissed from his university post (and two years later is expelled from the Akademie der Wissenschaften)
	Second Bitterfeld Conference on Culture and Politics
	Death of Otto Grotewohl
1965	Law on Uniform Socialist Education System, applying to all levels of education
	Eleventh Plenum of SED Central Committee decides on the widespread repression of dissent

1966	First nuclear power station comes on stream
1967	Volkskammer passes the Law on Citizenship of the GDR
1968	New constitution of the GDR comes into effect
	East German troops take part in the Warsaw Pact invasion of Czechoslovakia
1969	Controversy over Christa Wolf's *Nachdenken über Christa T.*
1970	Meeting between Willi Stoph (Chairman of the Council of Ministers) and West German Chancellor, Willy Brandt, in Erfurt
1971	Private telephone communication between East and West Germany is restored after 19 years
	Erich Honecker succeeds Ulbricht as First Secretary of the SED (3 May)
	Honecker promises 'no taboos' for committed socialist artists
	Transit Agreement between the GDR and the Federal Republic
1972	Cultural liberalization is heralded by the reception of Ulrich Plenzdorf's novel *Die neuen Leiden des jungen W.*
	Signing of the Basic Treaty between the GDR and the FRG (21 December)
1973	Death of Walter Ulbricht
	GDR joins UN
1974	International recognition is achieved when the USA takes up diplomatic relations with the GDR (Britain and France having done so in 1973)
1976	Expatriation of Wolf Biermann leads to prolonged confrontation between intellectuals and the SED leadership
1977	SED functionary Rudolf Bahro publishes *Die Alternative* in the Federal Republic, a critique of communist government, and is arrested
	Maxie Wander, *Guten Morgen, du Schöne*
1979	Punitive measures are taken against 'dissident' intellectuals
1980	Relations between East and West Germany deteriorate after the Soviet invasion of Afghanistan
1981	First of a series of peace conferences between the cultural intelligentsia from the GDR and the FRG, prompted by the increasing superpower nuclear confrontation
1982	Soviet Union stations SS-21 missiles in the GDR
1983	Peace demonstration by 100,000 in Dresden
	Peace campaigner Roland Jahn is expelled from the GDR
	West Germany signs a credit agreement (for 1 billion DM) with the GDR
	Christa Wolf, *Kassandra*
1984	Planned visit by Honecker to the Federal Republic is cancelled
1986	GDR and FRG sign an Agreement on Culture covering education, libraries, museums, radio and television, sport, and youth exchanges
1987	Writers' congress debates the abolition of censorship
	A rock concert in front of the Reichstag building in West Berlin leads to fighting between East Germans and the GDR police

Honecker finally makes the first official visit by a GDR head of state to the Federal Republic (7–11 September)

1989 Regular demonstrations outside the Nikolai Church in Leipzig (beginning in August)

Massive demonstration (500,000) in East Berlin demanding reform (4 November)

GDR celebrates it 40th anniversary (7 October), followed by the fall of Honecker (18 October) and the resignation of the Politburo (7 November)

Opening of the Berlin Wall (9 November) and the dissolution of the *Stasi*

1990 SED renamed the PDS (Party of Democratic Socialism) under Gregor Gysi

First free democratic elections to the Volkskammer (18 March), with the CDU the largest party (40.8%)

Treuhand Agency set up to dispose of East German industry

Treaty signed in Moscow restoring full sovereignty to Germany (12 September)

GDR joins the Federal Republic of Germany in accordance with Article 23 of the *Grundgesetz* (3 October)

1945 Radio stations established under Allied control in major German cities

Potsdam Conference (17 July–2 August) at which the Allies announce their intention of establishing democracy in Germany

Frankfurter Rundschau founded in the American zone

1946 First edition of *Der Ruf*

Nuremberg Trials concluded (October)

Licensed press established

Reopening of the universities

1947 British and American zones of occupation are merged (1 January; French Zone joins in April)

First edition of *Der Spiegel*

Marshall Aid announced

Founding of Gruppe 47 (10 September)

1948 Regional radio stations founded

Currency Reform in the Western zones (20 June)

Berlin Blockade (June until May 1949)

1949 Proclamation of the *Grundgesetz* (23 May) and the founding of the Federal Republic, with Bonn as the capital

First elections to the Bundestag (August–September) with Konrad Adenauer (CDU) elected Chancellor and Theodor Heuss (FDP) President

1950 Nation-wide demonstrations against rearmament

1951 First post-war Wagner Festival at Bayreuth

Death of Arnold Schönberg

1952 Signing of the German Treaty and the suspension of the Statute of Occupation

First edition of *Bild-Zeitung*

The Federal Republic

1954	West Germany wins the World Cup at football
	ARD begins television broadcasting
1955	Following the proclamation of (limited) sovereignty the Federal Republic enters NATO (9 May—formation of Warsaw Pact including the GDR, 14 May)
	First *Documenta* exhibition in Kassel
	Death of Thomas Mann
1956	Founding of the Bundeswehr (followed by the introduction of conscription)
	Death of Gottfried Benn and Bertolt Brecht
	German Communist Party banned
1957	In the federal elections the CDU/CSU gain an absolute majority (for the only time in the history of the Federal Republic)
1958	*Kampf dem Atomtod* begins its campaign against nuclear weapons
	Gleichberechtigungsgesetz (Law on Equality between the Sexes) comes into force
1959	Günter Grass, *Die Blechtrommel*
	SPD agrees the Godesberg Programme (13 November)
1960	Adolf Eichmann is kidnapped by Israeli agents (tried in 1961 and executed in 1962)
1961	Erection of the Berlin Wall (13 August)
1962	Beginning of the *Spiegel* Affair with the arrest of its editor, Rudolf Augstein
	Oberhausen Manifesto of the Young German Cinema
	First nuclear reactor comes on stream
1963	ZDF begins broadcasting
	President Kennedy visits the Federal Republic and West Berlin
	Adenauer resigns as Chancellor (15 October) to be replaced by Ludwig Erhard
1964	Herbert Marcuse's *One-Dimensional Man* appears in the USA (and in Germany in 1967)
1965	Peter Weiss, *Die Ermittlung*
	First edition of Hans Magnus Enzensberger's *Kursbuch*
1966	Congress 'Crisis of Democracy' held in Frankfurt (with speakers including Bloch, Habermas, and Enzensberger)
	Grand Coalition formed between CDU/CSU and SPD (1 December)
1967	Death of Konrad Adenauer
	Demonstration against the Shah of Persia's visit to Berlin, with the student Benno Ohnesorg killed by the police
	Bundestag passes *Filmförderungsgesetz* establishing subsidies for the cinema
1968	Assassination attempt on the SDS leader Rudi Dutschke
	Bundestag passes Emergency Laws (30 May)
	Action Committee for the Liberation of Women founded in West Berlin
1969	Federal elections lead to the first SPD/FDP coalition, led by Willy Brandt

Founding of Verband deutscher Schriftsteller, the writers' union

Death of Karl Jaspers and Theodor Adorno

1970	Baader–Meinhof terrorist group founded (renamed Rote Armee Fraktion in 1971)
	Federal Republic signs the Warsaw Treaty recognizing the Oder–Neiße Line
1971	*stern* publishes a declaration by 374 women admitting to illegal abortions
	Fifteen film-makers (including Wenders and Fassbinder) found the Filmverlag der Autoren
	Willy Brandt is awarded the Nobel Peace Prize for his *Ostpolitik*
1972	*Radikalenerlaß* (Decree on Extremists) is agreed by Brandt and the *Länder*
	Leading members of the Rote Armee Fraktion are arrested
	Heinrich Böll is awarded the Nobel Prize for Literature
	Olympic Games are held in Munich, with a team from the GDR allowed to compete
	Signing of the Basic Treaty between the FRG and the GDR (21 December)
1973	End of the Vietnam War
	Federal Republic joins UN
1974	Brandt resigns as Chancellor, to be replaced by Helmut Schmidt
	Heinrich Böll, *Die verlorene Ehre der Katharina Blum* (the film version by Volker Schlöndorff and Margarethe von Trotta is released in 1975)
1975	Baader–Meinhof trial begins
1976	Bundestag passes legislation allowing for abortion under certain conditions
1977	First edition of *Emma*
	Industrialists' leader Hanns-Martin Schleyer is kidnapped (and later killed) and Andreas Baader, Gudrun Ensslin, and Jan-Carl Raspe are found dead in their cells
1978	Kluge, Schlöndorff, Fassbinder, Reitz, and others make *Deutschland im Herbst*
1979	NATO 'dual track' decision on the modernization of its nuclear weaponry
	American TV series *Holocaust* is broadcast in West Germany
1980	Founding of the Greens as a federal party
1981	Wave of squatting hits West Berlin and other cities
1982	Easter Marches are resumed for the first time since 1968
	Death of Rainer Werner Fassbinder
	End of social–liberal coalition; Helmut Kohl (CDU) becomes Chancellor
1983	In the federal elections the Greens enter the Bundestag
	Peace movement holds the biggest rally in its history with over 500,000 in Bonn
1984	Official survey reveals that 50 per cent of trees in West Germany are damaged
	Edgar Reitz, *Heimat*

1985	Death of Heinrich Böll and Axel Springer
	Günter Wallraff, *Ganz unten*
1986	Nuclear reactor disaster at Chernobyl
	Death of Joseph Beuys
1987	Brandt resigns after 23 years as Chairman of the SPD
	Berlin celebrates its 750th anniversary
	Reagan and Gorbachev sign INF agreement removing medium-range missiles from Europe
1988	Death of Franz Josef Strauß (CSU)
1989	Opening of the Berlin Wall (9 November)
1990	German Monetary Union (1 July)
	German unification in accordance with Article 23 of the *Grundgesetz* (3 October)
	First all-German elections (2 December) with Kohl re-elected Chancellor

Index

360 Index

372 Index